America's Johannesburg

America's Johannesburg

Industrialization and Racial Transformation in Birmingham

Bobby M. Wilson

The University of Georgia Press
Athens

Paperback edition published in 2019
by the University of Georgia Press
Athens, Georgia 30602
www.ugapress.org
© 2000 by Rowman & Littlefield Publishers, Inc.
Additional materials © 2019 by the University of Georgia Press
All rights reserved

Most University of Georgia Press titles are
available from popular e-book vendors.

Printed digitally

Library of Congress Cataloging-in-Publication Data
Names: Wilson, Bobby M., 1947– author.
Title: America's Johannesburg : industrialization and racial transformation
    in Birmingham / Bobby M. Wilson.
Other titles: Industrialization and racial transformation in Birmingham
Description: Paperback edition. | Athens : The University of Georgia Press,
    2019. | Series: [Geographies of justice and social transformation] |
    "Originally published by Rowman & Littlefield Publishers, an imprint of
    The Rowman & Littlefield Publishing Group, Inc. Copyright © 2000"—
    Title page verso. | Includes bibliographical references and index.
Identifiers: LCCN 2019035591 | ISBN 9780820356273 (paperback) |
    ISBN 9780820356280 (ebook)
Subjects: LCSH: African Americans—Alabama—Birmingham—Social conditions.
    | African Americans—Alabama—Birmingham—Economic conditions. |
    Birmingham (Ala.)—Social conditions. | Birmingham (Ala.)—Economic
    conditions. | Birmingham (Ala.)—Race relations. |
    Industrialization—Alabama—Birmingham—History. |
    Capitalism—Social aspects—Alabama—Birmingham—History.
Classification: LCC F334.B69 N476 2019 | DDC 305.8009761/781—dc23
LC record available at https://lccn.loc.gov/2019035591

For Theodore Speigner

Contents

Foreword to the 2019 Edition

America's Johannesburg explains how shifting combinations of power and difference—in the forms of capital, extractive and manufacturing capacity, railroads, state structures, and, most crucially, labor—shaped the smoldering core of Birmingham, Alabama. The district came into being after the U.S. Civil War. It was made out of land seized by settler colonial expansion mixed with imported remnants of the plantation system—including profits that had been turned into cash before slavery's labor lords became landlords. Constantly rocked by conflict, Birmingham rapidly developed into the urban hub of a mining and ironmaking region—and later, and less successfully, a steelmaking region.

Capitalism requires inequality, and racism enshrines it. "Racial capitalism" in a phrase summarizes this ordinary feature of political economic life. Parsing out these co-constitutive interdependencies is as urgent as ever. We need, and Professor Wilson offers, insights into ongoing dynamics that enable action rather than descriptions of effects that are difficult to tell from despair.

In the final third of the nineteenth century, capitalism was churning in worldwide crisis. Many of the significant geopolitical shifts of that period were spatial fixes for drastic instabilities, including the hand-in-hand rise of Progressivism and apartheid/Jim Crow, and the rapid expansion of colonialism and imperialism, including the Scramble for Africa.

Professor Wilson's compact book focuses a wide lens on political economy at global, national, regional, urban, and community scales in order to examine the spatial form and social meaning that made Birmingham a North American precursor to the South African hotspot founded the following decade. It might seem self-evident that the Alabama settlement would become a central place in the Black Freedom struggle: so deliberately and dramatically was it weighted by relationships and ideologies accumulated from the greater plantation South. But as Professor Wilson reminds us, things are not as simple as they seem. In the context of extra-local forces from above and social movement from below, crosscut by unstable identities, we do well to give our full attention to who fought whom, how, and to what end. This is the book's purpose—to chart the inventiveness and conflicts of social actors who enliven categories of racial capitalism rather than track those categories as static units of analysis.

The churn occasioned by capitalism can only be fully understood by studying down to the ground. The forces of race, capital, skill, state, social reproduction, and intra-capitalist competition worked to make and remake the region. What capacities, habits, and tendencies might be inferred from the evidence—to imagine both competing world-making activities underlying the struggles detailed in *America's Johannesburg*—while the overlapping and interlocking devastations of racial capitalism in the contemporary world.

GEOGRAPHY AND THE STUDY OF RACE AND RACISM

In the modern discipline's early years—emerging around the same time as the founding of Birmingham and Johannesburg—environmental determinism explained difference understood as race, and justified hierarchy and deliberately produced inequality, by asserting that the peoples of the planet had differentiated into "races" due to the cumulative effects of climate, landscape, and associated cultural and productive activities of such environments. This type of study insisted that racialism, and therefore its violent organizational enactment as racism, reflected a natural order. Cedric Robinson reminds us that such racialism did not suddenly appear in the late nineteenth century to justify the violence of war, exploitation, and conquest but rather consolidated from existing social and interpretive practices that formed the ground of capitalism itself in rural England—between and among people all of whose descendants might have become white. While the imperial and colonial uses of geography as a discipline were already palpably apparent to conquered, enslaved, and colonized peoples including—by their very absence—victims of genocide, the Nazi campaign to destroy all designated rival humans in the European context brought mainstream geography into disrepute. Environmental determinists had embraced eugenics and other population improvement schemes. For them the only thing that changed more slowly than nature was culture.

After a suitable period of political irrelevance, during which a particular kind of cultural geography inspired development of ethnographically sensitive spatial inquiry, post–World War II geography advanced the study of race and racism under the quantitative revolution by studying areal differentiation. This work used mapping and statistical analysis to portray locations and effects of race-as-category according to indicators such as income or education, employment or illness, migration or redevelopment-induced dislocation. The complex procedures informing the research were belied by the flatness of the findings—because the categories of analysis seemed as sturdily static as they had been under environmental determinism, if for mostly unrelated reasons.

In the broad context of anticolonial and freedom movements of the long mid-twentieth century, many thinkers brought the study of race and racism into conversation with a broad range of intellectual and disciplinary traditions, building on the extensive arc of such work in order to find ways to lift movements more effectively. The scholarly and theoretical wing of the Black radical tradition is an accumulation of such analytical engagement, overlapping in significant ways with the Birmingham (UK) Center for Contemporary Cultural Studies. The purpose of the work is to deepen consciousness by revealing the constant experiment of politics as we make the world, though not under conditions we choose or desire. Social construction helpfully names this type of analysis because of its emphasis on making together, whether through conflict or cooperation, reproducing or interrupting relations of power and difference such that difference become less rather than more fatal. Professor Wilson shows social construction in action—*as* action—by laying bare how a brutally competitive corner of US racial capitalism battled to survive and grow through an ever thickening, but never secure, struggle for local domination through "race-connected practices."

Capitalist exploitation does not at every moment reveal its differentiating tendencies, which can nevertheless always be found. White supremacy is a particular instantiation of racism rather than its entire scope. Thus one can use Professor Wilson's work to think about other places, not because they read off from white supremacy to imitate its aims but rather because the level of detailed attention necessary to do close work shows itself in *America's Johannesburg's* methodology. It retains an openness to revision while remaining true to purpose. Working from the ground up demands a theoretical armature capable of holding a body of evidence. As Professor Wilson explained to a student, for him Marxism is a skeleton and his task—the work—is to put flesh on the bones. The social is the flesh in time-space.

BLACK GEOGRAPHIES AND THE CONTINUING SIGNIFICANCE OF AMERICA'S JOHANNESBURG

Bobby M. Wilson grew up in North Carolina in the freedom-fighting twentieth century. He tells us that periodically, in those dangerous times, his grandfather would pull up in his pickup truck and say, "Come on. Get in. We're going to march today." Black people make life. The socio-spatial character of struggle grounds meaning in the making of place, thanks to a viscerality that feels precise but is always provisional.

What, though, makes Black Geographies a field? Is it diasporic consciousness in action? Is it the sum of areal experiences? Is it bigger or smaller than Black Studies? As senior scholar John Bracey said at a gathering to review and debate Black Studies after forty years, "This isn't where we were headed, but this is where we're at." An entire infrastructure of thought underlies Black Geographies (and indeed Black Studies). We are several generations into the institutionalized work, and now more than ever we can work from and with intellectual ancestors and current theorists including Walter Rodney, Angela Y. Davis, Stuart Hall, C. L. R. James, Claudia Jones, Joy James, Paul Gilroy, Denise Ferreira da Sliva, Edouard Glissant, Frantz Fanon, Françoise Vergès, Achille Mbembe, Clyde A. Woods, and so many others. Yet new struggles that demand acknowledgment of specificities must, along with the research informing their trajectories, resist from within the constant blows that fracture movements back into the exact categories that freedom requires us to dissolve.

America's Johannesburg is a required text for teachers, researchers, and organizers. Its methodological openness has already made a substantial contribution to better research in geography, American Studies, and the various oppositional studies programs that have developed in U.S. universities over the past half-century. By revealing in its structure and meticulous development how to explain socio-spatial change over three quarters of a century of racial capitalism, *America's Johannesburg* provides a clear model for how to research related phenomena in a variety of contexts past and present. What's perhaps most appealing in the book is its deliberate thoroughness. Professor Wilson wrote a book intended for use in Black struggle that, in reciting devastations, mostly repeats the need for struggle without necessarily showing how to fight. In a word, this book's achievement is double: its relentless specificity combined with scalar audacity is a model for research about *and* action in distinct yet densely interconnected geographies of dislocation, resistance, and revolution.

Ruth Wilson Gilmore
August 9, 2019
Lisbon

Preface

This book seeks to reveal the history and evolution of race-connected practices in Birmingham, Alabama, and to explain how the city and its institutions acted to restrain or assist individual and group actions that fostered such practices. It attempts to uncover the reasons underlying these practices and their historical effects. The book is intended to give people of color the information and knowledge they need to better understand their situation—an essential requirement for gaining and exercising power. It is hoped that this work will serve to generate critical debate on the social construction of race and place as capitalism continues to restructure itself in a global and changing world.

Acknowledgments

Various sections of this book are revised and expanded versions of previously published materials. I have received valuable suggestions from the many reviewers of this and other works. In particular, I thank W. David Lewis of Auburn University for his critical insights on the industrial history of Birmingham and the members of the archival staff at the Birmingham Public Library, especially Marvin Whiting, for their valuable research guidance over many years. I also thank my friends and colleagues Ruth Gilmore, Clyde Woods, and David Organ for their encouragement during many stimulating discussions; also Jim Blaut, Dick Peet, and most of all Anne Buttimer, who inspired me in so many ways, for their many insights about critical geographical and societal issues.

Most of all, I thank my family, Joy, Ulrica, Cedric, and Vanessa, for giving me the space and time to work on this project, for I was not always there as much as I should have been. Thanks also to my mother and father, Ora Virginia Wilson and Bobbie H. Wilson, for teaching me to be persistent in things in which one truly believes.

Finally, financial support from the Comprehensive Minority Faculty Development Program at the University of Alabama at Birmingham made it economically possible for me to devote time to writing this book.

1

Introduction: Race and Capitalist Development

A distinction is made in private life between what a man thinks and says about himself and what he really is and does. In historical struggles one must make a still sharper distinction between the phrases and fantasies of the parties and their real organization and real interests, between their conception of themselves and what they really are.

—Karl Marx, *Political Writings*

From Birmingham's earliest days, the city's industrialists used race-connected practices as part of a strategy designed to increase their profits and maintain dominance. They succeeded well on both fronts: within twenty-five years of the city's founding, it was known as "the industrial city of the South"; it also came to be known, in later years, as America's Johannesburg.

Although much has been written about Birmingham as a chapter of U.S. civil rights history, lacking is a critical analysis of the city's own history and the race-connected practices that led to the civil rights movement.[1] Race-connected patterns and structures are deeply engrained and not easily discernible without an understanding of the larger structural and institutional forces that shaped and molded them. This book seeks to uncover those forces.

From the beginning of industrial capitalism in Birmingham, blacks were a significant part of the labor force. Owners of production used race-connected practices to regulate the struggle between themselves and workers and used racial (as well as gender and ethnic) divisions of labor to restructure production to make it more profitable. However, there have been only a few attempts to explain racial divisions.[2]

This book situates race primarily in a historical-geographical materialist context. According to Karl Marx, history is the struggle between capitalists and workers. Historical materialism emphasizes the antagonistic relationships among classes of people, whereas classical economics stresses class harmony. The mode of production determines the material quality of life and the social relations among classes, making it a most pervasive force. Marx's theory, as David Harvey noted, could offer the best critical analysis of social reality and is

> the most powerful of all the explanatory schemata available. It has the potentiality—largely unrealized in actual work—to get at matters as diverse as built environment formation and architectural design, street culture and micropolitics, urban economy and politics as well as the role of urbanization in the rich and complex historical geography of capitalism.[3]

Social and geographical realities result from the material production of life and not from an otherwise self-contained inter- or intrasubjective process. Such an approach demands historical research on the evolution of social forms and understanding of how the past shapes the present.[4] Marx's theory of capitalism is critical for analyzing the historical construction of race-connected patterns, and this book uses his theory as an instrument to examine the social transformation of race and place in Birmingham.

Historical materialism must take note of the historical conditions of blacks as a part of the working class. One cannot conceive of the proletariat as a "universal class" or submerge black oppression in a bogus universality. Race-connected practices result from the material production of life. A major failing of Marx's account of the working class as a historical subject was its inability to encompass the differentiated interests and motives of this class. Leonard Harris wrote,

> A basic feature of historical materialism, however, requires that we should begin from the standpoint of what people are by virtue of how in fact they live, produce, and reproduce themselves; how they in fact shape and reshape their world in actual praxis; how they manifest, shape, and reshape their species being as active agents from within their own history. If we begin from this standpoint, the interest of the working class is differentiated because its interest includes ontological commitments in praxes.[5]

To understand better the role of class actors in the formation of race-connected practices, this book also incorporates the conceptual framework of the French school of political economy called the regulationist school. Classical Marxian theory does not fully account for regional or locational differences in modes of regulation and regimes of accumulation, so, by drawing on regulation theory, this book examines the transformation of race-connected practices in Birmingham from the antebellum period to the Fordist phase of capitalist development. (Although Birmingham is a postbellum city, the forces that led to both race-connected practices and industrial growth originated in the antebellum period.)

Regulation theory did not focus specifically on race as a factor in capitalist development. Nevertheless, it provides valuable insight into the connection between class formation and patterns of racial domination. Regulatory processes provide a context for race-connected practices in Birmingham. The mode of social regulation defines the social context in which economic reproduction occurs. The transformation of race-connected practices reflects fundamental changes in local governance and modes of social regulation in capitalism.

Regulation theory, however, has often ignored material and discursive practices as they relate to local governance, practices that urban regime theory incorporates in its analysis. Using both theories, we can focus more on the regional and local scales, where neglect of historical-materialist analysis is serious. Blacks in Birmingham had to overcome not only the restraints of national modes of social regulation but also a vicious local regime strongly tied to the antebellum era that thrived on the exploitation of cheap black labor for half a century. Regulatory processes as defined by regulation and regime theories can be used to contextualize the governance of regional and local regimes.[6]

Regulationists distinguish between "extensive" and "intensive" *regimes of accumulation* in capitalism; each represents a distinct pattern of economic evolution. Each regime is further distinguished by "competitive" and "monopoly" *modes of regulation* that reproduce the fundamental capitalist property relationships and guide the prevailing regime of accumulation. The mode of regulation largely depends on the political sphere, the domain of sociopolitical struggles, which represents a set of codified social relations that guide and sustain the capital accumulation process. The coupling of a type of accumulation and regulation defines a specific regime.[7]

During the initial phase of industrial capitalism in the United States, the seemingly inexhaustible supply of low-paid, poorly organized immigrant workers made possible an extensive regime of capital accumulation that guaranteed a high rate of profit and more capital accumulation. This regime generated absolute surplus value through productive techniques by applying methods to lengthen the working day and expand the labor force.

With an intensive regime, growth takes place mainly through investment in fixed capital or machinery. It can generate relative surplus and create the potential for regular increases in both productivity and mass consumption. Marx noted in *Capital* that although real wages might rise with increases in accumulation, a growing disparity (increasing polarization) between capitalist and worker usually accompanies the rise. Greater disparities count in human society. Machines or technology drive down unit labor costs by increasing productivity in relation to wages. Thus, workers gain relatively little or nothing from increases in labor productivity.

The regulationists' "competitive mode" of social regulation is based on the nineteenth-century liberal notion of free and competitive markets. Craft controls were in effect, but prices and wages were determined competitively. This mode of regulation produced Marx's bourgeois variety of capitalism. Racial-repressive labor systems, however, produced another kind of capitalism at particular historical stages. Thus, for most of U.S. industrial history, an intensive regime with a competitive mode of regulation was more characteristic of capital accumulation in the North than in the South. Even in the North, however, the regime stopped far short of substantive racial equality. The competitive mode resulted in differences in wealth, power, and social status, all of which were often defined along racial and ethnic lines. Segmentation of labor along racial or ethnic lines is a major feature of a competitive and intensive regime of accumulation. As the workplace became more mechanized, capitalists relegated certain racial or ethnic workers to un-skilled work positions. Such inequalities were described as natural, or rational, and were derived mainly from market forces.

The monopoly mode of regulation includes scientific management, an oligop-olistic pricing system, and a complex system of determining wages that involves the social regulation of consumption norms. For regulationists, this mode is based on corporate power, which made possible the fordist regime of accumula-tion.[8] By late-twentieth-century capitalism (post-Fordism), such a regime had made the demand for black labor less essential than it had been at any previous stage of capital development.[9]

The transformation of race-connected practices in Birmingham was not solely the result of local motivations, capacities, and cooperation; rather, these were fa-cilitated by shifts in the mode of social regulation within capitalism itself. Both national and regional modes of social regulation influenced local race-connected practices. Antebellum Alabama rejected an intensive regime of capital accumula-tion based on wage labor in favor of an extensive regime based on black slavery, and many of Birmingham's early industrialists were deeply rooted in the antebel-lum plantation order. Race-connected practices were not derived solely from market forces and were major obstacles to the development of free competitive la-bor markets. If the outcome of the Civil War had been different, then Alabamians would have worked their mines and mills with black slaves.[10] Instead, planters re-lied on a monopoly mode of social regulation and, according to Shearer Davis Bowman, "wielded a degree of formal and direct authority over their menials that was absent from the relations of English landlords with their tenants and the day-laborers hired by those tenants."[11] The mode of social regulation is premodern, of the master–servant form, which John Stuart Mill described in his *Principles of Po-litical Economy* as one in which

> the lot of the poor, in all things which affect them collectively, should be regu-lated *for* them, not *by* them. They should not be required or encouraged to think for themselves, or give to their own reflection or forecast an influential voice in the determination of their destiny. It is the duty of the higher classes to think for them, and to take the responsibility of their lot, as the commander and officers of an army take that of the soldiers composing it. . . . The rich should be *in loco parentis* to the poor, guiding and restraining them like chil-dren. . . . They should be called on for nothing but to do their day's work, and to be moral and religious. Their morality and religion should be provided for them by their superiors, who should see them properly taught it, and should do all that is necessary to insure their being, in return for labor and attachment, properly fed, clothed, housed, spiritually edified, and innocently amused.[12]

Following the war, planters retained the authority to regulate an extensive regime of accumulation characterized by a repressive economic structure that exploited free blacks on a scale almost equal to that of the slave regime. Whites demanded that blacks be relegated to the lowest position in society, unable to compete with them on any terms. This monopoly mode of social regulation for whites over blacks meant Birmingham was able to manifest racism on a scale unknown in U.S. industrial history. Birmingham's early industrialists and managers favored a regulatory model built on the institution of slavery that became the basis for what Carter Wilson called "dominant aversive racism."[13] They produced, according to W. David Lewis,

> a particularly severe form of exploitation and social problems of enormous long-range consequence. Only in South Africa, where black workers burrowed for gold in the Main Reef, Johannesburg's equivalent of [Birmingham's] Red Mountain and the Warrior coal beds, did a similar situation come about. Pictures taken in the 1880s of Birmingham and the faraway city on the Witwatersrand have an uncanny likeness.[14]

As in Birmingham, South Africa's pattern was

> one of integrating blacks into the industrial work force as the principal source of labor but under conditions that would prevent them from developing the political and economic leverage that is normally acquired by working classes in a modernizing society.[15]

The low quality of Birmingham coal deposits and South Africa's gold ores may have created a need for both to limit wages. Certainly, race-connected practices in Birmingham's coal and iron industries distinguished the city from other industrial cities in the United States. Not until the civil rights movement of the 1960s did blacks confront this legacy. Birmingham, however, stopped short of enforcing an apartheid that permitted more direct coercion of South Africa's black population. George Fredrickson noted that apartheid provided additional security for a white population that was smaller in number than that in the United States or Birmingham.[16]

STRUCTURE OF BOOK

Chapters 2 through 4 discuss the origin of and reasons for race-connected practices in capitalist development, the role of the state in sustaining these practices, and how the restructuring of capitalism may produce changes in these practices. The antebellum regime and its role in capitalist development in the South are discussed in chapters 5 and 6. Chapters 7 through 9 then examine the rise and the fall of "Reconstruction" and what they meant for race and the southern political economy as well as the development of the Birmingham regime.

Chapters 10 through 13 document the types of labor systems used in Birmingham during the early phase of industrial capitalism, when there was almost no competition between blacks and whites for jobs despite a racially repressive labor system, and when, at times, there was equality in wages between blacks and whites who did similar tasks. These social and political conditions eventually gave way to black–white competition and white supremacy, which became fixtures in the region's social and spatial fabric. Chapters 14 through 17 examine the growth of corporate power, which signaled the coming of Fordism. The southern shift of this regime restructured the southern political economy and race-connected practices, making possible civil rights gains.

NOTES

1. David J. Garrow, *Birmingham, Alabama, 1956–1963* (Brooklyn: Carlson Publishing, 1989); David J. Garrow, *Bearing the Cross: Martin Luther King, Jr., and the Southern Christian Leadership Conference* (New York: William Morrow, 1986); Robert Gaines Corley, "The Quest for Racial Harmony: Race Relations in Birmingham, Alabama, 1947–1963," (Ph.D. diss., University of Virginia, 1979).

2. Sophie Bowlby, Jane Lewis, Linda McDowell, and Jo Foord, "The Geography of Gender," in *New Models in Geography: Political-Economy Perspectives*, vol. 2, ed. Richard Peet and Nigel Thrift (London: Unwin Hyman, 1989), 157–75; see also Liz Bondi, "Feminism, Postmodernism, and Geography: Space for Women," *Antipode* 22, no. 2 (August 1990): 156–67.

3. David Harvey, *The Urban Experience* (Baltimore: Johns Hopkins University Press, 1989), 3.

4. Ann Markusen, *Regions: The Economics and Politics of Territory* (Totowa, N.J.: Rowman & Littlefield, 1987), 11.

5. Leonard Harris, "Historical Subjects and Interests: Race, Class and Conflict," in *The Year Left 2: Toward a Rainbow Socialism, Essays on Race, Ethnicity, Class and Gender*, ed. Mike Davis, Manning Marable, Fred Pfeil, and Michael Sprinker (London: Verso, 1987), 103–4.

6. See Mickey Lauria, "Introduction: Reconstructing Urban Regime Theory," in *Reconstructing Urban Regime Theory: Regulating Urban Politics in a Global Economy*, ed. Mickey Lauria (Thousand Oaks, Calif.: Sage Publications, 1997), 1–9.

7. M. Aglietta, *A Theory of Capitalist Regulation: The U.S. Experience*, trans. D. Fernbach (London: NLB, 1979); see also Robert Brenner and M. Glick, "The Regulation Approach: Theory and History," *New Left Review* 186 (1991): 45–119.

8. Aglietta, *A Theory*; Brenner and Glick, "Regulation."

9. Manning Marable, *How Capitalism Underdeveloped Black America: Problems in Race, Political Economy and Society* (Boston: South End Press, 1983), 33.

10. W. David Lewis, *Sloss Furnaces and the Rise of the Birmingham District: An Industrial Epic* (Tuscaloosa: University of Alabama Press, 1994), 34.

11. Shearer Davis Bowman, *Masters and Lords: Mid–19th-Century U.S. Planters and Prussian Junkers* (New York: Oxford University Press, 1993), 20–21, 34.

12. John Stuart Mill, *Principles of Political Economy*, vol. 2 (Boston: Charles C. Little and James Brown, 1848), 319–20.

13. Carter A. Wilson, *Racism: From Slavery to Advanced Capitalism* (Thousand Oaks, Calif.: Sage Publications, 1996), 116–17.

14. Lewis, *Sloss Furnaces*, 83.

15. George M. Frederickson, *White Supremacy: A Comparative Study in American and South African History* (New York: Oxford University Press, 1981), 204.

16. Frederickson, *White Supremacy*, xxi, 240.

2

The Origin of Racism: Discursive and Material Practices

Neither Greeks nor Romans evolved prejudices of color and race. Frank Snowden wrote,

> The Greeks and Romans developed no doctrines of white superiority unsupported by facts or theoretical justifications for a color bar.
>
> The presence of a large number of Negroes in a white society, according to some modern views, gives rise to anti-Negro feeling. Ethiopians were far from rare sights in the Greco-Roman, particularly the Roman, world. Yet the intense color prejudice of the modern world was lacking. Although it is impossible to estimate the Negro element in the classical world in terms of precise statistics, it is obvious that the black population in Greece and Italy was larger than has been generally realized.[1]

Furthermore, during the Middle Ages, Europe was more isolated from, and ignorant about, the people and geography of the world than the Romans and Greeks had been centuries earlier.[2] Beyond their ecumenical world, space was "weakly grasped," terra incognita, and there was little contact with other races.[3] This rare contact was, however, enough for racism to exist as a discursive practice in precapitalist societies. For example, according to Robert Miles, enough information about Africans was available in manuscripts and printed travel accounts to place a "strain on a series of fundamental English beliefs: the genesis of mankind, the nature of beauty. . . ."[4] This racial discourse lacked a systematic theory of racial superiority, and no such theory about the African image preceded the slave mode of production.[5] Racial prejudice was not apparently responsible for the *initial* introduction of slaves into the U.S. colonies. George Fredrickson noted that at first enslaved people were considered heathens or captives in war and a form of property. The justification for their enslavement was not racial; it was seen as the will of God that some people rule and others are ruled. Fredrickson wrote, "The stereotypes about blacks and blackness held by some Englishmen on the eve of colonization were opinions casually held—beliefs that were 'not actively malignant' and that would not, under all circumstances, have led directly to societal racism."[6]

Initially, African slaves who accepted Christianity and baptism could not be held in perpetual bondage. As black slavery spread, however, Europeans began to equate whiteness with Christianity, and freedom and blackness were associated with heathenism.[7] It was believed that blacks could never have virtue or wisdom, and they could never become Americans because they could never *look* like English Americans. In the Christian context, blackness and darkness symbolized evil, death, and sin; whiteness and light represented virtue and wisdom. Blacks who assimilated Christian religious doctrine no longer had any claim to freedom or equality. According to Edgar Thompson, "visible physical differences loomed to become the chief marks around which to organize doctrines and beliefs of deeper biological differences."[8]

A body of customs, judicial sanctions, and statutes evolved to institutionalize the enslavement of Africans in the New World.[9] Enlightenment thinking replaced the traditional view of humans as children of God with one of humans as physical beings who were part of the natural world. Thus, according to Antonio Gramsci, French materialists of the eighteenth century based equality on the "reduction of man to a category of natural history, an individual of a biological species, distinguished not by social and historical qualifications but by natural gifts."[10]

Enlightenment thinking asserted the universality of human nature but only in terms of human values expressed in European society. Thinking along these lines, Birmingham's founder, industrialist John T. Milner, wrote, "The negro has no monuments, worthy of being noted in the history of his race, except such as have been produced by his labor, in a condition of servitude. . . . He is simply following the laws of his nature, as it has been known always, and from the beginning of time."[11]

In the American South, wrote Frederickson, planters' racist republicanism produced a marriage between egalitarian democracy and biological racism that "pandered at once to the democratic sensibilities and the racial prejudices of the 'plain folk.'"[12] Milner and his contemporaries believed that the laws of nature decree that whites must control blacks, and the ultimate form of control is slavery. This doctrine maintained interclass solidarity between southern slaveholders and non-slaveholders.

Although the *idea* of equality, or erasing differences, may be a value of the modern nation-state, Tzvetan Todorov noted that "actual equality does not prevail."[13] These are the elements of one of the most successful "ideological bluffs" of the bourgeois intellectuals.[14] Thus, the authors of the U.S. Constitution wrote of equality, but in reality there was only inequality. Racial slavery was unjust, but the Christian and moral nation constructed a notion of justice maintained in injustice that produced racial prejudice.[15] Winthrop Jordan explained that, in Christian and democratic societies, "where actual equality does not prevail, [but] the ideal of equality becomes a shared value . . . emphasis is placed on apparently irrefutable and 'natural' physical differences."[16] It was morally and naturally correct to enslave Africans who could never be Americans because they could never *look* or *behave* like Euro-Americans.[17] White supremacy was "not the fault of the coloured man, nor of the white man, nor of Christianity, but an ordination of Providence, and no more to be changed than the laws of nature."[18]

Long after slavery had ended, white southerners continued to talk of the natural or the biological incapacity of blacks.[19] C. Vann Woodward quotes Thomas Pearce Bailey, a southern educator at the turn of the twentieth century who set down the "racial creeds of the Southern people":

> (1) Blood will tell. (2) The white race must dominate. (3) The Teutonic peoples stand for race purity. (4) The Negro is inferior and will remain so. (5) This is a white man's country. (6) No social equality. (7) No political equality. (8) In matters of civil rights and legal adjustments give the white man, as opposed to the colored man, the benefit of the doubt, and under no circumstances interfere with the prestige of the white race. (9) In educational policy let the Negro have the crumbs that fall from the white man's table. (10) Let there be such industrial education of the Negro as will best fit him to serve the white man. (11) Only Southerners understand the Negro question. (12) Let the South settle the Negro question. (13) The status of peasantry is all the Negro may hope for, if the races are to live together in peace. (14) Let the lowest white man count for more than the highest Negro. (15) The above statements indicate the leanings of Providence.[20]

Blood does not always tell, however. In only a few places in the world might one find completely isolated groups—in other words, absolute genetic homogeneity. World capitalism itself has drawn people into juxtaposition and facilitated interbreeding, such as the appropriation of African women for the sexual pleasure of slave masters of European descent. Yet, the idea of race as a natural construct continues to function as a way to group people. In the United States, putting people into "white" and "nonwhite" categories is deeply embedded in discursive practices.

These practices have led to a plethora of studies to determine whether certain skin colors are associated with certain behaviors. Thomas Sowell, for example, reasoned that West Indians, Brazilian blacks, and American blacks should have similar economic experiences; he found, however, West Indians to be "much more frugal, hard-working, and entrepreneurial" than American blacks whereas "Brazil has larger black–white disparities than the United States in education and in political participation." On the basis of these findings, he argues that racism may play a less significant role in economic advancement than is commonly supposed.[21] More recently, Dinesh D'Souza has argued that because slave owners also enslaved members of their own race, slavery could not have been a racist institution.[22]

These arguments accept race as a scientific and natural construct, but it has no scientific basis. An exchange between a U.S. journalist and the late "Papa Doc" Duvalier of Haiti reveals the absurdity of such thinking. When the reporter asked what percentage of the Haitian population was white, Duvalier answered 98 percent. The journalist expressed doubts, but Duvalier insisted his answer was correct. When the journalist asked, "How do you define white?" Duvalier responded, "How do you define black in your country?" The journalist explained that in the United States anyone with any black blood was considered black. Duvalier replied, "Well, that's the way we define white in my country."[23] In short, nothing in the human genetic composition justifies racism, and no genes exist for white supremacy. Theodosius Dobzhansky said, "To be equal before the law people need not be identical twins."[24]

Race and racism belong in the social and the political realms, not the biological one. Speaking of the modern era, Ruth Benedict noted, "There has never been a time when civilization stood more in need of individuals who are genuinely culture-conscious, who can see objectively the socially conditioned behaviour of other peoples."[25] History, not nature has produced racism.[26] It is a social construction and a political act. More specifically, Ashley Montagu noted, it is "the deliberate creation of an exploiting class . . . seeking to maintain and defend its privileges against what was profitably regarded as an inferior social caste."[27] Members of a privileged class may enslave members of their own race, but the basis of class privilege in the United States was mainly racial, not cultural. According to Manning Marable, "Whiteness was fundamentally a measure of personal privilege and power, not a cultural statement."[28]

Racial discourse enabled the ruling class to exercise hegemony by supplying the system of belief that kept the masses from questioning their rulers' actions. Contrary to Marxist theory, the rule of one class over another does not depend totally on economic domination; the ruled must also accept the belief system of the ruling class.[29] Indeed, one interesting aspect of southern political development is the support given to the planter class by the southern white laboring class. Oliver Cox stated, "Planters so thoroughly propagandized the white common people of the South that they actually helped the master class to fight the Civil War in the interest of the continued exploitation of black labor on an extremely low level."[30]

Rulers are carriers of prevailing cultural traditions and guardians of racial or ethnic identities. Even the white working class is not totally free. To be free, according to David Roediger, this class must emancipate itself from the notion of "whiteness." It must question why people think they are white, rather than questioning the notion of race in general. Is it possible for those who call themselves white to stop thinking in terms of "whiteness"? Roediger continues,

> While whiteness nor blackness is a natural construct, whiteness is infinitely more false and precisely because of that falsity, more dangerous, than blackness. . . . It is a more brittle and fragile form of social identity that can be fought. . . . We must focus our political energies on exposing, demystifying and demeaning the particular ideology of whiteness, rather than calling into question the concept of race in general. . . . Whiteness describes not a culture but the absence of a culture. . . . It is the empty and therefore terrifying attempt to build an identity based on what one isn't and on whom one can hold back.[31]

Ian Haney Lopez wrote that whiteness is defined through a process of "negation, systematically identifying who was non-White," which Lopez noted was embraced by the court. As opposed to establishing the parameters of whiteness, the court established the non-whiteness of Chinese, South Asians, and so on.[32] Whiteness may be culturally fragile, but it is politically and economically powerful. It is an idea "whose material effects pervade and predominate all social relations."[33] From the Gold Coast of Africa to the black belt in the American South to the industrial North, the discourse of whiteness shattered black identity. Racial practices relegated blacks to the back of the bus and into low-skill jobs, and segregated schools and residential areas. According to Stanley Greenberg,

> Actors most closely identified with the emerging capitalist order helped "modernize" racial domination, using racial divisions to circumvent the labor market, placing the imprimatur of race on state institutions. Racial stratification, rather than "peeling off" with "modernization," was incorporated into the developing labor market and modern state.[34]

Racial discourse became a key feature of the capitalist mode of social regulation. It erased and marginalized the history and cultural discourse of blacks for the sake of capital accumulation. Cox noted, "Because of the world-wide ramifications of capitalism, all racial antagonisms can be traced to capitalist people, the white people of Europe and North America."[35]

RACISM AND THE CULTURAL LOGIC OF CAPITALISM

Any analysis of the experiences of blacks in Birmingham or any other place in the United States must recognize the importance of slavery in determining the material position of blacks in the overall division of labor as well as the discursive forms accompanying that position. Slavery was not marginal; it produced a regional power. American capitalism was not the product of a single dialectic. In any society, one may find a great variety of forms of exploitation associated with production for a market. Capitalism is not a unified, singular, and total entity but uncentered, dispersed, plural, and partial.[36] Slavery was one of many ways in which surplus was appropriated from workers; it grew by meeting some needs of the capitalist mode of production.

Slavery has always been strongly dependent on the capitalist world market. According to Raimondo Luraghi, it was "born *inside* a world dominated by capitalism, subject to its economic laws, linked to it by something like an umbilical cord."[37] In a letter to P. V. Annenkov, Marx wrote,

> Direct slavery is as much the pivot of our industrialism today as machinery, credit, etc. Without slavery no cotton; without cotton no modern industry. Slavery has given value to the colonies; the colonies have created world trade; world trade is the necessary condition of large-scale machine industry. . . . Slavery is therefore an economic category of the highest importance.[38]

Slavery yielded a high enough level of primary accumulation for a rising class to undermine the power of feudalism in Europe, where, according to James Blaut, capitalists gained

> the necessary experience and the necessary capital to commence a subsequent phase of the industrial revolution in Europe. From the plantations also, and from the now-rapid transformation of production in Europe, the capitalist acquired the power to begin at last the conquest of precapitalist societies in Asia and Africa and thus to inaugurate the stage of *colonial imperialism*, quite well described by Marx and Engels.[39]

Capitalists in New York and Liverpool, England, depended on cotton produced with slave labor. The slave plantation supplied this raw material to industry in both Europe and the northern United States. The slave mode of production offered expanding markets for manufactured goods and generated agricultural exports that dominated transatlantic commerce and stimulated diversified enterprises in New England and the Middle Atlantic U.S. cities. Cotton represented 50 to 60 percent of the value of total U.S. exports during the decades before the Civil War. Some 25 percent of the South's cotton went to supplying New England's rapidly growing textile industry, and the remainder went mainly to Great Britain.[40] Slavery provided much of the initial capital needed to inaugurate laissez-faire capitalism in the United States.[41] Black slavery's purpose was to accumulate capital. Thus, racism has both a material basis and a material effect.[42]

THE EXPANSION OF CAPITALISM

Waves of capitalist expansionism between 1415 and the early 1800s resulted in the enslavement of Africans.[43] Henri Lefebvre wrote that capitalism survives and grows "by occupying space, by producing a space."[44] In this sense, geography itself depends on the laws of motion of capitalist development.[45] During the increased commercial competition of the Middle Ages, geographical knowledge became a valued commodity because of the need to command space.[46] Global capitalism is not new; it is an inherent feature of accumulation. European states with vast sea power journeyed to nearly every part of the globe. In 1500, these European powers controlled 9 percent of the world's land; by 1800, 35 percent, which increased to 67 percent by 1878.[47] Spain and England were the most successful practitioners of global expansion, which enlarged the capitalistic "world economy." The Portuguese and the Dutch participated less in the expansion itself, acting instead as intermediaries in global trade, a role that allowed them to dominate the Indies.[48]

By the end of the nineteenth century, capitalists had successfully extinguished the communal land title of premodern societies in North America by expropriating and transforming land into private property.[49] Divesting the original inhabitants of their land was essential to the material success of early capitalists. This stage was one of "primitive accumulation." In the United States, primitive accumulation took the form of Indian removal. The 1830 Indian Removal Act gave

Andrew Jackson, who had been a long-time proponent of allowing whites to take Indian land, authority to carry out massive, government-directed deportation of Indians. This process made land and other resources available to an emerging capitalist class and produced a homogeneous space, the abstract space of capital, which transcended national, regional, religious, and kinship ties and was positioned above other powers to mobilize resources on a national and international scale. Homogenization of space simplifies the mobility of capital—a necessary condition of capitalism. According to Frederickson,

> Land hunger and territorial ambition gave to whites a practical incentive to differentiate between basic rights and privileges they claimed for themselves and what they considered to be just treatment for the "savages" who stood in their path, and in the end they mustered the power to impose their will.[50]

White supremacy provided the foundation for the expansion of capitalism and for removing Indians from their land. Benedict noted that modernity threw "many civilizations into close contact and . . . the overwhelming response to this situation is nationalism and racial snobbery."[51] The modern nation-state, in ensuring that whites could be united in a common nationality, denied freedom to people of color. As white America attempted to ensure its independent and totalizing culture, the character of the "negro" became, in the words of Jordan, "a dumping ground" for everything not white.[52] Whites, in contrast, became "a category of people subject to a double negative: they are those who are not non-White."[53]

Racial exploitation for material gain developed among Europeans with the rise of capitalism and its modernist cultural form, nationalism. Black slavery provided the initial material base for institutional racism and race-connected practices. Blacks entered capital–labor relations in the United States through slavery, and the South has never fully shaken that legacy. Southern slaveholders produced an especially virulent racism that gave shape to class hegemony, which emerged as the closest thing to a pure slaveholding class found in the New World.[54]

NOTES

1. Frank Snowden, *Blacks in Antiquity* (Cambridge, Mass.: Harvard University Press, 1970), 183.

2. Oliver C. Cox, *Caste, Class and Race: A Study in Social Dynamics* (New York: Modern Reader Paperbacks, 1970), 326.

3. David Harvey, *The Condition of Postmodernity: An Enquiry into the Origins of Cultural Change* (Cambridge, Mass.: Basil Blackwell, 1989), 241.

4. Robert Miles, *Racism and Migrant Labor* (London: Routledge and Kegan Paul, 1982), 99.

5. Oscar Handlin and Mary F. Handlin, "Origins of the Southern Labor System," *William and Mary Quarterly*, 3d series, 7 (1950): 199–222; Eric William, *Capitalism and Slavery* (New York: Russell & Russell, 1961), 7, 19; see also M. Nikolinakos, "Notes on an Economic Theory of Racism," *Race* 14 (1973): 365–81.

6. George M. Fredrickson, "Toward a Social Interpretation of the Development of American Racism," in *Key Issues in the Afro-American Experience,* ed. Nathan I. Huggins, Martin Kilson, and Daniel M. Fox (New York: Harcourt Brace Jovanovich, 1971), 243; see also George M. Fredrickson, *White Supremacy: A Comparative Study in American and South African History* (New York: Oxford University Press, 1981).

7. Fredrickson, *White Supremacy,* 84–85; see also Leon F. Litwack, *North of Slavery: The Negro in the Free States, 1790–1860* (Chicago: University of Chicago Press, 1961), 163.

8. Edgar Thompson, *Plantation Societies, Race Relations and the South: The Regimentation of Populations* (Durham, N.C.: Duke University Press, 1975), 116.

9. Mary Frances Berry, *Black Resistance, White Law: A History of Constitutional Racism in America* (New York: Meridith Corp., 1971); Winthrop D. Jordan, *White over Black: American Attitudes Toward the Negro, 1550–1812* (New York: W. W. Norton, 1977).

10. Antonio Gramsci, *Prison Notebooks,* ed. and trans. Quintin Hoare and Geoffrey Nowell Smith (New York: International Publishers, 1971), 362.

11. John T. Milner, *Alabama: As It Was, as It Is, and as It Will Be* (Montgomery, Ala.: Barrett and Brown, 1876), 149, 150.

12. Fredrickson, *White Supremacy,* 155.

13. Tzvetan Todorov, "'Race,' Writing, and Culture," in *"Race," Writing, and Difference,* ed. Henry Louis Gates, Jr. (Chicago: University of Chicago Press, 1986), 372.

14. Thomas Bates, "Gramsci and the Theory of Hegemony," *Journal of the History of Ideas* 36, no. 2 (1975): 363.

15. Alexander Saxton, *The Rise and Fall of the White Republic: Class Politics and Mass Culture in Nineteenth-Century America* (London: Verso, 1991), 42.

16. Todorov, "'Race,' Writing, and Culture," 372.

17. Jordan, *White over Black,* 341.

18. Quoted in Leon F. Litwack, *North of Slavery,* 21–22.

19. John H. van Evrie, *White Supremacy and Negro Subordination: or, Negroes a Subordinate Race* (New York: van Evrie, Horton and Company, 1868); Charles Carroll, *The Negro a Beast: or, in the Image of God* (St. Louis: American Book and Bible House, 1900); William Calhoun, *The Caucasian and the Negro in the United States* (Columbia, S.C.: R. L. Bryan Co., 1902); William B. Smith, *The Color Line: A Brief in Behalf of the Unborn* (New York: McClure, Phillips & Co., 1907); Robert W. Shufeldt, *The Negro: A Menace to American Civilization* (Boston: R. G. Badger, 1907).

20. C. Vann Woodward, *Origins of the New South, 1877–1913* (Baton Rouge: Louisiana State University Press, 1951), 355–56.

21. Thomas Sowell, *Ethnic America: A History* (New York: Basic Books, 1981), 219; Thomas Sowell, *The Economics and Politics of Race* (New York: William Morrow & Company, 1983), 103.

22. Dinesh D'Souza, *The End of Racism: Principles for a Multiracial Society* (New York: Free Press, 1995), 74–79.

23. Quoted in Barbara J. Fields, "Ideology and Race in American History," in *Region, Race, and Reconstruction: Essays in Honor of C. Vann Woodward,* eds. J. Morgan Kousser and James M. McPherson (New York: Oxford University Press, 1982), 146.

24. Theodosius Dobzhansky, *Mankind Evolving: The Evolution of the Human Species* (New Haven, Conn.: Yale University Press, 1962), 13.

25. Ruth Benedict, *Patterns of Culture* (Boston: Houghton Mifflin, 1934), 10–11.

26. Fields, "Ideology," 152.

27. Ashley Montagu, *Man's Most Dangerous Myth: The Fallacy of Race* (New York: Oxford University Press, 1974), 39.

28. Manning Marable, *Race, Reform, and Rebellion: The Second Reconstruction in Black America, 1945–1990*, 2d ed. (Jackson: University Press of Mississippi, 1991), 190.

29. James Joll, *Antonio Gramsci* (New York: Penguin Books, 1978), 120; see also Gwyn A. Williams, "The Concept of 'Egemonia' in the Thought of Antonio Gramsci: Some Notes on Interpretation," *Journal of the History of Ideas* 21, no. 4 (1960): 587–99; Joseph Femia, "Hegemony and Consciousness in the Thought of Antonio Gramsci," *Political Studies* 23, no. 1 (1975): 29–48; Bates, "Gramsci," 351–66.

30. Cox, *Caste*, 416.

31. David Roediger, *Towards the Abolition of Whiteness: Essays on Race, Politics, and Working Class History* (London: Verso, 1994), 12, 13.

32. Ian F. Haney Lopez, *White by Law: The Legal Construction of Race* (New York: New York University Press, 1996), 27.

33. Lopez, *White by Law*, 169.

34. Stanley B. Greenberg, *Race and State in Capitalist Development: Comparative Perspectives* (New Haven, Conn.: Yale University Press, 1980), 408.

35. Cox, *Caste*, 322.

36. J. K. Gibson-Graham, *The End of Capitalism (as We Knew It): A Feminist Critique of Political Economy* (Cambridge, Mass.: Basil Blackwell, 1996), 250–65.

37. Raimondo Luraghi, *The Rise and Fall of the Plantation South* (New York: New Viewpoints, 1978), 48.

38. Marx to P. V. Annenkov, Brussels, 28 December 1846, reprinted in Karl Marx, *The Poverty of Philosophy* (New York: International Publishers, 1971), 188.

39. James M. Blaut, "Imperialism: The Marxist Theory and Its Evolution," *Antipode: A Radical Journal of Geography* 7 (1975): 11. This work is generally called the William thesis after Eric William's *Capitalism and Slavery*; see also John Rex, *Race Relations in Sociological Theory*, 2d ed. (London: Routledge and Kegan Paul, 1983); James M. Blaut, "Where Was Capitalism Born?" *Antipode: A Radical Journal of Geography* 8 (1976): 1–11.

40. Harold D. Woodman, *King Cotton and His Retainers: Financing and Marketing the Cotton Crop of the South, 1800–1925* (Columbia: University of South Carolina Press, 1990), ix.

41. Saxton, *Rise and Fall*, 247; William, *Capitalism and Slavery*, 210.

42. Miles, *Racism*.

43. Blaut, "Imperialism," 1–19.

44. Henri Lefebvre, *The Survival of Capitalism* (London: Allison & Busby, 1976), 21.

45. Richard A. Walker, "Two Sources of Uneven Development Under Advanced Capitalism: Spatial Differentiation and Capital Mobility," *Review of Radical Political Economics* 10, no. 3 (1978): 28–37; David Harvey, *The Limits to Capital* (Oxford, U.K.: Basil Blackwell, 1982) 373–412.

46. Harvey, *Condition*, 244.

47. Anthony R. de Souza, "To Have and to Have Not: Colonialism and Core-Periphery Relations," *American Geographical Society's Focus* (Fall 1986): 14–19.

48. Fredrickson, *White Supremacy*, 20–21.

49. Fredrickson, *White Supremacy*, 4.

50. Fredrickson, "Toward"; Fredrickson, *White Supremacy*, 5.

51. Benedict, *Patterns*, 10.

52. Jordan, *White over Black*, 552.

53. Lopez, *White by Law*, 27–28.

54. Eugene D. Genovese, *The World the Slaveholders Made* (New York: Pantheon Books, 1969), 237.

3

The State's Role in Sustaining
Race-Connected Practices

Existing interests and ideologies associated with racial dominance in the colonial United States have had a significant impact on the role and status of people of color.[1] The state has also played an important role in sustaining racism because the economy depends on slavery, and the state depends on the economy. The U.S. Constitution supported the practice of slavery. For example, article one, section two, of the Constitution counted each slave as three-fifths of a human being for purposes of congressional representation and direct taxation. This method may have diluted southern slaveholders' representation in Congress, but it sustained the institution of slavery. Furthermore, article one, section nine, mandated that the states could not interfere with the transatlantic slave trade until 1808, but slave traders brought more than 50,000 slaves into the United States after 1808. The end of transatlantic slave trade brought an increase in domestic trading between states, and the surplus of slaves and slaveholders occupied the expanding territories. Article four, section two, required that fugitive slaves be returned to their owners.[2]

White supremacy and affirmations of racial inferiority were vital to the political success of the National Republicans, a federalist regime that governed the United States from 1812 to 1828. If blacks were to remain in the United States in large numbers, it was thought to be better to enslave them than to let them become a discontented underclass demanding full citizenship and finding common ground with the growing numbers of propertyless and poor European Americans.

The state lent significant support to the idea of colonizing free blacks, as proposed by the American Colonization Society. Its officers included many of the country's political elites—James Madison, Andrew Jackson, Henry Clay, Daniel Webster, Stephen Douglas, Francis Scott Key, and others.[3] The organization operated on the assumption that blacks could never be incorporated into the nation-state, but the movement was out of step with the political-economic trends of the time. Colonization would require massive governmental intervention in a period when federalism was falling into disfavor and laissez-faire capitalism was on the rise. In addition, slavery was such an economic asset that the states rejected every attempt to interfere with it. Thus, in 1828, the U.S. Senate Foreign Relations Committee rejected the idea of black colonization, fearing it would create a labor vacuum and raise the price of labor.[4]

JACKSONIAN DEMOCRATS

With the victory of Andrew Jackson in the 1828 presidential election, laissez faire, decentralized democracy, and states' rights replaced the federalist regime. In both the North and the South, the issue of slavery was placed in the hands of local white electorates.[5] Jackson showed distaste for blacks and brought white supremacy to the center stage.[6] From 1828 through the 1850s, the federal apparatus controlled by Jacksonian Democrats legitimized a social and political order built on the supposedly "natural" distinction of race. The South was nearly unanimous in its support of this program. Georgia cast 100 percent of its vote for Jackson; Tennessee gave him 95 percent; Alabama and Mississippi, more than 80 percent; North Carolina, 73 percent; and Virginia, 69 percent. South Carolina, which had no popular vote, gave its eleven electoral votes to Jackson. In the 1832 election, Jackson did even better. He ran unopposed in Alabama, Georgia, and Mississippi.[7]

The Jackson era represented a changing of the guard. The older political elites, who could trace their lineage to the country's founding fathers, were replaced by lower-level "upstarts." In a sense, Jackson's movement was the people's in that it extended liberal democratic rights to a poorer class of whites and made the United States perhaps the most truly democratic republic the world had ever seen.[8] At the same time, Jacksonianism sanctioned the marriage between racism and democracy and overcame the contradiction between the Declaration of Independence and the practice of black slavery. The Jacksonian Democrats believed the absolute basis of freedom was lack of economic dependence on other men. J. Mills Thornton noted, "Jacksonian ideology emphasized the notion that freedom is autonomy—that is, the absence of external forces manipulating one's life—the existence of slavery quite naturally came to seem an essential bulwark of freedom."[9] By guaranteeing that very few white men would ever have to depend directly on other white men for their sustenance, slavery saved white common laborers from depending on the wealthy planter class.[10] All white men could, as George Fredrickson wrote, become "aristocratic" and preserve a rank-ordered society without reducing the white lower class to an inferior status.[11] Essentially, slavery elevated the common southern white to a social position that averted the need for what Karl Marx called the class struggle.[12]

The opposition to Jacksonianism—the Whig Party—represented the old political elites. In the South, the Broad River group, wealthy planters who migrated from Virginia to Georgia in the 1780s, bought land in the Tennessee Valley in 1809 and acquired large land holdings in the southern black-belt region a decade later. Raimondo Luraghi said this class was "socially a scion of the seigneurial class of

Europe. . . . Ideologically it was a scion of the Italian Renaissance."[13] It played an important role in early Alabama politics but lost power to the Jacksonians. The planter class had social and economic influence, but it lacked political power for most of the antebellum period. Writing about Alabama, Thornton noted,

> At no time did large planters control—or even come close to controlling— the legislature, numerically. Throughout much of the antebellum period they were a very small part of the legislature, and even in the final decade of these years, when they did increase their role, they represented no more than a quarter of the seats.[14]

But, as Lewis noted,

> Along with their ownership of large estates and many slaves, the strong interest of Broad River people in promoting internal improvements and manufacturing disproves the idea that wealthy planters, as a class, opposed industrial development. What prevented them from implementing their visions was a lack of political power.[15]

Like the Jacksonian Democrats, the planter class sought individual freedom. However, while the Democrats worked toward this end by opposing state economic intervention, the planter class sought to extend its affluence with state aid. Linking laissez-faire economics to their notions of freedom and liberty, Alabama's Jacksonian Democrats refused federal aid for internal improvements and blocked the development of an industrial city in the state's mineral district during the antebellum period. From the economic crisis of 1837 until the middle of the 1850s, they defeated all attempts to seek governmental assistance for corporations and opposed the chartering of banks and railroads. Thornton noted that such behavior represented "the embodiment of all the insecurity of small farmers in the midst of plantations, or the poor in the midst of plenty, of a new state in the midst of old."[16]

Despite these differences, the two classes could act jointly on race matters. The Whigs offered no alternative to black slavery. Across the South, they emphasized whites' southern identity, and in no southern state did any Whig-sponsored economic issue challenge this identity.[17] Southern politicians may have disagreed on issues such as accepting federal funding for internal improvements, but all were anxious to present their position on the issue of race and slavery as especially sound. Thus, despite the planter class's lack of political power, it attained many of its goals related to slavery. By legitimizing racism as a way to distinguish their poorer constituents from black slaves, the Democrats produced a coalition that included the slaveholders. Thus, Jacksonian Democrats joined planters to support the expansion of both homesteading and slavery into the western territories, a position that briefly included the support of western farmers. They invigorated a racist social climate that denied democratic rights to free blacks in northern states, but the planter class's support for black slavery did not dampen its commercial spirit.[18] It was the Jacksonian Democrats that dampened this spirit by opposing any form of capital accumulation as a threat to freedom. Yet, they supported slavery—unfree labor.

For Jacksonians, wage labor was the antithesis of freedom and liberty; to sell one's labor was to work like a slave. Antagonism between the growing class of white wage laborers and black slaves started in the United States following its declaration of independence. In the 1800s, slanderous terms, such as "coon" and "buck," wrote David Roediger,

> had more than ambiguous or multiple meanings; they had trajectories that led from white to black. More than that, each of them went from describing particular kinds of whites who had not internalized capitalist work discipline whose places in the new world of wage labor were problematic to stereotyping Blacks.[19]

Southerners argued that northern capitalists worked laborers for more hours than slaveholders worked black slaves. According to Ann Markusen, Southerners also claimed that white wage workers were more oppressed than slaves because the value of slaves as commodities that reproduced intergenerationally "encouraged an ideology of paternalism on the part of slaveholders, who as a class protected their slaves from a too-killing pace of work."[20] Southerners called northern free wage labor "wage slavery."[21]

The Jacksonians believed that black slavery promoted "equality among the free by dispensing with grades and castes among them; therefore, it preserve[d] republican institutions"; its abolition, they said, would make the white commoner virtually a slave of the rich man.[22] Orestes Brownson, a labor reformer, called the wage system "a cunning device of the devil, for the benefit of tender consciences, who would retain all the advantages of the slave system, without the expense, trouble, and odium of being slaveholders."[23] Reaffirming Jeffersonian democracy, he asked that every person become an independent proprietor and possess enough goods to provide for their wants. Comparing free wage labor with unfree labor assumes that freedom is an economic category. Frederick Douglass emphasized that it was far more. He was fond of pointing out that his old position on the plantation was available, but he had never found anyone wanting to take his place.[24]

Of more importance, equating free wage labor with slavery was problematic for an intensive regime of capital accumulation. Questioning the legitimacy of wage labor threatened the very nature of such a regime. Without wage labor, could there be capitalism? The antebellum South lacked wage labor, which Adam Smith considered indispensable to the existence of capitalism.[25] Wage earners represented only 0.6 percent of Alabama's population in 1850 and 0.8 percent in 1860. The value added in manufacturing per capita for those years was only $2.98 and $5.29, respectively, compared with $36.02 and $50.66 for the Northeast.[26] In 1860, Alabama still had not developed a factory system; most establishments were small shops employing few workers. As late as 1900, wage earners were still less than 3 percent of Alabama's population. In 1860, the South—with one-third of the country's population—accounted for only 9.5 percent of the capital invested in the nation's industries.[27] According to one Alabama critic, the slave system did not generate investments,

> in a way to advantage the people and promote state welfare. . . . What becomes of the twenty million dollars which our commerce distributes annually among the planters of Alabama? The Census of 1850 states that in Alabama one million dollars only is invested in manufactures, a portion in twelve cotton factories, and fourteen forges and furnaces, as compared to Georgia's two million and Tennessee's three million.[28]

REPUBLICANS

Whereas the Jacksonians tied freedom and wage labor to black slavery, the new Republican Party connected the issue of freedom to the sale of public lands in the West and produced a more powerful political regime.[29] In this view, the right to property was the foundation for liberalism and capitalism, and any attack on financial assets was an attack on all property rights. With the rise of capitalism land became an important financial asset. As early as 1829, George Henry Evan of the *Working Man's Advocate* established the foundation for a new political regime by tying the issue of wage labor to the sale of public land in the West. Evan called for access to public lands not simply for the sake of those who would move West but as a benefit for those who would remain in eastern cities as wage laborers. The option of taking up land, he argued, would draw labor away from cities and a shrinking labor force would force employers to advance wages and reduce rents. In contrast, the lack of access to land made wage laborers into slaves.[30] Horace Greeley of *The New York Tribune* took up this idea in 1845:

> The freedom of the public land to actual settlers, and the limitation of future acquisitions of land to some reasonable amount, are also measures which seem to us vitally necessary to the ultimate emancipation of labor from thralldom and misery. What is mainly wanted is that each man should have an assured chance to earn, and then an assurance of the just fruits of his labors. We must achieve these results ye; we *can* do it. Every new labor-saving invention is a new argument, an added necessity for it. And, so long as the laboring class must live by working for others, while others are striving to live luxuriously and amass wealth out of the fruits of such labor, so long the abuses and sufferings now complained of must continue to exist or frequently reappear. We must go the root of the evil.[31]

Access to land alone does not necessarily reduce the exploitation of labor. It could be argued that the availability of unoccupied land could prevent workers from becoming stronger. Friedrich Engels noted that lack of available land in England made the English working classes more inclined to agitate than American workers, who had the option of becoming subsistence farmers.[32] At the same time, the threat of wages increasing to a level that would eliminate profit provided the ruling class with a powerful incentive to attempt to legally coerce and immobilize the labor force. Because land was available in the upland South, whites became subsistence farmers there. In Jefferson County (future site of Birmingham), 80 percent of the white male population owned farms in 1850.[33] In contrast, in seventeenth-century England and the Netherlands, where land was scarce and labor plentiful, there was less of an incentive to enslave labor.[34] Although differences in access to land would still result in differences in wealth, power, and social status, some considered these differences more acceptable than those imposed by the rigid racial hierarchy of the slave system. Frederick Jackson Turner saw the existence of free land, the frontier, as very important to the preservation of republican principles.[35] The Republican Party did not maintain an antislavery stance; it was a prohomestead party. According to John Commons, "Its position was identical with that of the workingmen. Only because slavery could not live on one-hundred-and-sixty-acre farms did the Republican party come into conflict with slavery."[36]

Northern voters supported the Republican Party not because slavery was anticapital but because slavery was incompatible with the liberal notion of a free and competitive market, which was the foundation of democratic republicanism. According to Barrington Moore, Jr., "Plantation slavery in the United States grew up as an integral part of industrialism and presented an obstacle to democracy much more than to capitalism."[37] Although U.S. capitalists supported the slave mode of production, they did not suspect that it would elevate the slaveholders to a position of significant power. As members of the Whig Party, however, slaveholders posed a serious threat to the regime of northern capitalists and Republicans, who increasingly saw themselves as struggling with an aggressive southern regime that sought to make slave labor the national norm. The result was a threat to the free-labor economy and to the development of a more intensive regime of accumulation because it would give slaveholders an advantage in the competition for land, labor, and capital. Republicans and northern capitalists saw the slave regime, as they had Native Americans, as an obstacle to their unrestrained exploitation of the entire country. James S. Allen wrote,

> Capitalist industry had to be assured, above all, of its own home market. This was the prime economic force which propelled the North in its struggle against the South. The bourgeoisie needed to dominate the whole country, to achieve national unity under its own wing, to explore, broaden, round out and conquer the market at home. This is the driving force of capitalism in progress, in the period of its expansion and growth.[38]

Free access to public lands, the idealistic vision of the Republican Party in the 1850s, attracted Whigs, Democrats, and those who believed that the western territories should remain free of slavery—the Free Soil Party.[39] The Republicans overcame northern capitalists' opposition to expanding free farmers into western territories by arguing that such expansion would stimulate manufacturing and

provide a food surplus for urban workers. In time, the rise of agrarian capitalism in the Midwest split the Jacksonian Democrats and isolated the South as the Republican regime—the regime of industrial capitalists. An "historic bloc" was formed, with midwestern farmers against the southern slaveholders.[40]

The Republicans accepted the new reality of wage labor—the new industrialism of banks, mills, factories, and industrial capital—but the Jacksonians' criticisms compelled Republicans to reconstruct the notion of wage labor to include the common white worker. They needed a way to explain why members of the free wage-laboring class were not slaves without raising the issue of whether the spread of wage labor was always and everywhere just. Thus, the Republican Party "did not ask white workers to consider themselves slaves nor devote themselves to slaves."[41] Doing this would liquidate the criticism of wage labor and in the process take away a part of the wage-laboring class from the Democrats. The Irish—an important contingent of the proletariat—were frequently called "niggers turned inside out," and blacks sometimes called "smoked Irish." However, the Republican regime reconstructed race in a way that let the Irish find refuge in whiteness. It "eased their assimilation as whites, and more than any other institution, it taught them the meaning of whiteness." Irish peasants could escape the racial oppression of the English by emigrating and becoming a part of the white race in the United States. They became "white," and "blacks" remained slaves, establishing the roots of conflict between the two groups.[42] Senator Lyman Trumbull, an Illinois Republican and a friend of Abraham Lincoln, declared in 1858, "We, the Republican party, are the white man's party. We are for free white men, and for making white labor respectable and honorable, which it can never be when Negro slave labor is brought into competition with it."[43]

Republicans definitively separated the wage labor issue from slavery but not without strong opposition from slaveholders. With the backing of Jacksonian Democrats, slaveholders were able to impose on the wider society a judicial system that shared their view of black slavery. In 1857, a southern majority on the Supreme Court attempted to fix the legal status of blacks forever in the *Dred Scott* decision, supported the expansion of black slavery into the western territories, and denied citizenship to all black slaves and their descendants. The Court ruled that

> rights of property are united with the rights of persons, and placed on the same ground by the fifth amendment to the Constitution, which provides that no person shall be deprived of life, liberty, and property, without due process of law. And an act of Congress which deprives a citizen of the United States of his liberty or property, merely because he came himself or brought his property into a particular Territory of the United States, and who had committed no offence against the laws, could hardly be dignified with the name of due process of law. . . . The right of property in a slave is distinctly and expressly affirmed in the Constitution. The right to traffic in it, like an ordinary article of merchandise and property, was guaranteed [sic] to the citizens of the United States, in every State that might desire it,

for twenty years. . . . Upon these considerations, it is the opinion of the court that the act of Congress which prohibited a citizen from holding and owning property of this kind in the territory of the United States north of the line therein mentioned, is not warranted by the Constitution, and is therefore void; and that neither Dred Scott himself, nor any of his family, were made free by being carried into this territory; even if they had been carried there by the owner, with the intention of becoming a permanent resident.[44]

The South regarded the decision as a great victory because it held that slaves were property, and slaveholders had the right, like any holder of property, to take their slaves into the free territories.

The Jacksonian Democrats argued that to deny this expansion would be an overtly discriminatory governmental action that violated their idea of freedom and individual liberty. On 2 February 1860, Jefferson Davis, later president of the Confederate States of America, introduced in the U.S. Senate a set of resolutions demanded by proponents of slavery. Davis's draft of the fourth resolution read,

Resolved, that neither Congress nor a territorial legislature, whether by direct legislation or legislation of an indirect and unfriendly nature, possesses the power to annul or impair the constitutional right of any citizen of the United States to take his slave property into the common territories, but it is the duty of the federal government there to afford, for that as for other species of property, the needful protection, and if experience should at any time prove that the judiciary does not possess power to insure adequate protection, it will then become the duty of Congress to supply such deficiency.[45]

The Senate adopted Davis's resolutions in May 1860.

Northern capitalists had to resist the decision or lose their reason for being. As capitalism must occupy and produce new space, the response to the *Dred Scott* decision and actions of the antebellum regime had to be "determinable, necessary, and obvious."[46] Lincoln's election to the presidency and the Republican regime destroyed any hope of achieving Davis's proslavery program, which gave Republicans the opportunity to create an economic policy more favorable to the development of an intensive regime of accumulation, especially in the western territories. Emancipation of slaves eliminated forever any threat of slavery expanding and left the West to free farmers and capitalists.

The existence of black slavery made it impossible for the white laboring class, in the North and the South, to come to grips with their class status in the United States. Marx noted, "Labour in a white skin cannot emancipate itself where it is branded in a black skin."[47] By spending all of its energy trying to distinguish itself from black slavery, the white working class did the dirty work needed to provide capitalism and its modernist cultural form the rationale for not only the continual exploitation of black labor but also the means to control it.[48] With the desire for liberation repressed, the white working class came to

want that which repressed it and developed somewhat of an Oedipus complex that

> stalled the development of a critique of wage labor in the U.S. working class history. . . . Only with black emancipation could a more straightforward critique of wage slavery, and a fierce battle over the meaning of free labor, develop. By that time the importance of a sense of whiteness to the white U.S. worker was a long-established fact both politically and culturally.[49]

The white race was a fait accompli.

With the end of the Civil War in sight, the fundamental question facing northern capitalists was whether to continue the system of racial oppression or institute a new system of social control. Lincoln, believing free blacks could not live harmoniously among whites, considered schemes for deportation and argued that all blacks should be returned to Africa. Speaking to a committee of blacks at the White House in 1862, he stated,

> You and we are different races. We have between us a broader difference than exists between any other two races. Whether it is right or wrong I need not discuss, but this physical difference is a great disadvantage to us both, as I think your race suffer very greatly, many of them by living among us, while ours suffer from your presence.[50]

He approved a scheme to transport blacks to a land grant in South America, arranged for colonization with the government of Haiti, and called for a constitutional amendment authorizing government-sponsored colonization.[51]

NOTES

1. George M. Fredrickson, *White Supremacy: A Comparative Study in American and South African History* (New York: Oxford University Press, 1981), 3–135.

2. Manning Marable, *How Capitalism Underdeveloped Black America: Problems in Race, Political Economy and Society* (Boston: South End Press, 1983), 4.

3. Leon Litwack, *North of Slavery: The Negro in the Free States, 1790–1860* (Chicago: University of Chicago Press, 1961), 24.

4. Litwack, *North of Slavery*, 158.

5. Fredrickson, *White Supremacy*, 149, 153–54.

6. George M. Fredrickson, *The Black Image in the White Mind: The Debate on Afro-American Character and Destiny, 1817–1914* (New York: Harper & Row, 1972), 25–32.

7. William J. Cooper, Jr., *The South and the Politics of Slavery, 1828–1856* (Baton Rouge: Louisiana State University Press, 1978), 11, 43.

8. Alexander Saxton, *The Rise and Fall of the White Republic: Class Politics and Mass Culture in Nineteenth-Century America* (London: Verso, 1991), 142–54; Fredrickson, *Black Image*, 20, 27, 41; Noel Ignatiev, *How the Irish Became White* (New York: Routledge, 1995), 68.

9. J. Mills Thornton III, *Politics and Power in a Slave Society: Alabama, 1800–1860* (Baton Rouge: Louisiana State University Press, 1978), xviii.

10. Thornton, *Politics and Power*; see also W. David Lewis, *Sloss Furnaces and the Rise of the Birmingham District: An Industrial Epic* (Tuscaloosa: University of Alabama Press, 1994), 15.

11. Fredrickson, *White Supremacy*, 155.

12. Wilbur J. Cash, *The Mind of the South* (New York: Alfred A. Knopf, 1941), 39.

13. Raimondo Luraghi, *The Rise and Fall of the Plantation South* (New York: New Viewpoints, 1978), 33.

14. Thornton, *Politics and Power*, 67.

15. Lewis, *Sloss Furnaces*, 15.

16. Thornton, *Politics and Power*, 18, 57, 67, 226.

17. Cooper, *The South*, 82.

18. Robert William Fogel and Stanley L. Engerman, *Time on the Cross: The Economics of American Negro Slavery*, vol. 1 (Boston: Little, Brown, 1974), 129.

19. David R. Roediger, *The Wages of Whiteness: Race and the Making of the American Working Class* (London: Verso, 1991), 100.

20. Ann Markusen, *Regions: The Economics and Politics of Territory* (Totowa, N.J.: Rowman & Littlefield, 1987), 60.

21. Markusen, *Regions*, 244.

22. Quoted in Thornton, *Politics and Power*, 206–7.

23. Quoted in Peter Camejo, *Racism, Revolution, Reaction, 1861–1877: The Rise and Fall of Radical Reconstruction* (New York: Pathfinder, 1976), 37.

24. Frederick Douglass, *Narrative of the Life of Frederick Douglass* (Wortley, U.K.: J. Barker, 1846), 98, 116.

25. Luraghi, *Rise and Fall*, 235.

26. U.S. Bureau of the Census, *Seventh Census of the United States, Manufactures, 1858*; U.S. Bureau of the Census, *Eighth Census of the United States, Manufactures, 1865*; Donald B. Dodd and Wynelle S. Dodd, *Historical Statistics of the South* (Tuscaloosa, AL.: University of Alabama Press, 1973); U.S. Bureau of the Census, *Manufactures*, Eighth Census, 1860.

27. *Manufactures*, 1860.

28. Quoted in Ethel Armes, *The Story of Coal and Iron in Alabama* (Birmingham, Ala.: Chamber of Commerce, 1910), 122.

29. Eric Foner, *Free Soil, Free Labor, Free Men: The Ideology of the Republican Party Before the Civil War* (New York: Oxford University Press, 1970), 27–29.

30. John R. Commons, "Horace Greeley and the Working Class Origins of the Republican Party," *Political Science Quarterly* 24, no. 3 (September 1909): 468–88.

31. Quoted in Commons, "Horace Greeley," 482.

32. From Friedrich Engels's Speech on the Republican Movement in England, in Minutes of the General Council of the First International, 28 March 1871, 165; also in *Marx and Engels on the United States*, Comp. Nelly Rumyantseva (Moscow: Progress Publishers, 1979), 233.

33. Henry M. McKiven, Jr., *Iron and Steel: Class, Race, and Community in Birmingham, Alabama, 1875–1920* (Chapel Hill: University of North Carolina Press, 1995), 14.

34. Fredrickson, *White Supremacy*, 55.

35. Frederick Jackson Turner, *The Frontier in American History* (Washington, D.C.: Government Printing Office, 1894).

36. Commons, "Horace Greeley," 488.

37. Barrington Moore, Jr., *Social Origins of Dictatorship and Democracy: Lord and Peasant in the Making of the Modern World* (Boston: Beacon Press, 1966), 428.

38. James S. Allen, *Reconstruction: The Battle for Democracy* (1865–1876) (New York: International Publishers, 1937), 19.

39. Foner, *Free Soil.*

40. Luraghi, *Rise and Fall*, 99.

41. Roediger, *Wages of Whiteness*, 87.

42. Ignatiev, *How the Irish*, 41, 76.

43. Quoted in Litwack, *North of Slavery*, 269.

44. *Dred Scott v. Sanford*, 19 Howard 393.

45. Quoted in Stanley I. Kutler, *The Dred Scott Decision: Law or Politics* (Boston: Houghton Mifflin Co., 1967), 182.

46. Kutler, *Dred Scott*, xvii.

47. Karl Marx, *Capital: A Critique of Political Economy*, vol. 1, trans. Ben Fowkes (New York: Vintage Books, 1977), 414.

48. Larry Sawers, "New Perspectives on the Urban Political Economy," in *Marxism and the Metropolis: New Perspectives in Urban Political Economy*, ed. William K. Tabb and Larry Sawers (New York: Oxford University Press, 1984), 12.

49. Roediger, *Wages of Whiteness*, 87.

50. Abraham Lincoln, *Collected Works*, vol. 5, ed. Roy Basler (New Brunswick, N.J.: Rutgers University Press, 1955), 371.

51. V. Jacques Voegeli, *Free but Not Equal: The Midwest and the Negro During the Civil War* (Chicago: University of Chicago Press, 1967), 43, 97.

4

Capital Restructuring and the Transformation of Race

Not only is race central to U.S. capitalist development, but it is also constantly reconstructed by ruling elites in their quest to exploit the working class and maintain hegemony. Society changes because capitalists are constantly changing the technical and social conditions of the labor process to increase production and ensure their domination over the means of production. The movement from "modernity," or industrial society, to "postmodernity," or postindustrial society, represented such changes during the late twentieth century. The term *restructuring* is often used to describe the effect of these changes. As Edward Soja wrote, this term

> conveys the notion of a "brake," if not a break, in secular trends, and a shift toward a significantly different order and configuration of social, economic, and political life. It thus evokes a sequential combination of falling apart and building up again, deconstruction and attempted reconstitution, arising from certain incapacities or perturbations in established systems of thought and action. The old order is sufficiently strained to preclude conventional patchwork adaptation and to demand significant structural change instead.[1]

Capitalists operate in a constant flux, as they attempt to find new markets, expand existing ones, and find cheaper methods of production and distribution. Capitalism is not a static system; it undergoes constant evolution.[2] Karl Marx noted, "All that is solid melts into the air."[3]

THE KONDRATIEFF CYCLE

For N. D. Kondratieff, economic restructuring is characterized by alternating long waves of relative expansion and contraction in the economy. Each of these waves lasts, on average, about fifty years in the historical development of capitalism (Figure 4.1). These long waves are an organic part of the capitalist system. In capitalism, there is complete interdependency among political and social development, war, economics, and finance. Unlike the basic Marxist thesis concerning the inevitability of capitalist crises, these cycles are self-correcting, and successive cycles are therefore repetitive.

Kondratieff viewed the long waves in terms of commodity price cycles in which relative movements of input and output prices regulate the rate of economic development.[4] Building on this work, others have pointed to basic innovations as the major trigger of long-wave economic fluctuations.[5] Because of his Marxist orientation, Ernest Mandel defined long waves as accelerations and decelerations of capital accumulation that affect employment.[6]

Two distinctive aspects of capitalism that have strong impact on employment are rapid modernization and depression. Modernization stimulates expansion of the economy and employment, causing an upswing in the Kondratieff cycle; but rapid modernization also can render the existing labor force and plants obsolete, leading to dislocation of economic activities and shifts in work force needs that may mean workers must acquire new skills, relocate, or both.[7] Downswings in the Kondratieff cycle coincide with a depression, during which demand for goods may decline because the lack of demand for labor causes the market incentive to collapse. Beyond alternations between modernization and depression, the pattern of the long waves is influenced by the ebb and flow of class struggle. According to Michael Marshall,

> It is the historical transformation of the *labour process*, rather than technology, which forms the hub of the process of industrial development, since it is only through the achievement of new forms of social subordination of labour to capital in production that the introduction and diffusion of new technical products and processes are accomplished. . . . I prefer to characterise the long waves in terms of their emergent social relationships of production.[8]

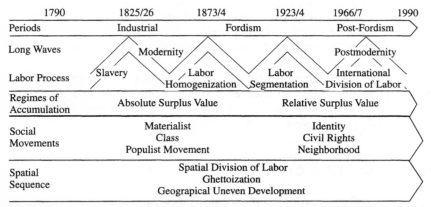

Figure 4.1   Kondratieff cycles along with concurrent labor, racial, and spatial effects.

Marx did not deal systematically with restructuring within the capitalist mode of production that may result from class struggles. For instance, he did not foresee the restructuring that produced a consumption norm so dominant that it co-opted the working class during what the regulationists call the Fordist phase of U.S. capitalist development. Regulation theory confronts the fact that capitalism has proven more durable than it was originally envisioned in classical Marxian formulations. It rejects the notion of the laws of motion of capitalism and instead probes particular forces shaping the development of a nation or a region. History did not provide a single path to capitalism. A. Lipietz wrote,

> The emergence of a new regime of accumulation is not written into the fate of capitalism even if it does correspond to some tendencies that can be observed. Regimes of accumulation and modes of regulation are outcomes of the history of human struggles: outcomes that have succeeded because they ensured some regularity and permanence in social reproduction. Thus, there is no sense in trying to comprehend any concrete social formation (even the currently dominant one) as a standardized, inevitable pattern. . . . Let us see how every country functions, what it produces, for whom, how, what the forms of wage relations are, what successive regimes of accumulation developed and why. And let us be very cautious when we attempt to throw a net over the world so as to catch the established relations between the regimes of accumulation of various national social formations.[9]

Regulation theory goes beyond the ahistorical approach of neoclassical economics to explain capitalist development. In the United States, the phases of capitalist development represent specific regimes of accumulation marked by important shifts in labor relations, technologies, and forms of industrial organization.[10] For example, the panic of 1837 initiated calls for industrialization in the antebellum South. The industrialization was a part of the upswing in the second Kondratieff cycle that began in 1849 and ended in 1873, when a downswing began that lasted until 1896 (see Figure 4.1).

The racialization of labor aided the 1849–1873 upswing. Leftover contempt for the laboring class from the colonial era persisted. Turning laborers with a peasant heritage into efficient factory hands proved a difficult and prolonged process, but because people will choose work for low wages rather than starve, they became attuned to the work discipline and the sense of time imposed by industrial capitalism. So, the displaced Irish, hungry and willing to work for the lowest wage, became a significant component of the country's unskilled labor force—but not until it was established that they were white. In the North, the Irish began to replace free blacks as early as 1838. A black newspaper, the *Colored American*, published:

> These impoverished and desperate beings—transported from the transatlantic shores, are crowding themselves into every place of business and of labor, and driving the poor colored American citizen out. Along the wharves, where the colored man once done [sic] the whole business of shipping and

unshipping—in stores where his services were once rendered, and in families where the chief places were filled by him, in all these situations there are substituted foreigners or white Americans.[11]

By the 1850s, these foreigners were a significant part of a cheap and exploited labor force that produced for capitalists the upswing in the second Kondratieff cycle. By 1873, a downswing in the second Kondratieff cycle occurred that actually contributed to the development of Birmingham, which was incorporated in 1871. Instead of investing in manufacturing, investors switched to investing in land, thereby contributing to the development of Birmingham and the state's mineral district. The racial impact of this downswing was the Compromise of 1877 and the southern populist movement that would have a major influence on race relations in Birmingham (see chapter 8). By the late 1890s, this downswing had ended, leading to a third upswing in the economy.

Between 1896 and 1920, the mode of regulation was essentially competitive. At the expense of blacks laboring in the mines and the mills, Birmingham became a major industrial city; and, with increased investment in more modern methods of production, the city became known as the "Pittsburgh of the South." The rapid rate of modernization, however, proved unstable and eventually led to a downswing that began in the 1920s and culminated in the Great Depression (see Figure 4.1). The competitive mode of regulation was unable to institutionalize the expanding mass consumption needed to underpin the expanding mass production, producing a downswing in the third cycle that hit Birmingham hard, and made the plight of blacks especially bleak.

Capitalism is resistant to the most catastrophic of economic crises. Antonio Gramsci compared the cultural hegemony of capitalism to the trench warfare system of World War I—although it was shelled, it still put up an effective resistance.[12] Thus, a major restructuring of the economy may not promote the necessary and sufficient catalyst for meaningful racial change or a successful class struggle, as demonstrated by the antebellum planters who survived the Civil War and attacks by radical reconstructionists. The Great Depression was to be the end of capitalism, but capitalism survived and delayed, perhaps forever, the development of a racially integrated society or the socialist worker.

The desire for economic recovery, not racial and social reform, guided most periods of restructuring. Restructuring can affect the form of race-connected practices.[13] They may undergo transformation; that is, change "shape, size, contours, purpose, function—with changes in the economy, the social structure, the system and, above all the challenges, the resistances to that system."[14] Restructuring can preserve and remake the racial order and race-connected practices or, according to Marc Allen Eisner, create "new contradictions that paradoxically threaten to dismantle them."[15] Such contradictions characterized the early phase of industrial development in Birmingham. While forces that produced a racially repressive labor force were at work, other forces contributed to interracial solidarity within the working class. Contradictions are a major feature of capitalism.

Critical theory seeks to expose the underlying forces that produce these contradictions. It rejects racism as a universal and unitary transhistorical phenomenon.[16] This rejection does not deny the ontological status of racism, but it is not necessarily reified. The recurrent features of racism that drove the historical emergence of black slavery, black sharecropping, black labor segmentation, black ghettoization, the black underclass, and so forth, may change form as capitalists restructure the regime of accumulation and mode of social regulation. A critical theory of race is not an essentialist theory of race but one that examines race within the context of the antagonism between capital and labor and the different modes of production.[17] Capitalism constantly restructures itself to increase accumulation, and it has undergone significant modifications since the nineteenth century. The failure of black liberalism in the twentieth century was its inability to understand the impact of this restructuring on the black community and responded realistically. As Michael Omi and Howard Winant noted, race involved

> an unstable and "decentered" complex of social meanings constantly being transformed by political struggle. . . . The crucial task . . . is to suggest how the widely disparate circumstances of individual and group racial identities, and of the racial institutions and social practices with which these identities are intertwined, are formed and transformed over time.[18]

Understanding this transformation is the task of a critical theory of race.

THE CRITICAL SPATIAL THEORY OF RACE

Care must also be taken not to disregard the subnational regional level, which may produce regimes of accumulation consolidated by regulations sustained by regional norms and forming a distinctive territorial capitalism.[19] A region or locality represents a unique intersection of settings for social action wherein racial and ethnic divisions often survive as a vital force for regulating the economy. According to Simon Duncan, understanding how larger political economic forces "worked at a general level seemed to have little connection with how people acted. . . . The locality seemed to offer something concrete rather than abstract."[20] The impact of capitalist regulation and restructuring on specific localities should be the focal point for a critical spatial theory that recognizes that all processes have local expression, which contributes to geographical variations. The cultural logic of capitalism assumes that growth overcomes geographical diversity. Marx accepted this assumption when he noted, "The workers have no Fatherland" and urged, "We must treat the whole world as one nation, and assume that capitalist production is everywhere established and has possessed itself of every branch of industry."[21] Thus, it could be argued that a focus on race and ethnicity would make working-class issues subordinate, undercut working-class struggles, and weaken international solidarity among workers. Focus on a particular place or location would have the same effect.

The transformation of race must be understood geographically as well as historically.[22] Those who accept race as a scientific construct assume that racism is constructed in one place very much as it is in another, but racism is not only historically specific; it is also geographically specific. The organization of local regimes has a direct impact on race-connected practices. These practices must be situated within a historical-geographical materialist context; the focus must be on the local regimes in changing economic situations that may affect race. An urban regime involves informal and formal arrangements that bring together public bodies and private interests to make, and act on, decisions in response to changes in the political economy or national and regional regulatory processes.[23] But, according to Marshall Feldman, "Urban regime theory inadequately theorizes the connection between local regimes and their wider institutional context, whereas regulation theory underestimates the importance of local actors and institutions."[24] By supplementing regulation theory with urban regime theory, we can focus on the role of a local regime in patterns of racial domination as it responds to changes occurring in the national mode of regulation and explain how political and economic elites form city-governing coalitions that fashion modes of regulation derived from the larger political economy.

Slavery established the mode of social regulation for Birmingham's first regime. Marx, who knew a great deal about slavery in the British Caribbean, wrote about slavery as though its effect was the same throughout the hemisphere, according to Elizabeth Fox-Genovese and Eugene Genovese.[25] It was not. The worlds made by slaveholders in the West Indies and Latin America differed from that in the United States, where slaveholders successfully resisted capitalist pressure longer. In the West Indies, slaveholders deserted their land, wrote Raimondo Luraghi, "to go to London to spend their money peacefully and to defend their interests," which proved a death blow to the planter class in that part of the world.[26] Confronted with a massive African presence, wrote Robin Blackburn, Caribbean slaveholders "were obliged to negotiate with, and make concessions to [a] slave elite" that served as an intermediate social buffer between themselves and their slaves. This elite was accorded modest corporate privileges that helped buttress the slave regime—privileges never accorded slaves or free blacks in North America. West Indians who immigrated to the United States resisted being cast in the same mold as their black North American counterparts, a fact that helps explain their relative economic success compared with many blacks born in the United States.[27] In the United States, wrote Edgar Thompson, "The plantation took two peoples originally differentiated as Christian and heathen and before the first century was over it had made two races."[28] In the South, an oligopolistic planter regime used race to regulate an extensive regime of accumulation.

A critical theory of race requires sensitivity to race in capitalist development; a critical spatial theory of race requires sensitivity to the ways in which capitalist development and restructuring transform the geography of places along racial lines. The idea behind a critical spatial theory is that capitalism (re)produces space. Classical economic theory, which many geographers have relied on to explain location, is ahistorical. It stresses the role of intrasocietal conditions and factors that reduce costs of production at a particular place; it does not analyze historical effects of different modes of production. Traditional geography assumes that space exists in a natural state and not as a socially constructed entity. A principal spokesperson for this traditional view, Ellsworth Huntington (1876–1947), wrote at least twenty-eight books and contributed to thirty others in his attempt to measure the influence of the natural environment on human progress. The physical environment does not fully explain the development of Birmingham. A critical spatial theory views spatial or regional development as a part of the general development of capitalism and not merely in terms of the location of endowed natural resources. New class and race relations had to be constructed before Birmingham could become the industrial city of the South, and the planter-based industrialists' regime played a significant role in reconstructing these relations. Likewise, the restructuring of capitalism has been an important factor in the reconstruction of race in Birmingham.

To understand fully the regime and mode of social regulation that transformed race and place in Birmingham, this book begins with the antebellum period. As Stanley Greenberg noted, "The South in particular, with its highly developed slave economy, clear and rigid racial-caste lines, and white monopoly of state power, provided the essentials for a racial order."[29] The planter-based regime, which produced a distinct racial and industrial pattern, took Birmingham down a route to industrialization that differed from most industrial places. The following chapters attempt to give empirical and interpretive substance to the conceptual arguments presented.

NOTES

1. Edward W. Soja, *Postmodern Geographies: The Reassertion of Space in Critical Social Theory* (London: Verso, 1989), 159.

2. Larry Sawers, "New Perspectives on the Urban Political Economy," in *Marxism and the Metropolis: New Perspectives in Urban Political Economy*, ed. William K. Tabb and Larry Sawers (New York: Oxford University Press, 1984), 4.

3. Karl Marx and Frederick Engels, *The Communist Manifesto* (New York: Penguin Books, 1967), 83.

4. N. D. Kondratieff, "The Long Waves in Economic Life," *Review of Economic Statistics* 17, no. 6 (November 1935): 105–14; Brian J. L. Berry, *Long-Wave Rhythms in Economic Development and Political Behavior* (Baltimore: Johns Hopkins University Press, 1991), 36, 37; see also Michael Marshall, *Long Waves of Regional Development* (New York: St. Martin's Press, 1987), 1–47.

5. Joseph A. Schumpeter, *Business Cycles: A Theoretical, Historical, and Statistical Analysis of the Capitalist Process*, vols. 1 and 2 (New York: McGraw-Hill, 1939), 87–102; Gerhard Mensch, Charles Coutinho, and Klaus Kaasch, "Changing Capital Values and the Propensity to Innovate," in *Long Waves in the World Economy*, ed. Christopher Freeman (London: Butterworths, 1983), 31–47; Simon Kuznets, "Innovations and Adjustments in Economic Growth," *Swedish Journal of Economics* 74 (1972): 431–51.

6. Ernest Mandel, "Explaining Long Waves of Capitalist Development," in Freeman, *Long Waves*, 195–201.

7. Frances Fox Piven and Richard A. Cloward, *Regulating the Poor: The Function of Public Welfare* (New York: Pantheon Books, 1971), 4–6.

8. Marshall, *Long Waves*, 86.

9. A. Lipietz, "New Tendencies in the International Division of Labour: Regimes of Accumulation and Modes of Regulation," in *Production, Work, Territory: The Geographical Anatomy of Industrial Capitalism*, ed. A. Scott and M. Storper (Boston: Allen & Unwin, 1986), 19, 25.

10. David Gordon, "Class Struggle and the Stages of American Urban Development," in *The Rise of the Sunbelt Cities*, ed. D. C. Perry and A. J. Watkins (Beverly Hills, Calif.: Sage Publications, 1977), 55–82; David Gordon, "Capitalist Development and the History of American Cities," in Tabb and Sawers, *Marxism*, 21–53; Michael Aglietta, *A Theory of Capitalist Regulation: The U.S. Experience*, trans. D. Fernbach (London: NLB, 1979), 111–50.

11. *Colored American*, 28 July 1838, cited in Noel Ignatiev, *How the Irish Became White* (New York: Routledge, 1995), 110.

12. Thomas Bates, "Gramsci and the Theory of Hegemony," *Journal of the History of Ideas* 36, no. 2 (1975): 363.

13. Peter Jackson, "Geography, Race, and Racism," in *New Models in Geography: The Political-Economy Perspective*, Vol. 2, ed. Richard Peet and Nigel Thrift (London: Unwin Hyman, 1989), 176–95.

14. A. Sivanandan, "Challenging Racism: Strategies for the '80s," *Race and Class* 25, (1983): 2.

15. Marc Allen Eisner, *Regulatory Politics in Transition* (Baltimore: Johns Hopkins University Press, 1993), 83–84.

16. Cornel West, "Race and Social Theory: Toward a Genealogical Materialist Analysis," in *The Year Left 2: Toward a Rainbow Socialism, Essays on Race, Ethnicity, Class and Gender*, ed. Mike Davis, Manning Marable, Fred Pfeil, and Michael Sprinker (London: Verso, 1987), 74–90; Michael Omi and Howard Winant, *Racial Formation in the United States: From the 1960s to the 1980s* (New York: Routledge and Kegan Paul, 1986), 57–69.

17. M. Nikolinakos, "Notes on an Economic Theory of Racism," *Race* 14 (1973): 365–81; Lucius Outlaw, "Toward a Critical Theory of 'Race'," in *Anatomy of Racism*, ed. Theo Goldberg (Minneapolis: University of Minnesota Press, 1990), 58–82; Paul Gilroy, "One Nation Under a Groove: The Culture Politics of 'Race' and Racism in Britain," in Goldberg, *Anatomy*, 263–82.

18. Omi and Winant, *Racial Formation*, 68, 69. Emphasis added.

19. Michael Storper and Richard Walker, *The Capitalist Imperative: Territory, Technology, and Industrial Growth* (New York: Basil Blackwell, 1989); B. Page and R. Walker, "From Settlement to Fordism: The Agro-Industrial Revolution in the American Midwest," *Economic Geography* 67, no. 4 (October 1991): 281–315.

20. Simon Duncan, "What Is Locality?" in Peet and Thrift, *New Models*, 222.

21. Quoted in Solomon F. Bloom, *The World of Nations: A Study of the National Implications in the World of Karl Marx* (New York: Columbia University Press, 1941), 24–25; Karl Marx, *Capital*, vol. 1 (New York: International Publishers, 1967), 581n.

22. Peter Jackson, "The Idea of 'Race' and the Geography of Racism," in *Race and Racism: Essays in Social Geography*, ed. Peter Jackson (London: Allen and Unwin, 1987), 3–19.

23. S. L. Elkin, *City and Regime in the American Republic* (Chicago: University of Chicago Press, 1987).

24. Marshall M. A. Feldman, "Spatial Structures of Regulation and Urban Regimes," in *Reconstructing Urban Regime Theory: Regulating Urban Politics in a Global Economy*, ed. Mickey Lauria (Thousand Oaks, Calif.: Sage Publications, 1997), 31.

25. Elizabeth Fox-Genovese and Eugene D. Genovese, *Fruits of Merchant Capital: Slavery and Bourgeois Property in the Rise and Expansion of Capitalism* (New York: Oxford Uni-

versity Press, 1983), 20; Eugene D. Genovese, *The World the Slaveholders Made* (New York: Pantheon Books, 1969), 3–20.

26. Raimondo Luraghi, *The Rise and Fall of the Plantation South* (New York: New Viewpoints, 1978), 48.

27. Robin Blackburn, *The Making of New World Slavery: From Baroque to the Modern, 1492–1800* (London: Verso, 1997), 586; Theodore W. Allen, *The Invention of the White Race: Racial Oppression and Social Control*, vol. 1 (London: Verso, 1994), 113.

28. Edgar Thompson, *Plantation Societies, Race Relations and the South: The Regimentation of Populations* (Durham, N.C.: Duke University Press, 1975), 116.

29. Stanley B. Greenberg, *Race and State in Capitalist Development: Comparative Perspectives* (New Haven, Conn.: Yale University Press, 1980), 32.

5

The Slave Mode of Production

What is a Negro slave? A man of the black race . . . A Negro is a Negro.
He becomes a slave *only in certain relationships.*

—KARL MARX, *Wage Labour and Capital*, 1849

Historians have hotly debated the material success of the slave mode of production for the South, yet profitability is a secondary issue, a diversion created by Alfred Conrad and John Meyer in 1964 and revived a decade later by Robert Fogel and Stanley Engerman.[1] To assess profitability, it is necessary to separate slave production as an individual enterprise from slavery as an economic system that can generate capital and economic growth.[2] Slavery generated high profits and growth rates where there was fresh land, a steady supply of labor, and strong demand on the world market for certain staples. Even slave-operated industries were often quite profitable.[3]

The North and the South, however, were not the products of a single dialectic. Slavery existed with capitalism to generate a "core" with a more intensive regime of accumulation in the North and a "periphery" organized close to an extensive regime of accumulation in the South. Even within the South, however, there were in effect two Souths—a slave South that grew and a nonslave South that existed at the subsistence level, almost a peasant economy. Fogel and Engerman's cliometric analysis that documents the high profitability of slavery focused primarily on the slave South. Roger Ransom found the wealth of the planters "overwhelming," averaging "almost six times the wealth reported by farmers in northern states." He noted that "farmers owning slaves reported an average of $33,906 of real and personal estate in 1860, whereas northern farmers reported an average of only $3,858." However, southern farmers with no slaves reported an average wealth of only $2,362—significantly below the average of northern farmers. In the two decades before the Civil War, per-capita wealth in the South was approximately 50 percent higher than that of the entire nation, mainly because of investment in slaves.[4] Indeed, because slaveholders had no inclination to accumulate capital except to invest in slaves, Jonathan Wiener argued that they were not capitalists.[5]

SLAVERY AS ANTICAPITALIST

Eugene Genovese argued that although slavery grew in the South to meet the demands of capitalists elsewhere, it simultaneously produced a ruling class antithetical to the capitalist mode of production, which explains the region's underdevelopment during the antebellum period.[6] The slave South was not of the capitalist world, wrote Raimondo Luraghi: "precapitalist in structure and antibourgeois in shape of mind."[7] Even Fogel and Engerman, who made an impressive case for the profitability and capitalist nature of slavery, contend it was noncapitalist in at least one significant respect: the "privatization" of political power. In the South, the state yielded a great deal of legal authority to the planter class, whereas in Europe the rise of capitalism was accompanied by a demand to centralize political authority in the state and weaken the feudal regime.[8]

The antebellum South had "a plantation economy embedded in a world market, but it also had a huge subsistence sector that severely circumscribed the penetration of market relations into the regional economy as a whole."[9] Slavery required the use of direct force. Robert Brenner notes,

> where the direct application of force is the condition for ruling-class surplus-extraction, the very difficulties of increasing productive potential through the improvement of the productive forces may encourage the expenditure of surplus to enhance precisely the capacity for the application of force. In this way, the ruling class can increase its capacity to exploit the direct producers, or acquire increased means of production (land, labour, tools) through military methods. Rather than being accumulated, the economic surplus is here systematically diverted from reproduction to unproductive labour.[10]

Direct force is dehumanizing. Dehumanized slaves will misuse the instruments of labor to prove their humanity, which makes production more costly. For this reason, the slaveholders selected none but the rudest and heaviest tools that required almost no skill to produce and were inefficient.[11] These tools enhanced even more the direct application of force to compensate for inadequate tools in the production process. In his *A Journey in the Seaboard States*, Frederick Law Olmsted wrote,

> I am here shown tools that no man in his senses, with us, would allow a laborer, for whom he was paying wages, to be encumbered with; and the excessive weight and clumsiness of which, I would judge, would make work at least ten per cent greater than with those ordinarily used with us. . . . So, too, when I ask why mules are so universally substituted for horses on the farm, the first reason given, and confessedly the most conclusive one, is that horses cannot bear the treatment that they always must get from the negroes; horses are always soon foundered or crippled by them, while mules will bear cudgelling.[12]

This observation suggests that the planter class was not concerned with innovations that would contribute to better treatment of the land and greater productivity. According to C. Post, the noncapitalist character of slavery blocked the slave master's "ability to reorganize the labor-process through technical innovation" and hindered the accumulation of capital.[13] The slave economy lacked diversification and wide-ranging knowledge of techniques suitable for capital accumulation. It restricted most slaves to unskilled repetitive tasks and discouraged expenditures for instruments of labor, which could have served to develop a regional market for industries.[14] It is the accumulation of investment capital to produce better instruments of labor that leads to technological progress and further capital accumulation. Better instruments would produce greater surplus value. As Genovese points out, black slaves had been accustomed to agricultural work in Africa, so raising productivity should not have been difficult.[15]

Gavin Wright, however, finds little evidence for the view of "associating slave labor with poor morale, semi-intentional carelessness, and technological backwardness."[16] "More likely," wrote Wright, "the agricultural practices simply reflected the low priority that planters placed on land investment and maintenance."[17] For instance, slaveholders rarely used a machine that allowed one laborer to plant as much cotton as two mules and four workers using conventional planting. A mule-drawn cotton picker was patented in 1850 by Samuel S. Rembert and Jedediah Prescott, but there were essentially no improvements on the original design until 1890, and another forty years passed before others made further advances. These gaps reflected the fact that the capital needed to maintain slaves is greater than that required to employ free labor, so less capital was available for investment in machinery.[18]

Slaveholders had to bear the cost of housing and maintaining slaves and rearing their children as well as other labor costs. Workers' consumption under slavery was indistinguishable from other production inputs: feeding and housing slaves differs little from seeding the field or maintaining production machinery.[19] Slaves were not variable capital but constant elements of the production process, which burdened the slaveholders with inflexible costs. Reducing the labor force by improving productivity was not considered economically feasible under the slave system, which required that all hands be constantly occupied. Any such effort would decrease the value of slaves. There was neither the incentive to invest in machinery nor the means to accumulate capital for such investment.

Free labor under capitalism enters the production process as variable capital—in other words, capitalists can increase or decrease the amount depending on economic circumstances, or they can replace labor with machinery. As variable capital, labor determines the value of the commodity being produced.[20] The amount of surplus value can be large or small, depending on the rate of labor exploitation. Free labor embodied in the production of a commodity adds to the market value of the finished product. One part of the labor process entails workers producing the value of their labor power necessary for basic subsistence, and the other part produces surplus value. One effect of capitalism is to distinguish more clearly between human consumption, as determined by variable capital, and consumption for production, which is constant capital. Constant capital—for example, plant and machinery—makes for qualitative efficiency in the production of a new commodity but gives up only as much value to the new commodity as required to produce the machinery.[21] In contrast, slaveholders directed their investments to the acquisition of more slaves and land, not better machinery, making economic progress quantitative and producing absolute surplus values.[22]

Variable capital gives capitalists power of real possession and the means to introduce new techniques into the labor process. A free-laboring industrial worker not only carries the responsibility of caring for a family but also can be released during a downswing. This ability puts labor and capital in a more competitive relationship than that of slaveholder and slave: the slaveholder has no such flexibility but must maintain slave labor or sell it; the relationship between capital and labor is more paternalistic than competitive. The wage-laboring system exploited labor more efficiently than slavery. Capitalists using wage labor did not have to absorb so much of the cost of developing labor as did slaveholders, especially during nonproductive years.[23]

One of many points that distinguish a Marxian analysis of production from that of classical economics is the effective canceling out of the labor value of machinery and raw materials from surplus value. Classical economics defines the value of manufactured products as determined by the relative cost of machines and raw materials as well as the cost of human labor. A more crucial omission is that classical economics conveys nothing about class relations that evolve in the production process. It is the class relations of production, not the producer's relation to the market, that determines the regime of accumulation.[24]

Slaveholding also meant planters had little incentive to reclaim soil. Theirs was essentially a one-crop agricultural economy with simple routines applied on a massive scale. Repeated planting of one crop exhausts nutrients, however, which combined with the potential movability of slaves contributed to the need for territorial expansion. Wright noted that slaves were not real property but personal property—that is, they were portable—which weakened the connection between slaveowners and the land they occupied. The value of investment in slaves was independent of the condition of the land, and slaveholders had little to gain from improved means of transportation because they were laborlords, not landlords. One result was that both population and communication were too sparse to permit development of a space-economy or territorial complex suitable for efficient circulation of capital.[25] Furthermore, capitalism requires not only accumulation of capital at a favorable site but also its circulation. Although urbanized space and transportation can ease circulation, in 1853, Alabama had only thirty towns with a population over 200.[26] Twenty years earlier, Indiana, with a population less than half the size of Alabama's, had seventy-seven towns of that size.

Slaves, unlike free labor, did not engage in exchange, which narrowed the sphere of circulation. The flow of capital is severely restricted. There is no circulation of the value of necessary labor time, i.e., wages, limiting the potential for capitalistic expansion. On the average, slaves received only 21.7 percent of the output on a large plantation.[27] In production based on variable capital, the entire basis is labor as exchange value and the creation of exchange value.[28] Because slaves did not consume the production of their labor and the free small landowners in the

South were mainly subsistence farmers, slaveholders alone provided the consumption norm—and, as a class, they were more interested in consumption for themselves than in accumulation for production. They enslaved blacks, wrote W. E. B. DuBois, "in order that they themselves should live more grandly and not mainly for increasing production."[29] This style marked their special status within southern society. According to Stuart Ewen, the planter class of the slave-owning South drew on

> the traditions of feudal Europe . . . [for] an iconography of power, a claim within history, legitimating the "peculiar institution" over which they held sway. The elaboration of a mannered, aristocratic style of life, across the antebellum South, masked a deep—ultimately fatal—contradiction in the structure of the plantation economy. From the eighteenth century onward, Southern elites carefully erected a detailed depiction of themselves as a leisured, landed class, presiding over happy and romantic rural principalities. From courtly manners to the studied consumption of European finery, Southern cavaliers expended enormous energy and wealth to situate themselves in magic kingdoms, ruled—benevolently—by themselves.[30]

The image was one of a leisured and landed gentry; the economic realities were quite different from those of a capitalist class. As Luraghi noted, they preferred to reveal "wealth, culture, and magnificent life, rather than to conceal money under plain clothes as the bourgeois did."[31] Slaveholders were materialists but not in terms of capital accumulation, which they condemned as godless materialism. Therefore, wrote Barrington Moore, Jr.,

> To hold down a subject population, they [slaveholders] have to generate an antirationalist, antiurban, antimaterialist, and more loosely, antibourgeois view of the world—one that excludes any conception of progress . . . policies are not advocated in order to make humanity happier and certainly not in order to make people richer.[32]

Excluding investment in slaves, the proportion of total investment spent for productive equipment (constant capital) was much lower than that spent for personal consumption.[33] This propensity to consume had a utilitarian function, providing, according to Genovese, "the facade necessary to control the middle and lower classes."[34] Historian Ulrich Bonnell Phillips noted that the slave system promoted leisure "by giving rise to an abnormally large number of men and women who whether actually or nominally performing managerial functions, did little to bring sweat to their brows."[35] Urbanization associated with a seigneurial civilization differs from that found in more capitalistic settings: for the seigneurial class cities are mainly places of consumption; for the bourgeois they are places of production.[36]

Could free white labor have been used in the antebellum South? Craft labor, a forerunner to industrial labor, was considered an inferior pursuit by poor southern whites, who preferred continuing to work the soil on small farms of the uplands.[37] Wrote Olmsted, "To work industriously and steadily, especially under directions from another man, is in the Southern tongue, to work like a nigger."[38] Jacksonian doctrine associating wage labor with slavery also slowed the development of a wage-laboring class, which helped to preserve slaveholders' very existence, their raison d'etre.[39] In the end, most craft tasks were left to slaves. Over half the people enslaved in the early nineteenth century were skilled artisans. Olmsted found them in every southern state; slave owners advertised them for sale, and those who lived in cities experienced a degree of freedom not found among the general slave population. Indeed, they were worth more as artisans in the cities than on the plantation. In Alabama, Olmsted observed that a black carpenter who was an accurate calculator and an excellent craft person sold for $2,000. One slave owner converted a plantation into an industrial school for slaves so he could profit from the high price paid for slave artisans.[40] During the Civil War, the southern iron industry used slaves extensively as puddlers, colliers, foundry workers, carpenters, and masons.[41]

Attempts were made to control slave competition in the few craft industries that existed during the antebellum period. An Alabama lawyer, Robert Tharin, supporting legislation forbidding the employment of slaves except as agricultural laborers or servants, said, "Let the nigger be confined to the cotton field, let no more negro black-smiths, and negro carpenters, and negro bricklayers, and negro wheelwrights be used to drive the poor white man to poverty and to idleness, that root of all evil."[42] For the most part, however, wage labor was considered undesirable.

Planters feared the development of an industrial capitalist class and a free working class within the South that could align with their counterparts in the North. Genovese argues that this fear caused slaveholders to distrust the idea of the industrial city in which they saw

> something incongruous with their local power and status arrangement. . . .
> The intrusion of bourgeois values so antithetical to plantation society was a grave threat to the foundations of slave society and the hegemony of the slaveholding class. . . . Successful reform movement meant the end of slavery and of the basis for the very power the planters were trying to preserve.[43]

Slaveholders as Capitalists

The planters' antagonism toward capital development did not prevent them from gaining considerable power in a country increasingly dominated by capitalists. The slaveholders, as Genovese notes, faced an unusually complex problem: they had to share power with an antagonistic northern bourgeoisie. On the verge of extinction, the slaveholders adopted the bourgeois mode of production and associated with the Whig Party. Some observers recognize the planters' high level of profit and growth but say they disguised deep structural weaknesses that condemned the South to underdevelopment, stagnation, and political disaster.[44] This condemnation was not because the region lacked industry but because its industrial economy was based on an extensive regime of accumulation and was subordinated to the plantation regime, which was based on slave labor. Richmond,

Virginia, was an important industrial city in the antebellum period and served as an outlet for surplus slaves who were leased by manufacturers. During the 1850s, the value of southern manufactured goods increased 95 percent compared to an increase of 85 percent for the United States as a whole. In 1860, the South had almost as many manufacturing establishments as New England, then the manufacturing core of the country, 20,631 versus 20,671, respectively.[45]

As long as slavery directed its mode of production to immediately local consumption, it preserved a somewhat noncapitalistic character. However, cotton exportation changed all that. According to Marx,

> as soon as peoples whose production still moves within the lower forms of slave-labor . . . are drawn into a world market dominated by the capitalist mode of production, whereby the sale of their products for export develops into their principal interest. . . . It was no longer a question of obtaining from him [the Negro] a certain quantity of useful products, but rather of the production of surplus-value itself.[46]

The slavery form of appropriation of surplus value differed from that of free labor but, for Marx, the logic of both was capitalistic. The notion that slavery was anti-capital and negated economic development in the South is based mainly on the fact that it was an abnormality in a world market dominated by free labor.

The antagonism toward capital accumulation came mainly from the Jacksonian Democrats, not from the slaveholders, who were Whigs and supported economic development. Jacksonian Democrats—not members of the planter class—were mainly responsible for the lack of urbanization in Alabama during the antebellum period.[47] In antebellum Alabama, not only were planters *not* antagonistic to industrial development, but—in an era of decentralized democracy and state's rights—they were capable of seizing regional political power and deeply influencing national politics for more than a half century.[48]

Economic motives alone do not necessarily mean an intensive and competitive regime of capital accumulation. The planters' route to industrialization was different from the classical route. Shearer Davis Bowman makes a distinction between the "creative entrepreneur," who initiates economic changes, and the "adaptive entrepreneur," whose skills are devoted to maintaining existing business relationships. Planters, like Prussian Junkers, were devoted to maintaining a monopoly mode of social regulation in the accumulation of capital. Slavery required monopoly control, which does not prevent the accumulation of capital. Bowman goes on to note that planters can be evaluated as capitalists without being labeled "modern." Planters were hostile to modernization because they were anti-egalitarians. They relied on nonmarket "political mechanisms" of repressive exploitation that made them capitalist but, contrary to Marxist theory, a capitalist economy has no one particular system of social relations, a special "mode of production." "Capitalism has been too protean a historical phenomenon to be identified with any particular mode of production."[49] In Birmingham, race-connected practices were key components of the mode of production.

NOTES

1. Alfred H. Conrad and John R. Meyer, *The Economics of Slavery and Other Econometric Studies* (Chicago: Aldine, 1964); Robert William Fogel and Stanley L. Engerman, *Time on the Cross: The Economics of American Negro Slavery*, Vols. 1 and 2 (Boston: Little, Brown, 1974), 158–90.

2. Eugene D. Genovese, *The Political Economy of Slavery: Studies in the Economy and Society of the Slave South* (New York: Vintage Books, 1967) 13–39; Gavin Wright, *Old South, New South: Revolutions in the Southern Economy Since the Civil War* (New York: Basic Books, 1986), 17–33.

3. Robert S. Starobin, *Industrial Slavery in the Old South* (New York: Oxford University Press, 1970), 146–89.

4. Roger L. Ransom, *Conflict and Compromise: The Political Economy of Slavery, Emancipation, and the American Civil War* (New York: Cambridge University Press, 1989), 51, 62; W. H. Baughn, "Capital Formation and Entrepreneurship in the South," *Southern Economic Journal* 16, no. 2 (October 1949): 162–63.

5. Jonathan Wiener, *Social Origins of the New South: Alabama, 1860–1885* (Baton Rouge: Louisiana State University Press, 1978); Wiener, "Class Structure and Economic Development in the American South, 1865–1955," *American Historical Review* 84, no. 4 (October 1979): 970–92.

6. Eugene D. Genovese, *The World the Slaveholders Made* (New York: Pantheon Books, 1969), 26.

7. Raimondo Luraghi, *The Rise and Fall of the Plantation South* (New York: New Viewpoints, 1978), 48.

8. Fogel and Engerman, *Time on the Cross*, 1, 129.

9. Elizabeth Fox-Genovese and Eugene D. Genovese, *Fruits of Merchant Capital: Slavery and Bourgeois Property in the Rise and Expansion of Capitalism* (New York: Oxford University Press, 1983), 17.

10. Robert Brenner, "The Origins of Capitalism: A Critique of Neo-Smithian Marxism," *New Left Review*, 104 (1977): 37.

11. Wright, *Old South*, 30.

12. Frederick Law Olmsted, *A Journey in the Seaboard Slave States, with Remarks on Their Economy* (New York: Dix & Edward, 1856), 46–47.

13. C. Post, "The American Road to Capitalism," *New Left Review* 133 (1982): 34.

14. Thomas Sowell, *Race and Economics* (New York: David McKay Co., 1975), 6.

15. Genovese, *Political Economy*, 70–81.

16. Wright, *Old South*, 30–31.

17. Wright, *Old South*, 30–31.

18. Genovese, *Political Economy*, 58.

19. Ben Fine and Ellen Leopold, *The World of Consumption* (London: Routledge, 1993), 259.

20. Karl Marx, *Capital*, vol. 1, trans. Eden and Cedar Paul (New York: E. P. Dutton, 1930), 191n.

21. To prove that surplus value cannot originate in the use of machinery and other materials, let L_i = labor value of commodity i (in hours), a_i = hours of labor currently employed in producing commodity i, A_i = labor value of machinery and raw materials used up in producing commodity i, and w = value of one hour of labor power. Then, $L_i = a_i + A_i$. Surplus value, s_i, is $L_i - a_iw - A_i$ and, by substituting L_i for $(a_i + A_i)$, $s_i = a_i(1 - w)$.

It is clear that A_i cancels, leaving only current employment of labor power that yields surplus value in the proportion $(1 - w)$, depending on the value of labor power. Since only the value of labor determines surplus value, Marx considered it to be variable capital. The employment of labor produces a value necessary for labor existence and a surplus value (i.e., a value over and above that necessary for existence). The value of machinery and material is not a part of surplus value and is considered constant capital. Proof of the value of labor as variable capital is taken from Donald J. Harris, "Capitalist Exploitation and Black Labor: Some Conceptual Issues," *Review of Black Political Economy* 8, no. 2 (Winter 1978), 7n.

22. Genovese, *Political Economy*, 17.

23. According to Cedric J. Robinson, *Black Marxism: The Making of the Black Radical Tradition* (London: Zed Press, 1983), 286, the cost of northern labor during the nonproductive years was "incurred by the socio-economic sectors of Ireland, Germany, Italy and England," the workers' places of origin.

24. Brenner, *Origins*, 25–92.

25. Wright, *Old South*, 17.

26. David Harvey, *The Urbanization of Capital* (Baltimore: Johns Hopkins University Press, 1985), 185–226.

27. Roger L. Ransom and Richard Sutch, *One Kind of Freedom: The Economic Consequences of Emancipation* (Cambridge, Mass.: Cambridge University Press, 1977), 3–4.

28. Karl Marx, *Grundrisse: Foundations of the Critique of Political Economy*, trans. Martin Nicolaus (New York: Vintage Books, 1973), 419.

29. W. E. B. DuBois, *Black Reconstruction in America* (Cleveland, Ohio: World Publishing Co., 1964), 35.

30. Stuart Ewen, *All Consuming Images: The Politics of Style in Contemporary Culture* (New York: Basic Books, 1988), 114.

31. Luraghi, *Rise and Fall*, 148.

32. Barrington Moore, Jr., *Social Origins of Dictatorship and Democracy: Lord and Peasant in the Making of the Modern World* (Boston: Beacon Press, 1966), 492, 496.

33. Baughn, "Capital Formation," 161–69.

34. Genovese, *Political Economy*, 18.

35. Ulrich Bonnell Phillips, *American Negro Slavery: A Survey of the Supply, Employment and Control of Negro Labor as Determined by the Plantation Regime* (New York: Appleton & Company, 1918), 397.

36. Luraghi, *Rise and Fall*, 68.

37. Holman Head, "The Development of the Labor Movement in Alabama Prior to 1900" (M.A. thesis, University of Alabama, 1955), 9.

38. Frederick Law Olmsted, *The Cotton Kingdom* (New York: Modern Library, 1969), 19.

39. Wright, *Old South*.

40. Frederick Law Olmsted, *A Journey in the Back Country* (New York: Schocken Books, 1970); Olmsted, *Journey in the Seaboard*, 553–54, 567.

41. Head, "Development," 14.

42. Robert S. Tharin, *Arbitrary Arrests in the South* (New York: John Bradburn, 1863), 75.

43. Genovese, *Political Economy*, 24, 141, 99; see also Genovese, *The World*; Fox-Genovese and Genovese, *Fruits*.

44. Fox-Genovese and Genovese, *Fruits*, 37.

45. *Manufactures of the United States in 1860*. Eighth Census, Bureau of the Census, Washington, DC: Government Printing Office, 1865).

46. Karl Marx, *Capital*, vol. 1, trans. Ben Fowkes (New York: Vintage Books, 1977), 345; *Grundrisse*, 513; see also David Roediger, "Precapitalism in One Confederacy: A Note on Genovese, Politics and the Slave South," *New Politics* 9, no. 11 (Summer 1991): 90–95.

47. J. Mills Thornton III, *Politics and Power in a Slave Society: Alabama, 1800–1860* (Baton Rouge: Louisiana State University Press, 1978).

48. Eugene D. Genovese, *Roll, Jordan, Roll: The World the Slaves Made* (New York: Pantheon Books, 1974), 26; Fox-Genovese and Genovese, *Fruits*, 60.

49. Shearer Davis Bowman, *Masters and Lords: Mid-19th-Century U.S. Planters and Prussian Junkers* (New York: Oxford University Press, 1993), 43, 88, 90, 94–95, 100.

6

An Extensive Regime of Accumulation Based on Slave Labor

The panic of 1837, part of the downswing in the first Kondratieff cycle, marked a major political turning point for the manufacturing, commercial, and financial interests organized as the Whig Party to oppose Jacksonian Democrats. In the years immediately after the panic, the citizenry tended to accept the Jacksonian position, holding mainly the Whigs responsible for the downturn. As the depression deepened, however, many Jacksonians came to reconsider their rejection of Whiggery. J. Mills Thornton III tells of the wealthy Mobile industrialist and politician Adam C. Hollinger's intellectual conversion during this time and his subsequent support of a strong Bank of the United States—an idea the Jacksonians had long opposed. As more Jacksonians joined Hollinger in supporting industrial development, their party's political power ebbed. Meanwhile, planters, realizing that manufacturing could bolster the region's economy, used their increasing political power to push for internal improvements and industrial expansion. The Whigs captured control of the Alabama Senate in 1849 and, by 1859, the center of power in the legislature had shifted toward planters with Whiggish goals. With this shift, Thornton noted, "The government becomes less and less the defender of the masses from the assaults of the few, more and more the tool of the social and economic elite. Indeed, the political and economic leaderships tend to merge." The planter class could now reevaluate the economy of the South vis-à-vis the industrializing North to keep pace while retaining its hegemony in the region.[1]

Although planters resisted any attempt to replace the plantation economy, they favored an extensive form of industrialization in which the plantation would be the primary market for manufactured goods supplied either by a few manufacturers subordinate to the planters or by slave artisans owned by the planters.[2] Within this context, Daniel Pratt, a cotton gin manufacturer, emerged in 1846 as the leading representative for industrialization in Alabama.[3]

Planters, however, feared that an intensive regime of industrialization would generate a large, class-conscious, urban proletariat that would threaten the institution of slavery. C. G. Memminger, who later became the Confederacy's secretary of the treasury, warned,

> Drive out negro mechanics and all sorts of operatives from our cities, and who must take their place? The same men who make the cry in the Northern Cities against the tyranny of Capital. . . . In our Cities, we see the operation of these elements—and if the eyes of the planting community are opened, the danger may be averted.[4]

To help placate the planters' fear, Pratt proposed "manufacturing villages," which he maintained would be

> healthier and more amenable to social control than cities. With a small, homogeneous population such villages were secure from the crime and social "-isms" which disrupted Northern urban life. Settled amid farms and plantations, and manufacturing items to serve the agricultural community, Pratt's factory villages promised to complement rather than supplant the cotton and slave system.[5]

This relatively extensive form of industrialization would not be a threat to slave labor (Pratt noted, "African slavery in North America has been a greater blessing to the human family than any other institution except the Christian religion"), nor would it challenge the planter class for hegemony.[6] Indeed, slave labor could be used to control free labor in manufacturing and to avoid the problems associated with it.

Although a few southern enterprises did employ both whites and slaves at the same factory or mine, there was no need for concern about class. White solidarity resolved class and caste conflicts, and racial antagonisms consistently subsumed class antagonisms between labor and capital. The proslavery argument convinced most non–slave owners—mostly Jacksonians who needed little convincing—that the slave mode of production brought economic advancement.[7]

Pratt walked a tightrope between the slaveholders' concerns and the need for regional industrialization. He and other reformers sought to reassure the planters that industrialization would not negate their class position, which depended on the value of their slaves. In 1860, Pratt himself used more than 100 slaves at Prattville to manufacture cheap cloth that slaveholders purchased for their slaves.

Although Birmingham did not exist as a physical entity before 1871, the city was conceived during the antebellum period as a slave-operated industrial city.[8] In 1859, Birmingham's founder and greatest supporter, John T. Milner, noted the region's potential for iron production:

> I am clearly of the opinion, from my own observation, that negro labor can be made exceedingly profitable in rolling mills. The want of skilled labor has hitherto been the grand objective to iron manufactures in the South. This is compensated for by the freedom of Southern states from that hindrance of Northern works, "strikes among the workmen." Making railroad bars is a mo-

notonous process. Each bar is the facsimile of the other, and the great labor consists in the heavy lifting and managing the heated masses in the *machines* or rolls. It requires no great mechanical skill even, for every point is done by machinery, that simply requires to be fed. A negro who can set a saw, or run a grist mill well, or work in a blacksmith's shop, can do work as cheaply in a rolling mill, even now, as white men do at the North, provided he has an *overseer*—a southern man who knows how to manage negroes. . . . I have long since learned that negro slave labor is more reliable and cheaper for any business connected with the construction of a railroad than white.[9]

Although in theory, industrial slave labor may have been less efficient than free labor over time, in the context of the antebellum South, slavery's inefficiency was not apparent. The stigma that poor whites and yeomen of the upland placed on wage labor often made them particularly intractable. One of Pratt's associates wrote of whites, "Brought up from the piney woods, many of them with no sort of training to any kind of labor; in fact, they had to learn everything, and in learning, many mistakes and blunders were made fatal to success."[10] Wages paid for southern free labor remained constant at $300 per annum from 1800 to 1861. An intensive regime of accumulation would have required releasing the rural population from the land to create a supply of wage laborers and urban consumers.[11] Free wage labor would have increased aggregate consumer demand and wealth in the region—a critical ingredient for such a regime and one the slave mode of production could not provide.

As whites overcame the stigma of wage labor, textile mills employed mainly rural poor whites of the upland, an area neglected under the slave mode of production, limiting blacks to menial, dirty, and hazardous jobs—"nigger work"— while white textile workers enjoyed the "benefits" of capitalist benevolence.[12] This pattern of industrial development left untouched the black labor supply that planters needed to maintain the sharecropping system. Nevertheless, wages remained low and contributed to a low consumption norm in the region.

The interests of the industrialists in the slave South were subordinate to those of the planters, who joined with them to develop an extensive colonial type of industrialization.[13] The countryside remained dominant; cities and towns along the railroad became mere trans-shipment points for export to distance markets.[14] The antebellum regime would not provide the production space needed for an intensive regime of accumulation. Transportation would tie stable, producing regions to the ports. Coal and iron ore would be mined, then shipped—like plantation crops—through the port of Mobile to other regions for processing. This process provided the best possible arrangement for planters; but, in 1852, Alabama had only 165 miles of track. By 1860, this number had increased to 743 miles through growing planter influence and the decline of the Jacksonian Democrats.[15] Railroad mileage in the North was still more than twice that in the South, although the South's area was more extensive.

The planters' industrial strategy presupposed, according to Eugene Genovese, "an adequate rate of material growth [for the South], but the South could not keep pace with an increasingly hostile North in population growth, manufacturing, transportation, or even agricultural development."[16] The dominance of the slaveholding class, wrote Genovese, "meant a Prussian road to industrial capitalism, paved with authoritarianism, benevolent despotism, and aristocratic pretension."[17] Barrington Moore, Jr., and others characterized the "Prussian route" as one that allowed a society to industrialize while the political and social system remained under the domination of a landed elite, who could preserve its position.[18] Raimondo Luraghi calls this political-economic arrangement the "seigneurial" system and notes that its deepest roots are in the Italian classicism of the Renaissance and not in Puritanism, which was the social base for bourgeois capitalists.[19]

Meanwhile, the non-South made the transition to a more intensive regime of accumulation based on free wage labor.[20] Although in 1860 the South had almost as many manufacturing establishments as did New England, it had only 2.47 establishments per 1,000 population compared with New England's 6.59 establishments per 1,000 population. The average capital investment per establishment for New England was $12,456; in the South, the figure was only $4,652. With a combined population, Illinois and Ohio had a greater capital investment than the entire South; in fact, the two states' average capitalization was twice as intensive as the average in the South. The South had only 159 establishments manufacturing cotton products; New England had 570. Only 16.3 percent of all such establishments were in the South, which had 28.2 percent of the population.[21] The urban population of the lower South was only 7 percent of the total population, compared with 37 percent in New England and Ohio and 14 percent in Michigan and Wisconsin.[22]

In Maryland and Virginia, the slave South attempted to become more competitive with the North. In these states, proximity to northern urban markets spurred significant progress in crop diversification and livestock improvement, which led to a reduction in the need for slaves. Surplus slaves were sold to obtain cash to invest in these estates, although slaves could be sold only in markets farther south, which needed access to virgin lands—where the wasteful methods of the slave system could be applied profitably. Slaves also could be used in mining and sugar milling in Mexico and the Caribbean and in mining, lumbering, and transportation enterprises in the U.S. West. Therefore, acquisition of new land could guarantee the continuation and expansion of the slave system.[23]

Many Northerners opposed the expansion of slavery, thereby contributing to the "free soil" movement. Genovese noted that this expansion had its political and social parallels: the need of the southern ruling class to maintain parity in the U.S. Senate or at least enough votes to protect its hegemony. For the planters, he wrote, "To agree to containment meant to agree that slavery constituted an evil. . . . Free-soil argument struck at the foundation of the slaveholders' pride and belief in himself."[24] Slaveholders were very pleased with the *Dred Scott* decision, which allowed slavery in the western territories.

Nevertheless, the geographical expansion of slavery represented a potential obstacle to an intensive regime of accumulation in the Midwest and to the developing economic relationship between the Midwest and northern industrial capital.[25] The Civil War removed this obstacle. According to Luraghi, "The Civil War had not so much the task of making free a complete capitalistic structure yet existing; but mainly that of creating the conditions for such a structure to grow, by sweeping away obstacles and joining all the states into a truly unified nation (the 'great Republic') and into an integrated market."[26] Canals and railroads would later connect the West with the Eastern seaboard and increase the profitability of western wheat and corn, and their derivatives that provided capitalists with raw materials.

The issue of states' rights and the possibility of war added urgency to planter demands for economic self-sufficiency. In 1854, Francis (Frank) Gilmer, a wealthy Alabama planter and merchant, chartered the South and North Railroad. Four years later, he commissioned Milner to lay railroad tracks connecting the southern and northern sections of Alabama. In 1860, the legislature, on Milner's recommendation, granted the rail line a loan of $663,135. In the following years, under the Confederacy, the state allocated aid sufficient to extend the railroad northward to a point near the future site of Birmingham (where Gilmer and Milner would build the first furnaces and rolling mills, and Pratt would be one of twenty-five shareholders).

Historically, the mass of peasants have achieved economic and political emancipation only when the formal abolition of feudalism accompanied the complete division of the seigneury. Harry Haywood wrote, "And wherever the formal abolition of slavery or serfdom was not accompanied by the expatriation of landlordism, political power either remained in the hands of the former landholding class, or was speedily regained by them."[27] Such was the case in Prussia, Japan, and other places, including the U.S. South. A major restructuring of the political economy was needed before the South would be able to produce an intensive regime of capital accumulation. The Civil War led to the creation of some preconditions for such a regime.[28] Although Pratt and other southern industrialists opposed secession, they could offer no viable alternatives to most planters, whose aristocratic tradition and ideology intensified their attachment to a premodern condition.[29]

According to Luraghi, when the war came, the southern planter class relied on an oligopolist mode of regulation to build a military-industrial complex without a "slaveless industrial bourgeoisie independent of planter control" and resorted "to forced industrialization."[30] To raise capital, the Confederacy floated its first public loan—$15 million—on 16 March 1861; the first $500,000 came from the state of Alabama. The Confederacy took over existing factories and constructed new facilities, creating, according to Luraghi, a mini-industrial revolution in the South without allowing a more modern capitalist class to rise.[31] To produce arms for the Confederacy, Pratt helped to organize the Red Mountain Iron and Coal Company just outside of the future site of Birmingham. At Selma, the Confederate government built a cannon foundry that cast big Brooke guns, which then were considered the best in the world. Nevertheless, the North, with its more intensive regime of accumulation and competitive mode of regulation, defeated the South, thereby eliminating the economic and political obstacles posed by the geographical expansion of slavery. Writing to Abraham Lincoln in 1864, Karl Marx identified the American working people as the "true political power of the North," referring to their resistance to slave power.[32] As Luraghi noted, the slaveholders "had to meet the North on its ground, industrial warfare. And there they lost."[33] In the South, slave labor had been and continued to be accepted in theory and practice. Class and caste relationships remained unchanged throughout the antebellum period and provided the mode of social regulation for an extensive regime of accumulation.[34]

NOTES

1. J. Mills Thornton III, *Politics and Power in a Slave Society: Alabama, 1800–1860* (Baton Rouge: Louisiana State University Press, 1978), 37–38, 91, 180, 292; Robert S. Starobin, *Industrial Slavery in the Old South* (New York: Oxford University Press, 1970), 11.

2. Eugene D. Genovese, *The Political Economy of Slavery: Studies in the Economy and Society of the Slave South* (New York: Vintage Books, 1967), 185–93.

3. Randall M. Miller, "Daniel Pratt's Industrial Urbanism: The Cotton Mill Town in Antebellum Alabama," *Alabama Historical Quarterly* 34, no. 1 (Spring 1972): 5–35.

4. Genovese, *Political Economy*, 199–200; quoted in Starobin, *Industrial Slavery*, 210.

5. Miller, "Daniel Pratt's," 11.

6. Quoted in Miller, "Daniel Pratt's," 32.

7. Starobin, *Industrial Slavery*, 209.

8. W. David Lewis, *Sloss Furnaces and the Rise of the Birmingham District: An Industrial Epic* (Tuscaloosa: University of Alabama Press, 1994), 85.

9. John T. Milner, *Report to the Governor of Alabama on the Alabama Central Railroad* (Montgomery: Advertiser Book and Job Steam Press Print, 1859), 44–45. Emphasis added.

10. Starobin, *Industrial Slavery*, 154–55.

11. Starobin, *Industrial Slavery*, 189.

12. Stanley B. Greenberg, *Race and State in Capitalist Development: Comparative Perspectives* (New Haven, Conn.: Yale University Press, 1980), 394; Starobin, *Industrial Slavery*, 214.

13. Genovese, *Political Economy*, 48–51; Jonathan Wiener, *Social Origins of the New South: Alabama, 1860–1885* (Baton Rouge: Louisiana State University Press, 1978); Gavin Wright, *Old South, New South: Revolution in the Southern Economy Since the Civil War* (New York: Basic Books, 1986), 22–23.

14. Barrington Moore, Jr., *Social Origins of Dictatorship and Democracy: Lord and Peasant in the Making of the Modern World* (Boston: Beacon Press, 1966), 111–61; see also Wiener, *Social Origins*.

15. Eugene Alvarez, *Travel on Southern Antebellum Railroads, 1828–1860* (Tuscaloosa: University of Alabama Press, 1974), 172; Lewis, *Sloss Furnaces*, 24–30.

16. Genovese, *Political Economy*, 4.

17. Genovese, *Political Economy*, 207.

18. Moore, *Social Origins*; for discussions of the "Prussian route" to industrial capitalism in the South, see Wiener, *Social Origins*, and Jonathan Wiener, "Class Structure and Economic Development in the American South, 1865–1955," *American Historical Review* 84, no. 4 (October 1979): 970–92.

19. Raimondo Luraghi, *The Rise and Fall of the Plantation South* (New York: New Viewpoints, 1978), 15–23.

20. Genovese, *Political Economy*, 157–79; Gavin Wright, *The Political Economy of the Cotton South: Households, Markets, and Wealth in the Nineteenth Century* (New York: W. W. Norton, 1978), 89–127; David R. Meyer, "The Industrial Retardation of Southern Cities, 1860–1880," *Explorations in Economic History* 25, no. 4 (October 1988): 366–86.

21. *Manufactures of the United States in 1860*. Eighth Census, Bureau of the Census, Washington, D.C.: Government Printing Office, 1865).

22. Genovese, *Political Economy*, 166, 171.

23. Genovese, *Political Economy*, 246; Starobin, *Industrial Slavery*, 214–22.

24. Genovese, *Political Economy*, 247, 250.

25. C. Post, "The American Road to Capitalism," *New Left Review* 133 (1982): 37.

26. Raimondo Luraghi, "The Civil War and the Modernization of American Society: Social Structure and Industrial Revolution in the Old South Before and During the War," *Civil War History* 18, no. 3 (September 1972): 241.

27. Harry Haywood, *Negro Liberation* (New York: International Publishers, 1948), 91.

28. Genovese, *Political Economy*, 207.

29. Starobin, *Industrial Slavery*, 229.

30. Luraghi, *Rise and Fall*, 113, 118.

31. Luraghi, "Civil War," 230–50.

32. *Marx and Engels on the United States*, compiled by Nelly Rumyantseva (Moscow: Progress Publishers, 1979), 168.

33. Luraghi, "Civil War," 246.

34. Starobin, *Industrial Slavery*, 231.

7

Reconstruction

Immediately after President Abraham Lincoln was assassinated and Andrew Johnson succeeded to the presidency, Johnson tried to put into effect the main parts of Lincoln's program for treatment of the defeated South. This program was to be very conciliatory toward the former slaveholding class. Johnson planned to continue the old governmental structure and show leniency. All confiscated property was returned, and the rights of Southerners to run for office were restored. In Johnson's third annual message to Congress, he explained his attitude toward blacks:

> It must be acknowledged that in the progress of nations, negroes have shown less capacity for government than any other race of people. No independent government of any form has ever been successful in their hands. On the contrary, wherever they have been left to their own devices they have shown a constant tendency to relapse into barbarism. . . . The great difference between the two races in physical, mental, and moral characteristics will prevent an amalgamation or fusion of them together in one homogeneous mass.[1]

During the summer and fall of 1865, southern states elected state officers and legislatures that restored the oligopolistic power of the former slaveholders and promptly passed laws, known as "Black Codes," severely restricting the political and economic rights of blacks.[2]

Clearly, freedom from slavery did not translate into a free and competitive labor market. Obviously not describing a competitive mode of social regulation, one Alabama planter noted,

> The nigger is going to be made a serf sure as you live. It won't need any law for that. Planters will have an understanding among themselves: 'you won't hire my niggers, and I won't hire yours;' then what's left for them? They're attached to the soil, and we're as much their masters as ever. I'll stake my life, this is the way it will work.[3]

Although the freeing of the slaves struck at the basis of the planters' wealth and power, they continued to hope the government would revoke emancipation. Some planters even ignored orders to free their slaves.[4] There were also radical reconstructionists, who opposed reinstatement of the planter regime and attempted to introduce a more competitive arrangement. In a speech in Lancaster, Pennsylvania, on 9 September 1865, Thaddeus Stevens, a Pennsylvania congressman and an ardent opponent of slavery, asked,

> How can republican institutions, free schools, free churches, free social intercourse, exist in a mingled community of nabobs and serfs; of the owners of 20,000 acre manors with lordly palaces and the occupants of narrow huts inhabited by "low white trash"? If the South is ever to be made a safe republic, let her lands be cultivated by the toil of the owners or the free labor of intelligent citizens. . . . The country would be well rid of the proud, bloated and defiant rebels. . . . The foundation of their institutions must be broken up and relaid, or all our blood and treasure have been spent in vain.[5]

For a time, the radicals seemed to gain the upper hand. After the 1866 elections, Congress passed a series of acts that set the stage for a period of intensely competitive politics that included the election of blacks to office. The Civil Rights Bill of 1866 repealed the Black Codes and conferred citizenship on former slaves; the 14th Amendment to the Constitution, in 1868, overturned the *Dred Scott* decision and granted citizenship to all people born or naturalized in the United States; and the 15th Amendment, passed in 1870, prohibited state governments from denying individuals the right to vote because of race and color. Conventions called in southern states to write new constitutions provided for the rights of blacks as free persons.

To break the economic and political power of the former slaveholding class, Thaddeus Stevens proposed establishing a system of small, independent farmers as the dominant southern agricultural pattern. He called on the government to confiscate the holdings of the South's 70,000 largest landowners and give forty acres each to a million adult freed men. The state would divide the remainder, an estimated 354 million acres, into farms for sale to the highest bidder.

While Stevens's proposal may have been intended principally to mock the former slaveholders, it was entirely consistent with the notion of democratic capitalism in which market competition and self-interest are supposed to play a major role in eliminating or relieving racial differences (e.g., competition in the labor market could lead to nondiscriminatory wages).[6] In short, Reconstruction could have led the South to eliminate political obstacles to developing a more competitive democratic capitalism. Planters were resentful and, according to Harry Haywood, depicted Reconstruction

> as a period of unrestrained violence, bloody terror, carnage, and rapine, in which the Negro is presented as a naive but semi-savage person who, freed from a benevolent slavery, roamed the land robbing and stealing, and venting his lust upon unprotected white womanhood; while in the background, di-

recting this horror, stalked the most sinister of all figures, the vengeful swaggering carpetbagger, a sort of Merchant of Venice, exacting his pound of flesh from a ruined and prostrate South.[7]

A whole literature was based on such distortions. David W. Griffith's *The Birth of a Nation*, published in 1915, depicted blacks during Reconstruction as ignorant lustful villains.[8] Birmingham's founder, John T. Milner, wrote,

> The experience of other emancipation States, had, without a single exception, proved that emancipation absolutely destroyed the value of the negro as a laborer, and the productiveness of any country once cultivated by them as slaves, rapidly went into insignificance, and nothingness, after they were left to themselves. *There is not a single exception to this rule anywhere in the history of the world.*[9]

Before the Civil War, Milner had written that the stagnation and inactivity of countries around the Gulf of Mexico were due to the "mistaken policy of the republican governments of liberating their slaves." He had noted, however, that these countries "are becoming rapidly anglicized, and have awoke from the long torpor."[10]

THE FAILURE OF RADICAL RECONSTRUCTION

Radical Reconstruction was not to be, nor was the postbellum South to develop a bourgeois capitalism like that described by Karl Marx. The federal government never provided the financial aid needed to rebuild the South; and, with the downswing in the second Kondratieff cycle, northern capitalists were willing to discard Reconstruction completely. As Gerald David Jaynes noted,

> The burden of a wartime economy had effectively forced the United States Treasury off the gold standard for internal commerce. A large federal debt had been incurred to finance the war and this had been accommodated with a large issuance of paper currency. The postwar northern economy was beset with price inflation, and many business interests were clamoring for a contraction of the quantity of paper currency. They argued that a decreased money supply and restoration of a gold-based hard money policy were the best procedures for combatting inflation and stabilizing the economy.[11]

Moves toward restoring hard money had, however, brought protests from farmers who favored payment in soft currency, or "greenbacks." This struggle produced the Greenback Party, the first exclusively populist-farmer alliance. Jaynes cites Edward Tobey, a financial expert of the time, who

> saw in the cotton industry a painless solution to the [economic crisis]. Tobey, and others, reasoned that since cotton was the number one export commodity of the United States, its supply essentially controlled the flow of gold to

and from the states. . . . The Tobey argument was simple. Not only would large cotton exports allow gold to be retained at home, but a surplus crop would induce a flow of gold to the United States. The resulting increase in the domestic supply of money would allow a contraction of the paper currency sans the debilitating effect of a depression, buoy the economy, and allow payment of the national debt.[12]

But, without black labor, cotton land would remain uncultivated. In addition, distributing free land to blacks and establishing a competitive labor system lessened the chances of producing cotton for export in sufficient quantity to reduce the federal debt.

Excessive rain, droughts, heat, and the ravages of insects cut agricultural production between 1871 and 1873. Cotton prices declined in the panic of 1873, part of the downswing in the second Kondratieff cycle. By 1878, an estimated 4.1 million acres of agricultural land were out of production—approximately 10 percent of cultivated acreage in 1870.[13]

These developments led former slaveholders to call with particular urgency for northern support for commercial and business development. Like other nations on the verge of extinction, the South wanted to connect with the inheritance of the bourgeois revolution. Northern capitalists were more than willing to accommodate. Capital scrambled into markets eroded by the slave regime.[14] The survival of capitalism depends on the continual production and reproduction of new markets, for, as Marx and Friedrich Engels noted,

> The bourgeoisie, by the rapid improvement of all instruments of production, by the immensely facilitated means of communication, draws all, even the most barbarian, nations into civilization. The cheap prices of its commodities are the heavy artillery with which it batters down all Chinese walls, with which it forces the barbarians' intensely obstinate hatred of foreigners to capitulate. It compels all nations, on pain of extinction, to adopt the bourgeois mode of production; it compels them to introduce what it calls civilization into their midst, i.e., to become bourgeois themselves. In one word, it creates a world after its own image.[15]

With the failure of radical Reconstruction, the South became more fully integrated into the capital world. Thomas Scott, president of the Pennsylvania Railroad, the country's largest corporation, helped broker an agreement between the Republican Party and southern conservatives seeking regional improvements. The Southerners agreed to support the Republican candidate for president, Rutherford B. Hayes, in return for a pledge of federal funds for internal improvements. The Compromise of 1877 resulted. According to John Agnew, "The state survives and prospers only if it can hold together the territorial coalition of places that gives it geographical form. This involves pursuing policies and distributing resources in a deliberate way to maintain legitimacy."[16] The 1877 compromise held the North and South together in a territorial coalition that produced demand for goods, trade, and commerce between the two regions. Northern investment in southern industries increased significantly—to the point at which the South was dependent on northern capital.[17] The compromise also gave the southern ruling class control over the mode of production in the region, effectively ensuring that postbellum capital development remained relatively premodern.

The downswing in the 1870s also led to struggles on many fronts: workers' strikes in northern cities, farmers' protests in the Midwest, and blacks' political and economic struggles in the South.[18] With high levels of labor exploitation in the North, workers argued also for northern Reconstruction, i.e., higher wages and better working conditions. Northern capitalists, having abandoned any notion of full Reconstruction in the South, responded quickly to workers' demands. Michael Reich noted that it was no coincidence that labor unrest reached a peak in 1877, "the same year that the North reneged on [southern] Reconstruction," giving the South a free hand over blacks in return for southern protection and support of their investments in the region.[19] Speaking in Atlanta, President Rutherford B. Hayes told blacks that their "'rights and interests would be safer' in the hands of the southern white man than in the care of the Federal government."[20] According to Howard Zinn, the year 1877 signaled that

> the black would be put back; the strikes of white workers would not be tolerated; the industrial and political elites of North and South would take hold of the country and organize the greatest march of economic growth in human history. They would do it with the aid of, and at the expense of, black labor, white labor, Chinese labor, European immigrant labor, female labor, rewarding them differently by race, sex, national origin, and social class, in such a way as to create separate levels of oppression—a skillful terracing to stabilize the pyramid of wealth.[21]

For Alabama, this signal meant rejecting a more competitive democratic capitalism in both agriculture and industry. Radical Reconstruction jeopardized a labor supply vital to cotton farming and threatened the flow of cheap cotton to the textile mills of the Northeast.[22] So northern capitalists agreed to "home rule" and settled for indirect control of the South's economy, even though military victory and economic hegemony had given them the power to resolve any problems that might arise. Home rule lasted eighty years, until in 1957 the government ordered federal troops into Little Rock, Arkansas, for purposes prohibited by the Compromise of 1877.[23]

The brief moment of Reconstruction had in some ways resembled Marx and Engels's "dictatorship of the proletariat"—the transitional period between the overthrow of the bourgeois state and the creation of communism. W. E. B. DuBois spoke explicitly of the possibility of Reconstruction becoming a "dictatorship of labor."[24] Marx held that the proletariat could exercise its power successfully only in a democratic way, and it has been argued that Reconstruction was the only period in U.S. history when blacks had real, effective power.[25] Many blacks had walked off the plantation and into the state legislature; after the Reconstruction Act of 1867 enfranchised blacks, twenty-seven won seats in the Alabama House of

Representatives and one to the Senate. During Reconstruction, Benjamin S. Turner and James Thomas Rapier became the first blacks to represent Alabama in Congress.[26]

However, Reconstruction is more commonly seen as, at best, an example of political democracy under capitalism.[27] Self-interest, not a concession to opposing social forces, motivated the ruling class to adopt Reconstruction. Any gains made since Reconstruction—by blacks, women, or other oppressed members of the working class—have required a struggle against the ruling class, and Reconstruction has come to symbolize "what might have been." Rapier was both the second and the last black to represent Alabama in Congress for more than a century.[28] The genuine bourgeois revolutionary current of radical Reconstruction lost out to what Jurgen Habermas termed a "revolution flowing backwards, one that clears the ground in order to catch up with developments previously missed out on."[29] In the end, Reconstruction only reorganized government in a way that assured industrial capitalists not only hegemony at the federal level but also control of state governments in the South. It did not include land reform: the government refused land grants to four million ex-slaves, although the grants would have required only a fraction of the land granted to railroad companies (an area greater than all of New England, New York, New Jersey, Pennsylvania, Delaware, and Maryland). What remained—laws guaranteeing equal rights for blacks, juridically and electorally, without land reform—were, at most, halfway measures.[30] Unlike serfs of Europe, who received rights to land on emancipation, wrote DuBois, "the American Negro slave was emancipated without such rights and in the end this spelled for him the continuation of slavery."[31]

A full Marxian transformation might have attracted poor whites, driven to reside on the worst land in the upland South, to ally themselves with blacks. Certainly, the idea of dividing the land equitably sent tremors through the ruling elites. Reconstruction achieved the goal of reconstructing the South for industrial capitalism, but it failed to provide economic and democratic rights for blacks.[32] It left the labor problem unsolved, and the ruling elites appealed to white solidarity against blacks. They sought no new alliance with the lower classes but wanted instead to exploit them and extract surplus value from their labor in the most efficient manner as possible. Thus, due to the failure of radical Reconstruction, postbellum modes of production in both agriculture and industry would remain more premodern than that of Marx's bourgeois variety.

NOTES

1. Quoted in Carter A. Wilson, *Racism: From Slavery to Advanced Capitalism* (Thousand Oaks, Calif.: Sage Publications, 1996), 91.

2. Roger L. Ransom, *Conflict and Compromise: The Political Economy of Slavery, Emancipation, and the American Civil War* (New York: Cambridge University Press, 1989), 230–31.

3. Quoted in Gerald David Jaynes, *Branches Without Roots: Genesis of the Black Working Class in the American South, 1862–1882* (New York: Oxford University Press, 1989), 103.

4. John Myers, "Black Human Capital: The Freedmen and the Reconstruction, 1860–1880" (Ph.D. diss., Florida State University, 1974), 17–46.

5. James A. Woodburn, *The Life of Thaddeus Stevens* (Indianapolis: Bobbs-Merrill Co., 1913), 527–28.

6. Jaynes, *Branches Without Roots*, 266.

7. Harry Haywood, *Negro Liberation* (New York: International Publishers, 1948), 164.

8. David W. Griffith, *The Birth of a Nation* (New York: The Epoch Producing Corporation, 1915).

9. John T. Milner, *Alabama: As It Was, as It Is, and as It Will Be* (Montgomery, Ala.: Barrett and Brown, 1876), 151. Emphasis added.

10. John T. Milner, *Report to the Governor of Alabama on the Alabama Central Railroad* (Montgomery, Ala.: Advertiser Book and Job Steam Press, 1859), 35.

11. Jaynes, *Branches Without Roots*, 9.

12. Jaynes, *Branches Without Roots*, 9.

13. Jaynes, *Branches Without Roots*, 200.

14. Jürgen Habermas, "What Does Socialism Mean Today? The Rectifying Revolution and the Need for New Thinking on the Left," *New Left Review* 183 (September–October 1990): 3–21.

15. Karl Marx and Friedrich Engels, *The Communist Manifesto* (New York: Penguin Books, 1967), 84.

16. John A. Agnew, "Sameness and Difference: Hartshorne's *The Nature of Geography* and Geography as a Real Variation," in *Reflections on Richard Hartshorne's The Nature of Geography*, ed. J. Nicholas Entrikin and Stanley D. Brunn (Washington, D.C.: Association of American Geographers, 1989), 128.

17. John W. Cell, *The Highest Stage of White Supremacy: The Origins of Segregation in South Africa and the American South* (Cambridge, England: Cambridge University Press, 1982), 147.

18. Jack M. Bloom, *Class, Race, and the Civil Rights Movement* (Bloomington: Indiana University Press, 1987), 34.

19. Michael Reich, *Racial Inequality: A Political-Economic Analysis* (Princeton, N.J.: Princeton University Press, 1981), 225.

20. C. Vann Woodward, *Origins of the New South, 1877–1913* (Baton Rouge: Louisiana State University Press, 1951), 46.

21. Howard Zinn, *A People's History of the United States* (New York: Harper & Row, 1980), 247.

22. Doug McAdam, *Political Process and the Development of Black Insurgency, 1930–1970* (Chicago: University of Chicago Press, 1982), 66–73.

23. C. Vann Woodward, "Yes, There Was a Compromise of 1877," *Journal of American History* 60, no. 1 (June 1973): 215–23.

24. W. E. B. DuBois, *Black Reconstruction in America* (Cleveland, Ohio: World Publishing Co., 1964), 219.

25. Elizabeth Ann Sharpe, "Was There a Dictatorship of the Proletariat in New Orleans During Reconstruction?" (Paper presented at Southern Labor Studies Conference, Birmingham, Ala., 21–24 October 1993).

26. Richard Bailey, *Neither Carpetbaggers nor Scalawags: Black Officeholders During the Reconstruction of Alabama, 1867–1878* (Montgomery, Ala.: Richard Bailey Publishers, 1991), 219, 240.

27. James S. Allen, *Reconstruction: the Battle for Democracy (1865–1876)* (New York: International Publishers, 1937), 24.

28. In 1992, Earl Hilliard became the first black to represent Alabama in the U.S. Congress since Reconstruction.

29. Habermas, "What Does Socialism Mean," 4.

30. Peter Camejo, *Racism, Revolution, Reaction, 1861–1877: The Rise and Fall of Radical Reconstruction* (New York: Pathfinder, 1976), 76–78.

31. DuBois, *Black Reconstruction*, 611.

32. Camejo, *Racism*, 83.

8

From Slave to Free Black Labor

> Economic reconstruction in the South after the Civil War required far more than repairing equipment, restoring neglected fields, and overcoming wartime shortages. It required a complete reordering of a slave society, the adjustment to, or, more precisely, the creation of a free-labor social system, with which blacks nor whites had much experience. This social revolution centered on agriculture.
>
> —Harold D. Woodman, *Agricultural History*

The development of a free black working class in the United States cannot be studied independent of the historical and social development of the postbellum economy of the South where the labor of former slaves was transformed into material elements of variable capital. Planters, recognizing their changed situation, urged blacks to continue working as laborers but to put "politics and the thought of social equality out of their minds."[1] In fact, over time, the loss of slave labor proved less significant to the planter class than might have been expected: Reconstruction failed to provide any opportunity for blacks to invest in land on a large scale, but coal mines and iron mills or tenant farming gave them a chance to sell their labor. Donald Harris wrote, "The first point to note about the position of black people in the U.S. capital–labor relation is that it is, for the most part, a position of labor and not of capital."[2]

In Alabama, Reconstruction effectively ended with the 1874 election, which brought so-called "redemption" for the planter class: population gains swelled the total vote, but the Democrats, then the political party of the planter class, added some 26,000 votes to their 1872 total, while the Republicans, the party of Reconstruction, gained only about 4,000. Republicans, therefore, represented only fifteen of the state's sixty-six counties in the Senate and twelve in the House. George S. Houston, a white supremacist and former slaveholder, was elected governor.

In the post-Reconstruction era, economic and social institutions operated to keep blacks landless and willing to work for low wages. The Democratic Party provided the political foundation for monopoly white power. Institutionalized racism and racial exploitation were more virulent than might be attributed to a competitive market; for example, black artisans were no longer allowed into the cities to ply their trades as they had been during slavery. The planters no longer enjoyed any benefit from this labor, so they no longer objected to white wage laborers doing these tasks.

The importance of whiteness increasingly eliminated any basis for competition between free blacks and whites in nearly every aspect of society. The Democratic Party controlled white voters by constantly reminding them of radical Reconstruction, and the Democrats intimidated black voters through social and economic coercion. Poor whites increasingly saw their class interests as at odds with those of blacks. According to Roger Ransom and Richard Sutch, emergence of a white tenant class brought blacks and middle- and lower-class whites into a more parallel situation than most whites found comfortable, and this discomfort led to open hostility toward blacks.[3] The Democratic Party eventually used this hostility to exploit politically both poor whites and blacks.

THE CLASS OF FREE BLACK WORKERS

The presence of a class of free black workers generated concerns on many levels about the material effects of a changing racial climate. Former slaves, fearing slavery would return, were suspicious of any situation that allowed their former masters to exact their labor and were quick to reject any arrangements resembling their former conditions, such as close white supervision and repetitive tasks. Paternalism no longer characterized black/white relations in the postbellum South.[4] Some southerners proposed voluntary emigration of blacks to Africa, but the postbellum regime rejected this idea because blacks provided an abundant and essential supply of cheap labor. Doubts about free black labor did, however, lead to a search for other sources of labor. As early as June 1869, a convention in Montgomery proposed a plan to encourage European immigration. Similar plans in Virginia and North and South Carolina also called for the creation of a commission, open information offices, distribution of pamphlets, and posting of agents at various places in Europe to attract workers. John Milner declared, "We must bring labor here that will be effective, or see our state given over to unthrifty, idleness, and weeds, as has been the case in every other country in the world where slave labor once formed the basis of agricultural wealth and was afterward set free."[5] A planter declared, "Another race of people will have to show them [blacks] how to labor and how to make it most profitable."[6] Milner made an extensive plea for "white men" to immigrate to Alabama, claiming potential workers had been dissuaded from moving to the state by the misperception that Alabama and the South were no longer productive. He attributed this misperception to the census of 1870:

> the most damaging comparisons have been held up and instituted as to the productiveness of our soils. Without explaining the condition and want of ef-

fectiveness of the labor cultivating our soils at that time, great tables and maps of comparison, founded only on the products of our soil at that time, are constructed and hung up, and commented on and circulated all over the civilized world, reducing the great crop producing empires of the South to a standard truly pitiable to contemplate. . . . Alabama has appeared before the world since the war only in the tattered garb of disappointment, distress and despair. . . . It is strange that the Agricultural Bureau of the nation, organized and paid for the purpose of finding out the difficulties, and promoting the interest of farming, should fail to find out what is the matter with the agriculture of the cotton States; and should attribute it to the selfishness of producers, in raising all cotton; the want of economy, and the prevalence of the same wasteful, thriftless habits of ante-war times; when the true cause— the *inefficiency* and *want of labor*—is seen and felt on every farm and in every field in the South.[7]

In other words, Milner associated low productivity with the failure of free black labor and the unwillingness of former slaves to work in the fields. "The only hope for the future prospect of this section is an immigration of laboring white people from abroad."[8]

The region had no history of immigration. The isolated southern labor market had produced few opportunities for immigrants and most European immigrants went to the North, not the South (Table 8.1)—partly because slave owners, to protect their tremendous investment, had blocked attempts to open the South to labor outside of the region.[9] (Foreigners might have been reluctant to go south for fear of being enslaved, but in practice, nearly all European immigrants became white upon crossing the ocean to the United States. The few who moved South across the Mason-Dixon Line became whiter.) European immigration meant that the North's rapidly growing industries did not need to proletarianize a farm population on a large scale, nor did they have to tap the free labor supply created by the emancipation. The postbellum South did, however, need a proletarianized labor supply to work its tenant farms and industries.[10] The lack of significant European immigration into the region also denied the South an important source of new ideas; foreigners contributed to many new industrial techniques that helped to produce the more intensive regime of capital accumulation in the North.[11]

When Alabama's campaign to attract immigrants failed, individual entrepreneurs started businesses offering white laborers for hire and advertised in newspapers in Mobile, Montgomery, and Huntsville.[12] But few local whites were willing to sell their labor, and many continued to work their small upland farms. Milner wrote, "The white people here, now, are educated and born nonproducers, and cannot, and will not labor [for others] in the fields."[13] In addition, hundreds of families left Alabama for the West, despite attempts by supporters of regional industrialization to stay the exodus.

Over time, as Woodman puts it, a "peculiarly southern free-labor system" developed.[14] In agriculture, three types of arrangements developed: wage labor, standing rent or tenancy, and sharecropping.

Table 8.1   1870 Distribution of Foreign Population

Region	Total Population	Foreign Born	%
Northeast	12,423,745	2,529,742	20.4
Connecticut	537,454	113,639	21.1
Delaware	125,015	9,136	7.3
Maine	626,915	48,881	7.8
Massachusetts	1,457,351	353,319	24.2
New Hampshire	318,300	29,611	9.3
New Jersey	906,096	188,943	20.8
New York	4,382,759	1,138,353	25.9
Pennsylvania	3,521,951	545,309	15.4
Rhode Island	217,353	55,396	25.4
Vermont	330,551	47,155	14.2
South	10,770,712	293,092	2.7
Alabama	996,992	9,962	1.0
Arkansas	484,471	5,026	1.0
Florida	187,748	4,967	2.6
Georgia	1,184,109	9,136	0.8
Kentucky	1,321,011	63,398	4.8
Louisiana	726,915	61,827	8.5
Maryland	780,894	83,412	10.6
Mississippi	827,922	11,191	1.3
South Carolina	705,606	8,074	1.1
North Carolina	1,071,361	3,029	0.3
Tennessee	1,258,520	19,316	1.5
Virginia	1,225,163	13,754	1.1

Source: U.S. Bureau of the Census, *1870 Census of Population, Ninth Census* (Washington, D.C.: Government Printing Office, 1872).

Wage labor, the first to appear after slavery, is the purest capitalist form. The tenant as a wage laborer produced surplus value that the landowner appropriated. In 1871, a convention of black farm laborers and Reconstruction leaders met in Montgomery, Alabama, and voiced support for wage labor over other arrangements. Delegates pointed to the advantages of this system in the development of agriculture using machinery and modern methods. In 1880, wage-organized plantations were found to be 35 percent more productive than those farmed under a sharecropping system.[15] During Reconstruction, federal law stipulated that the employer had to guarantee the necessities of labor and set the workday at ten hours.

Under the wage-labor arrangement, planters organized gangs (or squads) that worked under a white overseer—as slaves had under slavery. A lien on the crops secured funds to ensure the laborer's wages, but these were forfeit if the laborer left the job before the contract expired.[16] Laborers who violated contracts worked for the county or the local government as part of the convict labor pool. Federal law allowed employers to deduct from wages for careless treatment of tools and equipment. Abuse of such deductions often left black laborers indebted to the employer on payday, which solidified employers' control over wage laborers.

A variation of the wage-labor system was the "standing wage," which originated immediately after the Civil War. Laborers worked for six months or a year before being paid their wages.[17] This delay limited their mobility and benefited land owners, but this system never dominated—partly because the employers wanted a level of control closer to that they had enjoyed under slavery. Thus, the number of wage laborers working on plantations gradually declined as other labor forms grew in importance.[18]

Standing rent or tenancy was a contractual arrangement in which, as Oscar Zeichner explained, the "tenant was recognized as having 'dominion over the lands' and to control 'the processes of agriculture unhampered by interference on the part of the landlord.'"[19] The tenant paid rent for use of the land and kept all crops produced. A lien on the crop secured the rent for the landlord. Standing rent can be seen as a self-exploitative form of sharecropping: tenants appropriated directly the surplus labor they produced; that is, in producing the crop, the tenants labored for themselves. This form of sharecropping is most likely to persist where social stratification is not pronounced. Like wage labor, tenancy never became a dominant productive form in the postbellum South.[20]

The planters' opposition to wage labor was prompted by lack of capital as well as their desire for control. Wage labor (and some more modern forms of sharecropping) required capital, which was lacking in the South after the Civil War.[21] The slave mode of production had drawn capital into the region through the "cotton factorage" system, under which commission merchants sold cotton for, and extended credit to, the planters.[22] Slaves represented constant capital—in other words, they were an asset that could be sold on the market or used as collateral for loans. Thus, emancipation eliminated at one stroke both credit and more than $3.5 billion invested in slaves; the total in Alabama was $200,000,000, half the assessed valuation of property in the entire state in 1860. Between 1860 and 1870, emancipation reduced the South's per-capita wealth by one-third.[23] Of the total wealth of the five cotton states of Alabama, Georgia, Louisiana, Mississippi, and South Carolina, 45.8 percent was eliminated.[24] By 1880, the South, which had 35 percent of the nation's population, had only 8.5 percent of bank deposits and one bank for every 58,130 people, compared with a national average of 1 per 16,000.[25] As Gerald David Jaynes wrote, "The true legacy of federal agrarian policy in 1865 was the failure to provide the financial assistance to southern agriculture that would have allowed a restructuring of a sounder credit system."[26] Jaynes attributes much of the race-related practices in the post-Reconstruction South directly to this failure.[27]

SHARECROPPING AS A PREMODERN PRODUCTIVE FORM

Sharecropping became the dominant form of production in southern agriculture after the Civil War. Neoclassical analysis has focused on how sharecropping is in harmony with principles of capitalist rationality, rendering such analysis essentialist. As Serap Ayse Kayatekin points out, "Despite the diversity of approaches within it, neoclassical theory fails to understand sharecropping as a historical and social analysis. What often emerges from neoclassical analyses is an unproblematized concept of sharecropping, defined in relation to a universal notion of 'rationality.'"[28] In the neoclassical view, sharecropping is superior to wage labor because the cropper had a sense of independence and bore some risk and so had a greater interest in the crop than the wage laborer.[29] Such incentive eliminated the need of supervision. For example, Peter Kolchin saw the cropper as "a partner of the landowner in a joint business venture that provided the freedmen with greater individual discretion, dignity and self-respect."[30] William McFeely claimed, "Freedmen became sharecroppers to be able to assert some independence and to survive in conditions that produced actual starvation in the South."[31] The risk inherent in sharecropping was intended to be negligible, and the method was supposedly as productive as other forms of contracts: the landowner could optimize tenant inputs by manipulating the rent and the size of the tenants' parcels.[32]

History and social analyses do not support these principles. The form of sharecropping that emerged in the South as early as 1865 and that became prominent was almost feudal in nature; it was a premodern labor process even though it was subsumed under capitalist relations.[33] Historians and others who blame lack of capital for the underdevelopment in the postbellum South see it as a major reason for sharecropping as well: sharecropping required little capital because the landowner made no cash payments before the crop was sold and was ensured the laborer would remain throughout the crop year. Susan Mann wrote, "By tying labor payments to the finished commodity rather than to specified time periods, sharecropping better ensured that the laborer would remain for the duration of the production cycle."[34] Some planters contracted to pay workers a share of the crop but at the end of the crop year forced them off the land without paying them their share.[35]

Lenin compared the system with slavery and feudalism:

> We are dealing here mainly with semi-feudal relationships or, what is the same from the economic point of view, with the semi-slavery system of sharecropping. . . . The share-cropping region, both in America and Russia, is the most backward region, where the toiling masses are subjected to the greatest degradation and oppression. . . . The American South is to the "liberated" Negroes akin to a prison, hemmed in, backward, without access to fresh air.[36]

Modern, productive forms of sharecropping exist. According to Kayatekin, sharecroppers can have a "subsumed class position, that of recruiters of wage labor" or actually exploit wage labor with the landowner. Both appropriate surplus value and have claims on it for providing the necessary means of production. "In yet another form, the sharecropper is the appropriator of surplus-value produced by wage-laborers and gives a cut of this surplus-value to the landowner for providing the land; this is the capitalist ground rent."[37]

Sharecropping can exist with little or no social stratification and in a competitive labor situation, but race-connected practices prevented any such situation in the postbellum rural South. Landowners opposed any forms of sharecropping that involved a degree of labor freedom (i.e., any form that did not ensure the planter a reliable supply of labor when needed).[38] Ransom and Sutch argue that transferring ownership of capitalized labor from slaveholders to the ex-slaves was not itself destructive to the southern economy; rather, it was the free blacks' failure to supply their labor that made agriculture a risky proposition.[39]

These attitudes reflect the fact that, after the Civil War, the former slaves' first impulse was to test their new freedom geographically. Many left the plantation for the cities and towns where officials of the Freedmen Bureau, a federal agency established to care for freed blacks, provided a safer environment than the remote rural areas of the planters' domain. The black population of Alabama's three largest cities increased 44.1 percent between 1860 and 1870 (Table 8.2). According to Ransom and Sutch, the ex-slaves also

> chose to exchange a fraction of their potential income for "free" time. . . .
> They duplicated (perhaps emulated) the work-leisure patterns of other free Americans. Adolescents in their early teens, women with children, and elderly men and women all worked significantly fewer hours per day and fewer days per year than had been the standard under the oppression of slavery. Even the adult men chose to work less.[40]

Overall, there was a 28 to 37 percent decline in hours worked per capita.[41] Milner, writing in 1876, estimated the labor value of "free negro labor in the South" to be between "32.8 and 36.3 percent of what it was before the war." Speaking of the effects of the Radical Reconstruction Acts of 1867, he asked,

> Is there any wonder that want, and gaunt, haggard despair prevails everywhere in the Black Belt, since 1867? If the reader in Alabama will only look to the end of that year, he will recollect that a sadly dark cloud settled there, over this part of Alabama, and from that time, until now, this section has been gradually growing poorer.[42]

Table 8.2   Black Population of State's Three Largest Cities: 1860 and 1870

City	Population		% Change
	1860	1870	
Mobile	8,404	13,419	59.7
Montgomery	4,502	5,183	15.1
Huntsville	1,654	2,375	43.6
Total	14,560	20,977	44.1

Source: Population of the U.S. in 1860, Eighth Census (Washington, D.C.: Government Printing Office, 1864); *Compendium of Ninth Census, 1870* (New York: Arno Press, 1976).

Milner and other figures of the postbellum regime attributed such behavior to "nature":

> It is of no use to blame the negro because he won't work, when left to himself, any more than there is in blaming him on account of the color of his skin. He is simply following the laws of his nature, as it has been known always, and from the beginning of time.[43]

However, freedmen possessed the legal right to the entire product of their labor, and they could act as they wished. Therefore, creditors were increasingly likely to see crop mortgages as inadequate security because there was no longer any guarantee that blacks would produce the crops. The lack of a guarantee contributed to the downfall of wage labor as well as the turn toward other, less modern methods of farming.

Sharecropping came to be linked with a system of exploitation that, according to T. H. Marshall, denied blacks the basic civil right "to follow the occupation of one's choice in the place of one's choice."[44] The possibility of choices is essential to modern agriculture. Immediately after the Civil War, the planter-dominated legislature passed a law prohibiting the "enticement" of black workers away from plantations where they had contracted to work. Another law defined as "vagrants" people who neglected employment on which they depended. Failure to pay the fine for this crime led to forced labor or exclusion from the city except with the consent of one's employer. These laws marked the beginning of the convict-labor system, which became a major source of inexpensive labor for Birmingham's early industrialists (see chapter 10). Vagrancy laws were officially repealed in 1867, but they reappeared under different names and remained on the books of many southern states into the 1930s.[45] De facto slavery was established by another law passed under Reconstruction that gave former slave owners custody of minors who had no visible means of support.[46]

Because the croppers' compensation was nearly always a share of crops that could be produced only with the aid of material goods furnished by the landowner—who provided management but little or no labor—feudal forms can be considered even when the sharecroppers provide some means of production (Table 8.3).[47] Sharecroppers needed to supply tools or draft animals as well as their labor.[48] Former slaves might have owned their labor, but the planters still owned at least some of the necessary instruments of labor, the land, and sometimes the farmer's house. Jaynes wrote that this arrangement "weakened the planter's control over production by transferring labor supply decisions to labor."[49] The form of sharecropping adopted was also consistent with the regional mode of social regulation. According to Kayatekin,

> Feudal forms of sharecropping exist in communities characterized by unequal distribution of land and other means of production. . . . Tenants are fully dispossessed from the means of production and frequently in such cases the means of production are provided by the owner of the land. In the postbellum U.S. South almost all the means of production were provided by the

Table 8.3   Planter–Tenant Relationships

	Sharecropping (croppers)	Share renting (share tenants)	Cash renting (standing tenants)
Landlord furnishes	Land, cabin, fuel, one-half fertilizer, tools, seed, work stock, and feed	Land, cabin, fuel, and one-fourth to one-third fertilizer	Land, cabin, and fuel
Tenant furnishes	Labor and one-half fertilizer	Labor, two-thirds to three-fourths fertilizer, tools, seed, work stock, and feed	Labor, fertilizer tools, seed, work stock, and feed
Landlord receives	One-half crop	One-half to one-third crop	Fixed amount of crop or lint cotton
Tenant receives	One-half crop	One-half to two-thirds crop	Entire crop less fixed amount

Source: George A. Davis and O. Fred Donaldson, *Blacks in the United States: A Geographic Perspective* (Boston: Houghton Mifflin Co., 1975), 122.

landowner to the cropper. . . . The performance of surplus labor by the sharecroppers was legitimized by a world view that placed blacks at the bottom of a hierarchical world order; manual labor was to be performed by those who were deemed to be inferior. . . .[Like the black slaves] the sharecroppers of the southern states were considered to be childish, incapable of independence, and thus needed to be protected and taken care of.[50]

In November 1867, Alabama's Reconstruction government issued a general order creating a crop lien in favor of the cropper. This order became law approximately one year later; however, the redemption legislature amended the act, making the cropper's lien subordinate to all other liens to ensure that croppers would pay production and subsistence loans at harvest time.[51] These new laws allowed planters to assure creditors that the supply of labor would be sufficient to produce crops.[52]

As proceeds from the croppers' share were never enough to pay debts to the landowner that had been incurred during the year, croppers' debts accumulated from harvest to harvest.[53] In effect, state law held that any crop produced by a sharecropper belonged to the landowner. This result provided the mechanism for extreme exploitation: sharecroppers became "day laborers," not partners; their only rights were to plant, work, and harvest crops.[54] By the end of the 1870s, every southern state had laws granting the landlord first liens on crops, effectively granting landowners the right to intervene in the sharecroppers' necessary labor time.[55]

However, the crop lien law did not distinguish between landowners and merchants, which meant the two groups were in competition for whatever surplus croppers could produce. On 8 March 1871, in an effort to eliminate merchants who granted credit to independent croppers, Alabama's planters proposed a lien law that repaid landlords first.[56] The crop belonged to the landowner, they argued, so merchants should not be able to claim a share until the landowner's share is secured.[57] Some planters were more devious: as the crop-lien laws gave crop loans precedence over any other obligation of the borrower, some planters decided to become merchants, thereby further increasing their economic and class dominance.[58] Merchant planters could also intervene in croppers' necessary labor time by directly controlling the quantity of goods the sharecroppers consumed, for the court ruled that consumer loans were necessary for production and, therefore, were covered by the crop-lien laws. Consumer loans were often given in kind, not cash.[59]

Cash loans to sharecroppers were often financed by northern banks, although the funds were distributed through local banks or through merchants who served as brokers for northern capitalists. Like the cotton factorage system, these local agents played an important role in bringing into the South the little capital that existed.[60] Katharine DuPre Lumpkin wrote,

> These banks all have correspondents in the large cities, not alone in the South, but in the North as well. Through these channels filter down one way the financial opinions of the large cities and large banks, and up the other way, the views of the interior upon the state of trade and the condition of the crops. . . . The crop notes, originally discounted by the country bank, will be found in the loan portfolios of the larger institutions of the cities, as the money to make and move the crop is sent out through the usual banking channels.[61]

According to one observer, this combination of merchant and landlord launched a system of usury unrivaled by any in history.[62] Interest on these loans ranged from 50 to 125 percent, with some merchants charging farm tenants a flat rate of 25 percent despite the length of the loan, at a time when short-term interest rates in New York ranged from 4 to 6 percent and never exceeded 8 percent.[63] Thus, northern finance capital helped preserve this noncapitalist form of sharecropping. Although only 1 to 6 percent of black-belt merchants were also members of the planter class, as both landlord and merchant the postbellum planter could reap huge profits; and, by the end of the nineteenth century, southern agriculture was dominated by a new landlord-merchant class.[64] According to Woodman,

> A Mississippi planter boasted that when he rented his land to former slaves he was able to receive an annual income from his land "amounting to nearly its

full value." In addition, he furnished renters supplies from his store, receiving a lien on their crops. "Now, my little piece here ain't more than a couple of a hundred acres," he concluded, "but it's paying me more than double what it did when I worked fifty niggers on it."[65]

Indebtedness combined with the commissary system gave the former slave-holders almost the same control over labor as had existed under slavery.[66]

> The status of tenancy demands complete dependence; it requires no educa-tion and demands no initiative, since the landlord assumes the prerogative of direction in the choice of crops, [and] the method by which it shall be sold. He keeps the records and determines the earnings. Through the commissary or credit merchant, even the choice of diet is determined. The landlord can determine the kind and amount of schooling for the children, the extent to which they may share benefits intended for all the people. He may even de-termine the relief they receive in the extremity of their distress. He controls the courts, the agencies of law enforcement.[67]

In some ways, there was a struggle between a rising merchant class and the old planter class over how to extract surplus value from croppers and how to control their consumption. Jonathan Wiener noted that the skill with which the planters defended their position in this struggle "suggests that the post-war planters pos-sessed a degree of class-consciousness reminiscent of their pre-war counter-parts."[68] The planters' success in making their liens superior led the merchants to use the same approach with the white yeomen of the hill country, transforming them into tenants, so the hill country's class structure increasingly resembled that of the black belt. The prospect of poor whites being on equal footing with black tenants and sharecroppers may have worried the planter class, but their fears were groundless. The class positions of workers in the two regions may have appeared to converge, but racist republicanism, antagonistic cultural traditions, and differ-ent social origins did not allow it. The yeoman farmer of the upland was first and foremost part of the white race, and the geography of the two regions reinforced this separation.[69]

Unlike wage laborers, sharecroppers are not hired as individuals; they and their families provide the labor force for production; this system resembles slavery, wherein the family was often the unit of labor.[70] Building the sharecropping system around the family unit increased the labor supply because women more often worked in the fields (Figure 8.1). The system also provided the most authoritarian system possible and reinforced individualist, rather than collectivist, solutions in a way that served the planters' interests and helped destroy agrarian democracy. In short, the failure of Reconstruction transformed the "peculiar institution" of chat-tel slavery into the equally peculiar institution of southern tenancy: the slave mar-ket, a symbol of the human chattel, gave way to the modernized plantation. Contrary to the neoclassical view, the southern sharecropping system never pro-vided blacks with a sense of independence and freedom.

Figure 8.1   Sharecropper family.

The new socioeconomic relationship between landowners and former slaves altered their spatial relationship as well. Clusters of workers' dwellings set near the landowner were abandoned and replaced by sharecropper housing dispersed over the plantation. William Cohen noted, "In subdividing the plantations into small plots, the planters yielded to the blacks' rejection of the gang system and to their aversion to white overseers."[71] This arrangement may have given the illusion of more freedom (Figure 8.2), but these shacks were usually at the edge of the plantation and often set two to three miles from one another, making democratic and collective action difficult.[72] The planters were preventing cohesion in a black society finally free to organize against its former slave masters.[73] Indeed, dispersion hampered the black population's ability to organize more than illiteracy or any other negative legacy of enslavement. Unlike factories, where workers labor together and alongside one another under a cooperative and specialized division of labor, familial sharecropping reinforced the isolation of the work setting.[74]

In this new rural south, plantations were cut into small plots, and landlords could realize economies of scale in management, although not in production. Therefore, croppers had to cultivate intensively but with little benefit from technology or mechanization. Restricting acreage meant a lower return per worker; for the laborer, it meant working harder to maintain a standard of living so acreage restriction effectively increased the laborer's exertions.[75] Wiener wrote that this new geography "marked not the creation of 'large-scale, thoroughly capitalistic farms' but precisely a move away from the classic capitalist organization of

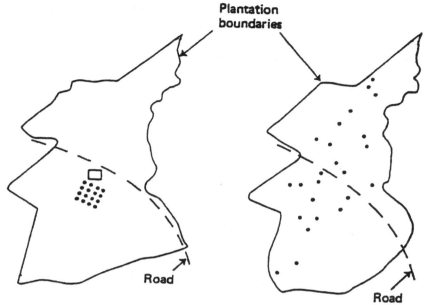

Figure 8.2 Pre-civil war and post-civil war plantation.
Source: George A. Davis and O. Fred Donaldson, *Blacks in the United States: A Geographic Perspective* (Boston: Hought Mifflin Company, 1975). 118.

agriculture."[76] In offering a share of the crop, landlords were capitalists, but they relinquished the right to be labeled "modern." For under the modern form of capitalism, according to Jaynes,

> The conservative validation of private ownership and profit have always been based upon the capitalist's willingness to bear risk while securing for the less enterprising laborers a guaranteed wage. The southern sharecropper bore all the burdens of an entrepreneur but was dispossessed of freedom of choice in making managerial decisions. . . . No government which allows its laboring population to mortgage its labor by enforcing debt peonage can claim to have free labor.[77]

The tenants' continuing indebtedness meant landowners had little or no incentive to adopt any innovations that increased the tenants' earning capacity. Doing so would have weakened or removed the basis of the landlords' control and ability to maximize the extraction of surplus labor.[78] Furthermore, landlords received only a share of the benefits of any investment. Tenants, for their part, would not invest in improvements because they would only add to the landowner's capital and, with contracts renewed annually, tenants had no long-term commitment to soil productivity. In short, sharecropping removed any incentive to invest in long-term improvements.[79] This effect continued well into the twentieth century. Whereas only 36 percent of the rented farms in the United States reported decreasing fertility of the soil in the 1930s, more than one-half of these farms in the

South reported a decrease. Greater numbers of croppers under a single landlord was correlated with greater loss in soil fertility.[80]

Sharecropping plantations, like slave plantations, were largely self-contained, with less need to rely on an urban-industrial economy. The more modern system of the Midwest led to the capitalization of agriculture, which increased demand for manufactured products and fed development of a manufacturing belt that extended from New England across the Great Lakes to Chicago. The southern mode of regulation meant that the rank-sized urban hierarchy, i.e., a wide range of different size cities, that developed within the manufacturing belt did not appear in the South until well into the twentieth century. Like the plantation before the Civil War, the landowner and the merchant, by providing all, restricted the development of a genuine money economy and of a market sufficient to justify the growth of industry in the region.[81] The merchants and commissaries, wrote Milner,

> all come from the class of non-producers, and are made for the purpose of keeping their commissions and other business alive, and not for the benefit of the producer. . . . If this business of advancing on cotton should stop in the Black Belt for one year, what little farming is done there, would cease. . . . Something must be done, and that soon. Either the army of nonproducers must break ranks, and fall to the ground, and go into the fields, or somebody must starve in Alabama.[82]

As a result, wrote Haywood, northern capitalists were able "to hold exclusive monopoly of the world's greatest source of raw cotton, and to maintain [their] cheap production for northern textile manufacturers."[83] Milner thought one solution for Alabama would be industrialization through the exploitation of the mineral district:

> Alabama is making her first marks in mineral development, and can compare with nothing in the amount and value of her actual productions. Pennsylvania is now the leading state in production of mineral values and will continue to be so in coal products for generations to come. But in iron Alabama will be up and even with Pennsylvania in less than twenty years. . . . In addition to the agriculture, we have now a basis for mining and manufacturing interests never known or understood before the war. If our fields were all barren, (which they are not), we have in our other industries the basis of great wealth waiting, as is our agriculture, only for capital and effective labor.[84]

Birmingham, the city that Milner conceived as a slave-based industrial city during the antebellum period, would become a reality in the postbellum period with industrial labor processes not so far removed from those of the planter-merchant class, which exercised "a degree of control over their work force far beyond that available to employers elsewhere in the Nation." This control extended beyond the fields into the arena of consumption.[85] Agriculture was the foundation of the southern political economy until the middle of the twentieth century, and planters' political and economic control had a profound influence on the development of industry in the South.[86] This control was particularly prevalent in Birmingham. Horace Mann Bond wrote,

> Alabama was more likely to witness the working of unsuspected economic forces than any other Southern state. Its natural resources were unique in the South; and, in an age when Coal was power, and Iron the other necessity for industry, it was already known that the Northern hill-country of Alabama had both in unexampled proximity. The bankers in Philadelphia and New York, and even in London, and Paris, had known this for almost two decades. The only thing lacking was transportation.[87]

NOTES

1. Quoted in J. Myers, "Black Human Capital: The Freedmen and the Reconstruction, 1860–1880" (Ph.D. diss., Florida State University, 1974), 99.

2. Donald J. Harris, "Capitalist Exploitation and Black Labor: Some Conceptual Issues," *Review of Black Political Economy* 8 (Winter 1978): 141.

3. Roger L. Ransom and Richard Sutch, *One Kind of Freedom: The Economic Consequences of Emancipation* (Cambridge, England: Cambridge University Press, 1977), 105; see also Edna Bonacich, "Abolition, the Extension of Slavery, and the Position of Free Blacks: A Study of Split Labor Markets in the United States, 1830–1863," *American Journal of Sociology* 81 (November 1975): 617–28.

4. Eugene D. Genovese, *Roll, Jordan, Roll: The World the Slaves Made* (New York: Pantheon, 1974) 110–12.

5. John T. Milner, *Alabama: as It Was, as It Is, and as It Will Be* (Montgomery, Ala.: Barrett and Brown, 1876), 208.

6. Quoted in Myers, "Black Human Capital," 126.

7. Milner, *Alabama*, 117, 209, 135.

8. Milner, *Alabama*, 146.

9. Gavin Wright, *Old South, New South: Revolutions in the Southern Economy Since the Civil War* (New York: Basic Books, 1986), 64–80.

10. James S. Allen, *The Negro Question in the United States* (New York: International Publishers, 1936), 120–21.

11. W. H. Baughn, "Capital Formation and Entrepreneurship in the South," *Southern Economic Journal* 16, no. 2 (October 1949): 168.

12. Quoted in Sylvia H. Krebs, "Will the Freedmen Work? White Alabamians Adjust to Free Black Labor," *Alabama Historical Quarterly* 36, no. 2 (Summer 1974): 154.

13. Milner, *Alabama*, 146. Based on Milner's statement, the low agricultural productivity of the South after the war could also be attributed to the failure of whites to labor in the field.

14. Harold D. Woodman, "Post–Civil War Southern Agriculture and the Law," *Agricultural History* 53, no. 1 (1979): 319–37.

15. "Proceeding of the Labor Convention: Wednesday, January 4, 1871," *Weekly State Journal*, 6 January 1871; Gerald David Jaynes, *Branches Without Roots: Genesis of the Black Working Class in the American South, 1862–1882* (New York: Oxford University Press, 1989), 243.

16. Peter Kolchin, *First Freedom: The Responses of Alabama's Blacks to Emancipation and Reconstruction* (Westport, Conn.: Greenwood Press, 1972), 36; see also Ransom and Sutch, *One Kind of Freedom*.

17. Jaynes, *Branches Without Roots*, 53.

18. Oscar Zeichner, "The Legal Status of the Agricultural Laborer in the South," *Political Science Quarterly* 55, no. 3 (September 1940): 412–28.

19. Zeichner, "Legal," 417.

20. Serap Ayse Kayatekin, "Sharecropping and Class: A Preliminary Analysis," *Rethinking Marxism* 9, no. 1 (Spring 1996/97): 28–57.

21. Woodman, "Post–Civil War"; Jaynes, *Branches Without Roots*, 243.

22. Harold D. Woodman, *King Cotton and His Retainers: Financing and Marketing the Cotton Crop of the South, 1800–1925* (Columbia: University of South Carolina Press, 1990), 194–95.

23. Baughn, "Capital," 163; Horace Mann Bond, "Social and Economic Forces in Alabama Reconstruction," *Journal of Negro History* 23, no. 3 (July 1938): 312.

24. Ransom and Sutch, *One Kind of Freedom*, 52.

25. Jack M. Bloom, *Class, Race, and the Civil Rights Movement* (Bloomington: Indiana University Press, 1987), 21.

26. Jaynes, *Branches Without Roots*, 244.

27. Jaynes, *Branches Without Roots*.

28. Kayatekin, "Sharecropping," 30.

29. N. S. Cheung, *The Theory of Share Tenancy* (Chicago: University of Chicago Press, 1969), 32–51; J. E. Stiglitz, "Incentive and Risk Sharing in Sharecropping," *Review of Economic Studies* 41, no. 126 (April 1974): 219–55; see also Jaynes, *Branches Without Roots*, 85.

30. Kolchin, *First Freedom*, 42.

31. William McFeely, *Yankee Stepfather: General O. O. Howard and the Freedmen* (New Haven, Conn.: Yale University Press, 1968), 163.

32. Cheung, *The Theory*.

33. R. Pearce, "Sharecropping: Towards a Marxist View," *Journal of Peasant Studies* 10, no. 213 (1983): 42–70.

34. Susan A. Mann, "Sharecropping in the Cotton South: A Case of Uneven Development in Agriculture," *Rural Sociology* 49, no. 3 (Fall 1984): 424.

35. Woodman, "Post–Civil War," 322–23.

36. Quoted in Allen, *Negro Question*, 33.

37. Kayatekin, "Sharecropping," 48.

38. Allen, *Negro Question*, 47.

39. Ransom and Sutch, *One Kind of Freedom*.

40. Ransom and Sutch, *One Kind of Freedom*, 6.

41. Ransom and Sutch, *One Kind of Freedom*, 6; see also Jaynes, *Branches Without Roots*, 228.

42. Milner, *Alabama*, 53, 160.

43. Milner, *Alabama*, 149.

44. T. H. Marshall, *Class, Citizenship and Social Development* (Chicago: University of Chicago Press, 1964), 82.

45. Mann, "Sharecropping," 423.

46. Kolchin, *First Freedom*; see also Krebs, "Freedmen," 151–63.

47. Kayatekin, "Sharecropping," 40.

48. Jonathan M. Wiener, "Class Structure and Economic Development in the American South, 1865–1955," *American Historical Review* 84, no. 4 (October 1979): 984.

49. Jaynes, *Branches Without Roots*, 31.

50. Kayatekin, "Sharecropping," 36, 37, 39. According to the U.S. Bureau of the Census, *Census of Agriculture, 1940*, vol. 3 (Washington, D.C.: Government Printing Office, 1946),

blacks comprised a little over one-fourth of the South's population in 1940, yet more than 50 percent of black tenants in the region worked under the noncapitalist form of sharecropping.

51. Woodman, "Post–Civil War," 329; see also Jaynes, *Branches Without Roots*, 147.

52. Jonathan M. Wiener, *Social Origins of the New South: Alabama, 1860–1885* (Baton Rouge: Louisiana State University Press, 1978), 69; Jaynes, *Branches Without Roots*, 185–90, 222, 312.

53. According to Harold Hoffsommer, *Landlord–Tenant Relations and Relief in Alabama*, FERA Research Bulletin, 2nd ser., no. 9 (Washington, 1935), 2, this practice persisted: in 1935, he found that 80 percent of the sharecroppers in Alabama had an indebtedness of more than one year's standing.

54. Jaynes, *Branches Without Roots*, 297, 313.

55. Kayatekin, "Sharecropping."

56. *Acts of Alabama, 1870–71* (Montgomery, Ala.: W. W. Screws, State Printer, 1871), 19.

57. Woodman, "Post–Civil War," 319–37.

58. Jonathan M. Wiener, "Planter–Merchant Conflict in Reconstruction Alabama," *Past and Present*, no. 68 (August 1975): 73–94.

59. Kayatekin, "Sharecropping," 37; Woodman, "Post–Civil War," 332.

60. Merle C. Prunty, "Two American Souths: The Past and the Future," *Southeastern Geographer* 17, no. 1 (May 1977): 1–24; see also Merle C. Prunty, "The Renaissance of the Southern Plantation," *Geographical Review* 45, no. 4 (October 1955): 466–82; and James S. Fisher, "Negro Farm Ownership in the South," *Annals of the Association of American Geographers* 63, no. 4 (December 1973): 478–89.

61. Katharine DuPre Lumpkin, *The South in Progress* (New York: International Publishers, 1940), 25–26.

62. Quoted in Horace Mann Bond, *Negro Education in Alabama: A Study in Cotton and Steel* (New York: Octagon Books, 1969), 121.

63. Thomas Clark and Albert Kirwan, *The South Since Appomattox* (New York: Oxford University Press, 1967), 90–91; Wilbur J. Cash, *The Mind of the South* (New York: Alfred A. Knopf, 1941), 152; Ransom and Sutch, *One Kind of Freedom*, 130; John Dollard, *Caste and Class in a Southern Town* (Garden City, N.Y.: Doubleday, 1957), 140; C. Vann Woodward, *Origins of the New South, 1871–1913* (Baton Rouge: Louisiana State University Press, 1951), 180.

64. Wiener, *Social Origins*, 112–14; Michael Schwartz, *Radical Protest and Social Structure* (New York: Academic Press, 1976), 58; Woodman, "Post–Civil War," 330.

65. Quoted in Woodman, *King Cotton*, 310–11.

66. More than one-fourth of the plantations in a study by T. J. Woofter, Jr., still had commissaries. (*Landlord and Tenant on the Cotton Plantation*, Research Monograph 5, WPA Division of Social Research (Washington, D.C.: Government Printing Office, 1936), 203.

67. Quoted in George A. Davis and O. Fred Donaldson, *Blacks in the United States: A Geographic Perspective* (Boston: Houghton Mifflin, 1975), 119.

68. Wiener, "Planter–Merchant," 93; see also Woodman, *King Cotton*.

69. Wiener, "Planter–Merchant"; Theodore W. Allen, *The Invention of the White Race: Racial Oppression and Social Control*, vol. 1 (London: Verso, 1994), 155.

70. Mann, "Sharecropping," 412–29.

71. William Cohen, *At Freedom's Edge: Black Mobility and the Southern White Quest for Racial Control, 1861–1915* (Baton Rouge: Louisiana State University Press, 1991), 20.

72. Robin D. G. Kelley, *Hammer and Hoe: Alabama Communists During the Great Depression* (Chapel Hill: University of North Carolina Press, 1990), 37.

73. Michael Reich, *Racial Inequality: A Political-Economic Analysis* (Princeton, N.J.: Princeton University Press, 1981), 228.

74. Mann, "Sharecropping," 415.

75. Ransom and Sutch, *One Kind of Freedom*, 99.

76. Wiener, "Class Structure," 984.

77. Jaynes, *Branches Without Roots*, 313, 314.

78. A. Bhaduri, "A Study In Agricultural Backwardness Under Semi-Feudalism," *Economic Journal* 83, no. 329 (March 1973): 120–37.

79. Jaynes, *Branches Without Roots*, 95–96; Ransom and Sutch, *One Kind of Freedom*, 102, 186.

80. Allen, *Negro Question*, 69.

81. Douglas F. Dowd, "A Comparative Analysis of Economic Development in the American West and South," *Journal of Economic History* 16, no. 4 (December 1956): 558–74.

82. Milner, *Alabama*, 148.

83. Harry Haywood, *Negro Liberation* (New York: International Publishers, 1948), 51, 57.

84. Milner, *Alabama*, 206, 207.

85. Woodman, "Post–Civil War," 336.

86. Allen, *Negro Question*, 36.

87. Bond, "Social," 310.

9

Development of the Birmingham Regime

With the reconstruction of place for industrialization, capitalists took possession of land and wrenched it away from the traditional form of property, thereby endowing it with exchange value. According to Henri Lefebvre, in the history of capitalism, real property played a major role only when "the relics of the former ruling class long owned not only the agricultural land but also the land suitable for building, and secondly, the relevant branch of production was dominated by trades and crafts."[1] After slavery, southern planters still owned the land but, having lost their slaves, they sought to invest more in land for its exchange value and to accumulate capital.

FROM LABOR LORDS TO LANDLORDS

The integration of regional space is important to the development of industrial capitalism. As production begins to rest more on industrial capitalism, it becomes more important to improve communication and transportation so as to conquer regional and national markets. After emancipation, southern investments increasingly went into transportation. Land values rose as a result, setting the stage for the development of Birmingham—which came to symbolize a new social order. Land, not labor, became the basis of wealth. In a free-labor economy, there is the tendency to increase wealth by investing in land. According to Gavin Wright,

> After emancipation, the "masters without slaves" were *landlords*, whose concern was to raise the value of output per acre, treating labor as a variable cost. Since land is fixed in place, what occurred was a pronounced localization of economic life. Farmers now reoriented their investments and their politics toward raising land yields and land values in particular localities. Local coalitions of landowners began to push for market, towns, railroads and eventually factories.[2]

Capitalism requires both the accumulation of surplus at a favorable site and the circulation of capital. Southern railroads received substantial aid during the postbellum period. Immediately after the Civil War, ten Alabama railroads received aid under a state law that allowed city and county governments to authorize the issue of bonds to pay for railroad expansion. In 1867, the Democrat-controlled legislature authorized the governor to endorse the first mortgage bonds of any railroad at the rate of $12,000 per mile, but only after the first twenty miles of new road were laid. In 1868, radical Reconstructionists amended the 1867 act to provide $16,000 per mile in five-mile increments that included tracks laid up to twenty miles past state boundaries.[3] Industrialist John T. Milner, of the South and North (S&N) Railroad, and John C. Stanton of the Alabama and Chattanooga railroad and field agent for Russel Sage, a northern financier and capitalist, joined to bribe members of the assembly in order to get more state aid, rescuing the S&N, which had already received substantial state aid in 1860, from financial ruin. Throughout the South, much of the state debt incurred during radical Reconstruction was marked for railroads, a natural byproduct of the penetration of capital in the new order established by the Civil War and emancipation.[4] The Alabama and Chattanooga and the S&N railroads received extravagant aid, accounting for almost 70 percent of the debt incurred by the state between the end of the Civil War and the end of Reconstruction and almost bankrupting Alabama. In 1868, the S&N Railroad received a low-interest loan from the state; in 1870, the state gave the Alabama and Chattanooga Railroad a low-interest loan of $2,000,000. The two railroads agreed to intersect at a strategic point in the mineral district where a great industrial city would be built.[5]

A planter-based coalition with interest in the S&N and the Alabama and Chattanooga railroads chose the Jones Valley as the site of Birmingham. This valley, one of many at the southern end of the Appalachian Mountains, is approximately five miles wide and fifteen miles long and lies between a mountain of iron ore and the Warrior coal fields. Near the center of the valley, the Alabama and Chattanooga (which ran northeast to southwest along the trough of the valley) intersected with the S&N (which extended north from Montgomery to Nashville). Milner convinced the president of the S&N, then John C. Stanton, to invest jointly in the development of a city on a tract of land near that intersection.

Stanton, a transplanted northern capitalist with experience in land investment, took a sixty-day option on land just east of the agreed-upon location. He failed to act on this option, a position he believed would be safe, because there was little capital in the state after the war. The sixty days passed, and a group of Alabama capitalists, including banker Josiah Morris and industrialist James W. Sloss, bought out the option, providing the site for the development of Birmingham, which was named for the industrial city in Great Britain. On 20 December 1870, James R. Powell, with financial backing from investors associated with the S&N, filed incorporation papers on the Elyton Land Company in the Probate Court of Jefferson County. Within eighteen days, engineers had surveyed 4,150 acres of field and forests that would become the site of Birmingham. However, Russel Sage and another northern financier, V. K. Stevenson, had acquired a majority of the state bonds endorsing the building of the S&N Railroad. They threatened to call in their bonds if the operation of the S&N was not turned over to the Alabama and Chattanooga railroad. To counter this threat, the S&N Railroad investors agreed on 19 May 1871, seven months before the incorporation of Birmingham, to allow the Louisville and Nashville (L&N) Railroad to take complete control of the railroad.[6]

Before the L&N takeover, Stanton, who was also a leader in the Alabama legislature during Reconstruction, had proposed extending the S&N to Chattanooga. Coal and iron would be shipped there, where it could connect with a line to New York. This extension would have made Chattanooga, not Birmingham, the "entrepot" of the mineral region.[7] Milner believed this plan would ruin his idea of a great industrial enterprise, with Alabama and Birmingham playing the same role in the Gulf and South that Pennsylvania and Pittsburgh were playing for the Atlantic states. Arguing against the Chattanooga idea, Milner contended that demand for coal would increase as more steam vessels appeared, especially in Gulf Coast trading. He made this argument in an 1859 report to the governor on the feasibility of a railroad in central Alabama:

> The Gulf of Mexico is destined soon to be the sea of the richest commerce the world ever saw: even now, one half the exports of the United States pass over this inland sea of ours. . . . The Commerce of the Gulf must be supplied with coal. The stormy capes and sunken reefs along the coast of Florida, that so hinder our commerce in going out, will protect our coal from competition from the Atlantic States; and Alabama must be to the countries around this central basin what Pennsylvania is to the Atlantic States. Her coal must drive their ships, their mills, and their machines.[8]

Some people thought Stanton's plan made sense in terms of the market for cotton, especially those who wanted a transportation system that would connect the cotton-producing plantation districts to the ports, bypassing the mineral district. Like colonizers, they were unconcerned with regional economic impact.[9] Indeed, many people opposed any investment in Alabama's mineral district. For example, a senator from the black belt, Judge Thomas A. Walker, characterized the district as "so poor that a buzzard would have to carry provisions on his back or starve to death on his passage."[10]

But in 1872, after Birmingham's incorporation, Daniel Pratt, with his son-in-law, Henry Fairchild DeBardeleben, acquired control of the Red Mountain Iron and Coal Company. Working with other mine and furnace owners, they began to produce coal and iron on a large scale in the Birmingham mineral district. With financial backing from the Elyton Land Company and the L&N Railroad, Levin Goodrich experimented with making iron with Alabama coke, and on 28 February 1876, made the first coke pig iron at the Pratt mines near Birmingham. Two years later, Daniel Pratt founded the Pratt Coal and Coke Company, and Birmingham was on the road to becoming "the industrial city of the South."

Not long afterward, DeBardeleben and a Kentucky iron master, Thomas T. Hillman, built the first iron furnace within the corporate limits of the city and named it Alice, after DeBardeleben's daughter. It started producing iron in 1880 and by 1883 employed 500 workers. Other industrialists began to build rolling mills, foundries, and pipe factories; and, by the early 1880s, eight Birmingham furnaces contributed to the state's ranking fifteenth nationwide in the production of ferrous metals. In 1886, the Tennessee Coal, Iron and Railroad Company (TCI), which until then had operated only in Tennessee, relocated to Alabama and consolidated other companies in the Birmingham district to become Alabama's largest and most powerful coal and iron company. By 1890, twenty-five blast furnaces were operating in the Birmingham district.[11]

There was opposition to Birmingham's development. The *Selma Times* of the black belt wrote that Alabama's mineral region would be "better off if all its furnaces were torn down, its mines filled with dirt, and its inhabitants put to planting cotton."[12] The Birmingham *Chronicle* responded, "Those who cannot catch this [industrial] spirit, as it permeates the South, will have to retire from high places and give room to new men."[13]

In 1885, testimony before a U.S. Senate Committee on the Relations between Labor and Capital suggested that opposition to industrialization in Alabama came from planters.[14] One witness testified, "The most pressing conflict was between planters and the industrial capitalists who threatened their labor supply, not between capitalists and proletarians."[15] Like the Prussian Junkers, planters may have been seeking to short-circuit urban centers to inhibit the growth of an urban bourgeoisie that could eventually take command of economic development.[16]

More recently, W. David Lewis has argued that opposition to Birmingham was primarily based on increasing economic rivalries among Alabama cities, such as Mobile, Selma, Tuscaloosa, and Montgomery, all of which had politically supported the idea of industrialization but eventually resented Birmingham's subsequent growth. As early as the late 1850s, support for industrialization extended to a class of town dwellers. Improved transportation and the growth of Birmingham produced competition between towns for market area, and some of the criticism of investment in the mineral district grew from this competition. Such investments and Birmingham's growth threatened the market areas of existing towns, particularly those relatively close to the mineral district. Lewis also noted that some criticisms were instances of residual Jacksonianism, which continued to oppose internal improvements. Whatever their cause, they did not reflect major opposition to industrialization from planters as a class.[17] When the Jacksonian Democrats no longer controlled the state's government, planter-based industrial forces saw an opportunity to build an industrial city in the mineral district and staff it with inexpensive, servile black labor.

What function does land have in the accumulation and circulation of surplus value under the capitalist mode of production? For Karl Marx, the key to any object's value is human labor: the quantity of labor, not the raw materials, used in producing a new commodity determines its value.[18] How then, asks David Harvey, "can raw land, not itself a product of human labor, have a price?"[19] Under the capitalist mode of production, land functions as a *condition* of production; that is, it can provide both the "means" and the "elements" of production. It provides the means of production in agriculture or mining, the raw materials used in the production process. Central Alabama's rich mineral district provided the means for producing coal and iron ore after the district was worked by former slaves and sharecroppers from the black belt. Land needed to *build on* makes it an element of production; it is not used directly in the production process but is still needed. The Elyton Land Company provided this element when it developed the Birmingham site.

The agreement to build a city near the intersection of two railroad lines increased the value of the land because it made the location more accessible. Between 1880 and 1890, railroad mileage in the South increased from 16,605 to 39,108 miles of track, or 135.5 percent, compared with the national expansion of 86.5 percent.[20] In 1890, the railroads accounted for half of the total capital in the United States and played a key role in the ascendancy of corporate capitalism.[21] To maximize the flow of goods and people, Birmingham's avenues were aligned parallel to the railroad lines running southwest to northeast along the trough of the Jones Valley. The railroad also opened Birmingham to interregional and national competition and contributed to urban agglomeration economies that further enhanced the circulation of capital. Marx wrote, "The more rapid and uninterrupted the supply of materials and *matieres instrumentales*, the smaller a supply does the capitalist need to buy. He can therefore much more often turn over or reproduce the circulating capital in this form, instead of having it lie around as dormant capital."[22]

J. H. von Thunen used the term "land rent," which is roughly equivalent to economic rent in classical economics, to explain the type of land use that would occur at any given location due to improved access.[23] Marx called land value that resulted from superior location due to improved transportation "differential rent one"; it decreases as distance from the most accessible area increases.

The value of land also depends on one's willingness to invest in the land. Marx called this capital flow "differential rent two." Planter capital financed the Elyton Land Company—in which nearly all of the investors were former slaveholders— but the development of Birmingham came at an opportune time in terms of overaccumulated capital in the country as a whole. Capital tends to accumulate in the primary circuit (i.e., the manufacturing or production sector), which contributes to overproduction. Too much capital in the manufacturing sector lowers the demand for goods and depresses prices; in other words, it brings a lower rate of profit.[24] When the profit rate lowers, investors search for other avenues and often turn to secondary and tertiary circuits—housing or built environment, health, education—that represent expenditures for the reproduction of labor, areas in which capitalists tend to underinvest. For this reason, investments in the physical growth of cities often occur during downswings in manufacturing.[25] According to David Harvey, this "spatial fix" takes place more for exchange-value than for use-value reasons—"investors were looking for a steady and secure rate of return on their capital."[26] A spatial fix contributes to long waves of investment in the built environment and usually coincides with downswings in the Kondratieff cycle. Investment in the secondary sector involves a higher proportion of variable, as compared with constant, capital, thereby generating a high rate of surplus value with a significant portion returning to construction firms, promoters, and speculators.[27]

The downswing in the second Kondratieff cycle (1873–1896) attracted speculators who were ready to invest in the built environment of the newly incorporated city of Birmingham (Figure 9.1). In its first year of existence, the Elyton Land Company subdivided the site into 50 × 140 feet lots on a rectangular grid and sold $80,000 worth of stock in the company (Figure 9.2). These funds provided a great deal of the financing needed to develop the site and attract investors from throughout the region.

Investments in the built environment may trigger demands for production in the primary circuit (as in the post–World War II suburbanization in the United States, which was part of the catalyst for the long industrial boom of the 1950s and 1960s).[28] Beginning in 1875, the Elyton Land Company, under the leadership of Henry M. Caldwell, concentrated more on promoting development of coal and iron resources than on land. However, a persistent downswing in the national economy brought the price of pig iron down from $40 to $8 per ton. Mining of coal and iron almost came to a stop, and the value of stock in the land company declined 50 percent. Investors then switched back to the secondary circuit, and building activity increased. In 1880, the average price re-

Figure 9.1   Illustrated scene of the Birmingham Real Estate Exchange by John Durkin.

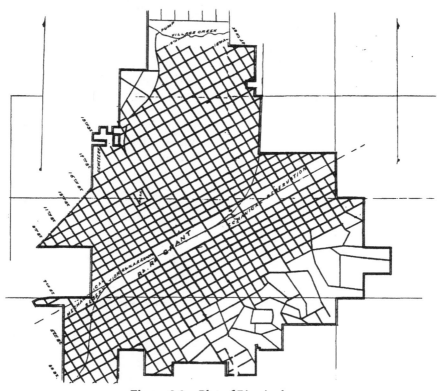

Figure 9.2 Plat of Birmingham.
Source: Elyton Land Company.

ceived for a lot sold was $200, increasing to $360 a year later, to $511 by 1882, and to $756 in 1883.[29]

From 1883 to 1887, residential developments paid off for investors in the Elyton Land Company, which declared annual dividends of 100, 95, 45, 340, and 2,305 percent on the value of the original capital stock.[30] Investors from all parts of the South converged on Birmingham and paid two to three times realistic prices. In response, Elyton's president noted at the annual stockholders meeting in 1886,

> There has been no decline in [land] values, but a steady increase. Birmingham has suffered less from the financial depression than almost any other city in the country and it has been remarked by more than one intelligent observer, that there seemed to have been no hard times in Birmingham.

He went on to say that for those interested in Birmingham, the depression may be "a blessing in disguise."[31] By 1887, the city boasted 437 real estate offices selling lots in suburbs extending as much as ten miles from Birmingham.

THE PLANTER-BASED INDUSTRIAL REGIME

The control exercised by the planter class made itself felt in all phases of the southern economy—not only in agriculture but also in industry.[32] The relationship between the planter class and the industrial capitalists in the postbellum South was complex and has been the focus of extensive debate among students of southern history.[33] In C. Vann Woodward's view, a rising commercial and industrial class had little more than a nominal connection with the former slaveholding class. These new leaders argued for a full industrialization that was radically different from that proposed by Daniel Pratt, who favored an extensive regime of accumulation based on slave labor. Thus, wrote Woodward,

> It would seem a mistake to assume that Redemption was in any real sense a restoration [of the slaveholding class]. Even though a few of the old names were prominent among the new leaders, Redemption was not a return of an old system nor the restoration of an old ruling class. It was rather a new phase of the revolutionary process begun in 1865. Only in a limited sense can it be properly called a "counter-revolution."[34]

Wilbur Cash, in contrast but for former slaves, redemption was a "counter-revolution" to Woodward, stressed the continuity of leadership and values between planters and southern industrialists, arguing that "the mind of the South" was continuous with the past. This continuity was particularly true in Alabama. John W. Cell likens a social class to a bus—riders may get on and off, but the bus and route remain the same even though riders getting on and off of the bus at designated stops "easily mistaken for the end of a journey." The postbellum South certainly did not signal the end of the planters' journey.[35] Indeed, their holdings increased after the war. In Marengo County, Alabama, the heart of the black belt, Wiener found,

> Between 1860 and 1870 the planter elite actually increased its relative wealth in real estate; it held a greater share of the real estate value five years after the war than it had when it began. The elite increased its share of the land value held by county residents by 8 percent between 1860 and 1870, from 55 to 63 percent.[36]

In 1881, Henry Grady, a strong supporter of industrialization in the South, noted,

> There is beyond question a sure but gradual rebunching of the small farms into large estates, and a tendency toward the reestablishment of a landowning oligarchy. Here and there through all the cotton states, and almost in every county, are reappearing the planter princes of the old time, still lord of acres though not of slaves.[37]

The plantation survived but in a different form, preserving the basis of planters' wealth.

Wiener noted that Alabama opted for a version of the "Prussian-type route" to development and not the classic capitalist path taken by England in the seventeenth and eighteenth centuries or by the northern states. On this basis, Wiener assumed that Alabama planters and industrialists represented two independent groups: the planter class turned the regime of capital accumulation over to the new, rising industrialist class while retaining control of the agricultural sector and politics.[38] In the words of Barrington Moore, Jr., industrialists exchanged "the rights to rule for the rights to make money."[39] Birmingham did not threaten the hegemony of planters who continued as landed elites during the postbellum period because both industrialists and planters depended on the exploitation of cheap black labor. As Woodward noted, "In some states, when the major offices were held by industrialists, the disproportionate voting strength of the Black Belt gave big landed interests a significant veto power. [And] until the end of the eighties any insurgency of the lower-class whites usually enabled the dominant industrial Redeemers to whip the landed interests into line."[40] The veto power of landed elites produced a space economy that kept industries out of, or at least on the edge of, the black belt, which was the domain of the planters.

Planters and their industrial counterparts contributed significantly to the white monopoly power base that regulated the regime of accumulation. "These two sources of power," stated Frances Fox Piven and Richard Cloward, "tend over time to be drawn together within one ruling class."[41] William Julius Wilson contended that the commercial and industrial elements' economic interests overlapped sufficiently to form a disciplined ruling class; and Dwight Billings noted that both depended on labor-repressive social relations to regulate the regime of accumulation.[42] The South moved toward industrial capitalism along a path characterized by the continuing exploitation of black labor; a monopoly mode of social regulation boosted the authority of planters and industrialists alike.

Postbellum Alabama did not, however, mirror the social conditions of Prussia. The southern road was founded on the institution of slavery and followed military defeat during the Civil War. The Prussian Junkers never attained as high a degree of control over their servile labor as did planters over slaves, and they eventually relied less on compulsory services and more on wage laborers, who resisted demands for increased labor while they became interested in producing their own marketable surpluses. The Confederacy's military defeat also entailed a more thorough collapse of planters' private authority than any experienced by nineteenth-century Junkers. The Civil War ended slavery without the sort of financial compensation and piecemeal implementation that accompanied the emancipation of serfs in Prussia.[43]

Junkers, unlike Alabama's planters, had to feudalize the bourgeoisie, drawing many over to their political and social points of view. There also were great differences between Prussian Junkers and Alabama planters in terms of economic and social values. Michael O'Brien noted,

> Alabama inherited an essentially laissez-faire political economy; the banks played no role in its industrialization; the planters were no aristocracy, nor

did they receive much deference beyond the prerogatives of wealth; Alabama had a democratic political system, notably in theory if less perfectly in practice; the bourgeoisie had no reluctance about making their political presence felt; the "Bourbon" regime developed no system of social welfare and, indeed, it reduced the scale of government activity. As Prussians, Alabamians cut a sorry figure.[44]

In reconsidering the Prussian thesis, Wiener noted that the "Prussian Road" was more of a metaphor for the South's distinct path to modernity than an actual description of what occurred.[45] Alabama's route had more in common with the political, racial, economic, and cultural circumstances of South Africa than with Prussia.

Finally, key Birmingham industrialists came directly from planter backgrounds. Industrialists and planters were not two independent groups. Birmingham's key industrialists were known as "mules"—an icon of southern agriculture and a suitable title, given their political, social, and personal ties to the planter class. Milner was the son of a slaveholding planter, who also participated in railroading and gold mining; Frank Gilmer was a wealthy planter impressed by the industrial potential of the mineral district; Joseph Bryan, a leading champion of southern industrialization and a key figure in the history of Sloss Furnaces, had been steeped from birth in the traditions of Virginia's planter aristocracy and was "first and foremost a Virginian." Another of Birmingham's key industrialists, James W. Sloss, began as a merchant but then owned several plantations that made him one of the state's wealthiest men. Thomas Seddon, who took charge of Sloss Furnaces in 1887, was the son of the Confederacy's secretary of war. Born on a Virginia plantation, he had managed a Louisiana sugar plantation before coming to Birmingham. Henry Fairchild DeBardeleben was a cotton plantation owner who migrated from South Carolina to Autauga County, Alabama. Enoch Ensley, who came to Birmingham from Memphis in 1881 and bought the Pratt Coal and Coke Company and later took control of the Alice Furnace Company, owned an inherited plantation in Mississippi from his father.[46] To this list of planter-based industrialists can be added James R. Powell of the Elyton Land Company.

In short, Birmingham industrialists were not new arrivals but men deeply rooted in southern seigneurial society and members of the old planter aristocracy who wanted to make money—to become owners of production, exploit the vast natural resources of Alabama's mineral district, and regulate the regime of accumulation. Unlike Prussia's industrialists, they needed no indoctrination: they fully identified with values of the seigneurial class. The planter-based industrial regime was not, however, simply a restoration of the seigneurial socioeconomic order, nor was the regime continuous with the past. Woodward was correct in this regard.

THE GROWTH OF INDUSTRIAL ENTERPRISES

The concentration of production in the mineral district started before the incorporation of Birmingham and attracted capitalists. As early as 1865, a Cincinnati firm invested in the Irondale Works in Jefferson County; two years later, the

Shelby Iron Company was developed as a result of the investments of fourteen New England capitalists.[47] Birmingham's development attracted attention and capital from abroad. The panic of 1873 forced the L&N into bankruptcy, and partial ownership of the railroad ended up in the hands of European capitalists. In 1875, Sir Isaac Lowthian Bell, president of the British Iron and Steel Institute, noted that the proximity of coal and iron in Alabama, Georgia, Tennessee, and West Virginia compared with the most favored localities examined in Europe.[48] In 1883, Birmingham's *The Iron Age* reported the arrival of two parties of English capitalists and stated, "Scarcely a week passes but the city is visited by capitalists from a distance."[49]

By the turn of the century, the United States had begun to compete successfully with European steelmakers internationally; the railroads and a growing economy were generating high levels of demand for steel and iron at home; and, in 1899, TCI produced the first steel made in large quantities from open-hearth furnaces in the South. Coal production also increased in Alabama from 13,000 tons in 1870 to more than 5.5 million tons by 1892. Six years later, the accumulation of foreign markets had made Birmingham the largest producer of pig iron in the country and the third largest in the world.[50] It was mainly this potential for production that earlier had moved Andrew Carnegie to declare, "The South is Pennsylvania's most formidable industrial enemy."[51]

Birmingham's steel production further increased the demand for coal, and by 1901 Alabama coal production exceeded 9 million tons. The state ranked fifth among twenty-seven coal-producing states and second only to West Virginia among southern and border states, and it doubled its production within ten years. In 1919, coal production remained about the same, but the value of coal produced in the state reached $37,300,000, an average of $2.08 per ton; nearly 50 percent of this production centered in the Birmingham area.[52]

U.S. firms often sent agents to Europe to drum up land sales. Foreigners also invested in state bonds and were reimbursed with land by states unable to honor their commitments; for example, in 1876, Alabama offered foreign investors land in exchange for defaulted 8 percent state bonds.[53] Foreign investors owned a majority of the stock of the L&N Railroad, which held approximately half a million acres of land in Alabama's mineral district.[54] In 1886, DeBardeleben used foreign capital to purchase 150,000 acres of rich ore and coal lands in the Jones Valley, where the industrial suburb of Bessemer would be developed. Using both foreign and domestic capital, DeBardeleben formed the South's largest industrial undertaking in this industrial suburb.[55] The introduction of foreign capital, however, did not alter the racial practices of the Birmingham regime: as absentee owners, foreign investors had little influence.

The panic of 1893 was a part of the downswing in the second Kondratieff cycle. When it ended, northern investment in the South accelerated and produced, according to Woodward, a "colonial economy." Birmingham should probably have heeded the advice of one northerner:

> Our capitalists are going into your country because they see a chance to make money there, but you must not think that they will give your people

the benefit of the money they make. That will come North and enrich their heirs. . . . Your people should not be dazzled by the glamour nor caught with the jingle of northern gold, but they should exact terms from these men that will be of benefit to the communities in which they may select to establish themselves.[56]

In the words of Woodward, the South became a "raw-material economy, with the attendant penalties of low wages, lack of opportunity, and poverty."[57]

REGULATING THE REGIME OF ACCUMULATION

The mode of social regulation provides the social context in which production occurs. It is composed of a complex ensemble of norms and habits, state forms, structures, practices, and customs.[58] Capitalism is not characterized by one particular mode of social regulation, but capital development in the postbellum South was. The Democratic state government helped guide and sustain Birmingham's planter-based regime; this Democratic Party was essentially the same as the Republican Party after radical Reconstruction and the compromise of 1877. Like the Republican Party, the Democratic Party strongly supported the notion of capital development. Its presidential candidate in 1876, Samuel J. Tilden, was a wealthy, conservative New York corporate lawyer friendly to capitalists' interests (capitalists often contributed to both parties).[59] The Republican Party was still known as the party of Reconstruction. The South neither could nor would forget that fact. Thus, the southern Democratic Party would provide the mode of social regulation. Birmingham industrialist James W. Sloss was closely associated with the state's most prominent Democratic leaders, including George S. Houston, who was elected governor in 1874. Both Houston and Sloss had economic interests in the L&N Railroad. The Democratic Party continued to effectively represent the interests of local capitalists. Houston's successor, State Senator Rufus W. Cobb, was the attorney for the L&N Railroad and the president of the Central Iron Works of Helena, an industrial suburb located just south of Birmingham. Cobb retained the position of president while serving as governor.[60]

The planter-based industrialists used their control of the state to obtain and maintain an inexpensive labor force. For example, the Reconstruction constitution set aside one-fifth of Alabama's total revenue for education, but the 1875 "redemption" constitution limited spending on education to $100,000 per year, and white property owners were not taxed for the education of blacks. Horace Mann Bond wrote, "It is obvious that an educated labor force, intelligent regarding rates of interest, cognizant of even the simplest methods of accounting would be a distinct liability to the system rather than an asset."[61] This statement was a clear echo of the past: slaveholders did not invest slaves' time in schooling. Education would have provided skills and opportunities the slaveholder had no intention of allowing slaves to seek.[62] Similarly, the opportunities available to black workers in the post-Reconstruction era required no education, and it is a great deal easier to control the mind of an uneducated worker than an educated worker. Carter Woodson noted in *The Mis-Education of the Negro*,

> When you control a man's thinking, you do not have to worry about his actions. You do not have to tell him not to stand here or go yonder. He will find his "proper place" and will stay in it. You do not need to send him to the back door. He will go without being told. In fact, if there is no back door, he will cut one for his special benefit. His education makes it necessary.[63]

Without the proper education, Woodson continues, one can easily "learn to follow the line of least resistance rather than battle against odds for what real history has shown to be the right course."[64] Thus, educating the black worker never became a high priority for the Birmingham regime, even in the twentieth century, because a strong back but a weak mind characterized the ideal worker. In 1912, John Fitch noted that one plant owner in the Birmingham area said he prevented labor trouble by hiring only workers who could not read and that there were not enough illiterates to go around.[65] In 1919, the state disbursed only $22,000 to educate blacks and $90,000 for whites; in 1928, the amount for whites increased to $140,000, but the amount for blacks declined to $20,000.[66] Because of this "miseducation," race-connected issues and practices were denied in community discourse, and this silence became the line of least resistance for many blacks.[67] For this reason, the struggle for civil rights had to begin in the education arena.

The redemption constitution also denied the state the power to borrow money except to support corporations, whereas the tax rate was set at a maximum seven and one-half mills. State monies also could be used to suppress insurrection, rebellion, or invasion.[68] The 1901 constitution convention produced a very regressive tax structure that remains in existence; a 1980 study found the state could increase its property tax rate as much as 66 percent and still rank among the lowest taxed states.[69] In the late 1990s, property and corporate franchise taxes accounted for only about 4 percent of Alabama's tax revenue, whereas income and sales taxes accounted for approximately 64 percent.

Jimmie Frank Gross noted that the 1901 State Constitution also included a clause limiting suffrage to those with "regular employment in some lawful business or occupation for the greater part of the last twelve months"—thereby tying the right to vote to capitalists' need for an accessible labor force.[70] (One representative from the Birmingham area, frequently plagued by strikes and seasonal unemployment, opposed this clause, stating, "We have quite enough traps set to catch all the negroes in Africa or anywhere else.")[71] The Birmingham representative apparently did not realize that the state was not only anti-black but strongly pro-capital. The availability of labor has no limit under capitalist development; an unlimited labor supply makes possible an industrial reserve army to keep down the cost of labor. A 1903 law prohibited "boycotting, unfair lists, picketing, or other interference with the lawful business or occupation of others."[72] Legislators defended it on the basis that government must protect property, and employers had a right to hire and fire whom they pleased.[73] The result was the development of a labor system as repressive as sharecropping.

The crop-lien system had its industrial counterpart. By issuing scrip, i.e., company currency, rather than cash and paying only monthly, industrialists could minimize their need for capital. Birmingham's industrial workers were often paid in scrip that allowed them to purchase goods only in the company commissary.[74] The commissary system compelled workers to buy at a particular price and imposed a surcharge of 10 to 25 percent to convert company scrip to cash—more where the proportion of blacks in the work force was high—on the grounds that the black worker had "no heed of tomorrow and lacks thrift."[75] Access to cash would have allowed workers to take off after each payday until their money ran out or give them time to seek work elsewhere. This reasoning was also behind the refusal to pay wages weekly or even monthly or, in some places, a postharvest labor payment system.[76]

The white monopoly on power rested on a one-party political system. The Democratic Party continued as the white man's party, with its single-minded focus on race as the dominant and persistent issue in southern politics.[77] The lack of political competition meant there were few surprises, which suited both local principals and owners outside of the region. A homogeneous and predictable political space also contributes to the accumulation and circulation of capital. For businesspeople overall, wrote Stanley Greenberg,

> Segregation and racially exclusive public policies are just so many constraints with which firms in a racial order must come to terms. Businessmen may decide that these constraints impose intolerable costs and must, therefore, be eliminated. But where business operates profitably and where attempts to tamper with racial practices elicit profoundly hostile public responses to capitalism and free enterprise, businessmen may simply place these constraints alongside other givens in management practice.[78]

All attempts to tamper with the racial order in Birmingham elicited hostile public responses, forcing local capitalists and businesspeople to incorporate race-connected practices to regulate the accumulation of capital.

THE ESTABLISHMENT OF CULTURAL HEGEMONY

> The system's *real* strength does not lie in the violence of the ruling class or the coercive power of the state apparatus, but in the acceptance by the ruled of a conception of the world which belongs to the rulers.
>
> —Antonio Gramsci

At first, black industrial workers came to Birmingham directly from slavery or through sharecropping. The wage-labor arrangement they encountered required them to become proletarianized, or acculturated to the industrialist's work order.

To do so, the ruling regime needed to establish cultural hegemony over the free black worker to sanction the extraction and organization of surplus on a more intensive level than under slavery or the sharecropper system. According to S. L. Elkin,

> The principal tasks of city governments in the privatist regimes, aside from not standing in the way of business growth, were to integrate into the existing political order the new workers required for industrial expansion and to provide whatever services and capital investment which were not readily forthcoming privately.[79]

Because slaves were not free, they worked only if they were forced. Slave owners thus retained a more "mercantilist" notion of time in contrast to that of the "liberal" view of human nature, whereby free-wage laborers are motivated because they share in an acquisitive spirit. This view does not mean that slave owners' time conceptions were not capitalist; they were merely preclassical or premodern. They clung to a preclassical view of workers, especially black ones. According to Mark Smith, slavery embraced a profit-oriented culture and "simultaneously retained an organic and hierarchical view of human relations. . . . [It] was as much about social control as it was about economic profit."[80] Control of slaves' time was of paramount social, moral, and political importance. It did not conflict with the planters' reliance on nature as the engine of plantation routine. They still followed nature, wrote Smith, introducing "clock time into seasonal and diurnal rhythms for the purpose of regulating labor and establishing plantation order."[81] Compared to the more time-oriented industrial capitalism, both slaves and sharecroppers came from a more task-oriented environment, where work was tied to the production of a finished commodity rather than to specified time intervals.[82] Sharecroppers, in particular, did not expect to labor a given amount of time day after day.

These differences in conceptions of time showed in workers' behavior in Birmingham during the early phase of industrial capitalism, which, according to Smith, "entertained a benign, liberal view of human nature whereby workers could be both regulated and motivated by time."[83] Former slaves and sharecroppers were not motivated. They did not always respond to the clocks and bells calling them to the mines and mills, and absenteeism was a major problem. The Sloss company needed about 269 workers but had to keep 565 on the payroll because most worked on the average less than half the month, and turnover was high.[84] Many refused to work at night. TCI found it could not use double shifts.[85]

Birmingham employers and newspaper editors argued that a basic condition of industrial capitalism—reliance on free-wage earners—increased blacks' irresponsible and menacing behavior. The Birmingham *News* wrote, "The Negro race is receiving little character training, little discipline, from the white race under the new economic conditions."[86] A company official complained that most blacks wanted only to live in the city and squander their earnings: "The chief use they have for it [money] is for three purposes—craps, women and whiskey."[87] (Such criticisms were not new: in Elizabethan times, according to Harvey, "Madness and unemployment were regarded as the same thing, while the advent of industrial capitalism had the effect of defining sickness as inability to go to work.")[88] What seemed menacing may have simply been behavior reflecting pride in the ownership of labor denied them for more than 200 years. Also, noted Robin Kelley, because most work under capitalism is alienating, especially when performed in a context of racial oppression, "We should expect black working people to minimize labor with as little economic loss as possible."[89]

Birmingham was not unusual in this respect. A preoccupation with the character and morals of working classes was a feature of privatist regimes everywhere during the early stage of industrial capitalism.[90] Capitalism had not created the cultural form that finally made all other cultural forms impossible.[91] An economic transformation does not mark only a major historical change or the emergence of a new elite; it also marks a cultural transformation. The cultural form that accompanied the rise of industrial capitalism required that the owners of production and the workers speak a common language and respond to the same clock. During the early phase of southern industrial capitalism, wrote Wayne Flint, southern workers' lives

> were still essentially rural, where labor might be back-breaking for a season. But once they had "laid crops by" in August, they had ample time for camp meeting revivals, visiting relatives, or just resting. After they picked cotton in the fall, the routine of their lives relaxed considerably until the following spring when crops needed planting. Although they had plenty of work to do, tending livestock, making baskets, clothes, and quilts, mending equipment, or other chores, *they controlled the pace of their lives.*[92]

In this premodern form, time was inscribed in nature, which determined when a particular task (e.g., harvesting the crop) would occur. Cotton was harvested when the weather allowed; otherwise the mules—and the farmer or sharecropper—rested or turned to another task. The length of the working day changed according to the task. There was no conflict between labor and "passing the time of day."[93] Talking of the immediate future, one was most likely to say, "I will meet you after I have finished what I am doing *now.*"[94] The notion of an exact appointment is not sensible when time is related to tasks that fluctuate with the seasons—from the intense labor at harvest time to idle hours at night or winter.

The rural South instilled this cyclical concept of time in the condition of blacks, who were fluid in their definition of the world. James Cone noted, "They are in the process of making history; things are in a state of flux. Nothing is nailed down." Capitalists and the modernist cultural form, in contrast, assumed "fixed definitions of things, because they have made them be what they are. For them history was in the past, that which has already happened."[95] Cyclical time implies that there is always next year, and time is never lost. Past, present, and future meld into one other to accentuate continuity within change.

These work rhythms were more humanly comprehensible than the temporal discipline required of industrial capitalism. Karl Marx argued that intensified work-rhythms could generate labor supply and management problems, especially when production is continuous.[96] Industrial capitalism values not the task but time, which rushes forward; the future becomes the present, and the present moment cannot be recaptured. Lefebvre wrote,

> With the advent of modernity time has vanished from social space. It is recorded solely on measuring-instruments, on clocks, that are as isolated and functionally specialized as this time itself. Lived time loses its form and its social interest—with the exception, that is, of time spent working. Economic space subordinates time to itself; political space expels it as threatening and dangerous (to power).[97]

Linear or modern time requires more discipline than cyclical time or time inscribed in nature. It includes working long hours and nights; it includes working time for the maintenance of labor and extra working time to produce the means of subsistence for the owners of the means of production. The more cyclical conception of time remained with black workers into the twentieth century. In 1907, when United States Steel (USS) took over TCI, it faced labor turnover in autumn so high it caused a drop in company earnings. The company attributed this to "the usual call at this season of the year for labor in cotton picking."[98] A general exodus also took place every winter, beginning in December when many workers went back for Christmas.[99] Flynt stated, "Unaccustomed to the steady work, rural-minded men often came to view industrial labor as a short-term palliative. They would leave their farms for a few months' work at a steel mill, then move on to another industrial job or back to the land.[100]

Harriet Beecher Stowe explained the work habits of free labor of the South and North in terms of natural factors: northern work was more intense because summers were brief and winters long; in the South, growth occurred year round, so there was no need for intense periods of work—an equal amount of production could be achieved with less labor. Gerald David Jaynes points out that Mrs. Stowe failed to realize that the conflict between northern capitalists and southern laborers was precisely because the capitalists "were not satisfied with an equal amount done with less labor, but wanted a greater amount done with equal labor."[101] They wanted to maximize working time devoted to producing their means of subsistence.

To instill the industrial notion of time into black workers' everyday routine, Birmingham capitalists sought to make other modes of living difficult, if not impossible. Industrialists, like the planters with sharecroppers, supported laws to control behavior and enforce a rigid work schedule.[102] In 1889, the editor of the Birmingham *Age-Herald* declared, "The negro is a good laborer when his labor can be controlled and directed." Industrialists demanded and got passed vagrancy laws similar to those enacted immediately after the abolition of slavery. (The state legislature passed the vagrancy codes in 1903 and 1907 to ensure industrialists an adequate and reliable supply of labor throughout the year.)[103] Birmingham waged an unrelenting campaign against vagrants, giving them the choice of going to jail or to work. The city went a step further, regulating saloons that attracted "undesirables" (against the opposition of local capitalists, who feared that it would cause workers to leave the area and hamper labor recruitment).[104] Through vagrancy laws and other means of control, a capitalist life eventually evolved. What became true for labor time, or the workspace, became true for leisure time, or domestic space.[105] According to J. L. Hammond and Barbara Hammond, the worker's

> daily life was arranged by factory hours; he worked under an overseer . . . ; if he broke one of a long series of minute regulations he was fined, and behind all this scheme of supervision and control there loomed the great impersonal system [of industrial capitalism].[106]

Edith Ward London, daughter of a Birmingham industrial manager, wrote in her diary,

> our household ran by the blowing of whistles. We were hustled out of bed by the 7:00 whistle. Daddy came to lunch when the big one blew at 12, and he was back home again for his game of tennis when the 3:00 whistle sounded. Whistles, snorting trains and even the big machinery clanking within the mill were commonplace to me. I had taken them for granted, as I had sunshine, as I had my father and mother's face.[107]

In 1888, Richard H. Edmonds, founder and editor of the *Manufacturers' Record*, a weekly newsletter, reported the triumphs of southern industrial capitalism over the more natural rhythms of the countryside: "The easy-going days of the South have passed away, never to return. . . . The South has learned that 'time is money.'"[108] Marx wrote, "Economy of time to this all economy ultimately reduces itself."[109]

Birmingham's ruling class accepted the idea of a free-labor system but exploited black labor by any means possible, barring slavery. As one Alabamian of the period said, "Emancipation had really changed nothing in the South. The Negro bears the same relation to us now, de facto, as before. We controlled his labor in the past (at our own expense) and will control it in the future (at theirs)."[110] The new industrial order in Birmingham, according to another, was nothing "but a continuation of the old."[111]

Had it not been for the Civil War and the Thirteenth Amendment, Birmingham would have been a center of slave-operated industries. Even with emancipation, the city perpetuated most features of an industrial slave regime.[112] Henry McKiven, Jr., wrote that the Democratic state government provided convict labor that competed with free miners and allowed the regime "to impose the system of scrip payment that deprived miners of a fair return for their labor."[113]

These and other repressive features meant that southern regimes relied less on investments from outside of the region than some scholars have assumed. The South devised a workable arrangement that used black and white labor consistent with white supremacy. In a series of studies on southern towns, William Warner and associates concluded that the separation between blacks and whites was caste-like in nature.[114] The system created what van den Berghe calls "Herrenvolk democracy," democracy for the master race but tyranny for the subordinate race.[115] Like slavery, this master–servant pattern of racial dominance regarded members of the subordinate group as childish, immature, and irresponsible—but lovable if they remained in their place. But, as Marx noted, "A people which enslaves another people forget its own chains."[116] These chains prevented Birmingham from producing a competitive democratic capitalism. Lewis wrote,

> Perhaps the most enduring prewar legacy that was handed on to Birmingham was the antebellum attitude that black people were members of an inferior race, best suited for menial tasks in a society where white men reigned supreme. . . . It is clear that many practices later used by firms that employed black convicts in the Birmingham District, including flogging and punitive confinement in "nigger boxes" that were "barely large enough for a prisoner to stand erect and lighted only by air holes to prevent suffocation," were also used by slaveholders before the Civil War.[117]

Although Birmingham was a postbellum city and the South's most industrialized city by the turn of the century, the mode of social regulation was clearly continuous with the antebellum past. This strong continuity with the antebellum past produced what Carter Wilson called "dominant aversive racism," which is what the civil rights movement had to confront.[118]

NOTES

1. Henri Lefebvre, *The Production of Space*, trans. Donald Nicholson-Smith (Oxford, U.K.: Basil Blackwell, 1991), 335, 336.

2. Gavin Wright, *Old South, New South: Revolutions in Southern Economy Since the Civil War* (New York: Basic Books, 1986), 34.

3. W. David Lewis, *Sloss Furnaces and the Rise of the Birmingham District: An Industrial Epic* (Tuscaloosa: University of Alabama Press, 1994), 50; C. Vann Woodward, *Origins of the New South, 1877–1913* (Baton Rouge: Louisiana State University Press, 1951), 9; William Warren Rogers, Robert David Ward, Leah Rawls Atkins, and Wayne Flynt, *Alabama: The History of a Deep South State* (Tuscaloosa: University of Alabama Press, 1994), 253.

4. Peter Camejo, *Racism, Revolution, Reaction, 1861–1877: The Rise and Fall of Radical Reconstruction* (New York: Pathfinder, 1976), 100–01.

5. Horace Mann Bond, "Social and Economic Forces in Alabama Reconstruction," *Journal of Negro History* 23, no. 3 (July 1938): 290–348. Bond noted that the creation of state debts did not result from the Reconstruction regime but from the activities of various capitalists working through both Republican and Democratic Party channels (343).

6. Bond, "Social," 343.

7. Ethel Armes, *The Story of Iron and Coal in Alabama* (Birmingham, Ala.: Chamber of Commerce, 1910), 244.

8. John T. Milner, *Report to the Governor of Alabama on the Alabama Central Railroad* (Montgomery, Ala.: Advertiser Book and Job Steam Press Print, 1859), 23, 26.

9. Wright, *Old South*.

10. Quoted in Armes, *The Story*, 110.

11. Martha Mitchell, "Birmingham: A Biography of a City of the New South" (Ph.D. diss., University of Chicago, 1946), 113.

12. Quoted in Jonathan M. Wiener, *Social Origins of the New South: Alabama, 1860–1885* (Baton Rouge: Louisiana State University Press, 1978), 157.

13. Quoted in Wiener, *Social Origins*, 188.

14. The industrial phase of capitalist development produced a great deal of conflict between capital and labor. In 1885, the Senate Committee on Education and Labor held a number of hearings throughout the country to examine this conflict.

15. Quoted in Wiener, *Social Origins*, 159.

16. Lawrence N. Powell, "The Prussians Are Coming," *Georgia Historical Quarterly* 71, no. 4 (Winter 1987): 650.

17. J. Mills Thornton III, *Politics and Power in a Slave Society: Alabama, 1800–1860* (Baton Rouge: Louisiana State University Press, 1978), 295; Lewis, *Sloss Furnaces*, 38, 72–73, 477–78.

18. Karl Marx, *Capital: A Critique of Political Economy*, Vol. 1, trans. Ben Fowkes (New York: Vintage Books, 1977), 125–77.

19. David Harvey, *The Urban Experience* (Baltimore: Johns Hopkins University Press, 1989), 90.

20. Woodward, *Origins*, 120.

21. Alfred D. Chandler, Jr., *The Railroads: The Nation's First Big Business* (New York: Harcourt, Brace and World, 1965), 9–12, 15.

22. Karl Marx, *Grundrisse: Foundations of the Critique of Political Economy*, trans. Martin Nicolaus (New York: Vintage Books, 1973), 825–26.

23. J. H. von Thunen, *Der Isolierte Staat in Beziehung auf Landwirtschaft und Nationalokonomie* (Berlin: Weegandt, 1875); P. Hall, ed., *von Thunen's Isolated State: An English Version of "Der Isolierte Staat,"* trans. C. M. Wartenberg (New York: Pergamon Press, 1966).

24. James O'Connor, *Accumulation Crisis* (Oxford, U.K.: Basil Blackwell, 1984).

25. Simon Kuznets, *Capital in the American Economy: Its Formation and Financing* (Washington, D.C.: National Bureau of Economic Research, 1961), 387–88.

26. Harvey, *The Urban Experience*, 80.

27. Lefebvre, *Production*, 336.

28. R. J. King, "Capital Switching and the Role of Ground Rent 1: Theoretical Problems," *Environment and Planning A* 21 (1989): 445–62.

29. Testimony by Henry M. Caldwell before the U.S. Senate Committee on Education and Labor, *Report of the Senate Upon the Relations Between Labor and Capital and Testimony*, IV, 48th Congress, 2nd Session (1885), 349–50.

30. Carl V. Harris, *Political Power in Birmingham, 1871–1921* (Knoxville: University of Tennessee Press, 1977), 21.

31. Quoted in H. M. Caldwell, *History of the Elyton Land Company and Birmingham, Ala.* (Birmingham, Ala.: Birmingham Publishing Co., 1892), 17.

32. James S. Allen, *The Negro Question in the United States* (New York: International Publishers, 1936), 9.

33. James C. Cobb, "Beyond Planters and Industrialists: A New Perspective on the New South," *Journal of Southern History* 54, no. 1 (February 1988): 45–68.

34. Woodward, *Origins*, 21–22, 20. Woodward qualified his view by noting that not all postbellum regimes were so aligned.

35. Wilbur J. Cash, *The Mind of the South* (New York: Alfred A. Knopf, 1941); Barrington Moore, Jr., *Social Origins of Dictatorship and Democracy: Lord and Peasant in the Making of the Modern World* (Boston: Beacon Press, 1966), 141–55; Jonathan Wiener, "Class Structure and Economic Development in the American South, 1865–1955," *Ameri-*

can Historical Review 84, no. 4 (October 1979): 970–92; John W. Cell, *The Highest Stage of White Supremacy: The Origins of Segregation in South Africa and the American South* (Cambridge, Mass.: Cambridge University Press, 1980), 107.

36. Jonathan M. Wiener, "Planter Persistence and Social Change: Alabama, 1850–1870," *Journal of Interdisciplinary History* 7, no. 2 (Autumn 1976): 240.

37. Quoted in Allen, *The Negro Question*, 97.

38. Wiener, *Social Origins*.

39. Moore, *Social Origins*, 437.

40. Woodward, *Origins*, 21.

41. Frances Fox Piven and Richard A. Cloward, *Poor People's Movements: Why They Succeed, How They Fail* (New York: Vintage Books, 1979), 1.

42. William Julius Wilson, *The Declining Significance of Race: Blacks and Changing American Institutions* (Chicago: University of Chicago Press, 1978), 56; Dwight B. Billings, *Planters and the Making of a "New South": Class, Politics, and Development in North Carolina, 1865–1900* (Chapel Hill: University of North Carolina Press, 1979), 99–100.

43. Shearer Davis Bowman, *Masters and Lords: Mid–19th-Century U.S. Planters and Prussian Junkers* (New York: Oxford University Press, 1993), 21, 48, 55.

44. Michael O'Brien, "The Nineteenth-Century American South," *Historical Journal* 24, no. 3 (September 1981): 762.

45. Alex Lichtenstein, *Twice the Work of Free Labor: The Political Economy of Convict Labor in the New South* (London: Verso, 1996), 8.

46. Lewis, *Sloss Furnaces*, 21, 55, 61, 139, 159; for more information on Joseph Bryan, see also James M. Lindgren, "'First and Foremost a Virginian,' Joseph Bryan and the New South Economy," *Virginia Magazine of History and Biography* 96, no. 2 (April 1988): 157–80; W. David Lewis, "Joseph Bryan and the Virginia Connection in the Industrial Development of Northern Alabama," *Virginia Magazine of History and Biography*, 98, no. 4 (October, 1990): 613–40.

47. Armes, *The Story*, 186, 196–97; Woodward, *Origins*, 150.

48. "Alabama: Its Iron Mountains and Coal Basin," *The Iron Age*, 15 July 1875, 1, 2.

49. "A Bright Future for Birmingham," *The Iron Age*, 12 April 1883, 2; also quoted in Woodward, *Origins*, 126.

50. Victor S. Clark, *The History of Manufactures in the United States*, Vol. 2 (New York: McGraw-Hill, 1929), 242–43.

51. *Manufacturers' Record* 15 (6 April 1889), 12–14.

52. U.S. Department of the Interior, U.S. Geological Survey, *Mineral Resources of the U.S., 1902* (Washington, D.C.: Government Printing Office, 1904); William B. Phillips, *Iron Making in Alabama* (Tuscaloosa: Geological Survey of Alabama, 1912), 151; Alabama Mine Inspector, *Coal Mine Statistics of State of Alabama for 1910* (Birmingham: Grant and Pow, 1911), 40; O. E. Kiessling, "Coal Mining in the South," *Annals of the American Academy of Political and Social Science* 153 (January 1931): 84.

53. H. Fry, *Financial Invasion of the U.S.A.: A Threat to American Society?* (New York: McGraw-Hill, 1980), 45.

54. Woodward, *Origins*, 126.

55. "Henry F. DeBardeleben," Birmingham Public Library, Archives, Hill Ferguson Historical Collection, File 3.36.

56. *Manufacturers' Record* 27 (June 7, 1895), 285.

57. Woodward, *Origins*, 291–320.

58. M. Aglietta, *A Theory of Capitalist Regulation: The U.S. Experience*, trans. D. Fernbach (London: NLB, 1979), 382; see also Robert Brenner and M. Glick, "The Regulation Approach: Theory and History," *New Left Review* 186 (1991): 45–119.

59. Camejo, *Racism.*

60. Woodward, *Origins*, 8; Bond, "Social," 336.

61. Horace Mann Bond, *Negro Education in Alabama: A Study in Cotton and Steel* (New York: Octagon Books, 1969), 141.

62. Roger L. Ransom and Richard Sutch, *One Kind of Freedom: The Economic Consequences of Emancipation* (Cambridge, U.K.: Cambridge University Press), 16–19.

63. Carter G. Woodson, *The Mis-Education of the Negro* (Trenton, N.J.: Africa World Press, 1990), xiii.

64. Woodson, *Mis-Education*, 96.

65. John A. Fitch, "Birmingham District: Labor Conservation," *Survey 27*, no. 14 (6 January 1912): 1527–40.

66. *Annual Report of the State Auditor*, 1919, 1928.

67. M. Desimone, "Racial Discourse in a Community: Language and the Social Construction of Race," *Journal of Negro Education* 62, no. 4 (Fall 1993): 414–18.

68. Woodward, *Origins*, 9.

69. Angie Wright and Duna Norton, "Land Ownership and Property Taxation in Alabama," Appalachian Land Ownership Task Force, Program for Rural Services and Research (Tuscaloosa: University of Alabama, 1980).

70. Jimmie Frank Gross, "Alabama Politics and the Negro, 1874–1901" (Ph.D. diss., University of Georgia, 1969), 243.

71. Cross, "Alabama," 253–54.

72. Anti-Boycott Bill, No. 329, H. 518 (1903).

73. Harris, *Political Power*, 217–18.

74. According to Irving Beiman, "Birmingham: Steel Giant with a Glass Jaw," in *Our Fair City*, ed. Robert S. Allen (New York: Vanguard Press, 1947), 111, 113, the commissary system existed until the 1940s. As a result of this system, he found that retail sales in Birmingham were 40 percent less than those in Atlanta, which had a population not much greater than Birmingham's. He noted, "Birmingham merchants long have been aware of the feudal hold TCI has on its workers through the commissary store system, which takes back a great part of their weekly wages. That money doesn't filter into general circulation."

75. *Proceedings of the Joint Convention of Alabama Coal Operators Association and United Mine Workers of America*, Birmingham, Alabama, 22 June 1903, 655.

76. Gerald David Jaynes, *Branches Without Roots: Genesis of the Black Working Class in the American South, 1862–1882* (New York: Oxford University Press, 1989), 46.

77. Douglas F. Dowd, "A Comparative Analysis of Economic Development in the American West and South," *Journal of Economic History* 16, no. 4 (December 1956): 558–74.

78. Stanley B. Greenberg, *Race and State in Capitalist Development: Comparative Perspectives* (New Haven, Conn.: Yale University Press, 1980), 142.

79. S. L. Elkin, "Twentieth-Century Urban Regimes," *Journal of Urban Affairs* 7, no. 2 (1985): 18.

80. Mark M. Smith, *Mastered by the Clock: Time, Slavery and Freedom in the American South* (Chapel Hill: University of North Carolina Press, 1997), 4–8.

81. Smith, *Mastered by the Clock*, 111.

82. Susan A. Mann, "Sharecropping in the Cotton South: A Case of Uneven Development in Agriculture," *Rural Sociology* 49, no. 3 (1984): 416.

83. Smith, *Mastered by the Clock*, 5.

84. U.S. Senate Committee on Education and Labor, *Labor and Capital*, 286–90.

85. Marlene Hunt Rikard, "An Experiment in Welfare Capitalism: The Health Care Services of the Tennessee Coal, Iron, and Railroad Company," (Ph.D. diss., University of Alabama, 1983), 60.

86. Quoted in Harris, *Political Power*, 187.

87. "Arbitration Commission Heard Much Testimony Yesterday," *Birmingham Age-Herald*, 16 August 1903, 5.

88. David Harvey, *Consciousness and the Urban Experience: Studies in the History and Theory of Capitalist Urbanization* (Baltimore: Johns Hopkins University Press, 1985), 51.

89. Robin D. G. Kelley, *Race Rebels: Culture, Politics, and the Black Working Class* (New York: Free Press, 1994), 22.

90. Jaynes, *Branches Without Roots*, 99.

91. Harry Braverman, *Labor and Monopoly Capital: The Degradation of Work in the Twentieth Century* (New York: Monthly Review Press, 1974), 139.

92. Wayne Flynt, *Poor but Proud: Alabama's Poor Whites* (Tuscaloosa: University of Alabama Press, 1989), 161. Emphasis added.

93. E. P. Thompson, "Time, Work-Discipline, and Industrial Capitalism," *Past and Present* 38 (December 1967): 56–97.

94. Joseph L. White, *The Psychology of Blacks: An Afro-American Perspective* (Englewood Cliffs, N.J.: Prentice-Hall, 1984), 6.

95. James H. Cone, *For My People: Black Theology and the Black Church, Where Have We Been and Where Are We Going* (New York: Orbis, 1984), 187.

96. Karl Marx, *Capital*, Vol. 2 (Moscow: Progress Publishers, 1967), 174–76, 246.

97. Lefebvre, *Production*, 95.

98. Quoted in Rikard, "Experiment," 59.

99. Alfred F. Brainerd, "Colored Mining Labor," *Transactions of the American Institute of Mining Engineers* 14 (1885–1886): 80.

100. Flynt, *Poor but Proud*, 161.

101. Jaynes, *Branches Without Roots*, 97–98.

102. Carl V. Harris, "Reforms in Government Control of Negroes in Birmingham, Alabama, 1890–1920," *Journal of Southern History* 38, no. 4 (November 1972): 567–600.

103. Harris, *Political Power*, 198–202.

104. Harris, "Reforms."

105. Dan Thu Nguyen, "The Spatialization of Metric Time: The Conquest of Land and Labour in Europe and the United States," *Time and Society* 1 (1992): 29–50.

106. J. L. Hammond and Barbara Hammond, *The Town Labourer, 1760–1832* (London: Longmans, Green & Company, 1917), 18–19.

107. Quoted in Marjorie L. White, *The Birmingham District: An Industrial History and Guide* (Birmingham, Ala.: Birmingham Historical Society, 1981), 80.

108. *Manufacturers' Record* 14 (3 November 1888), 11.

109. K. Marx, *Grundrisse: Foundations of the Critique of Political Economy*, trans. Martin Nicolaus (New York: Vintage Books, 1973), 173.

110. Quoted in Thomas Wagstaff, "Call Your Old Master—'Master': Southern Political Leaders and Negro Labor During Presidential Reconstruction," *Labor History* 10, no. 3 (Summer 1969): 337.

111. Quoted in Wiener, *Social Origins*, 216.

112. Lewis, *Sloss Furnaces*, 14, 34.

113. Henry M. McKiven, Jr., *Iron and Steel: Class, Race, and Community in Birmingham, Alabama, 1875–1920* (Chapel Hill: University of North Carolina Press, 1995), 78.

114. William L. Warner, "Introduction," in *Deep South*, eds. Allison Davis, Burleigh Gardner, and Mary Gardner (Chicago: University of Chicago Press, 1941); John Dollard,

Caste and Class in a Southern Town (Garden City, N.Y.: Doubleday, 1957); see also Oliver C. Cox, *Caste, Class and Race: A Study in Social Dynamics* (New York: Monthly Review Press, 1970), 333, 336, for a critique of race caste. Cox attempted to show that race relations are "political-class" relations that developed from the need of the white exploiting class to control its labor supply. Castes constitute "a natural status system" and are more permanent than class. Black and white in the South constitute a status system that is "a temporary society intended to continue only so long as whites are able to maintain the barriers against their assimilation." (503)

115. Pierre L. van den Berghe, *Race and Racism* (New York: Wiley, 1967), 17–18.

116. Quoted in Ralph Fox, *Marx, Engels and Lenin on Ireland* (New York: International Publishers, 1940), 42.

117. Lewis, *Sloss Furnaces*, 31.

118. Carter A. Wilson, *Racism: From Slavery to Advanced Capitalism* (Thousand Oaks, Calif.: Sage Publications, 1996), 78–117.

10

Industrialization with Inexpensive Labor

There is nothing wanting here in Central Alabama, but capital and labor, and even our negro labor, from some cause, does better in the coal and iron business than in farming.

—John T. Milner, *Alabama*, 1876

Location played a role in Birmingham becoming the industrial city of the South, but access to an abundant supply of raw materials alone was not sufficient: an adequate amount of labor was required for the production process that gives those materials their value.

Gavin Wright noted that Alabama emerged with the South "in the 1870s as a low-wage region in a high-wage country."[1] Whereas the planter class had favored high-priced labor before the Civil War because it owned labor, planter-based industrialists favored an accessible, controlled, and inexpensive labor force. John Milner believed that free black workers "could do better in the coal and iron business than in farming" but only through the "superior vigor of Anglo-American people." He said black workers must have an "*overseer—a Southern man* who knows how to manage negroes."[2]

The early industrial phase of capitalist relations of production needed a large reserve labor army that was nearby, mobile, and replaceable. The black belt's large black labor pool allowed the Birmingham regime to increase easily the absolute size of its labor force when necessary; this ability in turn promoted the development of a large black industrial working class (Table 10.1). In 1870, a year before Birmingham was founded, Jefferson County listed no black nonagricultural workers. Elsewhere in the state, most black nonagricultural workers were in domestic and personal service, but they were increasingly employed in the extractive industries, especially before large-scale mechanization was introduced. Thus, in 1880, Jefferson County showed only fifty-six blacks employed as railroad hands but 306

Table 10.1   Distribution of the Black Population

Year	Birmingham			Jefferson County		
	Total	Black	% Black	Total	Black	% Black
1870	—	—	—	12,345	2,506	20.3
1880	3,086	—	—	23,272	5,053	21.7
1890	26,178	11,269	43.0	88,501	32,142	36.3
1900	38,145	16,565	43.4	140,420	56,917	40.5
1910	132,685	52,305	39.4	226,476	90,617	40.0
1920	178,806	70,230	39.3	310,054	130,291	42.0
1930	259,678	99,059	38.1	431,493	167,957	38.9
1940	267,583	108,914	40.7	459,930	179,150	39.0
1950	326,037	130,035	39.9	558,928	208,616	37.3
1960	340,887	135,113	39.6	634,864	219,542	34.6
1970	300,910	126,310	42.0	644,991	206,464	32.0
1980	284,413	158,200	55.6	671,324	223,716	33.3
1990	265,968	168,277	63.3	651,525	228,521	35.1

Source: U.S. Bureau of the Census, *U.S. Census of Population, 1870–1990* (Washington, D.C.: Government Printing Office).

mine workers; in the larger Birmingham district (a four-county area) 163 of the 389 miners were black. By 1890, 3,600 of the 8,000 miners in the state were black; and in 1900, 9,700 of 18,000 miners were black.[3] That year, one union local of the United Mine Workers of America (UMWA) located in the Birmingham industrial suburb of Pratt City had more than 1,500 black and white members.[4] (Nationwide, more than 20,000 members of the UMWA were black; they worked mainly in the bituminous coal fields of Alabama and West Virginia.)[5]

Access to a large pool of inexpensive, exploitable labor made it possible for Birmingham to develop an extensive regime of accumulation, which kept wages low and hours long. Karl Marx wrote,

> The one who came to the market as the owner of money leaves it striding forward as a capitalist; the one who came to the market as the owner of labor power, brings up the rear as a worker. One of them, self-important, self-satisfied, with a keen eye to business; the other, timid, reluctant, like a man who is bringing his own skin to market, and has nothing to expect but a tanning.[6]

The exploitation of labor defined class relations in a way that made clear who the winners would be. Robert Fogel and Stanley Engerman, authors of *Time on the Cross*, compared the material lot of slaves to that of free workers to support their claim that many studies on the treatment of slaves contained numerous exaggerations: "Slave agriculture was not inefficient compared with free agriculture."[7] But, as T. Thomas Fortune of the *New York Age*, the leading black editor of the 1890s, pointed out, to suggest any comparison with slave labor is to acknowledge the harshness of the free wage-labor system that gave birth to a social condition more "excruciating in its exactions, more irresponsible in its machinations than any other slavery."[8]

Machines allow a regime to reduce the number of workers and become more intensive (i.e., to produce more units of a commodity in a given time). According to Richard Peet, "Increasingly, a relative surplus population arises," producing "more-or-less a permanent underclass of unemployed and, therefore, poor people."[9] The value of labor becomes a smaller portion of the value of each commodity. Workers lose control over their labor and become alienated from the product of that labor. As improvements are made in the means of production, more of the working day is given to producing for the owners and less is dedicated to the value necessary for the workers' subsistence. This change increases constant capital compared with variable capital and lowers the workers' value in the eyes of capitalists.[10]

In 1901, according to the *Labor Advocate*, a weekly newspaper of the Birmingham Trades Council,

> As far as the employees are concerned, the term "labor saving machinery" is a misnomer. In not a single instance has its introduction resulted in shortening the hours of toil. The only result so far has been to throw many out of employment and to reduce the wages of those who were so fortunate as to get work. The advantage is altogether with owners of the machine, who have grown rich on the profits.[11]

For instance, it was reported that, by the turn of the century, machinery in the mills and factories of Great Britain equaled the labor power of 500 million wage earners. In Massachusetts, machines did the work of 50 million. For free wage earners, machines complicated the industrial problem.[12]

Mechanization, or investments in fixed capital, come to industries in different ways and at different times. With its abundant supply of cheap labor, the South lagged significantly behind the North in mechanization. In 1883, J. W. Sloss, president of the Sloss Company, estimated that each northern iron furnace could produce forty, fifty, or sixty tons per day, whereas a southern furnace produced only twenty or thirty tons.[13] In 1880, less than 5 percent of the Alabama labor force was engaged in manufacturing and mechanical pursuits, compared with more than 50 percent of the labor force in Rhode Island and Massachusetts (Table 10.2). Some historians have attributed this imbalance to natural factors, claiming, for example, that the new cotton-producing areas of the Southwest were able to use wage labor and labor-saving technology because of a more favorable climate and better soil. (Yet, according to Susan Mann, "The cotton-producing areas of the Southwest were able to utilize wage labor largely because of the introduction of labor saving technology," not climate.)[14] Others point to the South's abundant natural resources, which meant that there was less need for machine labor for extraction.[15] Also, the South's two major crops, cotton and tobacco, are naturally fragile, which made it difficult to mechanize the harvest, and both have a lengthy production time, which is associated with less intensive capitalist development.

The primary obstacle to mechanization in the South was more social than technical or natural. Lack of capital combined with a cultural ethos that demanded control of labor at almost the level known under slavery led planter-based regimes of the black belt and Birmingham to build on the exploitation of

Table 10.2   Percentage of Total Gainfully Employed in All Occupations Engaged in Manufacturing and Mechanical Pursuits, 1880 and 1900

	1880		1900	
	Total	%	Total	%
Northeast				
Rhode Island	116,979	56.5	191,923	52.7
Massachusetts	720,774	51.4	1,208,407	46.9
Connecticut	241,333	48.1	385,610	45.8
New Hampshire	142,468	40.7	178,719	42.5
New Jersey	396,879	40.4	757,759	40.4
Pennsylvania	1,456,067	36.3	2,448,589	40.1
Maine	231,993	31.3	276,777	31.8
Ohio	994,475	24.4	1,545,952	30.0
Vermont	118,584	22.1	134,933	26.8
New York	1,884,645	33.4	2,996,474	34.5
Delaware	54,580	25.9	72,996	31.1
South				
Alabama	492,790	4.6	763,188	10.3
Arkansas	260,692	4.3	485,795	7.3
Florida	91,536	9.2	201,570	16.0
Georgia	597,862	6.0	864,471	9.9
Kentucky	519,854	11.8	752,531	14.2
Louisiana	363,228	8.4	536,093	10.1
Mississippi	415,506	3.2	645,123	4.8
North Carolina	480,187	7.1	716,742	12.7
South Carolina	392,102	5.0	570,995	10.3
Tennessee	447,970	8.1	727,587	11.1
Texas	522,133	5.8	1,033,033	7.8
Virginia	494,240	12.8	662,415	16.6
West Virginia	176,199	14.9	325,663	20.8

Source: U.S. Bureau of the Census, *Population of the United States at the Tenth Census, 1880,* Vol. 1, Table 29, pp. 712–13; U.S. Bureau of the Census, *Abstract of the Twelfth Census of the United States, 1900,* Table 64, p. 85.

inexpensive black labor. Southern regimes generally sought out and maintained more labor-intensive industries than the North; Birmingham wanted economic results without investing in machinery and methods characteristic of a more intensive regime of accumulation.[16]

Heywood Fleisig has shown that technology suitable for southern agriculture was available and could have been profitably employed as early as the late 1800s. For instance, there were at least 242 cotton harvesters patented in the nineteenth century, including one that incorporated the basic principle of the modern cotton picker. The gasoline tractor was available in the 1890s and went into mass production in 1903, but it was not introduced in the South on a large scale until

World War II. In 1920, northern states had six times as many tractors per acre of cropland as the Deep South. Until the 1930s, only about 1 percent of all plows were drawn by tractors in the South.[17]

Similarly, coal mining was much less mechanized in Alabama than in other major coal-producing states. In 1902, machines mined only 2.9 percent of the coal produced in the state, compared with 51.4 percent for Ohio and 35.6 percent for Pennsylvania (Table 10.3). The only states with a smaller proportion of their coal mined by machines were minor producers. Some attributed this lack of mechanization to little competition: Alabama mines did not at first compete in the market of the U.S. manufacturing belt, but the mines were captive to the state's iron and utility companies, which reduced the pressure to mechanize. (Also, Birmingham's foundries and rolling mills made products from cast and wrought iron, so they did not produce at levels compatible with a high degree of mechanization.)[18] As late as the 1920s and 1930s, the optimum production level of a foundry iron furnace in the Birmingham district was only 425 to 475 tons per day compared with almost twice that amount for a northern furnace.[19]

Jack Bergstresser argues that the characteristics of the region's raw materials, not lack of markets or technological inferiority, restricted production of iron and coal. The nature of the coal seams encountered meant that many of the Sloss mines were small drift mines averaging less than 100,000 tons per year. The quality of the coal did not allow economies of scale that could support a high level of mechanization, a fact that dictated a slower and less mechanized path of technological evolution than seen in Pittsburgh.[20]

Birmingham's industrialists were forced to invest heavily in technology to remove impurities in Red Mountain ore and Warrior coal. Still, despite complications, southern iron and coal industries remained more labor intensive than those in the North into the 1930s. Practically all coal was loosened and loaded by hand; such labor accounted for more than 50 percent of mining employment in Alabama until the 1920s. According to Robert Louis Cvornyek, coal miners "combined a considerable degree of physical strength, manual dexterity and technical knowledge."[21] TCI did not undergo a major modernization until it was absorbed by U.S. Steel in 1907. (George Gordon Crawford, then president of TCI, had been

Table 10.3   **Percent Machine Mined Coal for Five Major Producers, 1898–1902**

State	Year				
	1898	**1899**	**1900**	**1901**	**1902**
Alabama	4.56	3.43	4.41	3.71	2.90
Illinois	18.36	24.90	19.73	21.12	21.59
Ohio	35.76	41.35	46.53	47.26	51.42
Pennsylvania	25.34	29.67	33.65	35.95	35.57
West Virginia	7.93	9.27	15.09	20.01	23.35

Source: U.S. Department of the Interior, United States Geological Survey, *Mineral Resources of the United States, 1902* (Washington, D.C.: Government Printing Office, 1904), 327.

reared on a Georgia plantation but was a major promoter of scientific development in both industry and agriculture.) Birmingham's other major company, Sloss-Sheffield, continued to rely on convict labor and the exploitation of cheap black labor until the 1920s.[22]

Bergstresser wrote that Birmingham's lack of mechanization suggested not backward labor-intensive practices but "a rational technological path" that "harmonized well with the smaller scale of mining operations dictated by the Birmingham District's difficult geological conditions." He also noted that this path harmonized well with "*an abundant supply of cheap labor, and a cultural ethos conducive to labor intensity.*"[23] In other words, the Birmingham regime considered an abundant supply of cheap and exploitable labor the key to economic growth and, with such labor available, felt less pressure to mechanize than its northern counterparts. As W. David Lewis notes, Birmingham industrialists used "selective mechanization":

> Using labor-intensive methods would help compensate for one of the South's greatest problems, a scarcity of capital. Levels of mechanization that were already becoming common in the North could be avoided by adopting new and advanced equipment only selectively, as required for operations that could not be performed in traditional ways.[24]

Mechanization may increase production—but it would also increase the demand for skilled labor and the costs of reproducing that labor. The planter-based regime preferred a labor force it could control. When Edward Uehling, a northern-born engineer for Sloss Furnace, devised a mechanical pig-casting method, the company did not adopt it. Adopting such a device, Lewis wrote, would have been

> antithetical to the entire economic and social milieu within which southern blast furnace practice existed. As had been true from the inception of ironmaking in the Birmingham District, the strategy governing production there was predicated upon taking advantage of low-cost black labor, close proximity to all the raw materials required for smelting, and short interior supply lines to compete with firms outside the region. This strategy compensated for one of the basic problems facing southern industrialists: their lack of the large amounts of investment capital that would have been needed for the degree of mechanization that northern iron and steel producers had been implementing since the 1870s.[25]

Isolation of the southern labor market also meant isolation of the capital market, which reinforced the regime's extensive nature. Southern representatives in Washington, D.C., would not push for federal projects, fearing they would lead to a more intensive regime of accumulation.[26] With few native technicians and no inflow of skilled labor, southern industry could not consider extensive mechanization as an alternative to labor-intensive technologies that used inexpensive raw materials.[27] In 1900, Andrew Carnegie, who earlier had declared the South "Pennsylvania's most formidable industrial enemy," taunted Birmingham: "You have all the elements but you cannot make steel."[28] From 1879 to 1919—when the North developed highly mechanized industries and increased demand for manufactured products brought an agro-industrial production complex to the Midwest[29]—Birmingham continued to produce far less than it could have under an intensive regime of accumulation.[30]

Lower wages did, however, allow southern mine operators to sell their coal for less than the northern operators did, which gave the South a competitive advantage. Selective mechanization and vertical integration also enabled the Birmingham district to produce foundry pig iron cheaply enough to sell it profitably.[31] The combination of low wages and market expansion produced a high rate of surplus value. In 1880, the manufacturing rate for Jefferson County was almost three times that for the United States as a whole, and for the iron industry the rate was over five times as high (Table 10.4). Less than two decades after slavery, Alabama ranked fifteenth in production.[32]

Capitalists can increase surplus value by prolonging the working day and increasing the pace and intensity of work. From its beginnings until the early 1900s, the coal industry standard was a ten-hour work day and a six-day week. Low wages, however, reduced effective demand in the region and contributed to the South's low consumption norm, which slowed development of an intensive regime of accumulation.

Table 10.4   Percent Rate of Surplus Value

Year	United States Manufacturing	Steel	Birmingham Area Manufacturing		Steel
1880	108	90	308		488
1890	125	71	315		(122)
1900	136	133	145		(285)
1910	138	112	123		(89)
1920	126	109	89		(83)
1930	163	137	193		NA
1940	169	101	219		(219)
1947	146	94	158		111
1954	162	135	182		153
1958	185	148	160		182
1963	209	157	256		290
1967	222	168	189	(111)	160
1972	235	152	166	(107)	111
1977	272	167	165	(126)	179
1982	302	130	235	(134)	137

Source: Data used in calculating rates of surplus from the U.S. Census of Manufacturing from 1880 to 1982.
Note: Value in parentheses pertains just to the production of iron and steel within the incorporated city of Birmingham.

THE POLITICAL ECONOMY OF CONVICT LABOR

During the early phase of development, convicts and the contract system supplied inexpensive labor in the Birmingham district. The convict-lease system was rooted in the slaveholders' world, and—as in that world—race was a central theme. It became a main pillar of white supremacy and a distinguishing feature of the South's regime of accumulation. According to James Cobb, "Instead of shouldering the burden of a growing prison population in a time of budgetary retrenchment they [local officials] simply took advantage of the cheap-labor orientation of New South Industry."[33] Convicts helped develop the mineral district and worked on the rail lines connecting Birmingham to outside markets. Birmingham industrialists did not entice black labor off tenant farms with promises of higher wages, according to Cvornyek, but tapped into a ready surplus of black prison labor. Convict labor was to Birmingham industrialists what the crop liens, anti-enticement laws, and vagrancy statutes were to the postbellum planters.[34]

Although the surplus value rate of convict labor was relatively high, the convicts' absolute production per capita was between two-thirds and three-fourths that of free labor. Employers were willing to pay for lower productivity; TCI President George Crawford explained, "The chief inducement for the hiring of convicts was the certainty of a supply of coal for our manufacturing operations in the contingency of labor troubles."[35] Controlled labor insured steady, predictable coal reserves and, therefore, helped undergird the early phase of southern capitalism. Employers leasing or contracting the labor of convicts noted its "regularity":

> Three hundred men, for instance, go to bed at night and three hundred men go to work in the morning, for 310 days in the year. There are no picnics, no general laying off to attend funerals of fellow workers, no excurisons. Practically a constant number of men are certain to be on duty every day.... Convict laborers cannot strike.[36]

Birmingham's industrialists supported anti-vagrancy ordinances as a means of labor control but also because they increased the ranks of convict labor.

Convict labor was also a prime means of transforming the essentially agrarian work force into an industrial one. It was often the unfortunate situation of many former black tenant farmers who became skilled coal miners. On release from prison, many convicts gravitated to or remained in the Birmingham area, adding to the "industrial reserve army" of free wage earners. In the early 1900s, approximately 50 percent of the area's black coal miners were ex-convicts.[37] (Another estimate was only 15 to 20 percent of the miners; in either case, the percentage was significant.)[38] In 1910, the U.S. Immigration Commission noted,

> After the convict has worked in the coal mines for several years he has learned a trade thoroughly. Not only does he become a trained miner, but owing to the system of rigid discipline and enforced regularity of work, he becomes through habit a steady workman, accustomed to regular hours. When his

term [in prison] ends he almost invariably . . . continues to be a coal miner for the reason that he does not know how to do anything else, and because he has been taught to do one thing well and to earn a good wage.[39]

Through the convict labor system, black workers were proletarianized. Stanley Greenberg noted that proponents of this system believed the cruel treatment and high death rates associated with working convicts in the mines left a "healthy impression on the minds of rural black laborers."[40] In terms of the difference between the value of the labor's marginal product and capitalists' cost for acquisition, subsistence, and reproduction of labor, convict leases may have been more exploitative than slavery had been. Slave owners were "labor lords," and each slave represented a certain capital outlay; but the slave owner had to provide for "the subsistence and reproduction of the *entire* slave community, including the aged, the infirm, and children," which costs more than simply maintaining just individual slaves who worked.[41] In contrast, employers who leased convicts were concerned only with individuals and actually paid less than what their workers needed to survive, and they could refuse to use any convict who did not produce enough. Therefore, although convict productivity was only about two-thirds that of wage labor, the low subsistence level often more than made up for the shortfall.[42]

The lease system of working convicts outside government restraint began in Alabama in 1866, when the penal code allowed county courts to hire "out such as are vagrants to work in chain-gangs or otherwise, for the length of time for which they are sentenced."[43] According to state prison reports, the number of convicts available for work outside of the prison walls increased significantly from 1871 to 1906; the convicts were overwhelmingly black (Table 10.5).

In some ways, convict leasing had noncapitalist elements. In Europe, the rise of capitalism generated a demand to centralize political authority in the state, but states using the convict-lease system yielded a great deal of legal authority to planters. Such an abdication of state authority amounted to a form of feudalism. According to Robert Cvornyek, lessors of convicts "cloaked with the authority of the state and armed with the instruments of violence and intimidation, behaved in many of the same reckless ways as slaveholders . . . [as convicts] perform dangerous and exhausting work under primitive conditions in undercapitalized mines."[44]

John T. Milner was one of the first in Alabama to employ prisoners in coal mining. In 1874, he contracted with the state for thirty convicts to work the New Castle Coal Company's farm and coal mine in exchange for a fixed sum. In 1879, the governor instructed those who wished to lease convict labor to bid on a per-capita rather than a fixed-sum basis. This system allowed the state to exact higher fees for convicts who were physically able to perform additional work.[45] In 1882, Alabama's legislature passed a law requiring sealed bids for the leasing of convicts, holding leaseholders responsible for providing housing and food, and mandating that convicts work under the direction of an officer paid by the state.[46] The effect was that convicted criminals not only served a term for the crime committed but also had to work for an additional time to pay for the cost of prosecution.[47] Contractors could not lease fewer than twenty state convicts, and the minimum had increased to fifty by 1896.[48]

Table 10.5   Average Number of Convicts on Hand in Alabama, October 1871 to August 1918

| | Average Number of Convicts on Hand | | | |
	State Convicts	% Black	County Convicts	% Black
Two-Year Period Ending October				
1871	271	77.8	—	—
1876	688	91.6	—	—
1878	873	88.3	—	—
1880	603	88.2	—	—
1886	559	85.1	—	—
1888	740	88.4	853	—
1892	1,185	85.6	915	—
1894	1,577	88.9	899	92.4
1896	1,710	87.5	745	93.4
1898	1,763	88.5	786	95.0
1900	1,744	90.4	622	92.9
1902	1,809	87.8	870	93.7
1904	1,874	87.8	800	94.0
1906	2,059	86.2	714	95.2
Four-Year Period Ending August				
1910	2,392	82.6	724	87.8
1914	2,609	86.3	612	86.8
1918	2,465	82.3	226	85.4

Source: Reports of the Inspectors of Convicts, October 1871 to August 1918.

The state "graded" convicts according to their physical ability. An 1879 law, using terminology from slavery times, classified convicts as "full," "half," or "dead" hands with different rates for each. In 1883, the state authorized the Board of Inspectors to grade convicts into four classes: a first-class convict would produce five tons of coal in a ten-hour work day; second-class, four tons; third-class, three tons; and a fourth-class, or dead hand, one ton. In 1889, the board tried adding an even lower, fifth classification to include convicts physically unable to dig coal but who could perform other tasks; eventually this classification was abandoned as mine operators could force "fifth-class" convicts to work the mines anytime.[49] Convicts were required to produce twice as much if they cut the coal with a mechanical device instead of a pick and shovel.[50]

In 1883, the Pratt mines operators paid the state $19 per month for a first-class worker, $18 for second-class, and $9 for third. For the fourth-class, or "dead" hand, the contractor paid only for maintaining a necessary subsistence level.[51] A first-class convict produced as much as a free miner whose wage was $45 to $50 per month, giving the firm that leased a first-class convict a competitive advantage of $26 to $31.[52] TCI may have earned a profit of almost $10 per work day from a first-class convict miner. One estimate placed average daily cost of food, shelter, clothing, and leasing fees at only 39 cents per convict, compared with an average daily wage of $1.75 for free-wage earners in the Birmingham district.[53] A first-class convict mining coal for TCI would produce a surplus rate of almost 900 percent. In one bid for convicts, the contractor specified,

> The amount we offer per month is the amount to be paid for full day work. . . . They [convicts] shall eat breakfast before leaving the prisons and shall begin work as early as they can see how to do the work or as it is safe to take them out, and shall be allowed one hour in which to get dinner, and shall work as late in the evening as it is safe to keep them out, and they can see how to do the work. . . .[54]

Nationwide, male convicts in the United States averaged nine hours per working day; females, 8.7 hours. In 1885, convicts produced goods with a market value of $28,753,999; only $1,672,515 of this value was derived from coal production. Goods produced under the lease system were valued at $4,101,935, or 14.6 percent of all goods produced by convicts. In Alabama, convicts working ten hours per day produced goods with a market value of $1,636,240, most of it from coal: convicts produced 18 percent of the state's coal and nearly all of the coal produced by convicts in the United States.[55]

Some firms were particularly heavy users of convict labor. Thus, in 1892, TCI worked 1,000 convicts at its Pratt mines to produce 493,055 tons of coal, 38 percent of all the coal produced at those mines. In 1894, the company leased 62 percent of the convicts leased by the state.[56] During the 1910–1914 period, state convicts produced more than four million tons of coal in the Birmingham district, of which 8.7 percent was produced just by convicts at TCI's Pratt mines (Table 10.6).

The leased convict-labor system bypassed many problems associated with free labor: there were no demands for higher wages or threats of strikes. Convict labor was also more mobile than free labor: mine operators could move workers around like other factors of production when circumstances demanded. The reliable la-

Table 10.6   Tonnage of Coal Produced by State Convicts Leased to Mining Companies in the Birmingham District, September 1, 1910, to August 31, 1914

Company	Tonnage	% of Convict-Mined Coal
TCI Pratt Mines	386,027	8.7
Sloss-Sheffield	1,386,562	31.2
Bessemer Coal, Iron	581,769	13.1
Red Feather Coal	548,858	12.4
Pratt Consolidated Mines	1,488,562	33.5
Montevallo Mining Co.	47,165	1.1
Total	4,438,943	100.0

Source: Quadrennial Report of the Inspectors of Convicts, September 1, 1910, to August 31, 1914 (Montgomery: Brown, 1914).

bor force allowed leading corporations in the South's coal and iron industry to consolidate their control and operations on a massive scale.[57]

Without wage incentives and no threat of dismissal, however, convicts had no reason to work at all. For this reason, leaseholders began the "task system."[58] An 1883 Alabama law established the notion of work "tasks" in the mines. Thus, in TCI's coal mines, the average task was three to four tons per convict per day. The punishment for not completing one's task was a "whipping." According to a former guard, "The warden and the deputy warden would do the whippin'. . . . The whipping was done with a two-ply strap as wide as your fingers, tied to a staff. The convicts were face down with their pants off. They were whipped on the hips and legs five to twelve lashes."[59] As it had for the slave owner, whipping reinforced control and asserted dominance.

After meeting the day's task, convicts could continue to produce coal and earn approximately 30 cents per ton.[60] In 1885, a convict testified before the U.S. Senate Committee on the Relations Between Labor and Capital that he could complete his five-ton task by "9 or 10 o'clock. . . . [then] Sometimes I cut five or six tons for myself at 40 cents a ton."[61] Even at 40 cents a ton, the surplus rate was more than 250 percent. In 1886, the lease system of working convicts in the United States produced a surplus equal to 272 percent of total expenses. The average market value of goods produced per convict in coal mining was higher than for any other industry using the lease system.[62] By 1893, TCI was paying its convicts 8 cents per carload of coal for every car over their task.[63]

Alabama consistently ranked first among the states in revenue from convict labor. By 1883, at least 10 percent of the state's revenue was derived from this source. Between 1890 and 1900, Alabama coal operators paid on average more than $100,000 per year to the state treasury (Table 10.7). In 1890, 4 percent of the state's revenue came from convict leases held primarily in Birmingham's mining district, and in 1898 the state obtained 6 percent of its total revenue from the hire of its convicts.[64] An average of $7 to $14 was earned per month per convict.[65] The U.S. Bureau of Labor reported that between 1903 and 1904 the state of Alabama earned a net profit of $144.54 per convict.[66] In 1916, the contracting of convict labor generated over $1.5 million for the state, almost 22 percent of its revenue; and, in 1920, it generated almost $2.5 million, 21 percent of all revenue.[67]

In Birmingham's extractive industries, expenditures for raw materials formed almost no part of the capital outlay, and mechanization was almost nonexistent. Upkeep of convicts was exceptionally low. According to Alex Lichtenstein, they were like "machines for whose rental a certain price is paid." The Birmingham regime was unwilling to replace them with mechanical devices—what Marx termed "dead labor."[68] All mining by convicts was manual. In 1880, sixty out of the 540 (11 percent) convicts leased by the state died, compared with 1.5 percent of convicts in nonleasing states. Death and disease rates were lower among the female prisoners, who lived under much the same conditions as the males but mainly performed outdoor tasks and could receive sufficient sunlight.[69]

The Sloss Company operated its own prison at Coalburg, northwest of Birmingham. Sloss acquired the property (originally owned by Milner) from Edward

Table 10.7   Annualized Gross Earnings to the
State of Alabama for the Hire of Convicts

Reporting Period	Annualized Gross Earnings
Mar. 1873 – Sept. 1873	9,150.64
Oct. 1873 – Sept. 1874	9,148.93
Oct. 1875 – Sept. 1876	9,875.00
Oct. 1876 – Sept. 1877	35,272.18
Oct. 1877 – Sept. 1878	43,892.30
Oct. 1878 – Sept. 1880	31,851.62
Oct. 1886 – Sept. 1888	51,666.48
Oct. 1890 – Sept. 1892	112,824.42
Oct. 1892 – Sept. 1894	120,368.39
Oct. 1894 – Sept. 1896	130,459.57
Oct. 1896 – Sept. 1898	138,540.62
Oct. 1898 – Sept. 1900	115,462.19
Oct. 1900 – Sept. 1902	162,626.71
Oct. 1902 – Sept. 1904	383,690.52
Oct. 1904 – Sept. 1906	294,637.54
Oct. 1906 – Sept. 1910	860,697.91
Oct. 1910 – Sept. 1914	687,445.93
Oct. 1914 – Sept. 1918	944,419.17

Source: Reports of the Inspectors of Convicts, March 1873 to
September 1918.

Tutwiler in 1887. Between 1893 and 1895, the company leased 1,926 convicts from the state. Female inmates worked the prison farm and did the washing and sewing for the male convicts, thereby lowering the cost of basic subsistence to the firm. Housing and sanitation were minimal. Convicts resided in rectangular log buildings with hinged boards that opened and shut to regulate ventilation through the spaces between the logs. Between 1893 and 1895, the annual death rate at the camp was ninety per 1,000 compared with a rate of thirteen per 1,000 for the general population of Birmingham. The company attributed this high mortality rate to the racial composition of the prison population, not to conditions at the camp; in other words, the explanation lay not in the realm of production but, in the words of Thomas Seddon, Sloss Company president, "a natural 'inherent' difference, absolute and uncontrollable by human agency."[70] These were the same natural conditions that supposedly caused the inferiority of blacks. Milner argued that blacks were prone to sickness and died "everywhere and under all circumstances" at rates two to five times higher than whites. Conditions were so horrendous at the Newcastle Coal Company operated by Milner that it was known as "the second black hole of Calcutta."[71]

However, Thomas Parkes, a physician concerned about the health condition of the convicts, found many conditions at the Sloss camp to be socially produced and controllable. He noted that the convicts showed signs of mental depression, which he associated with a lack of exposure to sunlight and poor diet. These factors also contributed to the spread of tuberculosis and high death rates. On Sundays and holidays, convicts remained inside and were allowed no contact outside of the prison enclosure. In the mines, breathing space did not exceed 500 cubic feet for each prisoner. Parkes found that convicts who worked in the larger mines had to walk three-quarters of a mile in a bent position through a low-ceiling tunnel before reaching their work area. These conditions he attributed to inflammation found throughout the prison population that produced high fever, which, when untreated, provided a breeding ground for tuberculosis.[72]

Before 1883, there had been no state requirement to inspect county convicts and, according to the president of the State Board of Convicts, they

> were abandoned to their fate with no law but [their] will. They were slaves
> without the restraints that thrown around the slave-owner by association, by
> society and by interest, and the celebrated horrors of the Middle Passage are
> rivalled by the stories of the former treatment of county convicts. Few knew,
> and fewer cared, what became of them. They were kept as long and dis-
> charged when the contractor pleased.[73]

In 1883, the governor ordered state inspection every three months, and the General Assembly enacted a law requiring the same of county convicts. There was, however, no provision for enforcement, so contractors' practices continued unchanged.

In 1901, the State Department of Convicts eliminated the leasing program and became directly involved in supplying labor for coal mining i.e., contracting of convict labor. Organized labor was in a weakened position at the time, so the state was able to appropriate convict labor at the same rate as free labor. Under this new arrangement, the state contracted with companies for coal mining at a per-ton rate. Until leasing, the state controlled the quantity of work performed and provided everything necessary for the convicts' basic subsistence. The *Fifth Biennial Report of Convicts* noted that the state contracted with TCI for 412 convicts to work the Pratt mines at 73 cents per ton and with the Sloss Company for 187 convicts to mine coal at 43 cents per ton—the same rates as free labor at these mines. State-leased convicts mined on the average 1,500 to 1,700 tons of coal per day, bringing to the state net revenue per man per month of $31.27 in the Birmingham mining district and $27.50 elsewhere between 1910 and 1914.[74] Although the president of the State Board of Convicts expressed reservations about convicts working in the mines, he admitted, "These contracts have been quite remunerative to the state."[75] Indeed they had: gross returns to the state more than doubled from $162,626 for the two-year period ending September 1902 to $383,690 for the two-year period ending September 1904 (see Table 10.7).

The state constantly sought to reduce costs. Average expenditures per man per month for convicts at a TCI mine declined from $11.50 in 1910 to $10 in 1911. In the same period at a Sloss mine, average cost decreased only a few cents, from $11.35 to $11.31.[76]

Convict labor, whether leased or on state contracts, deprived free wage earners the benefit of their labor. During a period of intense labor struggles, from 1905 to 1908, TCI paid double the normal rate for convict leases and hired almost 2,000 convicts from Jefferson County alone.[77] Convict labor also lowered the cost of work done in the mines by free labor, which contributed to many of Birmingham's social and economic problems. In 1889, a state legislative investigating committee computed that TCI—the state's largest mining company and largest lessee of convicts—had saved $200,000 in wages since 1886 by using convicts.[78] The depressing effect on wages is shown by a U.S. Industrial Commission report on workers in Chicago's cooperage shops, where use of convict labor had led to a 30 percent decline in wages for free workers between 1875 and 1885.[79] A 1905 U.S. Bureau of Labor survey of 296 penal institutions showed that companies operating under contract and piece-price systems paid $3,077,012 for labor that would have cost $5,393,853 under the free labor system. Leased convicts cost only $404,188, but the total value of this labor at free labor prices would have been $1,355,796.[80]

Of the total value of goods produced in Alabama with convict labor, 81.8 percent was sold outside of the state, compared with an average of 65.3 percent per state nationally. The figure for coal was even higher: Alabama contractors and lessees of convict labor sold 92.4 percent of the coal they produced outside of the state.[81]

To defend their own producers, many states required those who sold convict-made products at retail to purchase an expensive license. In the 1890s, Canada barred the importation of pig iron from twenty-three furnaces in Alabama and Tennessee because they relied on coal and coke produced with convict labor.[82] In 1900, the U.S. Industrial Commission recommended legislation to prevent interstate traffic in prison-made goods to protect free labor.[83]

According to Richard Peet, wages paid to free labor covered "some socially defined wants to keep the workers relatively content and to fuel economic growth."[84] By keeping this money out of circulation, the convict system deprived both the marketplace and the wage earner. The editor of the *Labor Advocate* noted,

> Had this amount of money been paid out to free men of the State, her toiling masses would not have been forced to go to soup houses for nourishment, and for the necessaries of life, neither would the various enterprises have had to make assignments [legal transfer of properties to creditors], neither would there have been such a depression of times in Alabama as there has been . . . to the farmers of Jefferson County . . . it deprives you of a market to sell your products . . . [if convicts were wage earners and free] it would give you quite a market for your vegetables.[85]

County Fee System

Closely related to the convict-labor system was the county fee system, which granted county sheriffs a fixed amount from the state to feed each prisoner. In Alabama near the turn of the century, approximately thirty cents per inmate per day was considered more than enough to provide for a healthy diet, and that amount was paid to sheriffs, who spent on average less than nine cents per day per prisoner and pocketed the remainder. The system encouraged sheriffs to keep their jails full and ensured mining companies of a steady pool of workers, often shackled and chained (Figure 10.1).

The county fee system, like the convict-labor system and crop liens, became a means of labor control. In 1904, the president of the State Board of Convict Inspectors reported to the governor that the system

> is a continual grief to every humane man having knowledge of the evils attending it. I am informed that it is not known in but few States, Alabama among

Figure 10.1   Convict laborers.

them, and I am of opinion that it should not be known anywhere. Everything pertaining to it, ought, in my opinion, be wiped out of existence by an act of the Legislature. . . . That this system is largely kept up by a desire for fees is to my mind too patent to admit of discussion. Hundreds and hundreds of persons are taken before the inferior courts of the country, tried and sentenced to hard labor for the county, who would never be arrested but for the matter of fees involved. . . . Large numbers of these people are arrested and carried before the courts and convicted and sent to the coal mines and lumber camps who are unable to do, successfully, any kind of work. They there drag out a miserable existence and die. Someone is responsible for their death.[86]

The state auditor's report for 1915 shows that the Jefferson County Sheriff's Department received $56,601 for feeding county convicts in that year.[87] Death rates among convicts leased from the county were higher than among those contracted from the state. For example, during the two-year period ending August 31, 1896, the death rate for state convicts was 13.6 percent compared with 24.3 percent for county convicts.[88] Also, the Sloss Company's Coalburg facility used mainly county convicts and had a higher death rate than TCI's Pratt mines that worked mainly state convicts (Table 10.8). Despite the criticism, county governments continued to use the fee system to provide convict labor under contract and lease arrangements. Sloss continued to use county convicts at Coalburg until the mines were depleted and then moved convicts west to a new mine on Flat Top Mountain. Shipments of coal from Flat Top began in September 1902, and the last remaining convicts from Coalburg were transferred by the end of October. State officials negotiated a new three-year contract with the company for convicts. With 425 convicts, the Flat Top mine produced 434,750 tons of coal by 1909.[89]

While Sloss clung to accustomed ways, TCI began to adopt policies "rooted in hard-headed business considerations . . . congruent with a wave of reformism that was sweeping the country at the time."[90] TCI's purchase by U.S. Steel (USS)

Table 10.8 Deaths at the Pratt and Coalburg Mines

	1893	1894
TCI Pratt Mines		
Total Prison Pop.	1,031	1,138
No. of Deaths	86	58
Rate per 1,000	83.40	50.96
Sloss Coalburg Mines		
Total Prison Pop.	562	589
No. of Deaths	56	49
Rate per 1,000	99.64	83.19

Source: "Report of State Health Officer to the Governor on Coalburg," in *First Biennial Report of the Inspector of Convicts,* September 1, 1894, to August 31, 1896 (Montgomery, Ala.: State Printers, 1896).

in 1907 and the appointment of George Crawford, a strong proponent of new labor-saving technology, as president, signaled a shift to a more intensive regime of
accumulation. Convict labor had no future in such a regime. TCI would later rely
on a program of welfare capitalism to ensure the stability of its free labor force.[91]

The maturing of industrial capitalism in the South produced rural dislocation,
urbanization, and economic depression—all of which swelled the available free-
labor pool, which was desirable within the context of the capitalist and racial order. Eventually, many of Birmingham's industrialists decided the fee system was
corrupt and, therefore, potentially threatening to a steady and reliable labor pool.
In 1910, the Birmingham Chamber of Commerce charged that the acute scarcity
of labor in the Birmingham district was due to petty persecution by deputy sheriffs eager to fill their jails. Although blacks were only 40 percent of the city's population, they accounted for 60 percent of arrests. In one month, there were 1,500
arrests from which many were convicted and became convict laborers. According
to Cvornyek, between 15 and 20 percent of coal miners in the Birmingham district started as convicts.[92] Owners of industries increasingly came to believe that
the extra labor gained from the fee system often did not compensate for the ha-
rassment of free black workers by local law enforcement officers. Blacks would
think twice about moving into the district, and those already in the area would be
reluctant to stay, creating a potential labor shortage for industrialists.

Thus, TCI moved to oppose the use of convict leasing and contracting to avoid
a threat to the development of a reliable labor pool.[93] The same factors that had
made convict labor expedient carried serious limitations as southern capitalism
matured. For example, the state obligated firms that leased convicts to maintain
them even during times when they had no use for their labor; this fixed cost made
firms vulnerable to economic swings.[94] This vulnerability may account for the
21.5 percent decline in the total value of work done and goods produced by convict labor in the United States between 1885 and 1895, a time when the number of
convicts increased 30 percent, from 41,877 to 54,244.[95] Alabama's overall earnings
from the hire of convicts still increased during this period (see Table 10.7).

End of the Convict Labor System

The shift in convict labor was not due to just economic factors. In 1911, an explo-
sion killed 128 convicts at the Pratt Consolidated mines, and political pressure to
end the system of working convicts outside of the prison increased.[96] Jefferson
County terminated the convict-lease system in 1913, and the number of black
convicts leased by counties in the state decreased 16.5 percent, from 636 in 1910
to 531 in 1914 (see Table 10.5).

Nevertheless, other counties continued to send prisoners to the Birmingham
area, and the state's contracts remained in force despite several attempts to pass
legislation abolishing the leasing and contracting of convicts. One obstacle was
the fact that the convict labor system was financially rewarding: in reporting a
state budget deficit of nearly a quarter of a million dollars in 1895, Governor
William Oates made clear that he could not dispense with the TCI lease without
losing a major source of revenue for the state.[97] The state also saw convict labor as
a way to ease the shortage of labor during the war years, between 1916 and 1919.[98]

In the 1914–1918 period, the state earned more than 3.5 million dollars from the hire of convicts, the largest amount ever earned (see Table 10.7).

Increasing national and local criticism eventually led the governor to end the convict-labor system. Convict labor was increasingly used directly for the "public account" (i.e., for the benefit of the state or its institutions). Between 1885 and 1895, the number of states using this system increased from fifteen to twenty-five, and the value of goods produced more than doubled; the number of states using leased or contracted convicts dropped from twelve to seven, and the value of goods produced by leased convicts declined 41 percent, and 50 percent for contracted convicts.[99] Alabama, one of the seven, did not eliminate the contracting of convicts until 30 June 1928, when it became unlawful to work state or county convicts in any coal mine in the state. In the fiscal year ending 30 September 1928, the state convict department reported a deficit for the first time.[100] Between 1885 and 1903–1904, the U.S. Bureau of Labor estimated that the number of convicts laboring under the public-account system increased 80.2 percent, whereas the number under the lease system decreased 60 percent.[101]

Convict labor did not have a significant impact on the economy of the nation as a whole. In 1886, for example, convicts produced less than 1 percent of the country's total mechanical products; in 1890, the total value of convict labor was only about $2.5 million, a little more than one-tenth of a percent of the total wages paid in the manufacturing industries in 1890. However, as the U.S. Industrial Commission reported, "These facts, however, do not invalidate the claim that locally and in certain industries the competition may be serious and of such proportions as to claim the most earnest attention."[102] Alabama had more convict contractors and lessees than any other state except Texas. In 1894, convicts represented 15 percent of all miners statewide, and 38 percent of miners were employed by TCI.[103] In 1902, Alabama produced only 4.3 percent of the market value of bituminous coal in the United States, but the state's convicts produced almost 38 percent of the value of all coal produced with convict labor in the United States between 1903 and 1904. In 1905, the U.S. Bureau of Labor found that convicts in penal institutions were a source of profit in Alabama, Florida, Mississippi, and Virginia.

The convict-labor system alone did not encompass a specific mode of production; it was one of several labor forms that supported an extensive regime of accumulation. Robert David Ward and William Warren Rogers stated, "Convict leasing was the Black Code of the New South. . . . It served government and industry to the great reward of both."[104] In 1928, the year Alabama ended the leasing and contracting of convicts, the legislature passed a gasoline tax to fund the use of convicts on the public-account system to maintain roads and other internal improvements (i.e., road gangs).[105] The state then became the direct exploiter of convict labor, on "chain gangs," which Lichtenstein calls "one of the region's most vicious racist local institutions."[106] Convict labor helped build and maintain a farm-to-market transportation network that integrated an isolated rural South into the national economy.[107]

Regardless of the financial rewards the state reaped via the convict-lease system, it was operated mainly as a means of labor control and recruitment—forced labor in an age of emancipation. In this regard, wrote Lichtenstein, the mind of the South was very much "continuous with the past. . . . Convict labor made modern economic development of the South's resources compatible with the maintenance of racial domination" and race-connected practices. Lichtenstein described those who used convicts, including some of the city's most prominent industrialists, as advocates of a "Prussian route" to development in that they preferred forced labor to free contractual labor.

> In fact, they were the quintessential New South capitalist entrepreneurs, directors of industrial firms, railroads, banks and real estate companies. But they were also "laborlords" as slaveholders had been before them, buying, selling, and exploiting the labor of convicts. This combination of "bourgeois" and "antibourgeois" characteristics points to a potentially new way of looking at an important sector of the ruling class of the New South.[108]

Reinhard Bendix could have been describing Birmingham's earlier industrialists when he wrote, "Men may be guided not only by considerations of utility and affinity, but also by a belief in the existence of a legitimate order of authority." A highly authoritarian, socially repressive mode of regulation is a much greater obstacle to democracy than to capitalism per se. It is a political obstacle to a particular kind of capitalism—a competitive democratic capitalism that can produce a more intensive regime of accumulation.[109]

THE FREE WAGE EARNER AND CONTRACT LABOR

Before the introduction of the large-scale factory system, demand for factory goods was either uncertain or insufficient to permit continuous, capital-intensive mass production of a particular product line. Then, workers could be controlled, and productivity increased in several ways: use of skilled craft workers (mainly during the pre-industrial era), supervision via authoritarian rule and physical compulsion, and internal contracting. All of these methods are based on the premise that workers knew more than anyone else about performing the detailed tasks involved.

Capitalists effected their control of workers through contracting.[110] In the early phase of industrial capitalism, subcontracting, or internal contracting, was common.[111] For example, before the 1890s, the steel industry used "internal contracting": contractors hired and fired workers, set their wages, disciplined them, and determined production methods.[112] In an era of labor segmentation, capitalists can purchase variable capital at different prices. Owners can exploit unskilled workers who labor under the supervision of skilled workers under contract. According to R. Nelson, although these contractors are effectively wage earners in terms of their relationship to the means of production, they strongly embraced a preindustrial vision of being

> managers as well as workers. The firm provided materials, tools, power, and a factory building. The employees—contractors—in turn agreed to manufac-

ture a particular object or component in a given quantity at a designated cost and by a specific date. Otherwise they retained virtually complete control over the production process. The contractor was thus an employee working for a day wage and an independent businessman working for an anticipated profit.[113]

These contractors saw production as a cooperative endeavor and themselves as equal partners with capital; contractors were masters of their work even while they relied on the owner's capital. A reciprocal interest resulted, and the contractor emerged as a "petit-bourgeois" element fully allied with capital against the interest of subordinate workers. Such a unity of labor and capital characterizes "petty commodity production"; capitalist production of Marx's bourgeois variety is predicated on a purer separation of labor and capital. In Birmingham's iron and steel community, wrote Henry McKiven, Jr.,

> Skilled workers thought of themselves as independent producers. This self-image flourished in a world of work divided into a multiplicity of units, each controlled by a craftsman. Independence at work distinguished metal tradesmen from laborers, most of whom were black, who carried out the orders of skilled workers. In the minds of craftsmen this independence also made them the equal of the men who owned the companies for which they worked.[114]

Pay was on a sliding scale based on quantity of production. The wages of unskilled helpers and subordinate workers were drawn from the earnings of their contractors, who shared in the risks and the fruits of production. This arrangement reduced the owner's direct role in determining wages.[115]

A combination of authoritarian rule and internal contracting best describes the working conditions of the free black wage earner during the very early phase of industrial capitalist development in Birmingham. Combined with the convict-labor system, this working condition ensured a reliable supply of labor. Some coal mines in Alabama, for example those owned by TCI, contracted with private operators and paid per coal car.[116] At times, convicts leased by the coal operators worked for free miners, who paid the mine operator for the convict's labor. For example, John Rutledge, when working as a miner at Helena (south of Birmingham), paid the mine operator one dollar per day for the convict's services.[117]

Contract labor accommodated the racial order and was consistent with the notion of white supremacy. Black unskilled workers usually labored for white contractors, reinforcing a "split" labor system. This split was explained on "biological" grounds: a Birmingham engineer, Alfred Brainerd, found black miners "somewhat slow and lazy" but adaptable to tasks requiring little skill.[118] Contracting also separated black workers from white workers, which the racial order demanded. DeBardeleben said that the division made production easier: "There is nothing left for us to do but to contract to such parties as can cope with and handle labor."[119] The contract system was a means of control.

In practice, this labor system resembled the one Milner had proposed in 1859 for his slave-based industrial city, where blacks would work under an overseer—a "southern white man." Under the convict-labor system, carefully selected white convicts, "trusties," supervised and disciplined gangs of black convicts inside the mines.[120] (The few black contractors working the mines were the exception.) Following slavery, McKiven noted, skilled white workers

> hoped to build a world where they would once again be accorded the status they believed they deserved. To help accomplish this end skilled metal workers established institutions to protect the rights and authority at work that were so central to their concept of their place in the social order. . . . Skilled white metal tradesmen relied on the traditional right to control access to their trades to counter the black threat. When they moved to Birmingham white craftsmen found few skilled black iron workers, and they intended to make sure this continued to be the case.[121]

The contract system helped maintain the white workers' sense of privilege: where blacks once had held a virtual monopoly on craft jobs, now they were no longer given the opportunity to learn such skills. W. E. B. DuBois wrote,

> Go into the North or South and ask to have pointed out to you the most prosperous and reliable colored man in that community and in the majority of cases, I believe, you will have pointed out to you a Negro who has learned a trade; and, in many cases, you will find that this trade was learned during the days of slavery.[122]

In the North, the flow of European immigrants made it easier to exclude blacks from skilled occupations.[123] According to F. Ray Marshall, "Negroes generally were frozen out of occupations they had formerly held and relegated to 'Negro' jobs in urban occupations. The jobs set aside for them were usually ones that whites would not take."[124] The result was a dual-labor market: whites got jobs in the primary sector with high wages, good working conditions, and good chances for advancement; blacks occupied jobs in the secondary sector, with low pay and poor working conditions. Only one black trade union was a member of the Birmingham Trade Council in 1883, and blacks in the trades earned 20 to 30 percent less than whites doing the same job.[125] A black clergyman of the African Methodist Episcopal Church addressed the problem before the U.S. Senate Committee on Education and Labor in 1885:

> With regard to our race, generally I can say that it is making some advancement in many respects, and would make more if the trades were open to our young men. The entrances to the different trades seem, however, to be closed against them to a very great extent. There seems to be disposition on the part of some laborers in some localities to shut our people out. While some colored parents, fathers especially, are anxious to have their sons learn trades, believing that to be the best means by which they can provide for their future usefulness, there are very few trades outside of the barber's occupation of which our young men have a chance to acquire a knowledge, and therefore they are mostly engaged about here in mining doing other subordinate work;

very few of them are learning trades. There are some labor [trade] organizations here which, while they have no definite rules forbidding colored men to enter, yet do practically exclude them.[126]

From 1865 to 1900, blacks were unable to compete directly with whites for trade and other skilled positions. In 1901, only 212 of the 2,425 skilled craftspersons in Birmingham were black.[127] Workers in the trades were experts who could offer advice; for blacks to play such a role to white customers would have violated the racial order.[128] The developing trade unions represented only the most highly skilled crafts workers, the "aristocracy of labor" that fought to maintain their privileged position.[129]

By contracting work to skilled white miners, coal operators could avoid responsibility for labor productivity problems by pointing the finger at the contractor while reducing capital outlays to a bare minimum.[130] For their part, black workers had to produce a surplus not only for the contractor but also for the mine operator. Black workers bore the brunt of any downward adjustment in the contractor's price; these adjustments came whenever the manufacturer decided that the contractor's profits were too high. The contractor faced constant pressure to reduce variable capital, which meant a high rate of black labor exploitation.[131]

The unequal relationship between black and white workers, and between the owners of capital and the contractors, kept the price of contracting very low. Like plantation owners who had hired overseers, industrialists depended on other laborers to control and exploit unskilled black wage earners. For example, owners of textile mills perpetuated a variation of the contract arrangement to exploit unskilled white workers when they allowed children to come in and help their parents.[132] Between 1885 and 1895, the number of boys under 18 employed in Alabama mills increased by 81 percent, and the number of young women rose by 158 percent. During the last decade of the nineteenth century, as the mills moved south, child labor in the United States increased 300 percent. By 1900, 25 percent of all southern mill workers were children between the ages of ten and sixteen.[133] The governor of Alabama, who was also the owner of the Avondale Cotton Mill in Birmingham, refused to send a representative to the Southern Child Labor Convention, which advocated the elimination of child labor.

Child labor, however, was not as prevalent in Alabama's coal and iron ore mines as it was in other states. According to estimates, Alabama's mine owners employed only 894 children ages ten to fifteen, 5.1 percent of all coal miners in the state, as compared with more than 14,000 in Pennsylvania, which represented 13.7 percent of that state's coal miners.[134] The availability of convict labor and cheap exploitable free black labor reduced somewhat the demand for child labor in the Alabama mines.

Increasingly, workers objected to the contract system on the grounds that it divided labor. As one miner said, "One man has no right to get the labor of another man. . . . Both share alike."[135] Fortune recognized that free black and white wage earners working under contracting have a "common cause, a common humanity and a common enemy; and that therefore, if they would triumph over wrong . . .

they must be united."[136] The *Labor Advocate* called for obliterating the color line between wage earners before all "sink into a condition of hopeless slavery nearly as bad as that from which [the black] race had been rescued."[137]

NOTES

1. Gavin Wright, *Old South, New South: Revolutions in Southern Economy Since the Civil War* (New York: Basic Books, 1986), 50.

2. John T. Milner, *Alabama: As It Was, as It Is, and as It Will Be* (Montgomery, Ala.: Barrett and Brown, 1876), 58; John T. Milner, *Report to the Governor of Alabama on the Alabama Central Railroad* (Montgomery, Ala.: Advertiser Book and Job Steam Press Print, 1859), 45.

3. Herbert G. Gutman, *Work, Culture, and Society in Industrializing America: Essays in American Working-Class and Social History* (New York: Alfred A. Knopf, 1976), 145; Paul B. Worthman, "Black Workers and Labor Unions in Birmingham, Alabama, 1897–1904." *Labor History* 10, no. 3 (Summer 1969): 375–407.

4. Holman Head, "The Development of the Labor Movement in Alabama Prior to 1900" (M.A. thesis, University of Alabama, 1955), 171.

5. Herbert Gutman, "The Negro and the United Mine Workers of America: The Career and Letters of Richard L. Davis and Something of Their Meaning: 1890–1900," in *The Negro and the American Labor Movement*, ed. Julius Jacobson (Garden City, N.Y.: Anchor Books, 1968), 49–127; Sterling Spero and A. L. Harris, *The Black Worker: The Negro and the Labor Movement* (New York: Athenaeum, 1968), 206–45, 352–82.

6. Karl Marx, *Capital*, vol. 1 (New York: International Publishers, 1967), 165.

7. Robert William Fogel and Stanley L. Engerman, *Time on the Cross: The Economics of American Negro Slavery*, vol. 1 (Boston: Little, Brown, 1974), 5.

8. T. Thomas Fortune, *Black and White: Land, Labor, and Politics in the South* (New York: Fords, Howard, & Hubert, 1884), 174–75.

9. Richard Peet, "Inequality and Poverty: A Marxist-Geographic Theory," *Annals of the Association of American Geographers* 65 (1975): 566.

10. Marx, *Capital*, 165.

11. "Only Way to Remedy," *Labor Advocate*, 23 March 1901, 1.

12. "Boon to People," *Labor Advocate*, 26 April 1902, 1.

13. Testimony of J. W. Sloss, president of the Sloss Company, before the U.S. Senate Committee on Education and Labor, *Report of the Senate Upon the Relatives Between Labor and Capital and Testimony*, IV, 48th Congress, 2nd Session, 1885, 299.

14. Susan A. Mann, "Sharecropping in the Cotton South: A Case of Uneven Development in Agriculture," *Rural Sociology* 49, no. 3 (1984): 419; see also Susan A. Mann and James M. Dickinson, "Obstacles to the Development of a Capitalist Agriculture," *Journal of Peasant Studies* 5, no. 4 (1978): 466–81.

15. James C. Cobb, *Industrialization and Southern Society, 1877–1984* (Chicago: Dorsey Press, 1984), 16–17.

16. W. E. B. DuBois, *Black Reconstruction in America* (Cleveland, Ohio: World Publishing Co., 1964), 185; W. David Lewis, *Sloss Furnaces and the Rise of the Birmingham District: An Industrial Epic* (Tuscaloosa: University of Alabama Press, 1994), 1–38.

17. B. I. Wiley, "Salient Changes in Southern Agriculture Since the Civil War," *Agricultural History* 13, no. 2 (1939): 65–76; Heywood Fleisig, "Mechanizing the Cotton Harvest

in the Nineteenth-Century South," *Journal of Economic History* 25 (1977): 704–6; Jonathan Wiener, "Class Structure and Economic Development in the American South, 1865–1955," *American Historical Review* 84, no. 4 (October 1979): 987.

18. Herbert R. Northrup and Richard L. Rowan, *Negro Employment in Southern Industry: A Study of Racial Policies in Five Industries* (Philadelphia: University of Pennsylvania Press, 1970), 11; Lewis, *Sloss Furnaces*, 210.

19. Jack Roland Bergstresser, Sr., "Raw Material Constraints and Technological Options in the Mines and Furnaces of the Birmingham District: 1876–1930" (Ph.D. diss., Auburn University, Auburn, Ala., 1993), 27.

20. Bergstresser, "Raw Material 31, 53."

21. Robert Louis Cvornyek, "Convict Labor in the Alabama Coal Mines, 1874–1928" (Ph.D. diss., Columbia University, 1993), 159; see also Keith Dix, "Work Relations in the Coal Industry: The Hand Loading Era, 1880–1930," *West Virginia University Bulletin* 78, no. 7-2 (January 1978), 8–14.

22. Lewis, *Sloss Furnaces*, 204–212, 296–326.

23. Bergstresser, "Raw Material," 31. Emphasis added.

24. Lewis, *Sloss Furnaces*, 3.

25. Lewis, *Sloss Furnaces*, 209–10.

26. Wright, *Old South*, 78.

27. Wright, *Old South*, 78. Lewis, *Sloss Furnaces*, 210.

28. Quoted in C. Vann Woodward, *Origins of the New South, 1877–1913* (Baton Rouge: Louisiana State University Press, 1951), 127.

29. Brian Page and Richard Walker, "From Settlement to Fordism: The Agro-Industrial Revolution in the American Midwest," *Economic Geography* 67, no. 4 (October 1991): 281–315.

30. Ann Harper, *The Location of the United States Steel Industry, 1879–1919* (New York: Arno Press, 1977).

31. Bergstresser, "Raw Material," 31.

32. The rate of surplus value, or rate of exploitation, is defined as surplus value $(1 - w)$ divided by variable capital (w). Surplus value was determined by subtracting production wages for a given commodity (w) from value added by manufacturing. The rate of surplus is positive as long as w is less than the value added. The higher the rate of surplus value, the larger the portion of value added to a commodity accruing to capitalists as surplus value and the smaller the portion accruing to labor as wages. See Phillips J. Wood, *Southern Capitalism: The Political Economy of North Carolina, 1880–1990* (Durham, N.C.: Duke University Press, 1986), 206–8, for a description of this method of determining rate of surplus value and problems associated with it.

33. Cobb, *Industrialization and Southern Society*, 69.

34. Cvornyek, "Convict Labor," 1, 3, 4, 8, 12; Lewis, *Sloss Furnaces*, 152–54; see also Alex Lichtenstein, "Twice the Work of Free Labor: Labor, Punishment, and the Task System in Georgia's Convict Mines," in *Race, Class, and Community in Southern Labor History*, ed. Gary M. Fink and Merl E. Reed (Tuscaloosa: University of Alabama Press, 1994), 151; Alex Lichtenstein, *Twice the Work of Free Labor: The Political Economy of Convict Labor in the New South* (London: Verso, 1996), 11, 72.

35. Quoted in Matthew J. Mancini, *One Dies, Get Another: Convict Leasing in the American South, 1866–1928* (Columbia: University of South Carolina Press, 1996), 58.

36. Shelby M. Harrison, "A Cash-Nexus for Crime," *Survey* 27, no. 14 (6 January 1912): 1546.

37. U.S. Senate, *Reports of the Immigration Commission, Immigrants in Industries*, Part I, Bituminous Coal Mining (2 vols.), 61st Congress, 2d Session, Senate Doc. 633, VII (1910), 218.

38. Harrison, "Cash-Nexus," 1548.

39. Quoted in Lichtenstein, *Twice the Work*, 86.

40. Stanley B. Greenberg, *Race and State in Capitalist Development: Comparative Perspectives* (New Haven, Conn.: Yale University Press, 1980), 221–22; Lewis, *Sloss Furnaces*, 309–10; Cvornyek, "Convict Labor," 138, 208.

41. Mancini, *One Dies*, 22.

42. Mancini, *One Dies*, 22–23.

43. *The Penal Code of Alabama.* Adopted by the General Assembly at Session, 1865–1866 (Montgomery, Ala.: Reid and Screw, 1866), 10–11. For a discussion of the convict lease system in Alabama, see Jack Leonard Lerner, "A Monument to Shame: The Convict Lease System in Alabama" (M.A. thesis, Samford University, Birmingham, Ala., 1969); and Robert David Ward and William Warren Rogers, *Convicts, Coal, and the Banner Mine Tragedy* (Tuscaloosa: University of Alabama Press, 1987).

44. Mancini, *One Dies*, 36; see also Cvornyek, "Convict Labor," 54, 56.

45. Cvornyek, "Convict Labor," 31, 38–39.

46. U.S. Senate Committee on Education and Labor, *Labor and Capital*, 438.

47. U.S. Senate Committee on Education and Labor, *Labor and Capital*, 440.

48. Laws Governing State and County Convicts, Article 2, Section 6528; Alabama Code of 1896, Sections 4476, 4477, 4478.

49. Mancini, *One Dies*, 192; Alabama Code of 1897, Section 4478; Cvornyek, "Convict Labor," 167–69.

50. Harrison, "Cash-Nexus," 1542.

51. U.S. Senate Committee on Education and Labor, *Labor and Capital*, 430, 438.

52. Mancini, *One Dies*, 105.

53. Cvornyek, "Convict Labor," 116, 121.

54. *First Biennial Report of the Board of Managers of Convicts, September 1, 1982–August 31, 1894* (Montgomery, Ala.: Brown Printing Company, 1894), 25–26.

55. U.S. Bureau of Labor, *Annual Report of the Commissioner of Labor, Convict Labor* (Washington, D.C.: Government Printing Office, 1905), 32–40; *First Biennial Report of the Inspector of Convicts, October 1, 1884–September 30, 1886* (Montgomery, Al.: Barrett and Company, State Printer and Binder, 1886), 21.

56. *Report of the Board of Managers.*

57. Lichtenstein, *Twice the Work*, 95, 103.

58. Alabama Code of 1897, Section 4479.

59. Quoted in Mancini, *One Dies*, 106–107; Cvornyek, "Convict Labor," 178.

60. Laws Governing State and County Convicts, Article 2, Section 6531.

61. Senate Comm. on Education and Labor, *Labor and Capital*, 435.

62. U.S. Industrial Commission, *Report of the Industrial Commission on Prison Labor* (Washington, D.C.: Government Printing Office, 1900), 23, 60.

63. Mancini, *One Dies*, 44–45, 48.

64. *Annual Report of the State Auditor*, 1883, 1898.

65. Mancini, *One Dies*, 102.

66. Bureau of Labor, *Annual Report*, Convict Labor, 189.

67. *State Auditor*, 1916, 1920.

68. Lichtenstein, "Twice the Work," 164.

69. Mancini, *One Dies*, 102.

70. Quoted in *Facts About Coalburg Prison: Doctor Parkes' Report Reviewed* (Birmingham, Ala.: Archives, Birmingham Public Library, n.d.), 8.

71. Quoted in Cvornyek, "Convict Labor," 31, 244.

72. Thomas D. Parkes, *Report on Coalburg Prison* (Birmingham, Ala., Committee on Health of Jefferson County Medical Society, 1895), 8.

73. *First Biennial Report of the Inspectors*, 23.

74. *Fifth Biennial Report of the Inspectors of Convicts* (September 1, 1902, to August 31, 1904); *Quadrennial Report of the Inspectors of Convicts* (September 1, 1910, to August 31, 1914), 15.

75. *Sixth Biennial Report of the Inspectors of Convicts*, (September 1, 1904, to August 31, 1906), 7.

76. "Convict Department, Its Management," Sworn Statement of Emmet O'Neal, Governor of Alabama Before Investigating Committee (Montgomery, Ala.: Brown Printing Company, 1913), 68–70; *Quadrennial Report of the Inspectors*.

77. Carl V. Harris, *Political Power in Birmingham, 1871–1921* (Knoxville: University of Tennessee Press, 1977), 204; Gutman, "The Negro," 112.

78. *Report of the Special Committee of the Alabama General Assembly to Investigate the Convict Lease System* (Montgomery, Ala., 1889), 28.

79. U.S. Industrial Commission, *Report on Prison Labor*. In 1885, Chicago cooperage workers not affected by convict labor earned an average of $623, but those in shops competing with convict labor earned average wages of $432. Although demand for such goods in Chicago, stimulated by the growth of the meat-packing industry, increased by 130 percent between 1875 and 1885, average weekly earnings of coopers in Chicago, where convict labor produced 67.8 percent of 1,099,776 packages sold in 1885, were much lower than that of coopers in cities where the influence of convict labor was negligible or nonexistent.

80. U.S. Bureau of Labor, *Annual Report, Convict Labor*.

81. U.S. Bureau of Labor, *Annual Report, Convict Labor*.

82. U.S. Industrial Commission, *Report on Prison Labor*, 23, 46–50; U.S. Bureau of Labor, *Annual Report, Convict Labor*, 42; Lichtenstein, *Twice the Work*, 94.

83. U.S. Industrial Commission, *Report on Prison Labor* 23, 46–50.

84. Peet, "Inequality," 565.

85. *Labor Advocate*, 10 March 1894, 1, 4.

86. *Fifth Biennial Report*, 15–16.

87. *Annual Report of the State Auditor*, 1915.

88. *First Biennial Report of the Inspectors of Convicts*.

89. Lewis, *Sloss Furnaces*, 310–11; Lichtenstein, *Twice the Work*, 103.

90. Lichtenstein, *Twice the Work*, 296.

91. Cvornyek, "Convict Labor," 303–4.

92. Martha Mitchell, "Birmingham: A Biography of a City of the New South" (Ph.D. diss., University of Chicago, 1946), 113–14; Cvornyek, "Convict Labor," 138.

93. Cvornyek, "Convict Labor," 309.

94. Lichtenstein, *Twice the Work*, 107–8, 124.

95. U.S. Industrial Commission, *Report on Prison Labor*, 7.

96. Ward and Rogers, *Convicts*.

97. Mancini, *One Dies*, 111.

98. Cvornyek, "Convict Labor," 316.

99. U.S. Industrial Commission, *Report on Prison Labor*, 7, 9, 44.

100. *State Auditor*, 1928.

101. U.S. Bureau of Labor, *Annual Report, Convict Labor*, 39–40.

102. U.S. Industrial Commission, *Report on Prison Labor,* 23.

103. U.S. Department of the Interior, U.S. Geological Survey, *Mineral Resources of the U.S., 1902* (Washington, D.C.: Government Printing Office, 1904); U.S. Bureau of Labor, *Annual Report, Convict Labor,* 45, 193–200; Cvornyek, "Convict Labor," 113.

104. Ward and Rogers, *Convicts,* 122.

105. Mancini, *One Dies,* 230.

106. Lichtenstein, *Twice the Work: Political Economy,* 168.

107. Cvornyek, "Convict Labor," 133; Lichtenstein, *Twice the Work: Political Economy,* 152–85.

108. Lichtenstein, *Twice the Work: Political Economy,* 9.

109. Reinhard Bendix, *Nation-Building and Citizenship: Studies of Our Changing Social Order* (Berkeley: University of California Press, 1977), 19; Barrington Moore, Jr., *Social Origins of Dictatorship and Democracy: Lord and Peasant in the Making of the Modern World* (Boston: Beacon Press, 1966), 141–55; Shearer Davis Bowman, *Masters and Lords: Mid-19th-Century U.S. Planters and Prussian Junkers* (New York: Oxford University Press, 1993), 90.

110. John Urry, "Capitalist Production, Scientific Management and the Service Class," in *Production, Work, Territory: The Geographical Anatomy of Industrial Capitalism,* ed. Allen J. Scott and Michael Storper (Boston: Allen & Unwin, 1986), 44; see also R. Nelson, *The Merger Movement in American Industry, 1895–1956* (Princeton, N.J.: Princeton University Press, 1959); D. Nelson, *Managers and Workers, Origins of the New Factory System in the United States, 1880–1920* (Madison: University of Wisconsin Press, 1975); David Stark, "Class Struggle and the Transformation of the Labour Process: A Relational Approach," *Theory and Society* 9, no. 1 (January 1980): 89–130; M. S. Larson, "Proletarianisation and Educated Labor," *Theory and Society* 9 (1980): 131–75; John Urry, "The Growth of Scientific Management: Transformations in Class Structure and Class Struggle," in *Class and Space: The Making of Urban Society,* ed. Nigel Thrift and Peter Williams (London: Routledge and Kegan Paul, 1987), 254–75.

111. John Holmes, "The Organization and Locational Structure of Production Subcontracting," in *Production, Work, Territory,* ed. Scott and Storper (Boston: Allen & Unwin, 1986), 80–106.

112. Nelson, *Managers;* Larson, "Proletarianisation"; Stark, " Class Struggle."

113. Nelson, *Managers,* 36.

114. Henry M. McKiven, Jr., *Iron and Steel: Class, Race, and Community in Birmingham, Alabama, 1875–1920* (Chapel Hill: University of North Carolina Press, 1995), 27.

115. Katherine Stone, "The Origins of Job Structures in the Steel Industry," in *Labor Market Segmentation,* ed. Richard C. Edwards, Michael Reich, and David M. Gordon (Lexington, Mass.: D. C. Heath and Company, 1975), 27–84.

116. "Miners, Pratt City in the Tells," *Labor Advocate,* 30 March 1894.

117. Testimony of John Rutledge before U.S. Senate Committee on Education and Labor, *Labor and Capital,* 305.

118. Alfred F. Brainerd, "Colored Mining Labor," *Transactions of the American Institute of Mining Engineers* 14 (1885–1886): 78.

119. Quoted in the *Bessemer Weekly,* 14 April 1894.

120. Milner, *Report,* 45; Cvornyek, "Convict Labor," 176.

121. McKiven, *Iron and Steel,* 27, 29.

122. W. E. B. Dubois, *The Negro Artisan* (New York: Octagon Books, 1968), 7.

123. Lucian B. Gatewood, "The Black Artisan in the U.S., 1890–1930," *Review of Black Political Economy* 5 (Fall 1974): 19–33.

124. F. Ray Marshall, *Labor in the South* (Cambridge, Mass.: Harvard University Press, 1967), 11.

125. Mitchell, "Birmingham," 124.

126. U.S. Senate Committee on Education and Labor, *Report of the Committee of the Senate upon the Relations Between Labor and Capital and Testimony Taken by the Committee*, 48th Congress, 1st Session, Vol. IV. (1885), 374–75.

127. Greenberg, *Race and State*, 332.

128. Raymond S. Franklin, *Shadows of Race and Class* (Minneapolis: University of Minnesota Press, 1991), 69–88.

129. Jeremy Brecher, *Strike* (San Francisco: Straight Arrow Books, 1972), 29.

130. Robin D. G. Kelley, *Hammer and Hoe: Alabama Communists During the Great Depression* (Chapel Hill: University of North Carolina Press, 1990), 63.

131. Jacques Gouverneur, *Contemporary Capitalism and Marxist Economics* (Totowa, N.J.: Barnes and Noble Books, 1983), 143.

132. Melvin T. Copeland, *The Cotton Manufacturing Industry of the United States* (New York: A. M. Kelley [1912] 1966), 2–3.

133. Hugh C. Bailey, *Liberalism in the New South: Southern Social Reformers and the Progressive Movement* (Coral Gables, Fla.: University of Miami Press, 1969), 162, 165, 179; Walter I. Trattner, *Crusade for the Children: A History of the National Child Labor Committee and Child Labor Reform in America* (Chicago: Quadrangle Books, 1970), 36–37, 40–41; Woodward, *Origins*, 226.

134. A. J. McKelway, "Conservation of Childhood," *Survey* 28 (June 6 1912): 1530. Percentages based on 1901 employment in coal industry provided by Edward W. Parker, "Coal," Department of Interior, U.S. Geological Survey, *Mineral Resources of the U.S.* (Washington, D.C.: Government Printing Office, 1904), 318.

135. *Proceedings of the Joint Convention of Alabama Coal Operators Association and United Mine Workers*, Birmingham, Ala., 22 June 1903, 260.

136. Fortune, *Black and White*, 235–36.

137. "The Laborers War," *Labor Advocate*, 2 April 1898, 1.

11

Noncompetitive Labor Segmentation and Laissez-Faire Race Relations

Although capitalist development as a historical process accommodated and elaborated race-connected practices, at times it also permitted a blurring of the racial order to ensure capitalists access to labor.[1] It is possible to see, in some instances, industrial capitalism as a force for the destruction of race-connected practices.[2] In addition, noncompetitive labor segmentation and the liberal notion of a free labor market characterized the early phase of industrial capitalism in Birmingham and, in the post-Reconstruction era, a stirring of laissez-faire race relations allowed for some class solidarity across racial lines.

For Karl Marx and Friedrich Engels, industrialization undermined the traditional social order and established new relations:

> The modern bourgeois society . . . has but established new classes, new conditions of oppression, new forms of struggle in place of the old ones. . . . Differences of age and sex [and race] have no longer any distinctive social validity for the working class. . . . All previous historical movements were movements of minorities, or in the interest of minorities. The proletarian movement is the self-conscious, independent movement of the immense majority, in the interest of majority.[3]

Industrial capitalism entailed a commitment to, first, a rational and secular outlook; second, contractual relations in place of status relations; and third, as a consequence of the first two requirements, impersonal markets. These commitments obviously had implications for race relations, as free and competitive market forces do not produce race-connected practices. According to Ellen Meiksins Wood,

> It is not so clear that racial or gender equality are antagonistic to capitalism, or that capitalism cannot tolerate them. . . . In fact, there is a positive tendency in capitalism to *undermine* such differences, and even to dilute identi-

ties like gender and race, as capital strives to absorb people into the labour market and to reduce them to interchangeable units of labour.[4]

For instance, in coal mines, where workers organized more along industry than craft lines, organizing necessitated more open racial policies than had been required for most craft unions.[5]

The emerging industrial order appeared incompatible with the constraints and immobility of a racial order in several ways.[6] Race-connected practices bar free competition. George Fredrickson noted that white-supremacist attitudes and policies originated in preindustrial settings, but

> Pursuing their rational self-interest, capitalists would have hired the best individuals for the job regardless of their ancestry, and workers would have freely sought out the best market for their labor. Inequality would have existed, but it would have been purely a matter of class rather than race.[7]

Industrial capitalism may have been a major cause of modern social and economic inequality, but it also sanctioned racial ideology and white supremacy to mask this inequality. Yet, it seems reasonable that the introduction of industrial capitalism would undermine, to some extent, such a racial order, at least in the short term. Noel Ignatiev noted,

> Under the capitalist system, all workers compete for jobs. The competition gives rise to animosity among them; but normally it also gives rise to its opposite, unity. It is not free competition that leads to enduring animosity, but its absence. Race becomes a social fact at the moment "racial" identification begins to impose barriers to free competition among atomized and otherwise interchangeable individuals.[8]

The competition for the black vote because of Reconstruction was fundamentally connected to the need for competition in the labor market, which produced, according to Gerald David Jaynes, nondiscriminatory wage and job policies.

> Within any geographical area in which all the laborers and employers were in close enough proximity to compete with one another directly there is little evidence of wage discrimination. Almost no source, white or black, employer or employee, visitor or resident, was aware of wage differentials between black and white agricultural workers. . . . Throughout the 1870s and certainly by the end of Reconstruction, the evidence related to the question of color discrimination in wages and employment opportunities outside agriculture is very different from that found for farm work. At this early period clear signs of the developing racial division of labor are evident. In unskilled labor, even in factories, the abundance of efficient and reliable black laborers made it impossible for whites to displace the indispensable pool of black workers. The refusal of unskilled whites to work with blacks under terms of equality was at best a poor bluff when they knew the employer could easily replace an entire force of striking whites with an equally productive number

of blacks. The consequence was that few sources report the existence of discriminatory wage policies for unskilled labor.[9]

Stephen DeCanio concluded that between 1880 and 1910 the South had a competitive economy in which black labor was not oppressed. Margin product factor pricing in agriculture was entirely consistent with the known levels of wage and sharecrop payments. He continues, "If anything, labor tended to receive a wage somewhat higher than the value of its marginal product."[10] Blacks as a whole were just as productive as whites as a whole.

After Reconstruction failed, racism continued to distort the South's economic institutions, although not to the point of completely undermining the competitive capitalist market. Until the 1890s, the Republican Party, which was the party of northern capitalists, continued to protest the treatment of southern blacks and offer new legislation to protect their rights. Repressive laws and acts of violence against blacks existed, but they were not instruments of economic exploitation in the labor market.[11] The mobility of the former slaves after emancipation was not just a test of their new freedom or a period of wandering. In fact, the 1890 census, the first to make racial distinctions pertaining to occupations, revealed that blacks' labor force participation was considerably higher than that for whites. Of blacks ten years of age and older, 58 percent were gainfully employed compared to 47 percent for whites.[12] William Cohen noted, "Like people everywhere in the modern world, [they] moved from one place to another in tune with the rhythms of the labor market, going where the promise of economic betterment was greatest."[13] The desire of blacks as a family unit to work fewer hours than under slavery seems both plausible and consistent with what was expected in a competitive labor market. According to Robert Higgs,

> Black men obviously valued the housekeeping and childrearing service of black women; and holding women off the labor market as showpieces in idleness—an oft-repeated claim—seems implausible in general, though conceivable in a few cases. Black parents after 1865 could sometimes choose to educate their children instead of sending them to the fields or to other employment. In brief, as a free man the black could respond to a variety of new opportunities, and one result was reduction in the aggregate amount of black labor supplied.[14]

Market pressures and the tendency to accept the liberal notion of a free and competitive market after Reconstruction meant Birmingham capitalists subjected black and white workers to almost the same discipline of control, nearly equalizing their wages. Yet, wrote Gavin Wright, "Wherever distinction had to be made, discrimination was the rule, and blacks had little prospect for advancement above the unskilled level, producing segmentation of labor along racial lines. The operation of market forces did little to improve this situation."[15] Despite the competitive nature of early industrialism, it neither displaced nor transformed a firmly established racial order. Any transformation, Herbert Blumer noted,

> is not merely in one direction. Instead, the traditional order may act back, so to speak, on the process of industrialisation blocking it at many points, forc-

ing it sometimes to develop alongside yet outside of the traditional order, and frequently assimilating it inside of the traditional structure of life. Thus, while industrialisation may have disruptive effects at certain points it may be held in check at other points, and above all may be made to accommodate and to fit inside of the traditional order at many other points.[16]

The strength of competition and self-interest cannot be dismissed as factors eliminating or ameliorating racial differences. The period between 1865 and 1900 was, as Fredrickson noted, "not a golden age of race relations, but it can nevertheless be characterized as a time when much separatism retained an informal and laissez-faire quality."[17] Late-nineteenth-century market forces permitted laissez-fare racism. If making a profit meant eliminating racial barriers, then business managers conformed; if making a profit meant accommodating the racial order, then businesspeople complied. Higgs noted that it was

> an interplay of two systems of behavior: a competitive economic system and a coercive racial system. Black people participated actively in the market economy as workers, investors, and consumers, but they acted under more constraints than the white participants in market activities. . . . With their dreams of quickly becoming landowners shattered, most blacks had no choice but to turn to the emerging free labor market for their salvation. And from the very beginning, market forces—mingled with recurring episodes of violence, intimidation, and fraud—predominated in shaping the economic future of the freedmen.[18]

Asked in 1883 by the U.S. Senate Committee on Education and Labor for evidence that the two races were averse to working together, a former president of the Shelby Iron Works in Alabama, John Lapsley, replied,

> No . . . Now, if this man . . . had been asked to sit down at a table with a Negro he would have considered it a gross insult, but he did not feel at all insulted at being asked to work with him in the field. . . . Anything but social equality the laboring white man of this country will stand. They won't stand that; but they have no objection to associating with the colored race as laborers, as far as my observation extends.[19]

Appearing before the same committee, the secretary of the Shelby Iron Works, Charles Hazard, supported Lapsley's contention:

> There are certain positions that I would rather have a white man fill than a negro. For instance, for an engineer for a locomotive I would rather have a white man than a negro. However, that may be because we have never tried negroes in these capacities.[20]

Whereas Thomas Seddon, president of the Sloss Company from 1888 to 1896, spoke of the "natural inherent" differences between black and white workers, J. W. Sloss, the company's founder in 1881 and its first president, noted that owners of production could make no improvement simply by replacing workers of one race with another.[21] Another Birmingham industrialist told the same Senate committee that, although it was difficult for blacks to get into more skilled occupations, those who held such positions were

> as good as white men; their yield is as good; they are steady workmen; they are reliable in every way, and their product is fully as good as anything we have got from white labor. In other departments, too, we have worked them generally with white men. We would have, for instance, a white man on one side of the rolls and a colored man on the other; we would work them in pairs in that way and we have no difficulty about it.[22]

With an abundant labor supply, an expanding market, and no black–white competition between workers, many of Birmingham's industrialists saw little need for controls and regulations concerning race. They were quick to dismiss race-connected practices as minor factors in the workplace. William Julius Wilson also noted,

> Although the available data support the view that a wage differential did exist in many industries during this period, particularly in the South, there is little indication that this represented management's efforts to divide the working class by developing a white labor aristocracy; rather the data suggest that management wanted to cut costs by allowing blacks to compete more or less freely in the open market and by discouraging black participation in labor unions.[23]

Fredrickson noted that this pattern was the dominant one in black–white economic relations until 1910. This pattern was not the result of competition between black and white workers. Most low-paying and unskilled jobs went to blacks, following antebellum precedent, as evidenced by the large number of black workers in Alabama's coal mines, where unskilled jobs dominated. Most whites accepted the notion that blacks did the dirtiest and most unpleasant work, and blacks and whites rarely competed for the same jobs. This lack of direct competition, along with the attempt to realize the nineteenth-century liberal ideal of a totally free labor market, made racial prejudice almost irrelevant in the workplace.[24]

In some industries, especially mining, when operators could not find enough blacks to do the dirtiest tasks, they recruited poor whites. In these situations, almost no wage difference existed between black and white workers. For example, in 1883, black and white workers at Pratt's Birmingham mines earned the same wages.[25] They traveled into the mines on the same coal car and stood in the same line to receive their pay. As late as 1898, TCI and Sloss Iron and Steel officials negotiated contracts with labor that provided "no discrimination is to be made in the distribution of work against the colored miners, but all competent colored men are to have an equal chance at work."[26]

Because blacks were readily exploitable and cut off from sources of real power, southern capitalists saw little danger to white supremacy from such occasional, peripheral breaks in the color line. C. Vann Woodward also presented evidence that the color line may have become less rigid in the 1880s.[27] Wilson wrote of an "unholy alliance between blacks and the white ruling classes prior to 1890 [that] actually prevented the racial code from becoming more severe." He found little empirical support "for the Marxist's contention that the capitalist class attempted to isolate the black labor force by imposing a system of racial stratification both in and outside of industries."[28] Capitalists manipulated both black and white workers as a class, rather than playing one race against the other to generate a higher rate of surplus. Instead of trying to produce a greater mass of use values with the same amount of labor, early industrial regimes increased the absolute size of the labor force, extending the scale of production based on identical norms, as opposed to developing a white labor aristocracy to divide the working class.

THE FORMATION OF A MORE HOMOGENEOUS WORKING CLASS

The proximity required of workers in the coal mines also made black and white workers share common working circumstances as they never had before. It was easier to mobilize them for collective action and, with no direct labor competition, it seemed possible that blacks and whites might unite as a class. Labor leaders took advantage of the segmentation of the labor force to organize all of the unskilled workers, and white and black workers often united briefly in a particular conflict.[29]

The Knights of Labor, which first appeared in Alabama in 1877, eight years after it was organized, took advantage of the lack of competition along racial lines to organize both black and white workers. Within two years, the Knights had twelve local organizations in the state, and a state assembly was organized at a convention in Birmingham in 1887.[30] The Knights rejected the wage system and the separation of labor and capital and attempted to organize all workers without regard to race. Holman Head wrote that the Knights sought to return laborers to the proprietary status they enjoyed during the pre-industrial era by establishing cooperative institutions to provide labor "a proper share of the wealth that they create."[31] The Knights built the industrial suburb of Powderly five miles west of Birmingham under a "cooperative plan" where, unlike company towns and commissaries, workers could own homes and share in the profits of community businesses.

The Knights attempted to organize skilled as well as unskilled labor. Craft unions had appeared as early as 1858 in the iron and steel industry, when a group of Pittsburgh iron puddlers founded the Sons of Vulcan; other crafts in that industry organized and joined forces as the Amalgamated Association of Iron, Steel, and Tin Workers in 1876.[32] Unlike unions organized along industry lines, these unions established barriers to protect their members. Skilled craft workers complained that in negotiations the Knights were often not familiar with a particular trade and that this limitation often led to participation in strikes that did not reflect their real concerns. In 1886, the trade unions withdrew from the Knights of Labor and joined other conservative unions to form the American Federation of Labor (AFL).[33] The AFL represented the skilled trades and considered itself of higher status in the labor community than the Knights or the United Mine Workers, which represented mainly unskilled workers.[34] In Birmingham, the AFL unions formed a trade council in 1889; the council represented more than 7,000 tradesmen by 1894, when Birmingham became one of the South's most unionized cities. Trying to smooth over differences between the Knights and the trade unions, the *Labor Advocate* (later the official organ of the trade council) wrote,

> There should be no quarrel between the Trade Unions and the Knights of Labor in this city. Both are important factors in advancing the interests of the working class. Each has its distinctive field, and there is no occasion for conflict. The Knights of Labor have never designed to supersede the American Federation of Labor. Their work is of a different character. The trade unions are organized from the different branches of skilled labor, and their object is the advancement of the interests of those branches. The order of the Knights of Labor, however, looks beyond this and seeks to bring within its fold all who toil with head and hand, uniting the efforts of all who labor in advancing the welfare of the toiling masses.[35]

Despite such pleas, the Knights declined in membership and influence as the trade unions grew. The Knights were forced to confront the fact that, although whites were willing to work alongside blacks and organize with them, whites would never consider social equality for blacks, especially in the highly skilled craft-oriented trades.[36] Nevertheless, the Knights' experiments with cooperatives and political involvement helped show the way for much of the populist movement in the South.[37]

THE POPULIST MOVEMENT

An established racial system involves more than the play of industrial forces. According to Blumer, "Racial alignment is shaped in major measure by nonindustrial influences, . . . resulting patterns of racial alignment permeate the industrial structure, and . . . changes in such patterns are traceable mainly to movements in social and political happenings."[38] No social movement in southern history epitomized such changes more than the populist movement that paralleled the period of laissez-faire race relations. As the frontier came to a close and opened land filled up, farmers made their best effort to reclaim their republic.[39] This movement had a rural base but expanded to include factory and mine workers in the Birmingham area, where, as they did throughout the South, populists sought strenuously to create an alliance with poor blacks.

A dual agricultural economy reinforced by geography contributed to this racial realignment. Before and after the Civil War, plantations were concentrated in the lowlands (i.e., the black belt), and the white yeoman farmers remained in the uplands (Figure 11.1).[40] The war weakened some of the planter hegemony and shifted

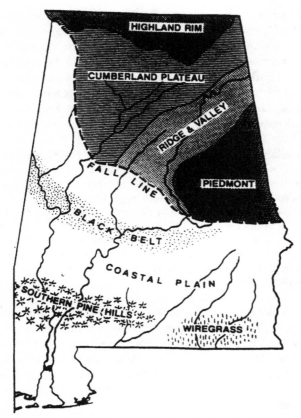

Figure 11.1   Physical geography of Alabama. Source: Virginia V. Hamilton, *The Story of Alabama* (Woodville, AL.: Viewpoint Publications, 1986), 13.

some cotton production toward the uplands; these shifts brought more political and economic prominence to the white yeoman farmers.[41] The class structure of the uplands also increasingly resembled that of the black belt as hill merchants transformed many white yeomen into tenants, bringing them into a class position almost parallel to that of black tenants in the black belt.[42] Thus, not only did lowland blacks move to Birmingham but white farmers, overwhelmed by debts and falling prices, came down from the uplands to work in the textile mills and the mines.

The populist movement grew among upland farmers and tenants who were opposed to both the planters and the industrial capitalists.[43] Many white smallholders who had joined in the campaigns to oust radical Reconstructionists believed they would be replaced by regimes favoring the small farmer over big business (i.e., by Jacksonian Democrats). Instead, the exploitation of upland farmers was so severe that it made them into a powerful force, so that for a time the coalition of industrial capitalists and white farmers against black labor fell apart.[44]

One of the first statewide agricultural organizations to appear in Alabama after the Civil War was the Grange, whose members were for the most part land owners and conservatives who supported wage labor over sharecropping. The Grange had some black members, but it was never in a position to make policy, so its discussions of racial problems mainly concerned blacks' status as laborers. By the mid-1870s, the organization had begun to decline.[45]

In 1878, discontented white yeoman farmers of the uplands organized a "Greenback Labor" party, which aligned with the Knights of Labor. Some black leaders reacted to the decline of radical Reconstruction by joining the Greenback Labor movement to express their resentment against the Republican Party. Willis Thomas, a black miner and social reformer, was a leader of the Greenback movement in Jefferson County, which had sixteen Greenback-Labor clubs by 1879.[46] The party organized both farmers and coal miners and created biracial committees that negotiated with capitalists. According to Wayne Flynt, it made the convict-lease system a major political issue, advocated full employment, and proclaimed, "Wealth should be the property of the laborer who produced it not 'idlers' who lived off the sweat of others."[47]

In the 1880s, a more militant and class-conscious organization appeared. The Wheel challenged the Interstate Commerce Commission and the state legislature to take action against the Louisville and Nashville Railroad for its unjust transportation rates. The Wheel appealed to small farmers, tenants, and sharecroppers and tried to find a common cause with the larger labor movement. In 1887, the group met in Birmingham to form a statewide Union Labor Party that would include many black delegates. This group could not organize effectively against the Democratic Party and, in 1889, merged with the more effective Farmer Alliance, an organization of white small farmers, which helped to oppose the Democrats during the economically depressed 1890s.[48]

The Farmer Alliance was the most important agricultural organization in Alabama between the Civil War and 1900. The depression of the early 1890s was particularly harmful to farmers, who had suffered major losses as the dollar had appreciated by 200 percent between 1865 and 1895. The alliance organized against northern capitalists who set artificially high prices for transporting farm products to market by rail.[49] During the period of the Pullman and Homestead strikes in the Midwest was when the alliance grew active in politics.

As early as 1888, the Knights of Labor and the Farmer Alliance held a joint convention in Montgomery, Alabama. They devised a platform advocating better pay and working conditions, revision of the convict-lease system, and government ownership of means of communication and transportation. One-third of the delegates were black, and they later formed 1,600 local associations throughout the state. The next year, convening in St. Louis, the Knights and the alliance took a strong stand on the political and economic rights of blacks. The Farmer Alliance merged with the Knights of Labor in 1890 and became known as the National Farmer Alliance and Industrial Union.

Although the alliance was openly defying the Democratic Party—the party that had supposedly "saved" the state from radical Reconstruction—some alliance members sought reform within the framework of the party, calling themselves Jeffersonian Democrats, the "true Democratic Party." Most regular members, however, did not support such a move, and in 1891 the Citizens Alliance formed as a third party.[50] This new party brought together upland farmers, blacks, and city and factory laborers who represented a threat to the politico-economic hegemony of the planters and the industrialist capitalists.[51]

Other unions in Birmingham also aligned themselves with the populists, who were blamed for much of the labor unrest in the city during the period. Nearly 5,000 miners held a convention in Bessemer on 13 October 1893 and adopted the name "United Mine Workers of Alabama"—not, at the time, associated with the UMWA—and offered membership to all mining workers, regardless of their occupation or race. Blacks contributed significantly to building the union, and during a coal miners' strike the following year, black and white miners exhibited great solidarity. According to Pinkerton Detective Agency reports sent to Governor Thomas Jones, Lichtenstein found, "Black strikers stood fast with their white counterparts and did not return to work; virtually all the strikebreakers came from outside the coal mining communities." Lichtenstein further noted, "Black willingness to remain out on a strike was a conscious decision, dictated not by fear or white 'control' but by conviction and collective solidarity."[52] The 1894 strike was unsuccessful, but later in the decade the UMWA, the national union, reinvigorated organized labor in the coal mines and began a campaign to rebuild the union that contributed to a remarkable record of labor activity in Alabama.[53]

Although blacks were sometimes used as strikebreakers, which intensified anti-black feeling among white workers, no all-white or racially segregated union formed in the mines. According to one black union member, "I believe that the United Mine Workers has done more to erase the word 'white' from the Constitution than the Fourteenth Amendment."[54] Another black labor official in the 1890s reminded nonunion blacks, "Labor organizations have done more to eliminate the color line than all other organizations, the church not even excepted."[55]

The UMWA forced Birmingham merchants to reverse their refusal to allow integrated unions in their meeting halls.[56] Until the early 1900s, several blacks held local and district UMWA offices and helped organize both black and white workers. Among them was B. L. Greer, a miner who was for six years vice-president of District 20, which covered the Birmingham area. In 1904, Greer characterized his relations with district officers and members as "harmonious."[57] The local union assigned three of the eight seats on the district's executive board to blacks, thereby guaranteeing black representation.[58] By 1900, mine operators throughout the state recognized the union, which negotiated contracts annually. By 1902, 65 percent of miners in Alabama belonged to the union, which was 50 percent black.

The lack of racial competition extended to housing. Birmingham had no ordinances about the residential separation of the races before 1900, and historical studies show little evidence of de facto ghettoization. The most commonly used measure of racial segregation is the index of dissimilarity (i.e., the percentage of blacks or whites who would have to move from a given neighborhood so that its population would reflect the racial composition of the city as a whole). In 1910, the average black–white dissimilarity index for northern cities was 59.2 compared with 89.2 in 1940; in southern cities for which data are available, the averages were 38.3 in 1910, 21 points lower than the average in the North, and 81.0 in 1940.[59] This latter figure reflects the high levels of residential segregation produced by increasing competition between blacks and whites during the Fordist phase of industrialization.

No such information is available for Birmingham's early years, but the lack of black–white competition and the nature of company housing suggest low dissimilarity scores. In company housing, superintendents, skilled and unskilled workers, blacks and whites, immigrants and convicts lived within walking distance of mines and mills.[60] DeBardeleben built his own home two blocks from his rolling mills; E. M. Tutwiler, developer of many mines in the Birmingham district, resided at a mining camp with several hundred black convict laborers.[61] David Corbin wrote, "By its contrived rigid structure, the company town, while giving the coal operators extraordinary forms of power over the miners, precluded the development of a social and political hierarchy based on color ethnicity, that is, a caste system, within the working class community."[62] At most, company houses segregated black and white workers by rows, with a black row and white row of housing often standing back to back; in some, blacks lived on the summits of steep hills overlooking the mines, and whites resided on the lower slopes.[63] Nevertheless, according to Corbin, the company town was usually "too small, its population too familiar, and social interaction too great to allow racial stereotyping and social distance and, hence, a culture of discrimination to flourish."[64] Company housing patterns socially and spatially reproduced the noncompetitive segmentation of labor, and, because workers did not own their homes, there was no housing competition between them. These patterns approached those seen in the South's antebellum cities, where there also was no competition between black and white workers and urban slave owners saw no need to segregate slave housing. The dissimilarity index between free blacks and whites was only 29.0 in 1860.[65]

The spatial pattern of company housing meant that black and white workers shared practical experiences; this shared experience also encouraged class solidarity. Intense spatial concentration of workers characterized Birmingham's housing patterns into the twentieth century. Hosea Hudson, a black labor leader in the 1930s, compared Birmingham with Atlanta:

> You miss one worker here [Birmingham], you get the other next door. But over there in Atlanta, you got to go from here over cross town to see the next steel worker. He'll talk well, but getting him to go from over yonder to over here and this one over here to meet together, that was the problem I had. And it kept me running around, just running around.[66]

In Atlanta, more a commercial and trade center than an industrial city, workers were dispersed throughout the area; but, according to Michael Storper and Richard Walker, "When large numbers of workers share the same, or similar conditions of work and neighborhood life the means of communications are better."[67] In the post-Fordist era, a flexible and mobile capital deprives labor of this crucial precondition of power.[68]

This company housing pattern may explain why perhaps the most important instance of racial cooperation among workers in the South occurred in and around Birmingham. The working class overcame racial barriers more than once in the years after Reconstruction. The large black population concentrated in Alabama's coal fields made organizing black workers a matter of basic self-interest for white miners. The Knights represented the first real attempt to unite black and white workers, and, according to Melton Alonza McLaurin, the last in the nineteenth century.[69] Racial violence and the opposition to racial equality kept the Knights from overcoming the segmentation of labor along racial lines, especially in the trades. However, briefly, there was harmony even between the Knights and the trade council, which achieved some successes in countering racial prejudice. This experiment was daring. It occurred less than a decade after Reconstruction.[70] As Woodward wrote of this period, "Never before or since have the two races in the South come so close together politically."[71] In Engels's terms, it was a period in which the U.S. working class made a step toward becoming a "class-for-itself" with the consciousness and identity to transcend racial, ethnic, and religious differences.[72] In assessing this period in Alabama, William Rogers wrote,

> To ascribe to the Populists a sustained and righteous desire to correct the wrongs done to Negroes in Alabama is to overstate the case. *Yet the Populists promoted the cause of the Negroes, admitted them to their councils, advocated their political and economic advancement. To ignore these efforts is to miss an important part of the agrarian movement.*[73]

The same solidarity between blacks and whites applies to the industrial labor movement. Labor leaders, aided by the lack of competition between blacks and whites and the tendency of capitalists to accept the liberal notion of a free labor market, organized interracial unions.[74]

NOTES

1. Stanley B. Greenberg, *Race and State in Capitalist Development: Comparative Perspectives* (New Haven, Conn.: Yale University Press, 1980), 129–47, 209–42.

2. Oliver C. Cox, *Caste, Class and Race: A Study in Social Dynamics* (New York: Modern Reader Paperbacks, 1970), 333.

3. Karl Marx and Friedrich Engels, *The Communist Manifesto*, ed. Samuel H. Beer (New York: Appleton-Century-Crofts, 1955), 9–10, 17, 21.

4. Ellen Meiksins Wood, *Democracy Against Capitalism: Renewing Historical Materialism* (Cambridge, Mass.: Cambridge University Press, 1995), 266.

5. Alex Lichtenstein, "Racial Conflict and Racial Solidarity in the Alabama Coal Strike of 1894: New Evidence for the Gutman–Hill Debate," *Labor History*, 36, no. 1 (Winter 1995): 64.

6. Herbert Blumer, "Industrialisation and Race Relations," in *Industrialisation and Race Relations: A Symposium*, ed. Guy Hunter (London: Oxford University Press, 1965), 220–53; Greenberg, *Race and State*, 129–47.

7. George M. Fredrickson, *White Supremacy: A Comparative Study in American and South African History* (New York: Oxford University Press, 1981), 199.

8. Noel Ignatiev, *How the Irish Became White* (New York: Routledge, 1995), 98.

9. Gerald David Jaynes, *Branches Without Roots: Genesis of the Black Working Class in the American South, 1862–1882* (New York: Oxford University Press, 1989), 259, 261.

10. Stephen J. Decanio, *Agriculture in the Postbellum South: The Economics of Production and Supply* (Cambridge, Mass.: MIT Press, 1974), 12, 13.

11. George M. Fredrickson, *Black Liberation: A Comparative History of Black Ideologies in the United States and South Africa* (New York: Oxford University Press, 1995), 97; Decanio, *Agriculture*, 13.

12. Robert Higgs, *Competition and Coercion: Blacks in the American Economy, 1865–1914* (Cambridge, Mass.: Cambridge University Press, 1977), 40–41.

13. William Cohen, *At Freedom's Edge: Black Mobility and the Southern White Quest for Racial Control, 1861–1915* (Baton Rouge: Louisiana State University Press, 1991), 45.

14. Higgs, *Competition and Coercion*, 40.

15. Gavin Wright, *Old South, New South: Revolutions in Southern Economy Since the Civil War* (New York: Basic Books, 1986), 13.

16. Blumer, "Industrialisation," 232.

17. Fredrickson, *White Supremacy*, 262.

18. Higgs, *Competition and Coercion*, 13, 37–38.

19. U.S. Senate Committee on Education and Labor, *Report of the Senate upon the Relations Between Labor and Capital and Testimony*, IV, 48th Congress, 2nd Session (1885), 165.

20. Committee, *Relations Between Labor and Capital*, 470.

21. Committee, *Relations Between Labor and Capital*, 288.

22. Quoted in Taft Research Notes on Alabama Labor History, "Black Workers" (Birmingham, Ala.: Archives, Birmingham Public Library, n.d.), 4.

23. William Julius Wilson, *The Declining Significance of Race: Blacks and Changing American Institutions* (Chicago: University of Chicago Press, 1978), 84.

24. Wilson, *Declining Significance*, 215; see also chapter 5.

25. Martha Mitchell, "Birmingham: A Biography of a City of the New South" (Ph.D. diss., University of Chicago, 1946), 124.

26. Quoted in Holman Head, "The Development of the Labor Movement in Alabama Prior to 1900" (M.A. thesis, University of Alabama, 1955) 168–69; see also Chris Evans, *The Histories of the United Mine Workers of America*, vol. 2, 1890–1900, microfiche (Chicago: Library Resources, 1970), 586–96.

27. George M. Fredrickson, *The Black Image in the White Mind: The Debate on Afro-American Character and Destiny, 1817–1914* (New York: Harper & Row, 1972), 203; C. Vann Woodward, *The Strange Career of Jim Crow*, 3rd ed. (London: Oxford University Press, 1974), 11–65.

28. Wilson, *Declining Significance*, 57. George Reid Andrews, "Comparing the Comparers: White Supremacy in the United States and South Africa," *Journal of Social History* 20 (Spring 1987): 591, noted that the same thing happened in South Africa, but much later. In 1922, South African mine owners and the state engaged in action to defeat the demands of white miners for systematic job discrimination in the workplace.

29. This period provided the basis for Herbert Gutman's defense of the classical Marxist notion that the class struggle would render race irrelevant. See Herbert G. Gutman, "The Negro and the United Mine Workers of America: The Career and Letters of Richard L. Davis and Something of Their Meaning: 1890–1900," in *The Negro and the American Labor Movement*, ed. Julius Jacobson (Garden City, N.Y.: Anchor Books, 1968), 49–127.

30. Melton Alonza McLaurin, *The Knights of Labor in the South* (Westport, Conn.: Greenwood Press, 1978), 39.

31. Head, "Development," 41.

32. Herbert R. Northrup, "The Negro and Unionism in the Birmingham, Ala., Iron and Steel Industry," *Southern Economic Journal* 10, no. 1 (July 1943): 27–40.

33. Fredrickson, *White Supremacy*, 222–23.

34. Carter A. Wilson, *Racism: From Slavery to Advanced Capitalism* (Thousand Oaks, Calif.: Sage Publications, 1996), 139–40.

35. "Let Us Have Peace," *Labor Advocate*, 19 July 1890.

36. Claudia Miner, "The 1886 Convention of the Knights of Labor," *Phylon* 44, no. 2 (June 1983): 147–59. According to Andrews in "Comparing," efforts to protect unskilled white labor from black competition in South Africa led to the Nationalist Labor Coalition, an alliance between conservative white elites and the white labor movement.

37. McLaurin, *Knights*, 39.

38. Blumer, "Industrialisation," 239.

39. Daniel Kemmis, *Community and the Politics of Place* (Norman: University of Oklahoma Press, 1990), 30.

40. Michael Reich, *Racial Inequality: A Political-Economic Analysis* (Princeton, N.J.: Princeton University Press, 1981), 220.

41. Horace Mann Bond, *Negro Education in Alabama: A Study in Cotton and Steel* (New York: Octagon Books, 1969), 125.

42. Jonathan M. Wiener, "Planter–Merchant Conflict in Reconstruction Alabama," *Past and Present*, no. 68 (August 1975): 73–94.

43. Reich, *Racial Inequality*, 232–33.

44. Peter Camejo, *Racism, Revolution, Reaction, 1861–1877: The Rise and Fall of Radical Reconstruction* (New York: Pathfinder, 1976), 151.

45. William Warren Rogers, *The One-Gallused Rebellion: Agrarianism in Alabama, 1865–1896* (Baton Rouge: Louisiana State University Press, 1970), 98–99, 145.

46. Herbert G. Gutman, "Black Coal Miners and the Greenback-Labor Party in Redeemer, Alabama: 1878–1879," *Labor History* 10, no. 3 (Summer 1969): 506–35.

47. Wayne Flynt, *Poor but Proud: Alabama's Poor Whites* (Tuscaloosa: University of Alabama Press, 1989), 246–47.

48. Rogers, *One-Gallused Rebellion*, 124–29.

49. Jack M. Bloom, *Class, Race, and the Civil Rights Movement* (Bloomington: Indiana University Press, 1987), 36.

50. Rogers, *One-Gallused Rebellion*.

51. C. Vann Woodward, *Origins of the New South, 1877–1913* (Baton Rouge: Louisiana State University Press, 1951), 252.

52. Lichtenstein, "Racial Conflict," 70, 72.

53. Robin D. G. Kelley, *Hammer and Hoe: Alabama Communists During the Great Depression* (Chapel Hill: University of North Carolina Press, 1990), 4–5.

54. Quoted in Herbert G. Gutman, *Work, Culture, and Society in Industrializing America: Essays in American Working-Class and Social History* (New York: Alfred A. Knopf, 1976), 192.

55. Gutman, *Work*, 132.

56. Paul B. Worthman and James Green, "Black Workers in the New South, 1865–1915," in *Key Issues in the Afro-American Experience*, eds. Nathan Huggins, Martin Kilson, and Daniel M. Fox (New York: Harcourt Brace Jovanovich, 1971), 47–69.

57. "Miners Convention," *Labor Advocate*, 18 June 1904, 1.

58. "Alabama Miners: Many Delegates Present," *United Mine Workers Journal*, 25 June 1908, 8.

59. Douglas S. Massey and Nancy A. Denton, *American Apartheid: Segregation and the Making of the Underclass* (Cambridge, Mass.: Harvard University Press, 1993), chap. 2.

60. Marjorie L. White, *The Birmingham District: An Industrial History and Guide* (Birmingham, Ala.: Birmingham Historical Society, 1981), 77.

61. White, *Birmingham*, 77.

62. David A. Corbin, "Class over Caste: Interracial Solidarity in the Company Town," in *Blacks in Appalachia*, ed. William H. Turner and Edward J. Cabbell (Lexington: University Press of Kentucky, 1985), 93.

63. Flynt, *Poor but Proud*, 117.

64. Corbin, "Class over Caste," 97.

65. Massey and Denton, *American Apartheid*, 19–26.

66. Quoted in Nell I. Painter, *The Narratives of Hosea Hudson: His Life as a Negro Communist in the South* (Cambridge, Mass.: Harvard University Press, 1979), 228.

67. Stanley Aronowitz, *The Politics of Identity: Class, Culture, Social Movements* (New York: Routledge, 1992), 5.

68. Michael Storper and Richard Walker, *The Capitalist Imperative: Territory, Technology, and Industrial Growth* (New York: Basil Blackwell, 1989), 154–82.

69. McLaurin, *Knights*.

70. Reich, *Racial Inequality*, 147, 245.

71. C. Vann Woodward, "Tom Watson and the Negro in Agrarian Politics," *Journal of Southern History* 4, no. 1 (February 1938): 21.

72. Friedrich Engels, *The Condition of the Working Class in England* (1844; reprint, Moscow: Progress Publishers, 1977), 21.

73. Rogers, *One-Gallused Rebellion*, 332–33. Emphasis added.

74. This period of U.S. capitalist regulation in the South has gone almost unnoticed by most labor historians, with the exception of Gutman, "The Negro and the United Mine Workers," and "Black Coal Miners and the Greenback-Labor Party."

12

Accommodating the Racial Order: The Rise of Institutionalized Racism

I want to give you niggers a few words of plain talk and advice. No such address as you have just listened to is going to do you any good; it's going to spoil
you. You might just as well understand that this is a white man's country as far
as the South is concerned, and we are going to make you keep your place. Understand that. I have nothing more to say.

—Williams C. Oates, future Alabama governor,
speaking at Tuskeegee University in 1894 (quoted in Scott and
Stowe, *Booker T. Washington: Builder of a Civilization*)

The period of laissez-faire race relations between 1890 and 1910 was a transitional
moment in the history of U.S. capitalist development. Although capitalism may be
structurally indifferent to racial identities, noted Ellen Meiksins Wood, "Its history
has been marked by probably the most virulent racisms ever known."[1] This laissez-
faire period coincided with what some people see as the nadir for blacks, a time
when there was a high incidence of lynchings and black victimization.[2] Lynching
has long been seen as a symbol of white power, and some recent works suggest that
it was a reaction to black insurgency—as manifested through the populist and labor movements—and increasing job competition. Threatened whites lynched
blacks who would not stay in "their proper place." Laissez-faire relations were not
acceptable to whites. Even whites willing to consider blacks equal partners in the
labor movement, according to Robin Kelley, found their acts and gestures "had to
be disguised and choked back; when white workers were exposed as 'nigger lovers'
or when they took public stands on behalf of African Americans, the consequences
could be fatal."[3] In other words, according to Wood, capital derives advantages
from racism, "not because of any structural tendency in capitalism toward racial
inequality . . . , but on the contrary because [it helps] disguise the structural realities of the capitalist system and because it divide[s] the working class."[4]

153

The alliance of farmers, blacks, and city and factory workers that characterized the populist movement was a threat to the hegemony of planters and industrialists, which led to some restructuring of the southern political economy. Old prejudices and suspicions, extending into both workplaces and homes, became institutionalized in the region's spatial and social fabric. Why this change was so long delayed reflects, according to C. Vann Woodward, "the strange career of Jim Crow" in the South.[5] Whites who had appeared at times to accept laissez-faire race relations began to support formal controls and regulation of blacks. Among these whites were Birmingham's founder, John T. Milner, one of the state's strongest advocates for regional industrialization.

If capital is truly mobile, then investment could flow where cost of production is less expensive (i.e., to the black section of the economy), thereby decreasing income and employment in the dominant white section. The white working class opted to continue the racial order, but that order could not be maintained without the support of the dominant society as well as state controls and regulation.[6] By the turn of the century, noted Paul Baran and Paul Sweezy, institutionalized racism had become the southern capitalists' main strategy for controlling labor and capital, which made black oppression and exploitation "as bad as it had ever been under slavery."[7] John Cell called this period "the highest stage of white supremacy."[8] In the 1880 Alabama gubernatorial election, the Greenback Party received only 42,343 votes against 134,411 for the Redeemer Democrats, the party of the planters and industrialists, whose monopoly on political and economic power made racism "respectable" and "scientific" and provided the foundation for the nation's racial system in the twentieth century.

THE DECLINE OF POPULISM

In 1892, the Democratic Party of Alabama nominated for governor Thomas Jones to run against the Populists' nominee, Reuben Kolb. In expressing his support of Jones, Henry DeBardeleben stated, "It is of great importance to the business men of the state to have you elected."[9] To accomplish their political aims, the Democrats first sought a constitutional convention to disenfranchise blacks, an idea they rejected when they realized the Farmer Alliance would have dominated any such convention. They decided to work through statute instead and enacted the "Sayre Law," under which precinct registrars, appointed by the governor, were empowered to select assistant registrars who certified eligible voters. This statute made it easier for the party in power, the Democrats, to add or delete names from the voting list and paved the way for manipulation and fraud that would ensure the party continued victory.

The Jeffersonian Democrats expected that white small farmers would be disenfranchised along with blacks, so they proposed a white-only primary that would do away with black votes altogether but retain those of the white small farmers. Redeemer Democrats and Populists objected. The proposal was clearly inconsistent with the Populists' objective of uniting blacks and whites, and, although it was consistent with the Democrats' white supremacy doctrine, they had denied blacks the vote since the end of Reconstruction without having to share power with upland white farmers. In short, by controlling black votes in the black belt, Democrats neutralized the political power of the white lower class and saw no need to accept such a proposal. No matter how blacks voted, Democrats always benefited.

This situation applied in 1892, when the Populists were defeated. The defeat did not prevent the Jeffersonian Democrats and Populists from combining their resources behind Kolb again in 1894. In that campaign, they emphasized the rights of miners when labor unrest was widespread in the Birmingham area. Jones was not running, but the fact that he had hired Pinkerton detectives to quell the unrest played an important role in the gubernatorial campaign, as it stimulated support among miners for Kolb, who also pledged to remove convicts from competition with free labor.

Two Republican groups met in Birmingham to support the Populists. They pleaded with blacks to neither register nor vote in the election, fearing that the Democrats would tally the votes in Democratic columns no matter how they were cast. According to one paper, the *Troy Jeffersonian*, a strong supporter of Kolb, "The best thing for the Negro voter to do in the coming registration and election is to keep hands off and let the white voters settle the matter between themselves."[10] However blacks responded to that advice, the Democrats won again. Their candidate, William Oates, received almost 30,000 more votes than Kolb, who carried only three black-belt counties.

In 1896, the Populists moved to broaden their political base by incorporating miners, city laborers, blacks, and Republicans. Previously, the planter and industrialist class had tended to dismiss populism by remarking, "emancipation freed the poor whites more than it did the Negro" or by comparing poor whites with peasants in the French Revolution.[11] This class then realized that the coalition could undermine the powers in place. They used race very effectively to defeat the populist movement and to strengthen their grip on the southern working class. Joseph Johnston, one of two contenders for the Democratic nomination for governor in 1896, called openly for white supremacy: "We do not believe in surrendering any section of our state to the control of the negro. . . . We do not believe he is fitted by birth, education or experience to engage in making or executing laws for the people of Alabama."[12] This statement forced the Populist Party to become more identified with blacks but, more important to voters, to become identified with the party of Reconstruction, the Republicans. In fact, Joseph Manning, a leader of Alabama's populist movement, left the Populist Party to join the Republican Party without finding a replacement. Association with Republicans and blacks was the death knell: the Populists failed again to defeat the Democratic Party.

Throughout the South, more Populists agreed to black disenfrachisement while Redeemer Democrats promised that poor whites would not be disenfranchised in the process. Woodward listed three arguments used to justify this arrangement between Populists and Democrats: (1) it would end the corrupt elections that had long disgraced southern politics; (2) without the Negro as arbiter between white factions, white men could divide freely again on basic issues and enjoy a vigorous political life; and (3) losing the vote would force the Negro to abandon false hopes, to find his "place," and consequently race relations would improve.[13]

More Populists came to believe that the black vote, concentrated in the black belt, prevented the white yeomen of the upland from exercising their rightful political influence. Thus, according to Woodward, it seemed, "The barriers of racial discrimination mounted in a direct ratio with the tide of political democracy among whites."[14] The Democrats saw disenfranchisement as a way to prevent a populist-like movement from threatening the racial order.[15] The Populist candidate for governor of Alabama in 1900 received fewer than 20,000 votes—10,000 less than the Republican candidate. Summing up the period, William Warren Rogers wrote,

> The Populists made an outright attempt to capture the black vote, an act that threatened the entrenched Democratic supremacy in every field. The Democrats adroitly used the Negro issue to brand Populism as a threat to southern institutions and to indict its leaders as either traitors or misguided idealists. This condemnation relieved Democrats of having to account for their shortcomings in the areas of education, penal reform, public roads, finance, and administration. *Negroes were the balance of power, and ironically their vote was used to maintain white supremacy.*[16]

The Democrats had no monopoly on white supremacy. In 1890, the chair of the Colored People's Convention declared that the Republicans had deserted blacks, "and undertaken to protect the capitalist and manufactures of the North."[17] According to Woodward, "The black man was beginning to feel toward his party much the same as the Southern white man was feeling toward his—that his vote was taken for granted and his needs were ignored."[18]

For a time, white Republicans of the South divided over the issue of disenfranchisement, but the lily-white faction gained ground during the 1890s. In Birmingham, they went so far as to expel blacks, leaving blacks with no major political party support. By 1916, this faction had convinced the national party to take the state organization from the blacks. As national Republican leaders increasingly aligned themselves with the southern planter class, blacks organized the "Abraham Lincoln Suffrage League of Alabama" in an attempt to persuade the party's national executive committee to honor the Fourteenth Amendment. The national committee refused to act, effectively ending black Republicanism in the state.

THE JUDICIARY AND RACE

Alabama's segregationist racial policies had the full backing of the judiciary. The courts viewed regulation by race as constitutionally "reasonable"; the state could still equally protect individuals. In 1883, this thinking led the Supreme Court to rule the Civil Rights Act of 1875 unconstitutional.[19] This ruling paved the way for the 1896 *Plessy v. Ferguson* decision, which upheld a state law that required separate passenger rail cars for white and black riders. The *Plessy* decision gave the South legal means to deny public accommodations solely on the basis of color (Table 12.1). In *Plessy*, the court held that issues of race existed in the realm of nature and were not socially constructed. Justice Henry Billings Brown expressed this finding in the majority opinion:

> We consider the underlying fallacy of the plaintiff's argument in the assumption that the enforced separation of the two races stamps the colored race with a badge of inferiority. . . . The argument also assumes that social prejudices may be overcome by legislation and that equal rights cannot be secured except by an enforced commingling of the two races. We cannot accept this proposi-

Table 12.1   Birmingham Segregation Ordinances

Ordinance	Description	Year
968	Unlawful for a black and white person to play with each other at game of chance.	1905
289	Separate accommodation for whites and blacks on streetcars.[a]	1910
308	Moving pictures of any prize fight between a white man and a negro prohibited.	1910
38-C	Segregated cemetery.	1911
1075	Nurses not to take white children into Negro homes.	1917
1130	Segregated blacks and whites in restaurants.	1917
1101-C	Racial segregation of residential areas.	1926
5066	Provided for segregated recreation facilities.	1930
5516	Separate accommodations in public buildings.	1930
5210, 5212	Employer required to provide separate toilet facilities for white and black workers.	1930
1413	Separate accommodation for whites and blacks on any jitney, bus, or taxicab in the city.	1944
798-F	Blacks and whites not to play together or in company with each other in checkers, baseball, softball, football, basketball, or similar games.[b]	1950

Source: The Code of Ordinances of the City of Birmingham, Alabama (Birmingham, Ala.: Mayor & Aldermen, 1905); *Abstract and Index of Ordinances of the City of Birmingham Passed Since the Adoption of the City Code of 1905*, compiled by J. P. Mudd, Assistant City Attorney, 9 August 1913; *The Code of City of Birmingham, Alabama*, enacted 18 September 1917 (Birmingham, City Commission); *The General Code of the City of Birmingham*, enacted 21 October 1930 (Birmingham, Alabama, City Commission); *Birmingham Racial Segregation Ordinances*, reprinted and distributed by the Birmingham Civil Rights Institute, 1992.
[a] Although no ordinances providing for segregated streetcars appeared until 1910, the 1905 city code book noted the case of *Bowie v. B.R. and Electric Co.*, 125 Ala. 397, which ruled that a streetcar company has the right to enforce separate accommodations for whites and blacks on streetcars.
[b] Amendment to ordinance 597 of the General Code of Birmingham, 1944.

tion. If the two races are to meet upon terms of social equality, it must be the result of natural affinities, a mutual appreciation of each other's merits and a voluntary consent of individuals. . . . Legislation is powerless to eradicate racial instincts or to abolish distinctions based upon physical differences and to attempt to do so can only result in accentuating the difficulties of the present situation. . . . If one race be inferior to the other socially, the Constitution of the United States cannot put them upon the same plane.[20]

Ironically, the only southern justice on the Court, John Marshall Harlan, a former slave owner, disagreed with the majority ruling:

The white race deems itself to be the dominant race in this country and so it is, in prestige, in achievements, in education, in wealth and in power. But in the view of the Constitution, in the eye of the law, there is in this country no superior, ruling class of citizens. There is no caste here. Our Constitution is color blind, and neither knows nor tolerates classes among citizens. . . . The law regards man as man, and takes no account of his surroundings or of his color when his civil rights as guaranteed by the supreme law of the land are involved. In my opinion, the judgment this day rendered will, in time, prove to be quite as pernicious as the decision made by this tribunal in the Dred Scott case.[21]

In commenting on his decision, Harlan assured whites that nothing he said threatened their power or status. For he grounded the decision on his concern that only "nurses attending children of the other race" were exempt from the ruling "a white man is not permitted to have his colored servant with him in the same coach, even if his condition of health requires the constant personal assistant of such servant."[22] Only as servants could blacks occupy the same space as whites on public transportation.

In *William v. Mississippi*, two years after *Plessy*, the Supreme Court upheld a lower court's decision that effectively disenfranchised blacks in Mississippi.[23] Three years later, the Alabama constitutional convention, strongly expressing the sentiments of the South's new racial policy, ratified a constitution that formally disenfranchised blacks in the state. Tom Heflin, a convention delegate, commented,

I believe as truly as I believe that I am standing here that God Almighty intended the negro to be the servant of the white man. . . . Nobody but the proud Caucasian cast his vote. . . . I do not believe that we are violating the Constitution of the United States. . . . I do not believe it is incumbent upon us to lift him [the Negro] up and educate him and put him on an equal footing that he may be armed and equipped when the combat comes.[24]

At the convention, a question arose concerning representation: if they could not vote, could blacks still be counted in determining the number of people in an electoral district? If the state did not count blacks, then the black belt, home of the planter class, could lose political strength to the upland, home of the yeoman class.

The planter class demanded that political representation be based on total population, not on voting population alone. Planters argued in terms of the paternalism that had supposedly characterized relations between master and slave. As one black belt delegate said, "The white people of the black belt are responsible for the civilization of the colored people, for their education, for their support and for their protection, and . . . have a right to representation in the law-making bodies of the state," which was to be based on the total population.[25] The new constitution not only called for representation based on total population but also included a provision forbidding any amendment changing the basis of representation. This provision guaranteed the planter class political domination of the state.[26]

The Fifteenth Amendment to the Constitution clearly states that no law can deprive blacks of their right to vote. Therefore, restrictions on voting could not be explicitly race based. Alabama's new constitution also eliminated many poor whites from the voting rolls; these men, who had fought in the Civil War so the southern elites could maintain their status, now sacrificed their right to vote to disenfranchise blacks for the sake of those same elites. Many white upland counties voted against the 1901 constitution, but the state's voters approved it by a vote of 108,613 to 81,734, and, according to Jimmie Frank Gross, "The planter class along with the industrialists triumphed once again."[27]

The Democrats' willingness to manipulate race hatred and fear worked to divide the working class and destroy its ability to make political and economic gains. Oliver Cox wrote,

> The "aristocrats" maintained their power not only by their exploitation of Negroes but also by their exploitation of poor whites, who are artfully played against colored people. . . . The Southern "aristocracy," as the modern capitalist ruling class of this area is sometimes called, could not endure without the hatred which it perpetuates between the white and black masses, and it is by no means unmindful of that fact.[28]

The political effects of the 1901 constitution were long lasting. As late as 1940, there were only 2,000 qualified black voters in the state; by 1954, the year of the *Brown* decision, the number had increased to only 50,000, which was less than 10 percent of the black population of voting age and only 6.3 percent of the total qualified voters in the state.[29] Still, the potential for black political domination existed in predominate black counties located in the black belt. In 1957, Alabama voters approved by a margin of 3 to 2 a constitutional amendment to abolish or alter the boundaries of Macon County to counter any possible threat of black political domination. But faced with how to incorporate the county into surrounding counties to dilute black political power and the possibility of more calls to abolish counties, the state legislature never acted to amend the constitution.[30]

Having eliminated the black vote, the 1901 constitution still concentrated political power in the black belt and southern Alabama. The legislative apportionment of 1901 showed 105 members in the House of Representatives of the state's legislature. Alabama's upland region added some new legislators, but the black belt remained heavily overrepresented. Thirty upland counties with an aggregate white population of 588,046 were alloted forty-five representatives. In twenty-one black-belt counties with only 187,939 whites, there were thirty-nine representatives. The fifteen counties in southern Alabama with a white population of 227,867, slightly more than the black population, which voted often with the black-belt counties, had twenty-one representatives. The combined white population of these two regions was less than the white population of the upland, yet they had fifteen more representatives than the upland.[31]

The 1901 apportionment produced thirty-five state senatorial districts. The twenty-one black-belt counties and ten southern Alabama counties constituted seventeen senatorial districts. Twelve of these districts had less than 20,000 whites each. The remaining upland counties and North Central Alabama comprised eighteen senatorial districts, and not one district had less than 20,000 whites. Nine of the eighteen districts had more than 35,000 whites each. Jefferson County, the location of Birmingham, had one senator and a white population of 83,489, or 5,000 more than the combined white population of seven southern Alabama counties, which had seven senators.[32] As late as 1956, twenty-eight black-belt counties, which had only 30 percent of the state's population, had over half of the votes in the legislature. At the extreme, again, was the Birmingham area's state senator who now represented 634,000 people as opposed to black-belt senators who represented on the average only 15,000.[33] Political domination by the black belt continued until the one-man, one-vote decision of the U.S. Supreme Court in 1962.[34]

Although judicial rulings made the federal government responsible for protecting the life, liberty, property, and equal rights of citizens against interference by the states, it left to the states the power of protecting these rights from individuals' interference. These rulings gave the states the power to enforce the Fourteenth Amendment, ruling that "relief from a great political wrong, if done, as alleged, by the people of the state and the state itself, must be given by them [the states] or a legislative and political department of the government of the U.S."[35] No federal agency accepted this judicial challenge as a way to remedy political wrongs against blacks; instead, many states enforced Jim Crow law as a legitimate exercise of their powers, contributing to the development of the modern nation-state.

RACIST DISCOURSE AND THE RACIALIZATION OF SPACE

Henri Lefebvre wrote that the modern nation-state "endeavors to mold the spaces it dominates, and it seeks, often by violent means, to reduce the obstacles and resistance it encounters there."[36] Dislocation, displacement, and division are the primary means by which capitalism and its modernist cultural form (re)produce space.[37] People on the racial and economic margins are shut away as a prophylactic move, to prevent polluting and infecting the body politics. Jews were not the first to be shut away in such a space. In 1314, when Germans came to Venice to sell and to buy, the Venetians decided to concentrate them in one building, the *Fon-*

daco dei Tedeschi, the "Factory of the Germans," to make sure that they paid their taxes. The building became a model for later and more repressive spatial forms of segregation that awaited Jews and others.[38]

In Baron Haussmann's restructuring of Paris in the 1800s, the newly designed boulevards, unlike the old winding streets, made it easier for police and soldiers to move into the working-class districts where there often were outbursts of social conflict. These broad avenues permitted army wagons to travel two abreast, allowing the militia to fire into the communities lying beyond the avenues. These boulevards also became a part of the new modern space where people from different classes could encounter one another, thereby blurring the lines among classes. These encounters so disturbed the bourgeoisie that they responded with more powerful designs that excluded the poor and the working class from certain spaces. The distinction between public and private space was renegotiated according to the bourgeois notion of social life on the boulevards. David Harvey wrote,

> Public investments were organized around private gain, and public spaces appropriated for private use; exteriors became interiors for the bourgeoisie. . . . The boulevards, lit by gas lights, dazzling shop window displays, and cafés open to the street (an innovation of the Second Empire), became corridors of homage to the power of money and commodities, play spaces for the bourgeoisie.[39]

The distance between the poor and the affluent increased as working-class neighborhoods were torn down and their residents relocated in the suburbs. The bourgeoisie were left in control of the city, and they sought to colonize the entire space with their blend of culture and capital—purifying space.[40]

Blacks were shut away to provide a purified space for the more desirable whites. In 1916, the U.S. Supreme Court ruled in *Buchanan v. Warley* that racial segregation was unconstitutional. For defenders of racial segregation, however, the court had left open a "reasonable" legal defense of racial segregation. Ten years later, Birmingham passed a comprehensive racial zoning ordinance, one of the most overt expressions of white supremacy ever put into law in the twentieth century. According to Charles Connerly and Bobby Wilson, the new code "was not some aberration of planning but was consistent with the mainstream of planning thought in the U.S.," which provided much of the resources and rationale for segregating black and white neighborhoods.[41] Areas zoned for blacks were preexisting black neighborhoods that contained approximately 42 percent of all households in the city in 1930 (Figure 12.1). They were located, wrote Blaine Brownell, throughout the city "along creekbeds, railroad lines or alleys, and they suffered from a lack of street lights, paved streets and other city services."[42]

When the U.S. Supreme Court upheld the constitutionality of zoning in 1926, Birmingham officials spoke optimistically about enforcing this zoning as

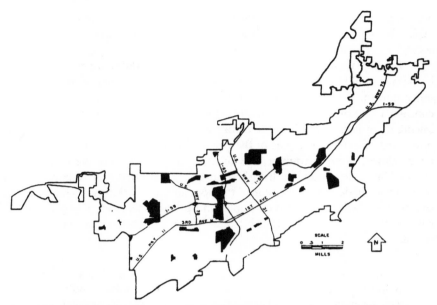

Figure 12.1 Source: Bobby M. Wilson, "Black Housing Opportunities in Birmingham, Alabama," *Southeastern Geographer* 17, no. 1 (May 1997), 49–57.

a tool to construct places along racial lines. The attorney defending the city's law noted,

> The effect of the decision is to sustain the validity of a typical zoning ordinance on all its essential features. This decision is so clearly in point as to very greatly increase the chance of Birmingham's zoning laws being upheld; it is so strong and so clearly in point that it may even have the effect of deterring anyone from testing the validity of our law.[43]

Birmingham argued that separation of the races through zoning was a proper use of police power because it protected both property value and life. Blacks were excluded from some residential areas not because of race but "solely because of the extraordinary and most exceptional injury to the public that will result from [blacks] exercising the right to live in a white residential area."[44] In other words, racial zoning prevented conflict that threatened the accumulation of capital. Birmingham argued also that its ordinance met the separate but equal test established by *Plessy v. Ferguson*:

> If the state can separate the whites and blacks in schools, on street cars and buses and in other public places, prohibit their intermarriage and biological integration outside the marriage relation, *solely* because of the harmful effect of such conduct on society, what prevents the same state from requiring whites and blacks to live in separate but equal, residential areas in Birmingham, *solely* because of the tremendously harmful effect on society of their living side by side?[45]

The ordinance did not prohibit blacks from owning property in areas zoned for whites. It only prohibited black occupancy. In defending its ordinance, the city noted that in *Buchanan v. Warley*, the municipality attempted to prevent a white property owner from disposing of his property to a black and argued,

> This attempt to prevent the alienation of the property in question to a person of color was not a legitimate exercise of the police power of the state, and is in direct violation of the fundamental law enacted in the Fourteenth Amendment of the Constitution preventing state interference with property rights except by due process of law.[46]

However, the city argued, the right to *occupy* real estate was not an absolute right protected by the constitution. Thus, the city could prohibit occupancy in the public interest and argued, in the spirit of capitalism, that property ownership has greater sanction than human rights or the right to reside where one chooses. Racial zoning did not threaten property rights, which energized the opinion that "property may be less readily subjected to restriction for the public good than liberty may be."[47] To limit property rights carried too great a price to avoid racial conflict.

The zoning ordinance thus allowed whites to own, but not occupy, properties in black neighborhoods, and absentee ownership was common in such neighborhoods. Blacks for the most part became renters, whereas whites became property and home owners—fragmenting further the working class. Due to the 1926 zoning ordinance, only 3.5 percent of the residential land zoned for blacks was owner-occupied, single-family, detached housing, compared with 61.5 percent of the land zoned for whites. Residential densities for Birmingham's black neighborhoods averaged 150 people per acre, ten times the density in white neighborhoods.[48] Blacks who could afford to move into better housing could find no neighborhoods in which they were allowed to buy or build a new house. Both of the small sections zoned by the city for black, single-family dwellings were fully occupied.[49]

True to the modern nation-state, racial zoning distinguished black communities and created sociospatial barriers to residential mobility to disempower them. Black leaders argued that confining blacks to areas with poor services made it less likely that they would remain in Birmingham, contributing to the high labor turnover in industries.[50] Zoning had been developed as a tool for rational land use planning, but it became a tool for accommodating the racial order.

Blacks who challenged the city's racial zoning faced threats, violence, and destruction of property. Bombings of black homes were so common that the city became widely known as "Bombingham." Not until the late 1940s did blacks contest the racial zoning ordinance in court, making Birmingham one of the last U.S. cities to defend such an ordinance.

In 1947, the U.S. District Court declared the Birmingham zoning ordinance unconstitutional. The city continued to enforce racial zoning nevertheless, and black property owners initiated a class action; again, the Court ruled the ordinance unconstitutional, the city appealed, and, finally, on 28 May 1951, the U.S. Supreme Court denied the city's petition for *writ of certiorari* to the Court of Appeals for the Fifth Circuit. This denial officially ended the city's racial zoning policy.[51] However, its effects on the city's social and spatial fabric continued, as de facto segregation persisted on a large scale.

NOTES

1. Ellen Meiksins Wood, *Democracy Against Capitalism: Renewing Historical Materialism* (Cambridge, Mass.: Cambridge University Press, 1995), 267.

2. Rayford W. Logan, *The Negro in American Life and Thought: The Nadir, 1877–1901* (New York: Dial Press, 1954).

3. Robin D. G. Kelley, *Race Rebels: Culture, Politics, and the Black Working Class* (New York: Free Press, 1994), 32.

4. Wood, *Democracy Against Capitalism*, 267.

5. C. Vann Woodward, *The Strange Career of Jim Crow*, 3rd ed. (London: Oxford University Press, 1974).

6. Stanley B. Greenberg, *Race and State in Capitalist Development: Comparative Perspectives* (New Haven, Conn.: Yale University Press, 1980), 285.

7. Paul A. Baran and Paul M. Sweezy, *Monopoly Capital: An Essay on the American Economic and Social Order* (New York: Monthly Review Press, 1966), 253.

8. John W. Cell, *The Highest Stage of White Supremacy: The Origins of Segregation in South Africa and the American South* (Cambridge, Mass.: Cambridge University Press, 1982).

9. Quoted in William Warren Rogers, *The One-Gallused Rebellion: Agrarianism in Alabama, 1865–1896* (Baton Rouge: Louisiana State University Press, 1970), 225.

10. Quoted in Rogers, *The One-Gallused Rebellion*, 282.

11. C. Vann Woodward, *Origins of the New South, 1877–1913* (Baton Rouge: Louisiana State University Press, 1951), 175–76.

12. Quoted in Jimmie Frank Gross, "Alabama Politics and the Negro, 1874–1901," (Ph.D. diss., University of Georgia, 1969), 204.

13. Woodward, *Origins*, 347–48.

14. Woodward, *Origins*, 211.

15. Michael Reich, *Racial Inequality: A Political-Economic Analysis* (Princeton, N.J.: Princeton University Press, 1981), 236–38.

16. Rogers, *The One-Gallused Rebellion*, 332–33. Emphasis added.

17. Quoted in Woodward, *Origins*, 218–19.

18. Woodward, *Origins*, 220.

19. William van Alstyne, "Rites of Passage: Race, the Supreme Court, and the Constitution," in *Race Relations and the Law in American History*, ed. Kermit L. Hall (New York: Garland Publishing, 1987), 564–99.

20. *Plessy v. Ferguson*, 163 U.S. 537 (1896).

21. *Plessy*, 537 (1896).

22. *Plessy*, 553.

23. *William v. Mississippi*, 170 U.S. 213 (1898).

24. Proceedings of the Constitutional Convention of Alabama, III, 2841, 2844–2845; IV, 4302–4303 (1901).

25. Quoted in Gross, "Alabama Politics," 261.

26. Jack M. Bloom, *Class, Race, and the Civil Rights Movement* (Bloomington: Indiana University Press, 1987), 48.

27. Gross, "Alabama Politics," 277.

28. Oliver C. Cox, *Caste, Class and Race: A Study in Social Dynamics* (New York: Modern Reader Paperbacks, 1970), 577.

29. "Registration of Negro Voters in Alabama in 1954," G. E. Pierce, Research Secretary, Alabama State Coordinating Association for Registration and Voting, Birmingham, Ala., unpublished paper, n.d., in Southern Research Council File 41.2.16.3.3 (Archives, Birmingham Public Library).

30. George Prentice, "Neighboring Counties Favor Boundary Change," *Montgomery Advertiser*, 18 December 1957, 1.

31. Joseph H. Taylor, "Populism and Disfranchisement in Alabama," *Journal of Negro History*, 34, no. 1 (January 1949): 410–27.

32. Taylor, "Populism," 426.

33. Hugh W. Sparrow, "Area With 30 Percent of State's People Has Over Half of Voters," *Birmingham News*, 20 May 1956, 6C.

34. *Baker v. Carr*, 369 U.S. 186 (1962).

35. *Giles v. Harris*, 189 U.S. 475 (1903); see also "The Alabama Decision," *Nation* 76, no. 1974 (30 April 1903): 346.

36. Henri Lefebvre, *The Production of Space*, trans. Donald Nicholson-Smith (Oxford: Basil Blackwell, 1991), 49.

37. Theo Goldberg, "'Polluting the Body Politic': Racist Discourse and Urban Location," in *Racism, the City and the State*, ed. Malcolm Cross and Michael Keith (London: Routledge, 1993), 45–60.

38. Richard Sennett, *Flesh and Stone: The Body and the City in Western Civilization* (New York: W. W. Norton, 1994), 228–37.

39. David Harvey, *Consciousness and the Urban Experience: Studies in the History and Theory of Capitalist Urbanization* (Baltimore: Johns Hopkins University Press, 1985), 204.

40. Harvey, *Consciousness*, 204; Scott Lash, *Sociology of Postmodernism* (London: Routledge, 1990), 35; Philip Cooke, *Back to the Future* (London: Unwin Hyman, 1990), 26–27; Chris Philo and Gerry Kearns, "Culture, History, Capital: A Critical Introduction to the Selling of Places," in *Selling Places: The City as Cultural Capital, Past and Present*, ed. Gerry Kearns and Chris Philo (Oxford, U.K.: Pergamon Press, 1993), 12.

41. Charles E. Connerly and Bobby M. Wilson, "Planning, Jim Crow, and the Civil Rights Movement: The Rebirth and Demise of Racial Zoning in Birmingham" (Paper presented at the Association of Collegiate Schools of Planning Annual Conference, 31 October 1992, Columbus, Ohio), 2, 22; see also Christopher Silver, "The Racial Origins of Zoning: Southern Cities from 1910–40," *Planning Perspectives* 6 (1991): 189–205.

42. Blaine A. Brownell, "Birmingham, Alabama: New South City in the 1920's," *Journal of Southern History* 38, no. 1 (February 1972): 28.

43. "City Zoning Law Declared Safe," *Birmingham Age-Herald*, 3 December 1926, 5.

44. United States Circuit Court of Appeals, Fifth Circuit, *City of Birmingham et al. Appellants v. Mary Means Monk et al. Appellees*, 185 F.2d 859. Brief and Argument of Horace C. Wilkinson, Attorney for Appellants (1949), 45.

45. *Birmingham v. Monk*, 54.

46. *Birmingham v. Monk*, 54.

47. "Constitutionality of Segregation Ordinances," *Michigan Law Review* 16 (1917–18): 111.

48. Bobby M. Wilson, "Black Housing Opportunities in Birmingham, Alabama," *Southeastern Geographer* 17, no. 1 (May 1977): 49–57.

49. Douglas L. Hunt, "More Facts About Negro Housing," Part I *Birmingham News*, 12 November 1947; 14; Part II, 14 November 1947, 18.

50. Connerly and Wilson, "Planning and Jim Crow," 17.

51. *Matthews v. City of Birmingham*, No. 286046 (N. D. Al., 1947); *Monk v. City of Birmingham*, 87 F. Supp. 538 (N. D. Al., 1949), reaffirmed on rehearing 185 F. 2d 859, U.S. Circuit Court of Appeals, Fifth Circuit, 1950.

13

Scientific Management and the Growth of Black/White Competition

Birmingham's planter-based regime never fully subscribed to the notion of a free and competitive labor market. Rather, it brought racism to center stage and institutionalized it for the sake of capital. Labor segmentation then resulted in a "racialized" class consciousness. Although this consciousness may have made it easier for blacks and whites to mobilize into separate collective action groups, they never saw themselves as equal partners in the same labor movement. Race was a constant social fact that barred free competition.

During Birmingham's early years, the contractural arrangement in the city's coal mines epitomized this segmentation. Workers paid at piece rates are interested in maximizing personal efficiency, even at the expense of the operator's machinery and tools. Even without a contract, free coal miners operated essentially as independent artisans, by cutting the coal in their assigned areas, blasting it loose, and loading it onto cars. The mine operator did not directly control the pace of production, but because wages were based on a piece-price system, workers could compete for control over production.[1]

Under conventional capitalist relations of production, the separation between labor and capital is cleaner. As long as Birmingham relied on petty production processes that entailed a cooperative relationship between skilled workers and employers, wrote Henry McKiven, Jr., workers "enjoyed a degree of economic, political, and social status that craftsmen in older industrial cities were rapidly losing." Elsewhere, in the 1890s and early 1900s, that relationship was increasingly strained.[2] Improvements in machinery and operating methods, which mark the maturing of industrial capitalism, made contractual and craft arrangements obsolete. According to Michel Aglietta, the restructuring of the social and technical conditions of labor meant replacing cooperation with "homogenization of labor, a spreading tendency to create more uniform working conditions among American workers."[3] This homogenization did not eliminate racial segmentation, however; it produced competition between black and white workers that reinforced segmentation.

As production reorganized, owners sought complete control over the plant. Workers resisted capitalists' attempts to increase productivity by lengthening the work day, and accumulation became dependent on transferring more knowledge from labor to management. Corporations began to practice what Frederick Taylor called "scientific management," a phenomenon that swept the United States in the second quarter of the twentieth century. Scientific management detailed how segmenting work tasks could radically increase productivity.[4] It produced a new class of experts and managers who further institutionalized labor segmentation.[5] True to the modernist cultural form, it wrested "know-how" from workers and put it within the corporation's management structure, thereby marginalizing workers, who were needed only to assemble the parts. According to David Stark, "As capitalists around the turn of the century sought to increase their output (and profits) in response to growing markets, they moved to abandon the subcontracting and helper system."[6]

This process actually started before the publication of Taylor's *Principles of Scientific Management*. It eliminated contractors in the Alabama coal mines near the turn of the century. On 10 May 1897, TCI abolished all contracting in its mines. By separating "planning" from "doing," theory from practice, skill from activity, and thought from action, scientific management stripped workers of their skills and disempowered them in the workplace, which damaged, and in some cases destroyed, working-class identity and culture.[7]

Scientific management brought legitimacy to the regime of bureaucrats and managers.[8] "Administrative" employees increased from 7.7 percent of total employment in 1899 to 18.0 percent in 1929, adding new complications to U.S. class relations. The movement for scientific management provided the basis for the appearance of a fully fledged service class in the United States between the two World Wars.[9]

The growth of a management class involved not only a struggle with workers, especially skilled craft persons, but also a contest with capital. Managers had to overcome resistance from owners or existing managers who, according to John Urry, "believed that 'scientific management' was an unnecessary expense that would undermine their own prerogatives." In testimony to the Special House Committee to Investigate the Taylor and Other Systems of Shop Management, Taylor reported that nine-tenths of the problem of carrying out "scientific management" came from existing managers, who preferred individual judgment or opinion to exact scientific investigation.[10] Eliminating this problem would also displace "aristocrats of labor," the skilled trader, to a position of much less importance. Jerry Lembcke wrote,

> [S]kill degradation created the possibility for capital to own and control in absentia, through its managers [and allowed the capitalist class to] . . . move its assets while maintaining a relatively stable existence for itself as a class. Workers, meanwhile, are pulled hither and yonder by the increasing ra-

pidity of capital's mobility, and their capacity to produce, much less reproduce, a collective culture is increasingly diminished by the last half of the twentieth century.[11]

This new mobility and replaceability of labor helped to undermine the traditional social order. According to Aglietta, the extraction of absolute surplus value had come to involve both increasing the absolute size of the working class and "a fundamental lack of differentiation between individual wage-labor units."[12] This change most affected industries that relied heavily on craft workers. Iron and steel makers sought to introduce technology that would reduce their dependence on skilled puddlers, mechanics, and rollers.[13] Coal mining was also affected, as machines replaced picks and shovels.

Over time, southern workers, like wage earners everywhere, became increasingly interchangeable elements of production, which made southern black labor compatible with the labor needs of capitalists elsewhere. New technologies combined with scientific management simplified many industrial work tasks. In 1902, Charles Schwab, a Carnegie Steel official, estimated that the company could train an agricultural worker of average intelligence to be a melter in six to eight weeks, whereas it would have taken two years to master the art of puddling.[14] Deskilling brought a marked decline in the number of skilled jobs in Birmingham's iron and steel industry during the first two decades of the twentieth century, and the number of semiskilled jobs increased. McKiven noted,

> Many skilled blacks worked as molders, an occupation that certainly did not require the level of skill it had demanded less than two decades earlier. Perhaps this deskilling lowered the stature of molding among whites, making it more acceptable to employ black molders. But workers in Birmingham still considered molding a skilled job, one that whites should therefore control. . . . Black representation in the many semiskilled positions created by technological innovation and economic expansion also increased.[15]

Reformers and supporters of industrial education no longer accepted the distinction once made between the trades and unskilled labor, the old occupational hierarchy. With deskilling, however, Birmingham's industrialists and civic leaders still recognized the need for educational institutions to upgrade the black worker. In 1900, the school board decided to build the first industrial high school for blacks.[16]

Homogenization forced southern industries to compete with northern regimes for labor. James Allen wrote that, first, in 1917, due to World War I, and again in 1922–1923, in the latter stage of the third upswing in the Kondratieff cycle, the demand for labor forced northern industrialists "to tap the hitherto practically untouched labor reservoir of the plantation country."[17] Black newspapers, some subsidized by northern capitalists, published articles encouraging the exodus of blacks from the South to work in northern industry.[18] Robert Abbott, editor of the *Chicago Defender*, was relentless in encouraging this exodus:

> The *Defender* invites all to come north. Plenty of room for the good, sober, industrious man. Plenty of work. . . . Anywhere in God's country is far better

than the Southland. . . . Come join the ranks of the free. Cast the yoke from around your neck. See the light. When you have crossed the Ohio river, breathe the fresh air and say, "Why didn't I come before?"[19]

During the War, labor agents from the North were so successful at recruiting labor from the Birmingham area that several local plants could not function properly.[20] The Birmingham regime responded by strengthening existing vagrancy laws to hold that "the burden of proof shall be upon the defendant to show that he is not a vagrant."[21] In 1912, Birmingham industrialists had already convinced the local government to raise the license tax for agents who came into the area to recruit black workers to $2,000. During World War I, coal companies convinced the city commission—over the objection of white labor unions—to raise the tax to $2,500 and also to require a $5,000 agent's bond.[22] In 1916, the city of Montgomery passed an ordinance that barred anyone from "enticing, persuading or influencing any laborer or other person to leave the city for employment at another place,"—a law similar to those that had kept former slaves from leaving the plantation after emancipation.[23] R. A. Statham of the *Labor Advocate* noted labor's opposition to such control: "When you place this outlaw tax against labor agents you are denying the negro of a privilege of seeking aid to better his condition. . . . You want him here for exploitation, and to keep labor down on the level of slavery times."[24]

Labor recruiters, like agents of the underground railroad during slavery, had to be very careful. An agent might walk briskly down the street through a group and, without gesturing, quietly say, "Anybody want to go to Chicago, see me."[25] Another agency distributed a pamphlet that declared,

> Let's go back North where there are no labor troubles, no strikes, no lockouts; large coal, good wages, fair treatment; two weeks pay; good houses; we ship you and your household goods; all colored ministers can go free; will advance you money if necessary; scores of men have written us thanking us for sending them; go now while you have a chance.[26]

Gary Kulik has argued that out-migration forced Birmingham industrialists to adopt more modern practices.[27] However, recruitment of black labor from the area did not affect the labor supply, especially not for unskilled labor. As W. David Lewis noted, despite out-migration, Birmingham's black population increased from 70,230 in 1920 to almost 100,000 in 1930, when it became the nation's eighth largest urban black population (see Table 10.1). Lewis continued, "Although large numbers of skilled black steelworkers may have migrated to northern cities, adversely affecting TCI, there remained a large pool of unskilled workers on which Sloss-Sheffield could draw."[28] The labor supply actually increased because the factors contributing to the out-migration were transitory. Large-scale migration ended when demand was satisfied. Allen noted, "The immigration law of 1924, which set low quotas, reflected the existence of a plentiful labor supply." Furthermore, the rapid rate of technological advancement in industry ensured a sufficient labor supply because it reduced demand.[29] Northern capitalists no longer needed the large black labor pool, which allowed the southern regimes a chance to survive a little longer, until the Great Depression produced permanent institutional and structural changes.

Labor homogenization made labor more mobile and helped to make a labor market, although not one market based on free competition. Rather, as race became more of a social fact, it promoted competition between groups, especially blacks and whites.[30] Eventually, large-scale migration to the industrial North produced direct competition in the North between blacks and whites for the same kinds of jobs. This competition became a chronic source of racial antagonism in the United States and led, by one account, to the outbreak of seventy-six race riots between 1913 and 1963.[31]

As white workers recognized that labor homogenization, or deskilling, had made blacks able to compete, they established artificial limits.[32] Efforts during the early part of the twentieth century to restrict black advancement came increasingly from the white working class. According to William Julius Wilson, "In this connection, then, the relationship between blacks and both working-class whites and the managers of industry seem to correspond more closely with the split labor-market theory of racial antagonism than with the orthodox Marxist explanations."[33]

The more radical racist whites terrorized blacks in nightly raids and hung and lynched them in a campaign of extermination. Williamson has argued that the southern ruling elites institutionalized segregation to protect blacks from the radical racists, especially in public accommodations.[34] Accommodating radical racists produced "horizontal segregation."[35] Protecting black workers from white workers, especially the more radical racists, later became part of a larger program of racial exclusion.[36]

Segregation, however, was not an attempt to *protect* blacks from radical racists but rather a source of security and stability for the ruling elites. Stanley Greenberg wrote, "Where commercial farmers [planter class] and dominant workers [whites] insist on the traditional race lines, businessmen will take the course of least resistance, opting for accommodation over endemic political conflict."[37] Capitalists always opted for accommodation over any political conflict that threatened the accumulation of capital. So, streetcar companies resisted enforcing segregation ordinances because of additional cost, although they eventually succumbed to pressure.[38] In Birmingham, McKiven noted, deskilling "generated considerable anxiety between white workers and the public. Because employers respected the social practices and values of the community and wanted to reduce the appeal of labor organizations, they maintained a Jim Crow system, albeit, one they controlled." McKiven goes on to note, "As early as the 1890s labor leaders, realizing that changes in the process of production could undermine union control of the racial division of work, began to look for new ways to regulate the employment of black workers."[39]

Mining companies increasingly provided separate pay booths and transportation facilities for black and white workers, and segregated seating arrangements were the rule at local union meetings and regional conventions. Richard Davis, the black United Mine Workers (UMW) official, observed that in the Alabama coal fields

> While white and colored miners worked in the same mines, and maybe in ad-joining rooms, they will not ride even on a work-train with their dirty min-ing clothes on together, nor will they in a miner's meeting sit together in a hall without the whites going to one side of the hall, while the colored occupy the other side. You may even go to the post office at Pratt City, and the white man and the colored man cannot get his mail from the same window. Oh, no, the line is drawn; the whites go to the right and the colored to the left.[40]

Birmingham's coal barons consciously played one race against the other. For ex-ample, in the coal strike of 1894, Henry DeBardeleben and the region's other coal barons threatened to permanently replace white miners with black ones.[41]

Laissez-faire race relations gradually gave way to an oligopolist mode of regu-lation that disenfranchised blacks by the end of the century. Lewis Jones noted that, although early capitalists to some extent

> took a benevolent attitude and encouraged the aspirations of competent Ne-groes who could never challenge their status, the Birmingham whites had memories of competition with Negroes for a secure place in the South and still saw in them a competitor who should not be given the least opportunity to compete.[42]

Under the oligopolist mode of regulation, to discriminate against blacks was to derive a large surplus value.[43] Growing racism would weaken even more an al-ready vulnerable labor market, making the period of laissez-faire race relations in the South transitory.

THE DECLINE OF BIRACIAL UNIONISM AND THE RECONSTRUCTION OF WORKPLACE

Workplaces were reconstructed along racial lines. The downswing in the second Kondratieff cycle and the Populists' attempt to unite poor people across racial lines convinced industrialists that they must act to avert a social revolution. In calling for a restructuring of working conditions at the turn of the century, the president of TCI noted,

> For years the authority exercised by the officers of this company over its coal mines had been growing less and less. The efficiency of the men, whether working by the day or on contract, was steadily declining and discipline had decreased with efficiency. . . . The conditions forced upon the manage-ment by the union had become intolerable. The authority over your property in their charge, as to what should constitute a fair day's work, and as to who should be employed, had to be restored and maintained, or all hope of per-

manent, successful competition with the products of other districts would have to be abandoned.[44]

In 1904, many mine operators in the Birmingham area, with a racial strategy in mind, called for open shops and rejected the existing wage scale, demanding lower pay and a return to the monthly payday. Commercial coal operators accepted the union's wage demands, but furnace operators and TCI did not, and the strike lasted twenty-six months. John Mitchell, president of the UMW, warned black workers, "If this fight was lost the colored miner would fall back to the old system in vogue a few years ago [the contract system], when he was compelled to do the work for which someone else received pay."[45] The United Mine Workers of America (UMWA) spent more than $500,000 in support of the strike, half the amount spent nationally on strike support for that year. Nevertheless, the mine operators' racial strategy proved successful. The strike failed, which proved a severe blow to the union, whose membership declined from 11,487 in 1903 to less than 4,000 in 1907.

Another strike in 1908 proved an even more severe blow to labor. Commercial operators, who had accepted union demands in 1904, asked for a 20 percent reduction in wages and the same conditions that prevailed in nonunion mines. As the strike continued, violence increased and race became a more significant factor. The governor of Alabama, an industrialist who had used convict labor, reported to UMW officials that "members of the legislature in every sector of Alabama were very much outraged at the attempts to establish social equality between white and black miners."[46] The *Birmingham Age-Herald* expressed regret at seeing "ignorant negro leaders" addressing crowds containing white workers: "As appalling as have been the murders and dynamiting growing out of the strike of the United Mine Workers in the Birmingham district, the worst thing yet done because of its far-reaching evil effect is the teaching and illustration of social equality in the mining camps."[47] In 1907, an official of TCI had characterized black employees as "shiftless, thriftless, sloppy, dirty . . . inefficient labor."[48]

According to Herbert Northrup, panicked union officials proposed to "transfer all of the Negroes out of the state and make the strike a 'white man's affair.'"[49] Speaking at a mass meeting supporting the strike, W. R. Fairley, of the national board of the UMWA, stated,

> They [operators] say that the state is overridden with hordes of negroes carrying guns with murder in their hearts. I would like to ask, if we have got those hordes in the coal mines of Alabama, who brought them here? Not the miners, but the operators, who now dare to make the charge. I would like to ask why they brought them here; they brought them here during the last strike to do what? To reduce the wages of the decent miners who were earning a living. But the hordes, as they are called, remind me of the old proverb that the worm will turn if you step too hard upon him. They didn't find that Alabama was a paradise; they didn't find they were being brought to the promised land where milk and honey flowed in abundance.[50]

It was not, however, the use of blacks as an industrial reserve army that defeated the union; it was the increasing inability to make economic and class issues paramount to race issues.[51] The ratification of the 1901 constitution, which had ensured that inability, which was a severe blow to biracial unionism. Speaking on labor's defeat, John P. White, then UMW vice president, commented,

> About 55% of the men who work in the mines of Alabama are negroes. The operators finding themselves defeated on the industrial field, resorted to drastic methods. The scenes were shifted gradually and the columns of the press began to teem with appeals to the prejudices and passions of men, and they injected the race question, claiming that the United Mine Workers of America were advocating social equality of the negro and the white man. Anyone who is a student of Dixie Land knows what effect this has upon the people of the South. . . . As everyone knows, the entire South is slumbering with that racial hatred, ready to break out in widespread conflagration. . . . Yet, it was necessary in order that the operators would not be defeated. . . . If these captains of industry . . . are able to destroy the dignity of labor and crush the hopes and aspirations of the men who toil by bringing up this ghastly specter of race hatred and social equality; then whenever a trade unionist desires improved conditions of employment; whenever he is unwilling to accept the dictations and tyranny of the employers, all that will be necessary to defeat him will be to inject the race question into the industrial cause, and that will suffice.[52]

The UMW's membership, which was half black, declined from 18,000 to only 700 between 1900 and 1910. The UMWA in Alabama struck again for higher wages in 1919 and again in 1920. Backed by state troops and the use of convict labor, TCI broke the strike and the union in Alabama, ending biracial unionism in the state for more than a decade.[53]

The UMW had a history of racial solidarity and tried to push for equality between black and white workers, but the hegemony of planter-based industrialists stopped the union from acting in accord with these principles. The 1901 constitution and the judiciary had provided TCI and other companies with the means and the mode of regulation to control the labor force and exploit racial competition for jobs. According to Jones, white supremacy

> affected all aspects of society, Birmingham [working class] whites thought about it all the time. Maintenance of it was essential to their conceptions of themselves and a measure of their well-being because they were the whites, nobodies who came from nowhere, in a situation of which they were not masters but overseers.[54]

Companies used both blacks' preoccupation with earning a living and whites' preoccupation with keeping blacks in their place. The result was social and economic injustice not only for blacks but for all workers. White workers were an instrument of domination that mediated the capital–labor relationship. De jure segregation provided a white monopoly on political and economic power that the

Birmingham regime used to segment labor and force racial competition *within* the wage-earning class and exploit this competition to extract "relative surplus value."[55]

TCI took advantage of the break in production caused by the 1904 strike to install new technologies representing the new condition of labor in coal production in Alabama. By the 1920s, Alabama miners no longer used picks and shovels, but machines that drilled holes and placed explosives and loaded coal onto shuttle cars. Finally, there came a new machine that replaced machines—the continuous miner, which, molelike, clawed coal directly from the vein and loaded it onto a conveyor.

The new methods and machines eliminated the need for considerable muscle power in mining so that mining was no longer considered "nigger work" but was in fact endowed with masculinist meaning. Michael Yarrow wrote, "Being able to do hard work, to endure discomfort, and to brave danger became an achievement of manliness."[56] Such "tough-mindedness" not only excluded women but also the black male who was not a "man." After 1920, black employment in the coal industry declined (Table 13.1).

As the homogenization of the labor process increased competition for jobs, black workers lost ground. In 1910, 64 percent of Alabama's black males were in unskilled manufacturing positions; a decade later, this proportion had increased to 92 percent, the highest percentage among southern states (Table 13.2).

The white working class, however, paid dearly for permitting the ruling class to instigate economic competition between the races. "We must not," according to Greenberg, "mistake the dominant worker's privilege as a member of the dominant section for his class position. Social status and political privilege do not necessarily translate into privilege or status in the labor market, though they may."[57] Certainly, they did not for most white workers; the prominence of race in the workplace also meant the exploitation of whites. Robert Norell tells of a U.S. Steel official, inspecting a Birmingham mill in the 1930s, who thought white workers in the skilled jobs of roller earned too much. He ordered the plant superintendent to cut the wage, adding that if the workers complained, "Tell them that we got a lot of barefooted colored men who want [those] jobs." Norrell goes on to say, "TCI management played on the insecurities of white workers to encourage opposition to change: 'If the lines of promotion are unified,' foremen warned white workers, 'these niggers are going to get your jobs.' "[58]

Table 13.1   Total Black Employment in Bituminous Coal Industry of Alabama

	1900	1910	1920	1930	1940	1950
Total miners	17,898	20,779	26,204	23,956	23,022	20,084
Blacks	9,735	11,189	14,097	12,742	9,605	6,756
Percent black	59.3	53.8	53.8	53.2	41.7	33.6

Source: U.S. Census of Population, 1900–1920; U.S. Census of Population, 1930, Vol. 4, Occupations by States, Table 11; 1940, Vol. 3, The Labor Force, Parts 2, 3, and 5, Table 20; 1950, Vol. 2, Characteristics of the Population, Alabama, Table 83.

Table 13.2   Percent of Black Males in Unskilled Manufacturing
Positions, 1910 and 1920, in Southern States

State	1910		1920	
	Total	% Unskilled	Total	% Unskilled
Alabama	32,604	64	56,384	92
Arkansas	15,718	77	22,658	76
Florida	25,492	70	34,688	70
Georgia	39,345	48	60,752	65
Kentucky	17,715	61	18,308	61
Louisiana	38,138	72	47,655	73
Mississippi	25,702	74	33,140	72
North Carolina	31,891	67	46,133	70
South Carolina	34,952	46	32,587	62
Tennessee	21,939	63	33,623	75
Texas	27,027	81	41,794	75
Virginia	39,737	68	52,109	64
West Virginia	4,207	68	4,932	64
Total	360,700	65	486,012	72

Source: Carole Marks, *Farewell—We're Good and Gone: The Great Black Migration* (Bloomington: Indiana University Press, 1991), 40–41.

Labor homogenization and deskilling that generated interest in racial segregation among white miners eventually produced massive suffering and poverty among whites in the Appalachian mining communities. Yet, whites would not join with blacks to fight exploitation. They were only too willing to obtain work, however small the income; they were "poor but proud." In 1960, almost 38 percent of white Alabamians had per-capita incomes of less than $1,500 per year. And, in 1970, more whites (93,614) than blacks (86,821) were below the poverty level, as the state became the third poorest in the United States.[59] If all blacks were poor, then this number still could not account for half of the country's poor. Although poor whites remained structurally distinct and in the majority throughout U.S. history, they somehow appeared absent or invisible. According to Andrew Hacker,

> Neither sociologists nor journalists have shown much interest in depicting poor whites as a "class." In large measure, the reason is racial. For whites, poverty tends to be viewed as atypical or accidental. Among blacks, it comes close to being seen as a natural outgrowth of their history and culture. At times, it almost appears as if white poverty must be covered up, lest it blemishes the reputation of the dominant race.[60]

Yet, throughout U.S. history, most of the poor people have been white.[61] For white labor, wrote W. E. B. DuBois, was "induced to prefer poverty to equality with the Negro . . . [and] would rather have low wages upon which they could eke out an existence than see colored labor with a decent wage." He further states,

> "There probably are not today in the world two groups of workers with practically identical [class] interest who hate and fear each other so deeply and persistently and who are so far apart that neither sees anything of common interest.[62]

Dubois's description of labor reflected the Marxian notion of a "class-in-itself." The white working class remained structurally distinct from the black working class "by fashioning identities 'not as slaves' and as 'not blacks.' "[63] The notion of a "class-for-itself" transcends racial and ethnic differences.[64] Marxists and neo-Marxists alike have been unable to subordinate race to class. Whether understood in Weberian or Marxian terms, we construct class position racially. Thus, we have the black middle class and the black underclass. Greenberg viewed the dominant wage-earning population as a "bounded working class," set off from the subordinate wage-earning population.[65]

Regardless of the color of labor, Cox sees race as "merely one aspect of the problem of the proletarianization of labor. . . . Racial antagonism is essentially a political-class conflict. The capitalist exploiter, being opportunistic and practical, will utilize any convenience to keep his labor and other resources freely exploitable."[66] Discrimination along racial lines serves the material interests of industrial capitalists, who used all of the forces of the southern race mythology to sustain the relations of production that produced surplus value but also racial violence and mass impoverishment. In Europe, a bourgeois class with few or no political or social ties to the old feudal order was the catalyst for a new economic order—industrial capitalism. In Birmingham, a bourgeois class with strong ties to the old political and social order of the planter class was the catalyst. The Birmingham regime, deeply embedded in southern planter culture, responded only briefly to changing market prices or labor demand in classical economic fashion. It was a brief period of laissez-faire race relations, a sidebar on the pages of U.S. race history, that helped to make this response possible. Segregation provided for white monopoly of political and economic power, and controlled black labor remained an integral part of the mode regulating the regime of accumulation in Birmingham. Given raw material constraints in the region, the route taken to industrialization may very well have been the most "rational technological path." For black workers, it was also the path to social and economic exploitation. Birmingham's industrialists adopted Taylor's system of management, which was not totally incompatible with traditional southern labor practices. Lewis noted,

> The firm could still recruit inexperienced African-Americans, hire fewer employees more selectively, put them on the job with minimal training, maintain low wage stales, and preserve rigid practices designed to keep black workers and white bosses in separate occupational roles. Sloss-Sheffield could thus embrace modernity and at the same time affirm its enduring commitment to southern values. . . . Mechanization notwithstanding, furnace crews were still solidly black except for supervisors, who were unvaryingly white.[67]

The race line remained. Birmingham did not easily abandon the old racial order. Again, only in South Africa's Johannesburg did a similar situation occur.

By the turn of the century, racism had so distorted the economic institutions of the South that it practically eliminated any workings of a competitive mode of regulation. State control and regulation of blacks, not the competitive market, dominated in the construction of race-connected practices. Making money required conforming to these controls and regulations that produced institutionalized racism. The material expression of this control is segregation, which "achieved a quasi-social elimination of blacks without eliminating their labor."[68]

NOTES

1. Alex Lichtenstein, *Twice the Work of Free Labor: The Political Economy of Convict Labor in the New South* (London: Verso, 1996), 128–29.

2. Henry M. McKiven Jr., *Iron and Steel: Class, Race, and Community in Birmingham, Alabama, 1875–1920* (Chapel Hill: University of North Carolina Press, 1995), 169.

3. Michel Aglietta, *A Theory of Capitalist Regulation: The U.S. Experience*, trans. D. Fernbach (London: NLB, 1979), 70; see also David Gordon, "Capitalist Development and the History of American Cities," in *Marxism and the Metropolis: New Perspectives in Urban Political Economy*, ed. William K. Tabb and Larry Sawers (New York: Oxford University Press, 1978), 25–63; and David Gordon, Richard Edwards, and Michael Reich, *Segmented Work, Divided Workers: The Historical Transformation of Labor in the United States* (Cambridge, Mass.: Cambridge University Press, 1982), 100–164.

4. Frederick W. Taylor, *Principles of Scientific Management* (New York: Harper & Brother, 1911); for a well-discussed historical treatment of scientific management, see also Harry Braverman, *Labor and Monopoly Capital: The Degradation of Work in the Twentieth Century* (New York: Monthly Review Press, 1974); Siegfried Giedion, *Mechanization Takes Command* (New York: Norton, 1948); and David Noble, *America by Design: Science, Technology and the Rise of Corporate Capitalism* (New York: Alfred A. Knopf, 1977).

5. John Urry, "The Growth of Scientific Management: Transformations in Class Structure and Class Struggle," in *Class and Space: The Making of Urban Society*, ed. Nigel Thrift and Peter Williams (London: Routledge and Kegan Paul, 1987), 80–106.

6. David Stark, "Class Struggle and the Transformation of the Labor Process: A Relational Approach," *Theory and Society* 9, no. 1 (January 1980): 101.

7. Daniel Nelson, *Managers and Workers: Origins of the New Factory System in the United States, 1880–1920* (Madison: University of Wisconsin Press, 1975), 48.

8. Timothy W. Luke, *Social Theory and Modernity: Critique, Dissent, and Revolution* (Newbury Park, Calif.: Sage Publications, 1990), 162.

9. John Urry, "Capitalist Production, Scientific Management and the Service Class," *Production, Work, Territory: The Geographical Anatomy of Industrial Capitalism*, ed. Allen J. Scott and Michael Storper (Boston: Allen & Unwin, 1986), 43–66.

10. John Urry, "The Growth," 265, 267.

11. Jerry Lembeck, "Class Analysis and Studies of the U.S. Working Class: Theoretical, Conceptual, and Methodological Issues," in *Bringing Class Back In: Comparative and Historical Perspectives*, ed. Scott G. McNall, Rhonda F. Levine, Rick Fantasia (Boulder, Colo.: Westview Press, 1991), 92.

12. Aglietta, *A Theory*, 70.

13. David Brody, *Steelworkers in America: The Nonunion Era* (Cambridge, Mass.: Harvard University Press, 1960), 27–49.

14. McKiven, *Iron and Steel*, 94.

15. McKiven, *Iron and Steel*, 122.

16. McKiven, *Iron and Steel*, 94–95, 118–21.

17. James S. Allen, *The Negro Question in the United States* (New York: International Publishers, 1936), 138.

18. Cedric J. Robinson, *Black Marxism: The Making of the Black Radical Tradition* (London: Zed Press, 1983), 295.

19. "Invites All North," *Chicago Defender*, 10 February 1917, 3.

20. Carl V. Harris, *Political Power in Birmingham, 1871–1921* (Knoxville: University of Tennessee Press, 1977), 226–27.

21. Quoted in Harris, *Political Power*, 201.

22. Harris, *Political Power*, 226.

23. Emmett J. Scott, *Negro Migration During the War* (New York: Arno Press and *The New York Times*, 1969), 76.

24. Quoted in Harris, *Political Power*, 226.

25. Scott, *Negro Migration*, 36–37.

26. Quoted in Allen, *The Negro Question*, 139.

27. Gary Kulik, "Black Workers and Technological Change in the Birmingham Iron Industry, 1881–1931," in *Southern Workers and Their Unions, 1880–1975*, ed. Merl E. Reed, Leslie S. Hough, and Gary M. Fink (Westport, Conn.: Greenwood Press, 1981), 22–42.

28. W. David Lewis, *Sloss Furnaces and the Rise of the Birmingham District: An Industrial Epic* (Tuscaloosa: University of Alabama Press, 1994), 392.

29. Allen, *The Negro Question*, 142–43.

30. Noel Ignatiev, *How the Irish Became White* (New York: Routledge, 1995), 98–99.

31. Stanley Liberson and Arnold R. Silverman, "The Precipitants and Underlying Conditions of Race Riots," *American Sociological Review* 30, no. 6 (December 1965): 887–98.

32. George M. Fredrickson, *White Supremacy: A Comparative Study in American and South African History* (New York: Oxford University Press, 1981), 229.

33. William Julius Wilson, *The Declining Significance of Race: Blacks and Changing American Institutions* (Chicago: University of Chicago Press, 1978), 83.

34. Joel Williamson, *The Crucible of Race: Black–White Relations in the American South Since Emancipation* (New York: Oxford University Press, 1984), 254.

35. Gavin Wright, *Old South, New South: Revolutions in Southern Economy Since the Civil War* (New York: Basic Books, 1986), 183.

36. Williamson, *The Crucible*.

37. Stanley B. Greenberg, *Race and State in Capitalist Development: Comparative Perspectives* (New Haven, Conn.: Yale University Press, 1980), 146.

38. Jennifer Roback, "The Political Economy of Segregation: The Case of Segregated Streetcars," *Journal of Economic History* 46, no. 4 (December 1986): 893–917.

39. McKiven, *Iron and Steel*, 114, 123–24.

40. Quoted in Herbert Gutman, "The Negro and the United Mine Workers of America: the Career and Letters of Richard L. Davis and Something of Their Meaning, 1890–1900," in *The Negro and the American Labor Movement*, ed. Julius Jacobson (Garden City, N.Y.: Anchor Books, 1968), 73–74.

41. Alex Lichtenstein, "Racial Conflict and Racial Solidarity in the Alabama Coal Strike of 1894: New Evidence for the Gutman-Hill Debate," *Labor History* 36, no. 1 (Winter 1995): 69.

42. Lewis W. Jones, "Fred L. Shuttlesworth: Indigenous Leader," in *Birmingham, Alabama, 1956–1963*, ed. David J. Garrow (Brooklyn: Carlson Publishing, 1989), 135.

43. A. Sivanandan, "Race, Class and the State: The Black Experience in Britain," *Race and Class* 17 (1976): 347–68.

44. "The History of the Tennessee Coal, Iron and Railroad Company, 1852–1932," prepared by W. B. Allen, unpublished (Archives, Birmingham Public Library, 1932), 48.

45. "President Mitchell in District No. 20: His Utterance Display Wisdom, Moderation and Firmness," *Labor Advocate*, 11 February 1905, 1.

46. Quoted in Richard A. Straw, "The Collapse of Biracial Unionism: The Alabama Coal Strike of 1908," *Alabama Historical Quarterly* 37, no. 2 (Summer 1975): 107–8.

47. Frank V. Evans, "Striking Miners Rally Near Mines at Dora," *Birmingham Age-Herald*, 8 August 1908, 1; Frank V. Evans, "The Social Equality Horror," *Birmingham Age-Herald*, 24 August 1908, 4.; see also Frank V. Evans, "Social Equality Talk Evil Feature of Strike," *Birmingham Age-Herald*, 22 August 1908, 1.

48. Quoted in Sterling D. Spero and A. L. Harris, *The Black Worker: The Negro and the Labor Movement* (New York: Athenaeum, 1968), 246.

49. Herbert R. Northrup, *Organized Labor and the Negro* (New York: Harper & Brother, 1944), 163.

50. "Eloquent Speech of W. A. Fairley Explaining the Miner Side," *Labor Advocate*, 31 July 1908, 1.

51. Spero and Harris, *The Black Worker*, 357.

52. "Vice-President White Tells Why Strike Was Called Off," *Labor Advocate*, 25 September 1908, 1.

53. Robin D. G. Kelley, *Hammer and Hoe: Alabama Communists During the Great Depression* (Chapel Hill: University of North Carolina Press, 1990), 5.

54. Jones, "Fred L. Shuttlesworth," 135.

55. Aglietta, *A Theory*, 70.

56. Michael Yarrow, "The Gender-Specific Class Consciousness of Appalachian Coal Miners: Structure and Change," in *Bringing Class Back In: Contemporary and Historical Perspectives*, ed. Scott G. McNall, Rhonda F. Levine, and Rich Fantasia (Boulder, Colo.: Westview Press, 1991), 385–410; Robin D. G. Kelley, *Race Rebels: Culture, Politics, and the Black Working Class* (New York: Free Press, 1994), 31.

57. Greenberg, *Race and State*, 276.

58. Robert J. Norrell, "Cast in Steel: Jim Crow Careers in Birmingham, Alabama," *Journal of American History* 73, no. 3 (December 1986): 676.

59. W. Flynt, *Poor But Proud: Alabama's Poor Whites* (Tuscaloosa, Ala.: University of Alabama Press, 1989) x, 358.

60. Andrew Hacker, *Two Nations* (New York: Charles Scribner's Sons, 1992), 100.

61. Cedric J. Robinson, "Race, Capitalism, and the Antidemocracy," in *Reading Rodney King/Reading Urban Uprising*, ed. Robert Gooding-Williams (New York: Routledge, 1993), 77.

62. W. E. B. Dubois, *Black Reconstruction in America* (Cleveland, Ohio: World Publishing Co., 1964), 680, 701, 700.

63. David R. Roediger, *The Wages of Whiteness: Race and the Making of the American Working Class* (London: Verso, 1991), 13.

64. John Rex, *Race Relations in Sociological Theory*, 2nd ed. (London: Routledge and Kegan Paul, 1983), 194.

65. Greenberg, *Race and State*, 276–78. The U.S. racial system also hurt white women, as black males were considered a threat not only to white males but also to the sexual purity of white women. Racism elevated white womanhood, according to David R. Goldfield, *Black, White, and Southern: Race Relations and Southern Culture, 1940 to the Present* (Baton

Rouge: Louisiana State University Press, 1990), 14, to "an exaggerated chastity, persons with no sexual feelings, delicate individuals who were not supposed to do much." One goal of the feminist movement has been to deconstruct this racist notion of white womanhood and reconstruct a new identity.

66. Oliver C. Cox, *Caste, Class and Race: A Study in Social Dynamics* (New York: Modern Reader Paperbacks, 1970), 333.

67. Lewis, *Sloss Furnaces*, 406, 423.

68. Carter A. Wilson, *Racism: From Slavery to Advanced Capitalism* (Thousand Oaks, Calif.: Sage Publications, 1996), 115.

14

The Growth of Corporate Power: The Emergence of Fordism

Most blacks in Alabama extolled the philosophy of Booker T. Washington, who sought to ally black labor with white capital. In 1895, he assured a predominantly white audience at the Atlanta Exposition that in exchange for industrial education and economic opportunities, blacks would not seek political rights; this idea became known as the "Atlanta Compromise." In 1907, Washington organized the Negro Business League, which supported the notion of a free and competitive market. He argued that individualism and the skilled, artistic professionalism that characterized the preindustrial era could improve the working status of blacks, not politics. According to Oliver Cox, these notions appealed to white supremacists for, however exalted Washington's motives,

> He declared: "We shall prosper in proportion as we learn to dignify and glorify common labor and put brains and skill into the common occupations of life. . . . No race can prosper till it learns that there is as much dignity in tilling a field as in writing a poem." Thus the white ruling class tended to agree with Washington when he advocated dignity in common labor—the doing of manual occupations efficiently and dignifiedly; that is to say, in essence, the doing of menial occupations contentedly . . . so long as Washington accepted the morality of capitalism, he had to conceive of the labor power of colored people in this fashion.[1]

Under Washington, Tuskegee Institute taught crafts with more relevance to the preindustrial than the industrial era. W. E. B. DuBois saw the university as a "paradox," teaching blacks to become prosperous and efficient when only industry and politics would free blacks economically and socially.[2]

Washington's idea of surrendering political rights for economic opportunities was doomed from the beginning because political rights and economic opportunities are inseparable. His philosophy of industrial education never considered the realities of the intensive regime of accumulation, which increasingly provided the underlying structure of the U.S. political economy at the turn of the century and never accounted for what C. Vann Woodward termed the "realities of mass production, industrial integration, financial combination, and monopoly." With fewer but larger economic units, corporate power increased, contributing to a more intensive regime of accumulation. Woodward continued,

> Since the Negro capitalist was nearly always a small capitalist, he was among the first to suffer and the last to rally under the new pressures. . . . The shortcomings of the Atlanta Compromise, whether in education, labor or business, were the shortcomings of a philosophy that dealt with the present in the past.[3]

By the turn of the century, falling rates of profit, overproduction, and underconsumption increasingly plagued capitalism in the United States, and monopolies and cartels emerged as an alternative to the competitive mode of regulation.

In 1886, the U.S. Supreme Court held that corporations were "persons" constitutionally protected by the Fourteenth Amendment—ironically, the amendment had been written in 1868 to protect the rights of freed blacks—effectively using the amendment as a means to protect laissez-faire capitalism against state intervention.[4] Thus, corporate mergers were no different from individual acquisitions of property, and corporations could do virtually anything they wanted. They were no longer special creatures of the state, but had been deemed separate and therefore private; the corporation was a natural entity. This ruling destroyed any special basis for state regulation of the corporation.[5] Charles Collins later wrote, in 1912, "It is not the negro, but accumulated and organized capital, which now looks to the Fourteenth Amendment for protection from state activity."[6]

Larger economic units can move toward financial independence by generating funds internally. The holding company that served as the initial vehicle for fusing financial and industrial capital would have been impossible without the 1886 ruling and later court interpretations. The corporation became the vehicle for the fusion of industry and finance into large monopolistic units called "finance capital" that could control key points of U.S. industry.[7]

In 1889, Birmingham industrialist Henry Fairchild DeBardeleben, whom local citizens often compared with Andrew Carnegie, had consolidated several small holdings into the DeBardeleben Coal and Iron Company, which was capitalized at $10 million (Figure 14.1). The consolidation brought under DeBardeleben's control seven blast furnaces, seven coal mines, and seven ore mines, including 900 coke ovens and several railroads and quarries. DeBardeleben exclaimed, "And every sheaf in the field rose up and bowed to my sheaf. I was the eagle and I wanted to eat up all the crawfish I could—swallow up all the little fellows, and I did it."[8]

In 1892, this firm consolidated with the Cahaba Coal Mining Company and its affiliate Tennessee Coal and Iron (TCI), thereby increasing TCI's landholdings from about 210,000 acres to 400,000 and making it the largest producer of bitu-

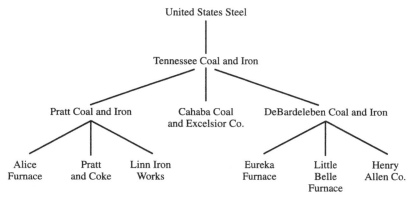

Figure 14.1 Consolidation of Birmingham's early industries.

minous coal and pig iron for the open market in the United States. According to its president, "By this very important union of interests, the three most important producers have become united instead of remaining in active competition."[9] In 1899, TCI also purchased the Sheffield Coal, Iron, and Steel Company (to eliminate, according to its president, "undesirable competition") and the Bessemer Rolling Mill. This move made Birmingham almost a one-company town.[10] In 1907, the consolidated TCI could accept an order from the Harriman Railroad for 150,000 tons of steel; TCI was, therefore, a direct challenger to Pittsburgh's U.S. Steel Corporation.

According to David Gerald Jaynes, the influence of capital and capitalists "on the industrial and employment philosophy of the developing southern mineral industries was knotted in a complicated web of profit seeking that meshed railroads, iron, and coal with the politics of state bond issues to help finance private industry and the utilization of cheap Negro labor."[11] TCI, obviously an example of this type of integration, had become one of the twelve largest U.S. firms by 1900.[12] Integration was, however, common among Birmingham firms. The proximity of the raw materials needed for iron production enabled firms such as Sloss and TCI to practice "backward integration." They obtained ownership of the mines and quarries that produced the raw materials.

TCI also practiced "forward integration" to control distribution and marketing of products that used pig iron, and Sloss sold iron directly to individual customers through its own sales department.[13] Unlike similar firms elsewhere, however, convict labor was crucial to the two companies' integration and consolidation.[14] The depression of 1893, one part of the downswing in the second Kondratieff cycle, hastened the growth of this new mode of production.

By finding more labor and new markets, the new corporate class had the power to overcome resistance from populist and working-class movements.[15] A new wave of colonialism followed. It included imperialistic adventures in the Pacific and the Caribbean that brought approximately eight million people of color under U.S. jurisdiction.[16] During this period, the United States began to replace Europe as the center of the world stage.

The rise of corporate capitalism in the United States stimulated a variety of demands for new state and national policies to curtail corporations' power. The Interstate Commerce Act of 1887 was the first in a long series of regulatory statutes. In 1890, Congress passed the Sherman Antitrust Act to maintain a competitive mode of regulation; other "progressive era" reforms included creation of the Federal Trade Commission (FTC). Some members of the corporate community favored such regulation. These members formed what Marc Allen Eisner called a "market regime" and what William Roy called the "entrepreneurial class segment" (see chapter 17), which divided the capitalist class.[17] Washington made his call for industrial education and black business development at the time of this split. As historian Benjamin Quarles stated, the program of his national Negro Business League "rested on the accepted values of the nineteenth century . . . at a time when reformers were beginning to plead for government aid in controlling aggressive monopoly, finance capitalism, exploitation of labor, and slums."[18]

However, nothing stopped the penetration of finance into industry. The Sherman Antitrust Act was too vague to halt the massive wave of corporate mergers and consolidations that occurred between 1897 and 1904. These moves were considered legal if other parties were theoretically free to enter the competition.[19] In Birmingham in the 1890s, a group of northern bankers and financiers assumed control of TCI affairs and eliminated regional control. In 1901, J. P. Morgan consolidated ten companies to produce the U.S. Steel Corporation. He said, "I like a little competition, but I like combination better. . . . Without control you cannot do a thing."[20]

A few years later, Morgan's U.S. Steel Corporation took advantage of the shortage of financial capital created by the Wall Street panic of 1907 to acquire TCI for more than $35,000,000 in U.S. bonds. U.S. Steel Corporation already controlled 60 percent of the steel production in the United States; purchase of TCI added 700 million tons to its iron ore deposits as well as two billion tons of coal and eliminated its strongest competitor in open-hearth rail production.[21] The *Birmingham Age-Herald* supported the corporation's entry into the area enthusiastically, claiming it would "make the Birmingham District hum as it never hummed before." The *Birmingham News* declared that the corporation would "make the Birmingham District the largest steel manufacturing center in the universe."[22]

Although the U.S. Steel Corporation did move its TCI subsidiary toward a more intensive regime of accumulation, it also used its monopoly power to eliminate part of Birmingham's competitive edge by charging customers at its Birmingham mills the price of steel produced at Pittsburgh plus the freight charge from Pittsburgh to the destination.[23] Pressure from southern customers forced the corporation to abandon this "Birmingham differential" pricing and, in 1909, it substituted the "Pittsburgh-plus" system, which priced steel to southern customers according to the price at Pittsburgh plus a differential of three dollars per ton and the cost of freight from Birmingham. (Birmingham boosters often blamed the U.S. Steel Corporation and the Pittsburgh-plus system for holding the city back, yet TCI had charged its southern customers on the same basis before becoming a subsidiary of the corporation. Thus, when steel bars sold for $30 a ton in Pittsburgh, they cost $37.60 when delivered to Knoxville from Birmingham or Pittsburgh, although the actual freight charge from Birmingham was only $2.60 a ton, and from Pittsburgh $7.60 a ton (additional profit for TCI).[24]

One of the first congressional investigations of the corporation's purchase of TCI occurred in 1909 before a subcommittee of the Committee on the Judiciary.[25] A 1911 investigation by the Senate Committee on the Judiciary, the Culberson Committee, reported,

> The effect and purpose of the purchase and absorption of the Tennessee company (TCI) were to monopolize the iron-ore supply of the country for manufacture, sale, and distribution among the several states and generally to eliminate the Tennessee company as a competitor in the manufacture, sale, and distribution of iron and steel products among the several States.[26]

A fifteen-month investigation by the U.S. House of Representatives Stanley Committee also concluded in 1911 that the U.S. Steel Corporation had wanted control of TCI to enter the open-hearth market with as little competition as possible; in the same year, the U.S. Attorney General sued the company.[27] In 1915, the court ruled in favor of the corporation, a ruling later upheld in the Supreme Court.[28] In 1924, the FTC outlawed the steel-pricing mechanism as a violation of the Clayton Act, which prohibited price discrimination; in response, instead of abolishing the Pittsburgh-plus plan, the corporation increased the number of bases from which it quoted prices; it abandoned this system only after considerable southern agitation in 1938.[29] None of the investigations or subsequent rulings hindered the growth and influence of TCI or other corporations. If the depression of 1893 set the stage for corporate capitalism, then the Great Depression (see chapter 15) institutionalized the corporations' hegemonic power.[30]

Although corporate power and influence increased, capitalists paid almost no attention to their workers' social/economic needs. Anything that increased the cost of living or workers' consumption norm could lead workers to demand higher wages, which would lower the rate of surplus value.[31] In the South, moreover, it would have meant higher wages for blacks, which was not permitted by a regime that based a part of its labor policy on exploiting unfree workers through the convict-lease and contractual system as well as free workers through the contractual systems. Living and working conditions in Birmingham epitomized this low consumption norm.

HOUSING AND WORKING CONDITIONS

You live in a company house
You go to a company school
You work for this company,
according to company rules.
You all drink company water
and all use company lights,

> The company preacher teaches us
> what the company thinks is right.
> —Carl Sandburg, "The Company Town"

Use of space is an integral part of the labor process of the prevalent mode of production.[32] The planter class controlled production under both slave and share-cropper systems, but the means of production differed spatially. The slave economy demanded maximum supervision as slaves worked in gangs and lived in housing grouped near the planter's residence. The sharecropper system demanded less supervision, as the plantation was subdivided into small parcels with tenant housing dispersed over the area.[33] Both slaves and sharecroppers, however, resided on plantation owners' properties. Likewise, black workers in Birmingham resided on industrialists' properties. Such spatial arrangements were a means of control.

The concentration of production that characterized the early form of industrial accumulation brought a need to house a large force of unskilled labor. Owners sought to meet this need by becoming directly involved in real estate, and many benefited from the real estate boom that Birmingham enjoyed at its inception. Meanwhile, much of the initial capital for industrial development came from profits realized from investment in land, and many of those investing in the built environment were Birmingham industrialists who organized land companies (Table 14.1). For example, in 1886, DeBardeleben and Sloss founded the Birmingham-Ensley Land Company with an initial capital investment of $450,000 and built the industrial suburb of Ensley for workers. By 1900, the great majority of blacks in Jefferson County resided in self-contained, company-built communities beyond the city limits; only 29 percent lived within the city of Birmingham (Figure 14.2).[34] Industrialists laid out housing in a rectangular grid, much as they did industrial facilities, without regard for land contours.

Table 14.1   Investments by Industrialists in the Built Environment

Land Company	Year Founded	Capital Stock	Industrialist
Ensley	1886	$10,000,000	Enoch Ensley
Birmingham Ensley	1886	450,000	Henry DeBardeleben James W. Sloss
Bessemer Land and Improvement	1887	2,500,000	Henry DeBardeleben
N. Birmingham, N. Highlands and N. Birmingham Building Association	1886	1,100,000	John and A. B. Johnston (of Georgia Pacific Railroad)
East End	1886	....	W. P. Pinckard
Leeds	1887	150,000	J. A. Montgomery
Gates City	1888	600,000	Robert Warnock
Pratt Land and Improvement	1886	....	Joseph Martin

Source: Marjorie L. White, *The Birmingham District: An Industrial History and Guide* (Birmingham, AL.: Birmingham Historical Society, 1981), 76–77.

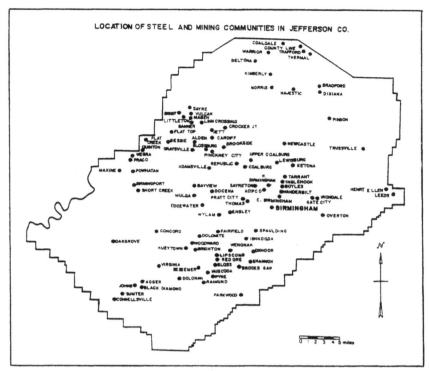

Figure 14.2   Location of steel and mining communities in Jefferson County. (Source: Marjorie Longenecker White, *The Birmingham District: An Industrial History and Guide* (Birmingham, Ala.: Birmingham Historical Society, 1981), 73.

In 1894, mine operators charged five dollars a month for one side of a cabin consisting of one room and a small kitchen. The fee for both sides was $10.[35] One turn-of-the-century lease agreement shows that workers who refused to do their assigned work were evicted from company housing. Eviction required only one day of written notice; a worker who refused to leave could be forcefully evicted without due process of law or could be obliged to pay—daily—a penalty equal to three times the rent. If the company used an attorney to evict, then the tenant paid the company's legal fees; tenants received no compensation for any improvements or repairs made to the property at their expense if the lease was cancelled.[36]

Capital invested in housing was immobile, so this arrangement made industry more dependent on locally reproduced social relations.[37] Company housing almost reproduced the social relations of the workplace, as Sandburg noted in his poem, "The Company Town." It was an appendage of the workplace. In company housing and the workplace, the company determined who had access to the community. According to Michel Aglietta, by excluding everyone but workers and family members living with them, employers could cut off workers "from individual ties of family, or bonds of neighborhood proximity or supplementary activity that [may] link them to a noncapitalist environment" (Figure 14.3).[38]

Figure 14.3   Policing company housing.

Company housing tied residents to the employer not only through work but also in life beyond the workplace, which constituted a social and spatial fabric suited to totalitarian capitalism. Workers did not even retain mastery over time beyond that given up in labor time to the capitalists. They lost their status as free workers or proletarians in the Marxian sense.[39]

Contemporary observers often hailed company housing as an improvement over rural housing or the tenements of northern industrial cities, but the quality varied considerably, ranging from hastily constructed one-room shacks to comfortable four-room houses for company officials. Workers had limited resources, so they had to accept whatever the company provided; in the Birmingham area, living conditions in company housing were extremely bad and contributed to high employee turnover. One TCI worker claimed that animals were better housed and told of cracks that "let in the moon and the snow."[40] The standard unit was a framed, single-family, two-room structure set on foundation posts with a composition-paper roof (Figure 14.4). One worker at TCI's Muscoda Camp south of Birmingham commented,

> There were no homes. Not anything you could call a home. The place here was half a wilderness, a mining camp of the worst order. The company had put up about forty-two planked shotgun houses. They charged you a dollar-and-a-half a room a month whether you lived in them or not. They simply took it off your pay. The houses were neither painted nor celled [sic], just planks knocked together.[41]

Figure 14.4   Housing in a coal mining community.

Working conditions were no better. Safe working conditions for blacks, who made up more than 50 percent of TCI's labor force, were particularly lacking. One observer described a mining camp as

> of the worst order. . . . There was no safety work of any kind. If a man was hurt, it was his look-out. . . . I've seen men go in there [the hospital] and have an arm or leg cut off as a result of an accident with the company lacking no responsibility at all. . . . [There was] a popular song that used to be sung here. . . . "Kill a mule, buy another, Kill a nigger, hire another. ". . . We had no school or churches. Sundays and paydays were days of madness and of riot and drunkenness. . . . There were always a few killings. Nobody paid any attention to them.[42]

The superintendent of another mine noted,

> There was no sanitation of any sort. The water was filthy and many "niggers" and white men died. Malaria was so common that if a man failed to show up for work, we just took it for granted that he was down with it. . . . Next to the mine office there was a dirty shack with two windows and a door that they called the hospital. . . .[43]

Of fifty cities with populations over 100,000 in 1909, Birmingham had the highest typhoid death rate, a rate of 59.7 per 100,000 population. In 1912, 8,000 cases of malaria were documented among TCI's approximately 40,000 employees and their families. The same year, working and health conditions produced accidents and illnesses so bad that miners averaged only twelve workdays per month. Alabama's per-capita appropriation for public health was less than one-fourth the national average; only Arkansas ranked lower.[44]

WELFARE CAPITALISM

The low consumption norm of Birmingham workers eventually threatened not only the workers' survival but also the interest of capitalists, who depended on a productive and loyal labor force. Rather than increase wages, however, some corporations turned to "welfare capitalism," an attempt to control labor costs by spending variable capital for social programs. Through its subsidiary, TCI, the U.S. Steel Corporation in particular launched the most comprehensive program in the region, which improved living and working conditions for thousands of citizens.[45]

TCI developed, or helped develop, approximately twenty racially segregated towns and villages within a fifteen- to twenty-mile radius of Birmingham, where 34 percent of the company's 45,000 workers resided. The most famous of these communities was Fairfield. Former President Theodore Roosevelt visited in 1911 and commended the developers: "It makes me proud, as an American, to see you and realize what you are doing and to see especially this, that you are avoiding the dreadful mistake that has so often been made of building up an industrial community where all attention was paid to machinery and none to the men."[46]

Another visitor, Jane Addams of Chicago's Hull House, noted the spatial arrangement with room left for land suited for use by children and for fresh air exercise, as well as detached houses, each with its garden spot:

> I am glad that [Fairfield] is getting away from the condition existing in Pittsburgh and other manufacturing centers—with their crowded tenements, no breathing places for the people, and tenements in which entire families live in one or two dark rooms. . . . I am glad to know that here the working man can secure desirable tenements of two, three and four rooms for a very reasonable rate. . . . We cannot build such tenements in Chicago.[47]

The company assigned a community director to each village whose task was to provide necessary community services as well as socialization that would make workers more efficient. Crawford, president of TCI, in a 1911 letter to James Farrell, president of the U.S. Steel Corporation stated,

> We have adopted as a policy the provision of better conditions of work and better conditions for our employees, and our plants are now kept neat and clean; the conditions of work have been made safer; our company houses are kept in good order, fences having been put around the yards, prizes offered

for the best kept premises and best gardens, drinking water supplies having been improved; bath houses have been erected at the mines; we have established night schools on technical subjects, lecture courses in the coal mines; furnished technical literature for libraries; and altogether we are taking an interest in the comfort and happiness of our employees during working hours and outside of working hours and, while we do not expect gratitude from them for this, we do expect that it will make it easier for us to secure the kind of labor that we want, and that the labor will be in condition to do better work. As a result, we are now getting the best labor in this district.[48]

Crawford goes on to describe the welfare program as a "very profitable investment," giving it credit for reducing labor turnover from 400 percent in 1912 to 145 percent by 1919 and to 13.3 percent by 1929. Because good municipal services were generally lacking in the rural south, a comprehensive welfare program could overcome the strong ties that bound many workers to the rural community and mold them into an efficient urban industrial labor force. Average number of days worked per month increased from 12 in 1912 to 18.3 in 1913, as working and health conditions improved and as workers accustomed to the task-oriented environment of the rural south adjusted to the more structural requirements of industrial capitalism. Whites, however, worked an average of 20.5 days, and foreign-born workers, 20.4. Blacks worked only 16.6 days.[49] It is not that blacks were less interested in working. Their ties to the rural communities were often stronger than that of whites, but absenteeim, which southern racist ideology defines as ineptitude, laziness, and shiftlessness, may also have been a form of informal resistance to racism that blacks continued to face in the workplace.[50]

The company-housing arrangement and welfare capitalism isolated workers and created a mode of living suitable to corporate capitalism.[51] Woodward credits this isolation with making black workers into efficient miners and "a stable bulwark against unionism."[52] Historians Ray Marshall and Paul Worthman also noted that the welfare program gave blacks a reason not to seek union membership, which they were already being denied.[53] Qualitative efficiency in the production process was maintained through the welfare program, which—like the sharecropping and crop-lien systems—made labor more controllable and dependent on the company.

Some companies initially resisted implementing such programs. At Sloss-Sheffield, which had policies still rooted in planter culture, according to John Fitch of the *Pittsburgh Survey*, working and housing conditions were "an abomination of devastation." Fitch also noted the opinion of the company president, Colonel John C. Maben, that any upgrading of conditions would be viewed as "coddling workmen," which threatened control over labor.[54]

Many employers, including Sloss, eventually embraced some form of welfare capitalism as the country entered the corporate phase of capitalist development. Unions, however, argued that there would be no need for such programs if companies provided decent wages, and that higher wages would also produce a larger tax base and, therefore, permit better public services.

NOTES

1. Oliver C. Cox, *Caste, Class, and Race: A Study in Social Dynamics* (New York: Modern Reader Paperbacks), 342–43, 344.

2. W. E. B. DuBois, "Federal Action Programs and Community Action in the South," *Social Forces* 19, no. 3 (March 1941): 375–80. Later, in *The Autobiography of W. E. B. Dubois* (International Publishers, 1968), DuBois admitted that his theory did not absolutely contradict Washington's. He acknowledged that neither he nor Washington had "understood the nature of capitalist exploitation of labor, and the necessity of a direct attack on the principle of exploitation as the beginning of labor uplift" (237). Those who argue that Washington deemphasized political rights for economic opportunities should note that he made a concerted effort to convince delegates to the Alabama constitutional convention not to disenfranchise blacks.

3. C. Vann Woodward, *Origins of the New South, 1877–1913* (Baton Rouge: Louisiana State University Press, 1951), 366–67.

4. The white working class is the most recent group to look to the Fourteenth Amendment. Corporate downsizing and relocation to countries where labor is less expensive reduced job opportunities in the United States during late-twentieth-century capitalism. Instead of attacking the root of this problem, white workers claim it is the result of reverse discrimination and call on the Fourteenth Amendment in attacking affirmative action programs.

5. *County of Santa Clara v. Southern Pacific Railroad*, 116 U.S. 138, 1132 (1886); Morton Horwitz, *The Transformation of American Law, 1870–1960* (New York: Oxford University Press, 1992), 65–107. Don Mitchell argued that corporations are creatures of the state, and thus can be regulated, in "State Restructuring and the Importance of Rights-Talk," in *State Devolution in America: Implications for a Diverse Society*, ed. Lynn A Staeheli, Janet Kodras, and Colin Flint (Thousand Oaks: Sage Publications, 1997), 118–38.

6. Charles W. Collins, *The Fourteenth Amendment and the States* (Boston: Little, Brown, 1912), 47.

7. Rudolf Hilferding, *Finance Capital* (London: Routledge and Kegan Paul, 1980), 21.

8. Ethel Armes, *The Story of Coal and Iron in Alabama* (Birmingham, Ala.: Chamber of Commerce, 1910), 239–42, 268–78, 335, 339.

9. "The History of the Tennessee Coal, Iron and Railroad Company, 1852–1932," prepared W. B. Allen, unpublished (Archives, Birmingham Public Library, 1932), 27.

10. "History," 38.

11. Gerald David Jaynes, *Branches Without Roots: Genesis of the Black Working Class in the American South, 1862–1882* (New York: Oxford University Press, 1989), 269.

12. Jaynes, *Branches Without Roots*, 270.

13. W. David Lewis, *Sloss Furnaces and the Rise of the Birmingham District: An Industrial Epic* (Tuscaloosa: University of Alabama Press, 1994), 225.

14. Alex Lichtenstein, *Twice the Work of Free Labor: The Political Economy of Convict Labor in the New South* (London: Verso, 1996), 95.

15. William G. Roy, "The Organization of the Corporate Class Segment of the U.S. Capitalist Class at the Turn of This Century," in *Bringing Class Back In: Contemporary and Historical Perspectives*, ed. Scott G. McNall, Rhonda F. Levine, and Rick Fantasia (Boulder, Colo.: Westview Press, 1991), 142.

16. C. Vann Woodward, *The Strange Career of Jim Crow*, 3rd ed. London: Oxford University Press, 1974), 72; see also Anthony R. de Souza, "To Have and to Have Not: Colonialism and Core-Periphery Relations," *American Geographical Society's Focus* (Fall 1986): 14–19.

17. Marc Allen Eisner, *Regulatory Politics in Transition* (Baltimore: Johns Hopkins University Press, 1993), 47–72; Roy, "The Organization."

18. Benjamin Quarles, *The Negro American* (Glenview, Ill.: Scott, Foresman & Co., 1967), 346.

19. Edward S. Greenberg, *Serving the Few: Corporate Capitalism and the Bias of Government Policy* (New York: Wiley, 1974), 96–97.

20. Quoted in Fortune, *U.S.A., the Permanent Revolution* (New York: Prentice-Hall, 1951), 76.

21. "Steel Corporation Acquires Tennessee Coal and Iron Co.," *The Wall Street Journal*, 7 November 1907, 3; "What U.S. Steel Has Acquired In the Purchase of T.C. 4I.," *The Wall Street Journal*, 8 November 1907, 2; see also Justin Fuller, "History of the Tennessee Coal, Iron, and Railroad Company, 1852–1907" (Ph.D. diss., University of North Carolina at Chapel Hill, 1966), 162–63; Marlene Hunt Rikard, "An Experiment in Welfare Capitalism: The Health Care Services of the Tennessee Coal, Iron and Railroad Company" (Ph.D. diss., University of Alabama, 1983), 46–47.

22. Quoted in Armes, *The Story*, 520–21.

23. Fuller, "History," 121–67; Rikard, "An Experiment," 27–29.

24. Victor S. Clark, *History of Manufactures in the United States* (New York: McGraw-Hill, 1929), 62.

25. Hearings Before a Subcommittee of the Committee on the Judiciary Relating to the Absorption of the Tennessee Coal, Iron and Railroad Company by the United States Steel Corporation (Washington, D.C.: Government Printing Office, 1909).

26. Absorption of the Tennessee Coal and Iron Co., 62nd Congress, 1st Session, Senate Document 44, Serial 6101 (Washington, D.C.: Government Printing Office, 1911), 22.

27. Hearings Before the Committee on Investigation of United States Steel Corporation, House of Representatives, 1911.

28. *United States v. United States Steel Corporation*, 251 U.S. 417, 1920.

29. Betty Hamaker Mullins, "The Steel Corporation's Purchase of the Tennessee Coal, Iron & Railroad Company in 1907" (M.A. thesis, Samford University, Birmingham, Ala., 1970), 86.

30. As Earl Ofari, in *The Myth of Black Capitalism* (New York: Monthly Review Press, 1970), 63, wrote in 1970, black businesses "never will be able to compete on the same level with the American corporate structure. Building a black Westinghouse or U.S. Steel is completely out of the question at this time."

31. David Harvey, *Consciousness and the Urban Experience: Studies in the History and Theory of Capitalist Urbanization* (Baltimore: Johns Hopkins University, 1985), 44.

32. Harvey, *Consciousness*, 44; David Harvey, *The Urban Experience* (Baltimore: Johns Hopkins University Press, 1989).

33. George A. Davis and O. Fred Donaldson, *Blacks in the United States: A Geographical Perspective* (Boston: Houghton Mifflin, 1975), 115–26.

34. Only West Virginia had more miners living in company housing than Alabama.

35. "How Miners Are Fleeced," *Labor Advocate*, 9 June 1894, 1.

36. House Lease of the Tennessee Coal and Iron Company, among ten printed documents compiled by Marlene Hunt Rikard, "The Black Industrial Experience in Early Twentieth Century Birmingham" (Birmingham: Alabama Center for Higher Education, 1979).

37. Kevin R. Cox and Andrew Mair, "Locality and Community in the Politics of Local Economic Development," *Annals of the Association of American Geographers* 78, no. 2 (June 1988): 307–25.

38. M. Aglietta, *A Theory of Capitalist Regulation: The U.S. Experience*, trans. David Fernbach (London: NLB, 1979), 154; see also House Lease in Rikard, "Black Industrial Experience."

39. Henri Lefebvre, *The Production of Space*, trans. Donald Nicholson-Smith (Oxford, U.K.: Basil Blackwell, 1991), 318–19.

40. Quoted in Marlene Hunt Rikard, "George Gordon Crawford: Man of the New South" (M.A. thesis, Samford University, Birmingham, Ala., 1971), 21.

41. Quoted in Rikard, "An Experiment," 48.

42. Quoted in Rikard, "An Experiment," 48–49.

43. Quoted in Rikard, "An Experiment," 131.

44. Rikard, "An Experiment," 131–32, 167.

45. Lewis, *Sloss Furnaces*, 296; George Brown Tindall, *The Emergence of the New South: 1913–1945* (Baton Rouge: Louisiana State University Press, 1967), 100.

46. Quoted in Rikard, "George Gordon Crawford," 28.

47. Jane Addams made these comments while attending the Child Labor Conference in Birmingham, 9–11 March 1911.

48. "History," 68–69.

49. Rikard, "An Experiment," 170.

50. In *Race Rebels: Culture, Politics, and the Black Working Class* (New York: Free Press, 1994), 4, Robin D. G. Kelley notes, "A lot of black working people struggled and survived without direct links to the kinds of organizations that dominate historical accounts of African American or U.S. working-class resistance." Absence from the workplace could be such a struggle.

51. James O'Connor, *Accumulation Crisis* (Oxford, U.K.: Basil Blackwell, 1986), 172; Gavin Wright, *Old South, New South: Revolutions in Southern Economy Since the Civil War* (New York: Basic Books, 1986), 170; for a comprehensive discussion of welfare capitalism, see Stuart D. Brandes, *American Welfare Capitalism, 1880–1940* (Chicago: University of Chicago Press, 1976).

52. Woodward, *Origins*, 364.

53. F. Ray Marshall, *Labor in the South* (Cambridge, Mass.: Harvard University Press, 1967), 74; Paul B. Worthman, "Black Workers and Labor Unions in Birmingham, Alabama, 1897–1904," *Labor History* 10, no. 3 (Summer 1969): 404.

54. John A. Fitch, "Birmingham District: Labor Conservation," *Survey* 27, no. 14 (6 January 1912): 1532.

15

The Great Depression and the Transformation of the Planter Regime

Mass production expanded during the 1920s as capitalists installed the new technologies of Fordist mass production. For one manufacturing establishment, 4,664 worker hours were required to build a car in 1912, but by 1923 only 813 worker hours were required.[1] W. David Lewis noted,

> Conditions were ripe in the postwar era for such effort; not only in the South but throughout the nation as a whole, manufacturing firms were achieving significant productivity gains. Investment capital was available at low interest rates, and the cost of equipment was declining relative to that of labor, inducing managers and owners to adopt new technologies to increase efficiency.[2]

Tennessee Coal and Iron (TCI), the U.S. Steel (USS) facility subsidiary in Birmingham, is an excellent example of this expansion. Its output of iron and steel was at such high levels by the late 1920s that New York financial experts called the city the "Pittsburgh of the South." During World War I, the company had invested $11 million in Fairfield Works, a massive new facility at Fairfield to supply steel for ship building at Mobile. This facility remained in operation after the war to make and repair railroad cars. In 1926, TCI built the first steel sheet mill in the South; in 1928, two new blast furnaces and sixty-three new byproduct coke ovens went into operation at Fairfield Works; in 1930, U.S. Steel invested $25 million and overhauled several mills in the Birmingham area. Such investments decreased dependence on inexpensive labor. Even Sloss-Sheffield began to modernize; in 1928, the company abandoned many antiquated facilities and by 1931 had completely mechanized its pig casting. Lewis noted that technically oriented executives held greater power than ever before.[3]

Workers gained little or nothing from increases in productivity, however. Wesley Mitchell in a review essay of these economic changes published in 1929 noted that in the manufacturing sector alone more than 825,000 blue-collar workers were let go between 1920 and 1927. Of the workers laid off by factories, 585,000 had to take up other occupations, leaving only 240,000 unemployed in the manufacturing sector. The net increase of unemployment for the whole nonagricultural economic sector exceeded 650,000 people. Although there had been an increase of 5.1 million employees in the nonagricultural sector between 1920 and 1927, the expansion of business, particularly the miscellaneous and mercantile occupations, made places for only 4.5 million new wage earners, which did not equal the number of new workers plus the old workers who had been displaced.[4] Employment declined and wages diminished in relation to production, setting the stage for the Great Depression. As Fordist technology spread, the price of constant capital (i.e., machinery) declined 50 percent relative to the price of labor during the first ten years after World War I. As a result of this decline, the ratio of constant capital to variable capital in manufacturing production increased by one-third, but factory employment declined about 6 percent.[5] More than 2.5 million jobs disappeared. As the depression worsened, the index of manufacturing employment, adjusted for seasonal variation, fell from 108 in August 1929 to 61 in July 1931, a 43 percent decline.[6] Hugo Black, a U.S. senator from Alabama during the depression and later a Supreme Court justice, expressed the problem succinctly:

> Throughout all the years the excuse for machinery has been that it would relieve human beings from the drudgery and slavery of long hours of constant toil. . . . With the use of machinery and efficiency we can produce . . . more than we can sell at home. . . . Instead of the advantage of improved machinery going to consumers and the men who work, it has gone to increase the tolls of those who own the plants; and they have built them and over-built them until they find themselves crucified on their cross of greed and unable to sell their product because they have robbed the laborer of the ability to purchase.[7]

Historically, the South, with its more extensive regime of accumulation, had produced at a level lower than the North, and its consumption norm had also been lower. As Fordist technology spread and competition between wage laborers increased, the worker's wage diminished as a portion of the value of products produced, contributing to the Great Depression. When coal mine operators used machines, they demanded a large wage differential between machine mining and pick-and-shovel mining. At one Birmingham mine area, the value of machine labor was set at seven to ten cents less per ton of coal; that is, the wage distributed to miners was seven to ten cents below the rate at that time. At the joint convention of the Alabama Coal Operators Association and the United Mine Workers of America in 1903, operators demanded a differential of 14.88 cents between pick mining and the air or punching machine and 18.81 cents with the chain or electric machine. The owner's rationale was that increased tonnage produced with machines meant the wage earner was adequately compensated and that the differential was needed to help pay for the depreciation of the machines.[8]

U.S. workers' wages, as a portion of the value of production, got increasingly smaller as capitalists made use of Fordist technology, appropriating even more of the working day as surplus value. In 1890, U.S. workers received $2.22 of every $10 worth of finished products, a surplus rate of more than 300 percent for the owners of production; by 1900, workers were receiving only $1.77, 17.7 percent of what their labor produced, which represented a surplus rate of more than 460 percent for the capitalists.[9] During the depression, the average wage declined from $28 per week in 1929 to $17 in 1932, and total aggregate income declined from $82 billion to $40 billion.[10]

The result was that labor could buy only a small, and decreasing, share of what it produced, a situation that contributed to the overproduction that produced the economic depression. Under the free market system, wages with high buying power are not expected. Labor is a commodity to be hired or bought for the lowest possible price; and, with the industrial reserve army of unemployed, labor organizations were ineffective in appreciably raising the wage scale, so consumers' buying power remained low. Low demand forced corporations to cut production, lowering their income from $11 billion in 1919 to $2 billion in 1928.[11] In 1929, the U.S. economy had the technological capacity to produce about $135 billion dollars worth of goods and services, but it could consume only about $94 billion worth of goods and services.[12] The USS corporation operated at 90.4 percent capacity in 1929 and at 17.7 percent in 1932; earnings declined 98.5 percent between 1929 and 1931, and in 1932, the company reported a loss of more than $70 million. In the nation as a whole, the total number of manufacturing establishments declined by one-third between 1929 and 1933. During this period, manufacturing output fell in value by more than 70 percent in Birmingham, compared with 50 percent in Atlanta and New Orleans.[13]

Construction activity also declined during those years, another indicator of worsening economic conditions.[14] The city's budget declined 35 percent between 1929 and 1935, which meant a reduction in both the number of public employees and their salaries. Industrial employment in Birmingham decreased by 52 percent between 1930 and 1933, and retail employment fell by one-third.[15] In 1933, TCI reduced weekly wages 50 to 75 percent and threatened to dismiss workers who questioned the policy.[16]

Birmingham was so strapped that President Franklin D. Roosevelt called it the city hit worst by the depression. Half of all families on relief in the state lived in the Birmingham area. In 1932, George Huddleston, a member of Congress from Birmingham, testified before the U.S. Senate relief committee that not more than 8,000 of Birmingham's 108,000 wage earners received their normal wages and 25,000 lacked work at all.[17]

Workers seeking economic assistance in Birmingham steadily increased, peaking at more than 33,000 cases by July 1933. Each involved several individuals, so that 25 to 35 percent of the city's population was receiving assistance, well in excess of ratios in either Detroit (8.5 percent) or New York City (15.5 percent).[18] Total black employment in Birmingham declined 30 percent during the depression. One contemporary researcher found, "At the height of the depression nearly 75 percent of blacks in Birmingham were without work."[19] Absentee owners made things worse, as they were reluctant to invest scarce capital in a location where they had no direct social ties. Congressman Huddleston argued for federal taxation as a means of redistributing income:

> There is plenty of political unrest in Birmingham. My people are desperate. They're in an agony of distress and starvation. They are likely to do anything. They have almost lost the power of reasoning. The situation is full of dynamite. There is intense resentment against everybody in public office. We are all to blame for the depression and all of us—the whole nation—should and must pay for it. It is unfair to make a local community like Birmingham, whose industries are largely owned in distant financial centers, try to take care of its own relief problems. There are, for instance, hundreds of railroad men out of work, some of them for two years, yet no railroad company contributed a cent to our local Community Chest. . . . How are we going to force these people to pay back part of the money they take from our people, except through Federal taxation?[20]

The Great Depression created, according to David Harvey, a whole style of thinking "in which questions of production and fundamental class relations were held in abeyance, a constant backdrop to a foreground of quite different political and economic concerns."[21] This thinking affirmed the government's responsibility for managing the economy and initiated the era of the Keynesian welfare state. The potential for high rates of accumulation produced the need for public works and social welfare programs. In Franklin D. Roosevelt's inaugural address, he called for putting people to work by "direct recruiting by the Government itself, treating the task as we would treat the emergency of a war."[22]

The Fordist regime became closely linked to the form and function of the Keynesian welfare state. Welfare programs and investment in housing, education, and health care expanded tremendously. This investment allowed labor to consume more, thereby sustaining an intensive regime of accumulation. In a 1938 study of the manufacuring sector, Frederick Mills found that although 51 percent of the decline in man hours worked was directly related to a fall in production, 49 percent was tied to rising productivity and labor displacement.[23] Thus, the integration of the worker as both producer and consumer became the signature of the Fordist-Keynesian welfare regime. The worker relinquished power over the labor process (i.e., the fight over the length of the working day) in return for higher wages and easy consumer credit to participate in the Fordist consumption norm.[24]

With welfare increasingly a state responsibility, capitalists felt no need to provide social benefits for their workers. In 1933, when the Federal Emergency Relief Administration (FERA) began functioning, TCI's president of intracompany communication stated, "We are contributing our proportion of the tax money which is being used to provide this relief and it's unfair for our employees to ask us to duplicate this expenditure by giving them direct relief."[25] The company dismantled its community service division; all community workers and directors were eliminated by 1946. On 15 August 1951, the company donated its hospital and dispensaries to a private foundation.

The welfare state also subsidized a large part of housing consumption. Construction activity collapsed with the depression, and the federal government sought ways to restore the demand for housing. One method was to provide more housing opportunities, and the provision of needed housing became a growing government responsibility. The Housing Act of 1934 was as significant as the Homestead Act of 1862; it produced the Federal Housing Administration (FHA), which subsidized a significant part of housing consumption by insuring mortgages, an area that had had little governmental presence before the depression. Financial institutions had protected themselves by requiring down payments of from one-half to one-third the price of the house and offering three- to five-year mortgages; with FHA insurance, banks were willing to lend 90 to 95 percent of the purchase price for terms of twenty to thirty years.

As the state's role in housing increased, TCI also withdrew from providing company housing. The number of houses owned by TCI declined 20.7 percent between 1935 and 1941 and, by the end of World War II, only 10 to 15 percent of its labor force lived in company housing, compared to almost half at the turn of the century. In 1950, the company sold eight of its villages to John W. Galbreath and Company of Ohio for $5,052,000. The average selling price of these houses was more than $3,000 amortized over twenty-five years, which provided an average monthly payment of $15 in 1950.[26] The Fordist regime also considered company housing near mines and mills a liability and not an asset. The proximity of housing to factories interfered with the firms' freedom of location and with the vertical integration of production activities in single sites, which had been made possible by Fordist technology.[27]

Thus, the labor process was linked to a separation between workplace and residence. It was in this context that FHA financing built much of the country's suburbs, totally reshaping much of the urban United States to fit the consumption norm of Fordism. The mass-produced tract housing that characterized working-class suburban communities and the automobile that provided transportation revealed the intimate relationship between the production process and the mode of consumption. Increasing distance between workplace and residence and the elimination of company housing diffused labor's discontent. It socialized part of the costs of the reproduction of labor power and facilitated the mobility of labor.[28]

Social reformers had played into the hands of Fordist capitalists by calling for working-class housing to be located away from industrial areas. This call had also contributed to the destruction of working-class identity and culture. As Stanley Aronowitz noted, the space of Fordism "deprived labor of one of the crucial preconditions of its power—industrial concentration. When large numbers of workers share the same, or similar conditions of work and neighborhood life, the means of communications are better."[29]

The rise of the Keynesian welfare state disrupted privatist regimes in Birmingham and elsewhere; these regimes had resisted state efforts to provide direct assistance. During a period of erratic and unorganized politics, these regimes attempted to placate aggrieved citizens and yet maintain the cooperation of the business and commercial elites.[30] A Birmingham official noted, "We do not favor federal appropriation to help local governments in meeting their emergency relief burdens. We believe that this is a matter to be handled locally and that the federal government has troubles sufficient of its own to engage fully its attention."[31] Needy Birmingham citizens had relied on the Community Chest, a consortium of civic organizations established in 1923 that provided assistance as early as 1927, when it detected significant increases in the number of applicants for relief.[32]

Nevertheless, the Fordist-Keynesian welfare regime produced new policies and institutions to regulate land, labor, and capital. The regime promoted industrial stability by carrying out government-supervised industrial self-regulation. According to Marc Allen Eisner,

> Organized industry actors (e.g., trade associations, labor unions, and agricultural commodity groups) formulated agreements designed to prevent deflation and maintain a base level of output without simultaneously stimulating competition. Thus there was, in essence, a government-sponsored system of cartelization on a sectoral basis.[33]

In the process, the class struggle was somewhat altered. As the state took on greater social and economic responsibilities for managing the economy, the class struggle no longer entailed just conflict between workers and capitalists; it also came to include conflict between the state and workers.

The two major pieces of the New Deal legislation—the Agricultural Adjustment Act and the National Industrial Recovery Act—created a system of supervised self-regulation designed to increase profits above the level that would have been possible under a market or competitive mode of regulation.[34] More important, they restructured the southern political economy away from the planter-based regime toward a more modern form of industrial capitalism. They also forced corporations and workers to form associations; where these associations did not exist, the government created them and vested them with significant public authority. The agricultural regulatory system placed a premium on large farms as well as farm associations that excluded blacks and tenant farmers in the South.

THE NEW DEAL AND SOUTHERN AGRICULTURE: AN AMERICAN ENCLOSURE MOVEMENT

The New Deal's economic and social transformation of the South was crucial to blacks. From 1870 to 1940, there was a net out-migration from the South of two million blacks; in the decade that followed implementation of the New Deal, the 1940s, net out-migration was 1.6 million.[35] The out-migration induced by northern industry's pull for labor in World War I reflected a transitory situation; it did not transform the South's neoplantation economy.[36] During the depression, 30 percent of the rural farm population in the South was black, and nearly 50 percent of southern blacks were still working in farming and related occupations. Almost 80 percent of the South's black farm operators were tenant farmers, and nearly 60 percent of these black tenant farmers were sharecroppers who worked for the planter class.[37] The New Deal jeopardized this arrangement, wrote James Allen: "Relief projects reduced dependency; labor standards raised wages; farm programs upset landlord–tenant relationships; government credit bypassed bankers; new federal programs skirted county commissioners and sometimes even state agencies."[38]

The greatest threat to the neoplantation economy came from the New Deal's Agriculture Adjustment Act (AAA), which created, according to Eisner, "a system of supervised self-regulation designed to increase farm incomes above the level that would have been possible under market conditions."[39] The AAA (re)produced scarcity to stabilize farm prices: farmers were paid a subsidy to reduce the amount of their acreage used for production. This reduction affected cotton acreage in the South by 53 percent, and the bulk of the benefits went to the biggest, most prosperous farmers, large land owners, and planters. The act required planters to share subsidies with their sharecroppers in the same proportion as proceeds from harvested crops, normally one-third to one-half, but wage-laboring farm workers received no portion of the subsidy. Clearly, planters stood to gain financially if they could reduce sharecroppers to the status of foot-loose wage laborers; in other words, AAA policies offered economic incentives for displacing tenants and cash to pay wages during peak labor periods. Arthur Raper wrote, "Many tenants are being pushed off the land while many others are being pushed down the tenure ladder, especially from cropper to wage-hand."[40] Between 1935 and 1940, wage earners increased by 50 percent, making the southern agricultural productive process more capitalistic.[41] In addition, because reducing acreage also reduced the need for tenant operators, many planters refused to sign tenant contracts. In the South, the total number of tenant farm operators declined from 1,449,295 in 1940 to 380,946 in 1959, a 73.7 percent decline; for black tenants the decline was almost 80 percent. Of the total number of tenants that were sharecroppers, the decline was almost 78 percent; for black sharecroppers, 75 percent. For Alabama alone, the trend was similar (Table 15.1).

In Arkansas, the planters' actions produced a revolt among sharecroppers that led to the formation of the Southern Tenant Farmers' Union in 1934. The union

Table 15.1 Tenant Farm Operators, 1940–1959

	1940	1959	% Decrease
South			
Tenant	1,449,295	380,946	73.7
Black	680,266	143,464	78.9
Cropper	541,291	121,037	77.6
Black	299,118	73,387	75.5
Alabama			
Tenant	136,244	32,228	76.3
Black	57,651	15,933	72.4
Cropper	41,370	16,618	59.8
Black	19,334	7,081	63.4

Source: 1940 Census of Agriculture; 1945 Census of Agriculture, volume 2, General Report; *1959 Census of Agriculture*, General Report.

worked to resist sharecropper evictions, violations of AAA contracts, and general mistreatment of tenants. Alabama's sharecroppers also organized union locals in several black-belt counties, where membership reached a high of 8,000. The union did little for landless tenants, however. Planters resented the idea of a share-croppers' organization, especially an interracial one, and threatened, beat, and arrested sharecroppers who were members.[42]

The Keynesian welfare state supported the Fordist regime's goal of integrating workers as both producers and consumers with measures such as the 1938 Federal Labor Standards Act. This support set the stage for higher wages in the South, where very low wages had long attracted industry.[43] The increased mobility of southern labor (caused in part by increased reliance on wage labor) also forced southern capitalists and planters to pay higher wages, although not as high as those outside of the region. The amount paid for picking 100 pounds of cotton went up 211 percent between 1940 and 1945.[44]

Although income in the South, especially for blacks, continued to lag behind that for the United States as a whole, the rate of increase was higher and tended toward convergence with other regions in the long term. For example, between 1953 and 1974, the median income of black families in the South doubled, from $3,350 to $6,730, compared to an increase from $4,547 to $7,808, or 72 percent, for the country as a whole; white median income in the South increased from $6,855 to $12,050, 76 percent, compared to an increase from $8,110 to $13,356, or 65 percent, for the country as a whole.[45]

The increasing cost of labor and New Deal policies pushed the South to accept the notion of an intensive regime of accumulation and to become more integrated into the national economy. Higher wages encouraged the planter class to turn increasingly to mechanization. New Deal agricultural policies, particularly price supports, promoted that transition by providing the dependable and stable income needed to mechanize. For the first time since the Civil War, southern farmers were given the option to substitute capital for labor on a large scale, and they chose to do so. In the 1930s, southern farmers purchased 96,645 farm tractors. Despite war time shortages, the number of purchases almost doubled between 1940 and 1945, increasing from 10,577 to 21,077 tractors. During this period, the number of farms purchasing tractors for the first time increased from 7,905 to 14,611, an 85 percent increase. In the decade after World War II, the number of tractors in Alabama's black belt increased by almost 200 percent and, during the 1960s, it increased by 40 percent.[46] The percentage of cotton harvested mechanically in the South increased from only 6 percent in 1949 to 78 percent by 1964.[47]

As southern agriculture became more modernized, farmers sought more land to pay for their investments in machinery and to keep themselves fully employed. According to Warren Whatley, "Mechanization required a production scale of almost 100 acres before becoming the most profitable technique."[48] In 1925, average acreage of cropland per farm in the South was less than forty acres and in Alabama approximately thirty acres.[49] Farm experts estimated that a farmer needed approximately fifty acres to justify a tractor and 100 or more acres of cotton to profit from a mechanical cotton picker.[50] By the 1970s, the acreage of cropland per farm in the South had increased to more than 130 acres and in Alabama to nearly 100 acres.[51]

The scramble for enough land to preserve economies of scale occurred at the expense of the small black land owner in the South, where racism was still paramount. Earl Caldwell noted that planters used both legal and extralegal means "that made a mockery of equal justice . . . to acquire acre after acre of property" from black land owners.[52] For instance, when many family members had an interest in the land, the courts could order "partition sale." Thus, the greater the number of heirs involved in the property, the easier it was for large landholders or speculators to convince an individual family member to sell his or her interest. This policy opened the way for forced partition sales.

Another method involved tax sales, which occur when the government auctions land to collect delinquent taxes. Anyone losing land in this way was given several years to redeem it but had to reimburse the buyer for expenses as well as pay interest, penalties, and other costs—sums beyond the means of many rural black land owners. Many were tricked into mortgaging all of their land for a loan worth only a fraction of its value, and many became victims of foreclosure sales. One Alabama planter told of getting 120 acres from a black land owner who borrowed just $175 but lost the receipt after repaying the debt.[53]

Finally, under the doctrine of "adverse possession," a person who moved onto idle property, used it, and paid taxes can claim the property after twenty years. The out-migration of blacks from the South significantly increased the number of idle properties.[54]

As a result of racism, the decline in the amount of black-owned land was significant throughout the region. In 1910, blacks owned approximately sixteen million acres of land in the South, including the spectacular Sea Islands off the coast of South Carolina and the Citronelle oil fields in Alabama. All of these holdings were lost through partition sales. Blacks lost land at a rate of 6,000 acres per week. By 1970, they owned less than six million acres, including land acquired since 1910, and in 1990 black-owned holdings were insignificant.[55]

The decline of sharecropping, growth of wage labor, and increased concentration of land ownership effectively made for an enclosure movement that forced not only blacks but also poor whites off the land. According to Victor Perlo,

> The new system of exploitation, involving "free" labor, extended to poor whites as well. As agriculture in the South became more concentrated, hundreds of thousands of small white farmers lost their land. Many became city workers. . . . They became subject to the same type of extreme exploitation as the Negro.[56]

The enclosure movement signaled the move toward a territorial production complex closely resembling that of the agro-industrial Midwest. Raper wrote, "The New Deal with its cotton restriction program, its relief expenditures, and its loan services . . . has rejuvenated the decaying plantation economy. Those who control the plantations are now experiencing relative prosperity."[57] The labor processes of the postbellum plantation were, nevertheless, subsumed more under capitalist relations than those of the antebellum plantation, which were swept away by the engine of modernity. As Jonathan Wiener found, "The Depression . . . was not a temporary setback that delayed the South's socioeconomic evolution; it was a crisis that brought about the collapse of the labor-repressive system and its transformation from the Prussian into the classic capitalist road to development."[58]

By the end of the 1940s, planters turned toward investments in tools and machines. John Deere and Allis Chalmers had entered the southern market with mechanical cotton pickers. The number of pickers increased from 107 before 1946 to more than 3,700 by 1953.[59] By the mid–twentieth century, a more mechanized southern agricultural system would serve a more intensive form of industrialization in the South, and a more intensive regime of accumulation would undermine the old planter-based extensive regime.

THE NEW DEAL AND INDUSTRY

The New Deal restructured industrial relations as well as agriculture in the South. The National Industrial Recovery Act (NIRA) established the Public Works Administration (PWA), which provided employment funded by FERA. The Works Division of the Alabama Relief Administration provided assistance by taking over and operating factories closed because of the depression. For example, the Birmingham Iron and Wood Work Shop employed relief workers to make wooden plow stocks, the Civil Works Administration employed 15,000 on public work projects, and hundreds more found employment on massive PWA programs. A single PWA project employed 2,000, another 500.[60] The local PWA director noted that construction projects accounted for 60 to 70 percent of emergency employment during the 1930s; these projects moved the city ahead thirty years in building improvements.[61] Approximately 12,500 of the state's 18,000 coal miners—more than 70 percent—were on relief in 1935, including more than 6,000 in Birmingham alone.[62] Although blacks experienced the highest rate of unemployment during the depression and received little federal relief due to racism, whites still accused the relief administration of providing more relief than needed to blacks.

The New Deal also led to the first comprehensive regulatory system for labor, and this system stimulated workers' efforts to organize. Labor organizers flocked to Birmingham to take advantage of the promise of collective bargaining offered by section 7(a) of the NIRA, which pledged

> 1) employees will have the right to organize and bargain collectively through representatives of their choosing, and will be free from the interference, restraint or coercion of employers of labor, or their agents, in the designation of such representatives.
>
> 2) no employee and no one seeking employment will be required as a condition of employment to join any company union or to refrain from joining, organizing, or assisting a labor organization of his choosing.[63]

Among the first to take advantage of this promise was the United Mine Workers of America (UMWA). Union leaders believed that the NIRA could be used to help the organization recover from the effects of institutionalized racism that had broken the union. The New Deal policy of allowing striking workers to apply for relief decreased capitalists' control and tilted the balance of power toward unions. Workers who qualified for relief were less dependent on the company, which may explain why thirty-eight companies representing 90 percent of Alabama's coal operators and 85 percent of commercial coal tonnage in District 20 decided on 14 March 1934 to sign an agreement with the UMWA to collect union dues and increase wages. By 1935, the union had enrolled 95 percent of the anthracite and bituminous coal miners in the United States. Under the leadership of William Mitch, District 20 membership increased from a low of 225 in the first decade of the twentieth century to 18,000 by the mid-1930s.[64] USS also signed an agreement with the Steel Workers Organizing Committee (SWOC) of the Congress of Industrial Organization (CIO) in 1937; the union received exclusive bargaining rights four years later. In 1949, the SWOC, since renamed the United Steelworkers of America, received the right to represent the ore miners and, through contract negotiations, eventually brought TCI more in line with national patterns.[65]

Although the NIRA guaranteed employees the right to bargain collectively, it did not oblige employers to cooperate, and failure to cooperate produced 70 percent of the cases coming before the National Labor Relations Board (NLRB), established to enforce section 7(a). Employers were also free to make agreements with company unions, which usually represented only a minority of the workers and did not represent labor's interests even when they observed the forms of collective bargaining. For example, DeBardeleben organized a company union to counteract the UMWA in Birmingham, and other independent coal operators organized the Progressive Mineworkers' Association. TCI created a new Industrial Relations Department to manage the company's Employee Representation Plan, which later became the Brotherhood of Captive Miners. Later, the company endorsed the United Association of Iron, Steel, and Mine Workers, which combined the Industrial Relations Department and the Brotherhood of Captive Miners, to discourage attempts of the International Union of Mine, Mill, and Smelter Workers to enroll blacks.[66] Horace Huntley noted that whites who joined Mine, Mill, and Smelter were called "communists" and "nigger lovers" by those opposed to the union, and opposition to the unions' egalitarian racial views eventually caused so many whites to leave that it became mainly black while the company union remained white—further reinforcing the segmentation of labor along racial lines. Still, a black majority in Mine, Mill, and Smelter represented black influence and power that threatened white supremacy and race-connected practices. Huntley also noted that TCI stopped hiring blacks in the hope of undermining black influence in the union.[67]

The NLRB often evaded questions concerning company unions. Senator Robert Wagner, after serving as chair of the NLRB, concluded that section 7(a) could be secured only if Congress passed new legislation protecting the principle of collective bargaining from employer-dominated unions. In mid-1935, Congress passed the

Wagner Act, which held that representatives chosen by most of the workers would be the exclusive bargaining agents for workers in that work unit. Eleven days later, the U.S. Supreme Court ruled the NIRA unconstitutional on the grounds that it delegated to the president power reserved for Congress.[68] The ruling gave new weight to the Wagner Act and its guarantee of collective bargaining. Still, many employers failed to abide by the act until it was upheld by the Supreme Court.[69]

At least for a time, the NIRA had raised the prospect of class solidarity between black and white workers. To express a commitment to industrial workers and interracial solidarity, some American Federation of Labor (AFL) leaders—many from the more radical UMWA or the Communist Party—established the CIO in 1935. The CIO organized workers in steel, auto, rubber, textile, ship building, meat packing, and many other industries; it was expelled from the AFL in 1938.[70] Hosea Hudson, a Birmingham black labor leader and member of the Communist Party during the 1930s, thought that the labor struggle, despite institutionalized racism, "raised the level of Negro–White unity and proved that black and white could unite like brothers and sisters to fight the class enemy . . . no matter what hard feeling might have existed between them."[71]

Allen wrote that the Birmingham proletariat

> is older and has had more experience in the class struggle than any other body of southern workers. The development of the class struggle in the Birmingham region cannot but produce salutary effects upon the white agrarian population, especially in those sections where the Negro croppers and farmers are already organizing and struggling (as in the Black Belt counties to the southeast of Birmingham where the Sharecroppers Union is strongly entrenched). Birmingham has become the key to unlocking the barriers which have prevented working class solidarity in the deep South and it can be a powerful generating center of the proletarian revolutionary movement. One of the elements of industrialization feared most by the landlord-capitalist rulers of the South, and which they succeeded in avoiding in the textile industry—the creation of a compact white *and* Negro working class—is asserting itself strenuously in the Birmingham area.[72]

However, although unions often succeeded in convincing whites to join blacks in contract negotiation, unions did not move whites to accept black demands for an end to race-based wage differentials, discriminatory seniority systems, and segregated facilities.[73] When the United Steelworkers of America took over the Birmingham locals of Mine, Mill, and Smelter, it installed all white officers and gave work preference to whites.[74] For Birmingham, racism remained, in the words of Norrell, "caste in steel."[75]

NOTES

1. Mortier W. LaFever, "Workers, Machinery, and Production in the Automobile Industry," *Monthly Labor Review* 19, no. 4 (October 1924): 737.
2. W. David Lewis, *Sloss Furnaces and the Rise of the Birmingham District: An Industrial Epic* (Tuscaloosa: University of Alabama Press, 1994), 365.

3. Douglas L. Smith, *The New Deal in the Urban South* (Baton Rouge: Louisiana State University Press, 1988), 12; Lewis, *Sloss Furnaces*, 383, 393, 404, 411.

4. Wesley C. Mitchell, "A Review," in *Recent Economic Changes in the United States*, Report of the Committee on Recent Economic Changes, President's Conference on Unemployment, vol. 2 (New York: McGraw-Hill, 1929), 877–78.

5. Smith, *The New Deal*.

6. Stanley Vittoz, *New Deal Labor Policy and the American Industrial Economy* (Chapel Hill: University of North Carolina Press, 1987), 4.

7. *Congressional Record*, 3 April 1933, 1115, 1127.

8. *Proceedings of the Joint Convention of Alabama Coal Operators Association and the United Mine Workers of America*, Birmingham, Ala. (22 June 1903), 191, 529–30.

9. U.S. Bureau of the Census, *Census of Manufactures*, 1890 and 1900.

10. Vittoz, *New Deal*, 4.

11. *Statistical Abstract of the United States: 1940* (Washington, D.C.: U.S. Government Printing Office, 1941), 310–46, 496, 804.

12. Harold Loeb, *The Chart of Plenty: A Study of America's Product Capacity Based on the Findings of the National Survey of Potential Product Capacity* (New York: Viking Press, 1935), 148.

13. Smith, *The New Deal*, 16–17.

14. Edward S. Lamonte, "Politics and Welfare in Birmingham, Alabama: 1900–1975," (Ph.D. diss., University of Chicago, 1976), 160.

15. Smith, *The New Deal*, 18–19.

16. Smith, *The New Deal*, 19.

17. Russel Kent, "Senate Hears of Distress in City," *Birmingham Age-Herald*, 6 January 1932, 5.

18. Smith, *The New Deal*, 63.

19. Quoted in George R. Leighton, "Birmingham, Alabama: The City of Perceptual Praise," *Harper's* 175 (1937): 225–42.

20. Kent, "Senate Hears of Distress in City."

21. David Harvey, *The Urban Experience* (Baltimore: Johns Hopkins University Press, 1989), 43.

22. Quoted in Basil Baruch, *The History of the New Deal 1933–1938* (New York: Capricorn, 1963), 58.

23. Frederick C. Mills, *Employment Opportunities in Manufacturing Industries in the United States*, National Bureau of Economic Research, Bulletin no. 70 (New York, 1938), 10–15.

24. Stanley Aronowitz, *The Politics of Identity: Class, Culture, Social Movements* (New York: Routledge, 1992), 225–28; Bob Jessop, "Post-Fordism and the State," in *Post-Fordism: A Reader*, ed. Ash Amin (Oxford, U.K.: Basil Blackwell, 1994), 251–79.

25. Quoted in Marlene Hunt Rikard, "An Experiment in Welfare Capitalism: The Health Care System of the Tennessee Coal, Iron and Railroad Company" (Ph.D. diss., University of Alabama, 1983), 279.

26. Rikard, "An Experiment," 323–324, 326.

27. M. Aglietta, *A Theory of Capitalist Regulation: The U.S. Experience*, trans. D. Fernbach (London: NLB, 1979), 84.

28. David Harvey, *Consciousness and the Urban Experience: Studies in the History and Theory of Capitalist Urbanization* (Baltimore: Johns Hopkins University Press, 1985), 52.

29. Aronowitz, *Politics of Identity*, 5.

30. S. L. Elkin, "Twentieth Century Urban Regimes," *Journal of Urban Affairs* 7, no. 2 (1985): 11–28.

31. Quoted in Lamonte, "Politics and Welfare," 165.

32. Lamonte, "Politics and Welfare."

33. Marc Allen Eisner, *Regulatory Politics in Transition* (Baltimore: Johns Hopkins University Press, 1993), 89.

34. Eisner, *Regulatory Politics.*

35. Between 1940 and 1970, almost 4.5 million more blacks left than entered the South; almost 80 percent of the country's black population resided in the South in 1940, and about 50 percent lived in the North by 1970. U.S. Bureau of the Census, *The Social and Economic Status of the Black Population in the United States: An Historical View, 1790–1978,* Current Population Reports, Special Studies Series P-23, No. 80 (Washington, D.C.: Government Printing Office, 1979).

36. James S. Allen, *The Negro Question in the United States* (New York: International Publishers, 1936), 142–43.

37. Allen, *The Negro Question.*

38. George Brown Tindall, *The Disruption of the Solid South* (Athens: University of Georgia Press, 1972), 31.

39. Eisner, *Regulatory Politics,* 87.

40. Warren C. Whatley, "Labor for the Picking: The New Deal in the South," *Journal of Economic History* 43, no. 4 (December 1983): 905–29; Arthur F. Raper, *Preface to Peasantry* (Chapel Hill: University of North Carolina Press, 1936), 7.

41. Gunnar Myrdal, *An American Dilemma: The Negro Problem and Modern Democracy* (New York: Harper & Brother, 1944), 253.

42. Gilbert C. Fite, *Cotton Fields No More: Southern Agriculture 1865–1980* (Lexington: University Press of Kentucky, 1984), 141–42, 145; for a discussion of communist influence on the sharecropper union in Alabama, see Robin D. G. Kelley, *Hammer and Hoe: Alabama Communists During the Great Depression* (Chapel Hill: University of North Carolina Press, 1990).

43. Alan Brinkley, "The New Deal and Southern Politics," in *The New Deal in the South,* ed. James C. Cobb and Michael V. Nomorato (Jackson: University Press of Mississippi, 1984), 97–115.

44. Jonathan M. Wiener, "Class Structure and Economic Development in the American South, 1865–1955," *American Historical Review* 84, no. 4 (October 1979): 990.

45. Census, Social and Economic Status.

46. Whatley, "Labor"; George B. Tindall, *The Emergence of the New South: 1913–1945* (Baton Rouge: Louisiana State University Press, 1967), 430; Stanley B. Greenberg, *Race and State in Capitalist Development: Comparative Perspectives* (New Haven, Conn.: Yale University Press, 1980), 115; Harry Haywood, *Negro Liberation* (New York: International Publishers, 1948), 111.

47. Jeremy Rifkin, *The End of Work: The Decline of Global Labor Force and the Dawn of the Post-Market Era* (New York: G. P. Putnam's Sons, 1995), 71.

48. Whatley, "Labor," 907.

49. U.S. Bureau of the Census, *Census of Agriculture,* Part 2, The Southern States (Washington, D.C.: Government Printing Office, 1927).

50. Fite, *Cotton Fields,* 188.

51. *1978 Census of Agriculture,* vol. 1, *Summary and State Data,* part 51 (Washington, D.C.: Government Printing Office, 1981); *1978 Census of Agriculture,* vol. 1, *State and County Data,* part 1, Alabama (Washington, D.C.: Government Printing Office, 1981).

52. Earl Caldwell, "Gaining Ground on Black Property," *Black Enterprise* (May 1978): 23.

53. Caldwell, "Gaining Ground," 23.

54. *Only Six Million Acres: The Decline of Black Owned Land in the Rural South*, sponsored by Clark College of Atlanta and the Rockefeller Brothers Funds (New York: Black Economic Research Center, 1975); Caldwell, "Gaining Ground," 21–24, 48.

55. *Only Six Million Acres*; Caldwell, "Gaining Ground."

56. Victor Perlo, *The Negro in Southern Agriculture* (New York: International Publishers, 1953), 71.

57. Raper, *Preface*, 6–7.

58. Wiener, "Class Structure," 991.

59. Jay R. Mandle, *The Roots of Poverty: The Southern Plantation Economy After the Civil War* (Durham, N.C.: Duke University Press, 1978), 91.

60. Lamonte, "Politics and Welfare," 233.

61. Smith, *The New Deal*, 107.

62. Wayne Flynt, *Poor But Proud: Alabama's Poor Whites* (Tuscaloosa, Ala.: University of Alabama Press, 1989), 330.

63. Quoted in Jeremy Brecher, *Strike* (San Francisco: Straight Arrow Books, 1972), 149.

64. J. Wayne Flynt, "The New Deal and Southern Labor," in *The New Deal and the South*, ed. James C. Cobb and Michael V. Namorato (Jackson: University Press of Mississippi, 1984), 73.

65. Stein, "Southern Workers," 183–222.

66. Smith, *The New Deal*, 190.

67. Horace Huntley, "Iron Ore Miners and Mine Mill in Alabama, 1933–1952" (Ph.D. diss., University of Pittsburgh, 1976), 49–50; 97–98.

68. *Schechter Poultry Corp. et al. v. United States*, 295 U.S. 490 (1935).

69. *Associated Press v. NLRB*, 301 U.S. 103; *NLRB v. Jones & Laughlin Steel Corp.*, 301 U.S. 1; *NLRB v. Freuhauf Trailer Co.*, 301 U.S. 49; *NLRB v. Friedman-Harry Marks Clothing Co.*, 301 U.S. 58; and *Washington, Virginia & Maryland Coach Co. v. NLRB*, 301 U.S. 142.

70. Carter A. Wilson, *Racism: From Slavery to Advanced Capitalism* (Thousand Oaks, Calif.: Sage Publications, 1996), 147–48.

71. Hosea Hudson, *Black Worker in the Deep South* (New York: International Publishers, 1972), 58.

72. Allen, *The Negro Question*, 126–27.

73. Michael Honey, "Industrial Unionism and Racial Justice in Memphis," in *Organized Labor in the Twentieth-Century South*, ed. Robert H. Zieger (Knoxville: University of Tennessee Press, 1991), 135–57.

74. Honey, "Industrial Unionism," 111–14.

75. Robert J. Norrell, "Caste in Steel: Jim Crow Careers in Birmingham, Alabama," *Journal of American History*, 73, no. 3 (December 1986): 669–94.

16

The New Deal and Blacks

The New Deal was guided by a desire for economic recovery, not racial reform, which explains its emphasis on creating jobs and on increasing demand. In Franklin D. Roosevelt's words, the goal was "the assurance of a reasonable profit to industry and living wages for labor."[1] In practice, this emphasis meant that the full weight of exploitation fell even more on blacks, who had become an increasingly marginalized group.

In the South, the New Deal brought major restructuring of the political economy, but it did not significantly alter the white power structure, which had as much or more control in the region as the federal government. Only eleven of the more than 10,000 Public Works Administration (PWA) supervisors in the South were black.[2] Alabama Senator Hugo Black supported the New Deal and authored legislation to limit the work week to thirty hours in plants producing goods for interstate commerce, but he also thought federal funds should be disbursed through state and local governments, not directly by Washington, D.C. This policy gave the southern white power structure significant control over federal programs.

Racism and anti-communism made racial cooperation within the ranks of labor nearly impossible. Birmingham's largest employer, Tennessee Coal and Iron (TCI), systematically organized violent action against radicals during the mid-1930s, including the flogging of Joseph Gelders, a representative of the National Committee for the Defense of Political Prisoners, who was investigating the imprisonment of Jack Barton, secretary of the Bessemer section of the Communist Party, one of several sections in the Birmingham area. Police reported Birmingham was the southeastern headquarters of the Communist Party and that it had more than 2,000 local members, 75 percent of them black. The City Commission, characterizing members of the Communist Party as anarchists, adopted an ordinance forbidding their assembly. A young commissioner of public safety, Eugene "Bull" Connor, informed union leaders that there was no such thing as a peaceful demonstration, and the City Commission president, an active member of the Ku Klux Klan, banned integrated labor meetings.

In response to mass meetings by the Communist Party, both Birmingham and Bessemer passed anti-sedition laws during the 1930s that made it illegal to possess more than one copy of any material advocating overthrow of the government.[3] The American Civil Liberties Union (ACLU) branded Birmingham one of eleven cities where "repression was continuous, not incidental."[4] In Atlanta, whites organized around the slogan "No Jobs for Niggers Until Every White Man Has a Job!"[5]

The Keynesian welfare state never fully realized the potential of the National Industrial Recovery Act (NIRA) to increase wages and employment for black workers. New Deal policies did not eliminate the existing wage differential between black and white workers; indeed, proponents of the Federal Labor Standards Act of 1938 were able to gather southern support because it did not threaten the racial status quo; and, although southern planters benefited from New Deal agricultural programs, according to W. David Lewis, industrialists "succeeded in forging alliances with Black Belt planters to block further change. . . . Ties between industrialists and wealthy planters that dated back to the days of the Broad River group [original members of the planter class] still lived on."[6]

Planters of the black belt continued to rely on the state to maintain the racial order and their class position. The Alabama Farm Bureau, the political arm of agriculture, was intimately connected with the U.S. Department of Agriculture's Extension Service and became a major force in county committees responsible for crop allotments and price support. According to Stanley Greenberg, the Farm Bureau consistently opposed racial integration, attacking the Civil Rights Act of 1964 as "unconstitutional and an infringement on the rights of property owners."[7] In 1966, the Civil Rights Commission found not one black among 201 people serving in county committees in Alabama.[8]

By raising wages and shortening hours, the NIRA even made many menial occupations, such as janitor, more attractive to whites, who quickly displaced blacks.[9] Higher wages for workers also increased the incentive for mechanization, which in turn produced job scarcity and surplus labor, reinforcing whites' interest in racial separation.[10] For example, TCI's employment policies changed drastically between 1938 and 1948, with the company hiring mainly white workers. Testifying before the congressional committee investigating the necessity for a federal fair employment act, a black iron ore miner recounted,

> I work for the TCI company. One reason why I want to support fair employment practices is because these people [blacks] down there are being denied the rights and privileges to have a job and to earn a decent living, because of their color. This particular company in the last two years almost quit hiring Negroes. They have whites about 100 to one.[11]

When the black percentage of the population in Birmingham was 40 percent, no more than 27 percent of the people hired at TCI during the 1950s were black.[12] Of those hired, most were in unskilled manual positions, and workers in jobs eliminated by machinery were laid off regardless of their seniority.[13] The mining industry laid off blacks in disproportionate numbers, violating the seniority rule. In 1950, blacks made up 43 percent of the population in the Deep South but were hired for only 21 percent of new nonagricultural jobs.[14] Employed blacks faced promotion policies designed along racial lines to ensure the continuing segmentation of labor and perpetuate the dominant–subordinate relationship between the races observed throughout Fordism. Many plants employing blacks were able to secure exemptions from wage and hour requirements. NIRA codes did not cover workers in agriculture and domestic services, who received little or no increase in wages, although they still had to pay the higher prices brought about by observing NIRA regulations.[15]

In 1940, more than half of the black wage earners employed outside of agriculture were service workers, most in domestic service; less than 12 percent worked as managers, proprietors, professionals, clerks, salespeople, supervisors, and crafts persons.[16] Most blacks employed in Alabama's bituminous coal industry in 1940 were in repetitive and unskilled occupations (Table 16.1). Nearly 75 percent of employed black males in the Birmingham area worked as laborers and operatives, as opposed to 25 percent of employed white males (Table 16.2). Of employed black females, 85 percent were in domestic and other services (laundries, for example). Many branch plants built in the South after World War II either did not employ blacks or relegated them to unskilled, low-paying positions.[17] Records of the Birmingham Office of the Alabama State Employment Service showed that service occupations and unskilled work accounted for 85 to 88 percent of black job placements between 1948 and 1951.[18]

In addition, blacks were rarely found among the ranks of organized labor. Increases in economic concentration and firm size should presumably bring increased labor power by facilitating collective action, which, according to Frances Fox Piven and Richard Cloward, "reverberating throughout an interdependent

Table 16.1 Bituminous Coal Industry, Employment by Major Occupational Groups and Race, Alabama, 1940

Occupation	Black		White	
	Number	Percent Employment	Number	Percent Employment
Professional	1	*	103	0.8
Managers	1	*	302	2.3
Clerical and sales	10	0.1	365	2.7
Craftmen and foremen	75	0.8	1,945	14.5
Operatives	9,496	98.9	10,576	78.8
Other	22	0.2	126	0.9
Total	9,605	100.0	13,417	100.0

Source: U.S. Census of Population, 1940, Vol. 3, The Labor Force, parts 2, 3, and 5, Table 20.
*Less than one-tenth of a percent.

Table 16.2   Occupation as a Percent of
Total Employment by Sex and Race for
Jefferson County, 1940

Occupation	Black	White
Professionals		
Males	2.4	8.6
Females	5.9	18.4
Sales and clerical		
Males	2.9	34.4
Females	2.3	55.7
Craftmen		
Males	7.4	24.6
Females	0.2	0.9
Operatives		
Males	42.0	23.3
Females	6.2	10.5
Services		
Males	12.8	3.9
Females	84.1	13.9
Labor		
Males	32.3	5.2
Females	0.8	0.7
Total		
Males	100.0	100.0
Females	100.0	100.0

Source: U.S. Bureau of the Census, *Census of Population, Characteristics of the Population,* Alabama, 1940.

and concentrated economy."[19] However, in 1930, at least nineteen unions excluded blacks, and ten others admitted black members only in segregated locals. The National Association for the Advancement of Colored People (NAACP) estimated that no more than 50,000 blacks were members of national unions, and more than half of them were members of the Brotherhood of Sleeping Car Porters. This number represented only about 3 percent of blacks employed in transportation, extraction of minerals, and manufacturing. The NAACP wanted to have a clause written into the Wagner Act barring discrimination by labor unions, but the American Federation of Labor (AFL) announced it would oppose the legislation if the clause were included.[20]

The 1955 merger of the AFL and the Congress of Industrial Organization (CIO) brought conservative white crafts persons back into dominance in the labor movement, further undermining efforts to desegregate unions and workplaces and unraveling any possibility of a coalition between the labor and civil rights movements.[21] Finally, in the 1960s, black worker and civil rights organizations began a serious attack on labor unions. Federal courts determined that many labor unions were responsible for widespread patterns of unlawful discrimination.[22]

The New Deal also limited blacks when it came to housing. In 1940, blacks occupied 66 percent of Birmingham's slum dwellings, although they were only 40 percent of the city's population. Alleys in almost every section of the city were lined with rows upon rows of shanties that lacked toilet facilities, gas, and electricity.[23] K. Taeuber and A. F. Taeuber, who studied housing patterns in fifteen U.S. cities, found that almost 60 percent of the actual housing segregation in Birmingham in 1940 was a product of black–white socioeconomic differences compared with an average of 43.3 percent for other cities.[24]

The Federal Housing Administration's (FHA) Underwriting Manual noted that property values would deteriorate if blacks moved into a predominantly white area, and the agency refused to guarantee mortgages on homes purchased by blacks in white communities.[25] The FHA's policy provided the justification for a 1949 city ordinance sponsored by then city commissioner, Eugene "Bull" Connor, making it a misdemeanor "for a member of the colored race to move into, for the purpose of establishing a permanent residence, or having moved into, to continue to reside in an area in the city of Birmingham generally and historically recognized at the time as an area for occupancy by members of the white race."[26]

In 1950, the Jefferson County Board of Health reported, "Practically every section of the city which is heavily populated by the Negro race might be considered as blighted areas."[27] The uniformly low economic status of blacks removed any meaningful distinction between race and class housing patterns. Residential segregation contributed to the stratification of the consumption norm along racial lines to produce racially marginalized spaces. Realtors and property owners entered privately into racial covenants. No white neighborhoods experienced black incursion during the 1950s.[28] According to Robert Thompson, Hylan Lewis, and Davis McEntire, a leading white mortgage banker in the 1950s could remark confidently that "Birmingham has no racial transitional areas."[29]

Historically, the condition of U.S. housing had convinced many people that the private sector alone could not provide quality housing and that the state's regulatory role in the provision of housing should be increased. Alabama Governor James Folsom, whose political philosophy had the ring of turn-of-the-century populism, declared in 1948, "One only has to look at the hundreds of families in this State, and especially veterans living in places unfit for habitation, the skyrocketing rents, etc., to ascertain whether or not private enterprise is taking care of the situation or is even making satisfactory progress."[30] Even the president of Birmingham's City Commission, W. Cooper Green, was for "the elimination of slums and blighted areas, dilapidated dwellings unfit for human habitation . . . therefore we favor publicly assisted low-rent housing as a means of supplying decent, safe, and sanitary housing for such low-income families."[31]

New Deal housing policy, however, clearly stipulated that public housing would not compete in the market in a way that could diminish demand for and profits from private housing. In addition, wrote George Davis and O. Fred Donaldson, "The public housing bureaucracy has been governed by the necessity of demonstrating to its critics that the housing being built is bare of any amenities which might be pleasing to the eye; public housing was to be for shelter only."[32] Thus, the quality and design of public housing provided almost no use-value for its residents.

In the late 1950s, blacks living near Birmingham's largest urban renewal project filed a class-action suit contending that the Birmingham Housing Authority, the local relocation agency, did not provide adequate housing accommodation for displaced families.[33] Residents who qualified for public housing also claimed that the agency pursued a policy of racial segregation that violated the Fourteenth Amendment. The federal district court dismissed the case because it involved two distinctly different classes of plaintiffs, one raising the Fourteenth Amendment but not the other.[34]

Such a rigid pattern of segregation made it possible for the owners of real estate who could monopolize ghetto space to exploit blacks.[35] It created barriers not only to geographical mobility but also to the circulation of revenues (e.g., wages, profit, interest, taxes, rent). These barriers allowed the extraction of monopoly rents and prices, trapping a given pattern of revenue circulation within its confines. Whatever their economic standing, blacks had no choice but to pay rent for housing in the areas set aside for them. This requirement, according to R. J. King, drove "their standard of living below that underlying the normal value of labour power at the time."[36] Richard Walker wrote, "It pays to promote it [segregation] as a kind of product differentiation to increase sales. It also pays to promote mutually supportive land values in order to secure the maximum level of rents; property investors would be foolish to dilute such values by randomly mixing people."[37]

In their attempt to influence and determine patterns of housing, realtors could be seen as "structural speculators." Their strategy was to generate monopoly and differential rents by influencing the larger arena of decision.[38]

When, after several years of the New Deal, the problems of poverty and race remained, many blacks questioned the assumption that all workers would benefit by increasing the power of organized labor.[39] The National Recovery Act (NRA), if anything, meant "Negro Run Around," "Negro Removal Administration," or "Negroes Ruined Again."[40] Marc Allen Eisner wrote,

> The centralization of power in the leadership of the unions, and the narrow set of issues addressed by the NLRB, fostered greater conservatism in the labor movement. . . . The New Deal's legacy in the regulation of labor was similar to its legacy in agriculture. The goal was to promote and supervise the organization of the regulated interests in hopes of promoting stability.[41]

W. E. B. DuBois and others saw the failure to aid blacks as inherent in the contradictions and failure of capitalism.[42] Although New Dealers would identify with the black struggle for equality, they would not do so to the detriment of capitalism.[43] Industrialists might come to believe that collective bargaining was essential to industrial peace, but that labor would have to enter into cooperative arrangements to ensure stability and the homogenized space required of a mobile and flexible capital. The Wagner Act helped to provide the framework for this arrangement.

Neither slum clearance nor urban renewal accomplished its goal of providing a decent home and suitable environment for every American family. They did, however, provide relief for powerful city institutions. In Alabama, urban renewal provided the space for one of the largest employers in the state, the University of Alabama at Birmingham and its medical complex. Urban renewal became a program, wrote Nancy Kleniewski,

> designed to stimulate economic growth by making cities more profitable places for capital to invest. Urban renewal was not a housing program and did not have housing production as its goal except where housing fit into overall plans for economic development and growth. Urban renewal programs were also largely initiated and carried out by local business-oriented groups with the assistance of federal and local governments.[44]

Although the Great Depression and the New Deal greatly undermined premodern modes of social regulation in the South, those elements of racial and class inequality derived from market forces became more dominant. The Keynesian welfare state benefited the advantaged at least as much as the disadvantaged and therefore reinforced and stabilized the system of class and racial inequality derived from market forces. Government intervention did not extend to support for civil rights. Agricultural workers and domestic servants, who were mostly black men and women, respectively, were left out of the core programs of the New Deal.[45]

NOTES

1. Quoted in Basil Baruch, *The History of the New Deal 1933–1938* (New York: Capricorn, 1963), 80.

2. Harvard Sitkoff, *A New Deal for Blacks, The Emergence of Civil Rights as a National Issue*, vol. 1: *The Depression Decade* (New York: Oxford University Press, 1978), 49.

3. Douglas L. Smith, *The New Deal in the Urban South* (Baton Rouge: Louisiana State University Press, 1988), 198.

4. Robert Ingalls, "Antiradical Violence in Birmingham During the 1930s," *Journal of Southern History* 47, no. 4 (November 1981): 521–44; see also Robin D. G. Kelley, *Hammer and Hoe: Alabama Communists During the Great Depression* (Chapel Hill: University of North Carolina Press, 1990), 72.

5. Quoted in Sitkoff, *A New Deal*, 36.

6. W. David Lewis, *Sloss Furnaces and the Rise of the Birmingham District: An Industrial Epic* (Tuscaloosa: University of Alabama Press, 1994), 426–27.

7. Stanley B. Greenberg, *Race and State in Capitalist Development: Comparative Perspectives* (New Haven, Conn.: Yale University Press, 1980), 123.

8. Greenberg, *Race and State*, 124.

9. David R. Goldfield, *Black, White, and Southern: Race Relations and Southern Culture, 1940 to the Present* (Baton Rouge: Louisiana State University Press, 1990), 28.

10. Gavin Wright, *Old South, New South: Revolutions in the Southern Economy Since the Civil War* (New York: Basic Books, 1986), 223–25.

11. Quoted in Committee on Education and Labor, *Federal Employment Practices Act,* H.R. 4453, 81st Congress, 1st Session, 1949, 254.

12. Herbert R. Northrup and Richard L. Rowan, *Negro Employment in Southern Industry: A Study of Racial Policies in Five Industries* (Philadelphia: University of Pennsylvania Press, 1970), 42.

13. Northrup and Rowan, *Negro Employment,* 42.

14. J. J. Persky and J. J. Kain, "Migration, Employment and Race in the Deep South," *Southern Economic Journal* 36, no. 1 (July 1970): 268–76.

15. John P. Davis, "A Black Inventory of the New Deal," *Crisis* 42 (May 1935): 141; Steve Valocchi, "The Racial Basis of Capitalism and the State, and the Impact of the New Deal on African Americans," *Social Problems* 41, no. 3 (August 1994): 347–62.

16. U.S. Bureau of Census, *Sixteenth Census of the United States: 1940 Population.*

17. Glenn McLaughlin and Stefan Robock, *Why Industry Moves South* (Washington, D.C.: Committee of the South, National Planning Association, 1949), 69.

18. L. T. Hawley, "Negro Employment in the Birmingham Metropolitan Area," in *Selected Studies of Negro Employment in the South* (Washington, D.C.: Committee of the South Reports, National Planning Association, 1955), 213–328.

19. Frances Fox Piven and Richard A. Cloward, *Poor People's Movements: Why They Succeed, How They Fail* (New York: Vintage Books, 1979), 97.

20. F. Ray Marshall, *The Negro and Organized Labor* (New York: Wiley, 1965), 53–85; see also Michael Honey, "Industrial Unionism and Racial Justice in Memphis," in *Organized Labor in the Twentieth-Century South,* ed. Robert H. Zieger (Knoxville: University of Tennessee Press, 1991), 135–57; Jill Quadagno, *The Color of Welfare: How Racism Undermined the War on Poverty* (New York: Oxford University Press, 1994), 23.

21. Quadagno, *Color,* 23.

22. Herbert Hill, "Myth-Making as Labor History: Herbert Gutman and the United Mine Workers of America," *Politics, Culture, and Society* 2, no. 2 (Winter 1988): 137.

23. "Health as an Indication of Housing Needs in Birmingham, Alabama and Recommendations for Slum Clearance, Redevelopment and Public Housing," Jefferson County Board of Health, Geo. A. Denison, M.D., Health Officer, 12 April 1950, 6.

24. K. Taeuber and A. F. Taeuber, *Negroes in Cities: Residential Segregation and Neighborhood Change* (Chicago: Aldine, 1965), 105–14.

25. Sitkoff, *A New Deal,* 50; see also Douglas S. Massey and Nancy A. Denton, *American Apartheid: Segregation and the Making of the Underclass* (Cambridge, Mass.: Harvard University Press, 1993), 54–55.

26. City Ordinance 709-F (1949).

27. "Health as an Indication of Housing Needs," 6.

28. Taeuber and Taeuber, *Negroes in Cities,* 105–14.

29. Robert A. Thompson, Hylan Lewis, and Davis McEntire, "Atlanta and Birmingham: A Comparative Study in Negro Housing," in *Studies in Housing and Minority Groups,* ed. Nathan Glazer and Davis McEntire (Berkeley: University of California Press, 1960), 58.

30. Report of the Joint Committee on Housing, *Slum Clearance,* 80th Congress, 2nd Session (Washington, D.C.: Government Printing Office, 1948), 5.

31. Joint Committee on Housing, *Slum Clearance,* 10.

32. George A. Davis and O. Fred Donaldson, *Blacks in the United States: A Geographic Perspective* (Boston: Houghton Mifflin, 1975), 136.

33. Robert J. Frye, *Housing and Urban Renewal in Alabama,* Bureau of Public Administration (Tuscaloosa: University of Alabama, 1965), 41.

34. *Watts v. Housing Authority of the Birmingham District*, 150 F. Supp. 552 (1956); Joint Committee on Housing, *Slum Clearance*.

35. P. A. Baran and Paul M. Sweezy, *Monopoly Capital: An Essay on the American Economic and Social Order* (New York: Monthly Review Press, 1966), 253.

36. R. J. King, "Capital Switching and the Role of Ground Rent 1: Theoretical Problems," *Environment and Planning A* 21 (1989): 449.

37. Richard A. Walker, "A Theory of Suburbanization: Capitalism and the Construction of Urban Space in the United States," in *Urbanization and Urban Planning in Capitalist Society*, ed. Michael Dear and Allen J. Scott (New York: Methuen, 1981), 393.

38. John R. Logan and Harvey L. Molotch, *Urban Fortunes: The Political Economy of Place* (Berkeley: University of California, 1987), 30.

39. Raymond Wolters, "Section 7a and the Black Worker," *Labor History* 10, no. 3 (Summer 1969): 459–74.

40. J. Wayne Flynt, "The New Deal and Southern Labor," in *The New Deal and the South*, ed. James C. Cobb and Michael V. Namorato (Jackson: University of Mississippi Press, 1984), 85.

41. Marc Allen Eisner, *Regulatory Politics in Transition*, Baltimore: Johns Hopkins University Press, 1993, 103.

42. Sitkoff, *A New Deal*, 56; W. E. B. Dubois, "Federal Action Programs and Community Action in the South," *Social Forces* 19, no. 3 (March 1941): 375–80.

43. Steve Valocchi, "The Racial Basis," 347–62.

44. Nancy Kleniewski, "From Industrial to Corporate City: The Role of Urban Renewal," in *Marxism and the Metropolis: New Perspectives in Urban Political Economy*, ed. William K. Tabb and Larry Sawers (New York: Oxford University Press, 1984), 205.

45. Edward S. Greenberg, *Serving the Few: Corporate Capitalism and the Bias of Government Policy* (New York: Wiley, 1974), 103–27, 130; Quadagno, *The Color of Welfare*, 19–24.

17

The Southern Shift of Fordism and Entrepreneurial Regimes

It is possible to talk about the U.S. capitalist class after the 1890s in terms of two segments, corporate and entrepreneurial. The entrepreneurial segment had stronger regional and local interests than the corporate segment.[1] In addition, entrepreneurial regimes were more concerned about local race issues than corporations doing business in the South during Fordism, and they even were willing to undermine the racial order and negotiate with civil rights leaders.

When asked whether his firm was evading its social responsibility in Birmingham at the height of the civil rights struggle in 1963, U.S. Steel (USS) President Roger Blough said, "For a corporation to attempt to exert any kind of economic compulsion to achieve a particular end in the social area seems to me to be quite beyond what a corporation should do."[2] A corporation can, however, spend several billions of dollars on new plants and products, and such investments can determine the quality of life for a substantial segment of society.[3] USS used what Kevin Cox and Andrew Mair called "strategies of multilocationality" to reduce its dependence on any one locality.[4] The corporation adopted practices that made its Birmingham properties subordinate to its interests and operations at other locations and that allowed it to evade social responsibilities within the community.[5]

Birmingham rejoiced when USS acquired TCI in 1907, but forty years later, Irving Beiman wrote that the corporation had treated Birmingham as a stepchild; this view became known as the colonial-imperialistic thesis, as it described Birmingham and the South as a region reduced to colonial status.[6] The historical dominance of an extensive regime of accumulation and premodern modes of social regulation facilitated such behavior. Of course, Birmingham and the South had had no reason to assume that USS, headquartered in Pittsburgh, would formulate policies based on regional and local interests.[7] Some local leaders, in fact, believe that USS used its monopoly power in Birmingham to pursue policies that barred firms that might compete with it for labor and that the corporation did so without regard for the effects such a policy might have on the community.[8] There is no proof that USS actively pursued such a policy; it is, however, true that no companies employing a large labor force moved into the city after the entry of USS.[9] Furthermore, no significant industrial agglomeration was associated with linkages between steel-producing and steel-using industries.[10]

In contrast, according to William Roy, owners in the entrepreneurial segment of this capitalist class "directly controlled the means of production on an individual, partnership, or family basis. Capital took the form of personal property: assets were fixed and tangible."[11] Such firms are vulnerable not only to swings in the economic cycle but also to local social conditions, such as changes in the ethnic and racial composition of the community.

With the increasing mobility of labor after the Great Depression, blacks became highly urbanized. By 1970, 81 percent of the black population was urban compared with only 49 percent in 1940.[12] The growth of a black proletariat in northern cities during the 1940s and 1950s added an urban black voting bloc to the already diverse political situation, and the entrepreneurial regimes that appeared in large northern industrial cities during this period were distinguished by coalitions reflecting ethnic and racial diversity. Mayor Daley of Chicago adjusted to the city's changing racial composition by co-opting emerging leaders in the black community.[13] Blacks could organize a territorially based political machine directly connected to the party headquarters.

Elsewhere in the North, political machines channeled black participation through what Ira Katznelson called citywide "buffer institutions." They were linked to the political machine but not a formal part of its decentralized structure. In these situations, power flowed in only one direction—from machine headquarters to the segregated black institutions. The machine hand-picked middle-class black leaders who "sponsored substantively unresponsive programmes calculated to bring rewards to the leadership-elite."[14] Thus, the northern black urban lower class came into the civil rights era with little experience in political participation. Civil rights politics were largely middle-class affairs from 1915 to the 1950s.[15]

In the South, in contrast, urban regimes as a whole had little need to placate blacks, as so many were emigrating from the region and those who remained wielded less influence than their northern counterparts. Southern regimes took advantage of the southern shift of Fordism, which produced new markets, and promoted business-oriented policies that set the stage for the so-called "sun belt" growth phenomenon in the late twentieth century.[16] In the Fordist model, successful industries and related firms extend into new territories to create what A. Lipietz called "peripheral fordism."[17] This process began with Henry Ford's own history. Soon after he introduced automatic assembly line production at his Highland Park, Michigan, Model-T plant, he began to expand into new, peripheral areas.[18]

The welfare state's willingness to intervene in local situations also weakened the southern planter-industrialist arrangement and provided the window of opportunity for Fordism after the depression, a period when U.S. capitalists enjoyed overwhelming competitive advantage. Northern capitalists directed and financed much of the industrial development of the South during that period and established branch plants that produced more than 70 percent of the Southeast's total value of products in 1939.[19] In the South, peripheral Fordism meant that regulation came increasingly from outside of the region.

During the 1940s, the southern shift of fordism made firm location an increasingly political question. With their blend of conservative progressive themes, entrepreneurial southern regimes pushed locally oriented growth policies while maintaining strong opposition to unions and the Keynesian welfare state.[20] In contrast to the true privatist regime that had controlled much of the South and, according to S. L. Elkin, "needed little in the way of public resources and new authority to realize its intention," entrepreneurial regimes depended a great deal on public resources and used their authority to encourage state policies that led to the creation of development commissions to entice capital.[21]

As early as 1935, Mississippi received legislative approval to use municipal bonds to construct facilities for industries. In the 1950s, the Birmingham Chamber of Commerce began a ten-year crusade to attract manufacturing to the area.[22] Alabama's Cater Act of 1949 and the Wallace Act of 1951—which was written by George Wallace, then a young state representative—gave local governments authority to set up industrial development boards that could exempt industries from local property taxes. By 1962, nine southern states, including Alabama, had embraced the idea of bond-financed, tax-exempt factories. This concept effectively transferred a municipality's borrowing advantages to private industry. By the end of the 1960s, southern states accounted for most of the industrial development bonds issued in the United States.[23]

Like Daniel Pratt and other industrialists of the antebellum era who feared that large urban agglomeration was a source of conflict between workers and capitalists, many Fordist corporations moved their plants into the South's rural areas and small towns and not the large cities, thereby taking factories to the fields.[24] The more urbanized and industrialized North became qualitatively less efficient for capitalists because of unionization, and the South provided a territorial production complex that allowed Fordism to escape. The rural South was better able than the urban North to (re)produce the class relations needed to maximize the Fordist regime's ability to dominate the social process of production and reduce workers' resistance to that domination.[25]

Rural industrialization also made it possible for many southern workers to stay on the farms, where work time was not only discontinuous but work tasks were also becoming more mechanized, giving farmers time to work in factories and supplement their income. The portion of southern farm operators reporting off-farm income increased from 28.5 percent in 1934 to almost 50 percent in 1954. Many, however, eventually left the farm to engage in nonagricultural pursuits full time.[26] Blacks living in the rural South commuted to the rural factories instead of to cotton and tobacco fields.

The southern shift of Fordism linked production and consumption norms over the region's economic space, but it brought no guarantee of improved job opportunities for southern blacks.[27] Ford himself, although considered one of the most progressive industrialists of his time, considered blacks a subordinate group and excluded them from most of his plants outside of Michigan.[28]

The proletarianization of blacks under fordism relegated them to the cellar of the industrial economy. Horace Mann Bond described the segmentation of labor in Alabama as a "labor pyramid with a mass of black common labor, with an intermediate layer of white skilled workers and middle class 'white collar' employees, and with the financiers and capitalists of these enterprises at the apex."[29] Blacks understood what was a "white" job and what was a "black" job. Still, the Fordist regime was not as socially repressive as the planter-based regime with its more premodern mode of social regulation.

Blacks became more politically aggressive and sought to overcome the forces that marginalized them. As entrepreneurial regimes depended on local social relations, they were particularly vulnerable to civil rights demonstrations and economic boycotts, and the entrepreneurial segment of the capitalist class in the South played a significant role in negotiations with local black leaders that set the stage for civil rights gains. The economic restructuring initiated by New Deal policies and Fordism transformed the mode of social regulation and race-connected practices. As modernization swept the South, the interest of the southern ruling class was no longer to protect white supremacy but to promote an agro-industrial production complex. By the 1960s, the Alabama Farm Bureau was not simply a collection of local farm committees but also involved a major insurance company, a real estate developer, and a wholesaler.[30]

With southern industries increasingly regulated by Fordist corporations outside of the region, the ruling class had on the eve of the civil rights movement fully accepted more modern modes of production. This transformation made possible a struggle for civil rights on an unprecedented scale. It forced local regimes to present their communities as qualitatively efficient in the production process. Protests from blacks and intervention by the Keynesian welfare state challenged prevailing ideas and customs. Productive state policies and marketplace laws disciplined the South to the point where local regimes increasingly viewed racial turmoil as antagonistic to potential capital accumulation. As early as 1955, the Montgomery bus boycott caused consternation among local businesspeople concerned about attracting new investments when civil rights activities made the city lose a DuPont facility and four other plants to competing cities.[31]

Speaking to the Rotary Club of Atlanta in 1961, Malcolm Bryan, president of the Federal Reserve Bank of Atlanta, warned that if the governments of southern states "failed in their responsibilities to maintain law and order, the investment of that capital or the location of that plant with us is dangerous; for all rational men know that a mob turned loose on one man, or one class of men, or on one property, or class of property can also be turned loose on another man, or other men, or other properties."[32]

Entrepreneurial regimes were more willing than planter-based regimes to sacrifice old racial beliefs and practices to maintain and attract new investments. This willingness contributed to significant civil rights gains in Birmingham and the South as a whole. It provided important leverage for the civil rights movement that challenged the racial status quo and eventually produced more biracial regimes. Atlanta became known as "a city that was too busy to hate" and produced one of the earliest biracial regimes in the South.[33] The more entrepreneurial regime of Birmingham ousted Connor, who continued to identify with the old racial order, and in July 1963 repealed all segregation ordinances. In 1969, Arthur Shores, a black civil rights lawyer, was appointed to the city council. Within less than a decade, the city had elected its first black mayor. Greenberg noted that the end of the racial order was unheralded: "By the late sixties, the Farm Bureau and white farmers had unobtrusively given up the race question; without sharecroppers, [but] with machines . . . they could afford to."[34]

The South's detour from the planter-based industrial arrangement replaced the racially repressive labor system of sharecropping with greater investments in constant capital. As black migration from the rural South to industrial cities increased, a closer association developed between segregation and urban-industrialization than between segregation and southern agriculture. The transformed planter class never came to the aid of Connor in Birmingham during the civil rights movement. He and his counterparts faced the civil rights challenge virtually on their own.[35] The more entrepreneurial regime helped to reshape race-related practices enough to make the overt racist politics of the planter-based regime obsolete. With this restructuring, premodern modes of social regulation no longer dominated the Birmingham regime, making possible a more racially inclusive city. According to Earl Black and Merle Black, this transformation of Birmingham and the South was nothing more than "the southernization of the old American dream—to make and keep a lot of money."[36]

NOTES

1. William G. Roy, "The Organization the Corporate Class Segment of the U.S. Capitalist Class at the Turn of This Century," in *Bringing Class Back In: Contemporary and Historical Perspectives*, ed. Scott G. McNall, Rhonda F. Levine, and Rick Fantasia (Boulder, Colo.: Westview Press, 1991), 139–63.

2. Quoted in Andrew Hacker, "Do Corporations Have a Social Duty?" in *The Corporation in the American Economy*, ed. H. M. Trebing (Chicago: Quadrangle Books, 1970), 122.

3. Andrew Hacker, *The Corporate Takeover* (New York: Harper & Row, 1964), 9.

4. Kevin R. Cox and Andrew Mair, "Locality and Community in the Politics of Local Economic Development," *Annals of the Association of American Geographers* 78, no. 2 (June 1988): 310.

5. George W. Stocking, *Basing Point Pricing and Regional Development: A Case Study of the Iron and Steel Industry* (Chapel Hill: University of North Carolina Press, 1952), 155.

6. Irving Beiman, "Steel Giant with a Glass Jaw," in *Our Fair City*, ed. Robert S. Allen (New York: Vanguard Press, 1947), 99–122.

7. Marlene Hunt Rikard, "George Gordon Crawford: Man of the New South" (M.A. thesis, Samford University, Birmingham, Ala., 1977), 187.

8. Rikard, "George Gordon Crawford," 187.

9. Douglas L. Smith, *The New Deal in the Urban South* (Baton Rouge: Louisiana State University Press, 1989), 116–17.

10. Charles E. Connerly, "Urban Rivalry and the South: Atlanta and Birmingham." (Paper presented at the Fifth National Conference on American Planning History, Chicago, 19 November 1993), 11.

11. Roy, "The Organization," 149.

12. U.S. Bureau of the Census, *The Social and Economic Status of the Black Population in the United States: An Historical View, 1790–1978*, Current Population Reports, Special Studies Series P-23, no. 80 (Washington, D.C.: Government Printing Office, 1979).

13. Milton Rakove, *Don't Make No Waves . . . Don't Back No Losers* (Bloomington: Indiana University Press, 1975), 259.

14. Ira Katznelson, *Black Men, White Cities: Race Politics and Migration in the United States, 1900–30, and Britain, 1948–68* (London: Oxford University Press, 1973), 113.

15. Martin Kilson, "Black Politicians: A New Power," *Dissent* (August 1971), 333–45.

16. John H. Mollenkopf, *The Contested City* (Princeton, N.J.: Princeton University Press, 1983), 213–53.

17. A. Lipietz, "New Tendencies in the International Division of Labour: Regimes of Accumulation and Modes of Regulation," in *Production, Work, Territory: The Geographical Anatomy of Industrial Capitalism*, ed. A. Scott and M. Storper (Boston: Allen & Unwin, 1986), 16–40.

18. Michael Storper and Richard Walker, *The Capitalist Imperative: Territory, Technology, and Industrial Growth* (New York: Basil Blackwell, 1989), 71.

19. G. McLaughlin and S. Robock, *Why Industry Moves South* (Washington, D.C.: Committee of the South, National Planning Association, 1949), 13–14.

20. Earl Black and Merle Black, *Politics and Society in the South* (Cambridge, Mass.: Harvard University Press, 1987).

21. S. L. Elkin, "Twentieth Century Urban Regimes," *Journal of Urban Affairs* 7, no. 2 (1985): 13.

22. Smith, *The New Deal*, 116.

23. James C. Cobb, *Industrialization and Southern Society, 1877–1984* (Chicago: Dorsey Press, 1988), 39.

24. Rodney A. Erickson, "The Filtering-Down Process: Industrial Location in a Nonmetropolitan Area," *Professional Geographer* 28, no. 3 (August 1976): 254–60; Rodney A. Erickson, "Corporations, Branch Plants, and Employment Stability in Nonmetropolitan Areas," in *Industrial Location and Regional Systems*, ed. John Rees, Geoffrey J. D. Hewings, and Howard A. Stafford (Brooklyn: J. F. Bergins Publishers, 1981), 135–53; Sam O. Park and James O. Wheeler, "The Filtering-Down Process in Georgia: The Third Stage in the Product Life Cycle," *Professional Geographer* 35, no. 1 (February 1983), 18–31.

25. David Gordon, "Class Struggle and the Stages of American Urban Development," in *The Rise of the Sunbelt Cities*, ed. D. C. Perry and A. J. Watkins (Beverly Hills, Calif.: Sage Publications, 1977), 55–82.

26. U.S. Bureau of the Census, *1959 Census of Agriculture*, vol. 2, *General Report* (Washington, D.C.: Government Printing Office, 1962).

27. Gavin Wright, *Old South, New South: Revolutions in the Southern Economy Since the Civil War* (New York: Basic Books, 1986), 264–66.

28. Carter A. Wilson, *Racism: From Slavery to Advanced Capitalism* (Thousand Oaks, Calif.: Sage Publications, 1996), 154.

29. Horace Mann Bond, *Negro Education in Alabama: A Study in Cotton and Steel* (New York: Octagon Books, 1969), 145; for a discussion of black labor in Birmingham, see also

Paul B. Worthman, "Black Workers and Labor Unions in Birmingham, Alabama, 1897–1904," *Labor History* 10, no. 3 (Summer 1969), 375–405.

30. Stanley B. Greenberg, *Race and State in Capitalist Development: Comparative Perspectives* (New Haven, Conn.: Yale University Press, 1980), 121.

31. Cobb, *Industrialization*, 110.

32. Malcolm Bryan, Address to the Rotary Club of Atlanta, 23 January 1961, in A. Meier and E. Rudwick, *Civil Rights During the Kennedy Administration, 1961–1963*, part 1: The White House Central Files and Staff Files and the President's Office Files, microfilm (Frederick, Md.: University Publications of America, 1986).

33. Alton Hornsby, "A City That Was Too Busy to Hate," in *Southern Businessmen and Desegregation*, ed. E. Jacoway and D. R. Colburn (Baton Rouge: Louisiana State University Press, 1982), 120–36; see also James C. Cobb, *The Selling of the South: The Southern Crusade for Industrial Development, 1936–1980* (Baton Rouge: Louisiana State University Press, 1982), 122–50.

34. Greenberg, *Race and State*, 125.

35. Greenberg, *Race and State*, 407.

36. Black and Black, *Southern Politics and Society*, 46.

18

Conclusion

Although ideologies associated with racial dominance may be grounded in natural differences, this book has demonstrated that to claim that race-connected practices are based on the natural realm is to understate the role of major historical and political developments associated with the rise of the modern nation-state and the restructuring of capitalism. The political workings of the Jacksonian Democrats and the Republicans, the southern disfranchisement movement, and the southern populist movement all played major roles in transforming race in Birmingham. Planters maintained tremendous economic and social influence that extended into the postbellum period, when the Republicans made major concessions to this class that transformed race.

Southern white labor may have shown more overt antagonism toward blacks than workers elsewhere, but it was the actions of the ruling elites that legitimized this antagonism. Stanley Greenberg noted, "Racial categories are real, not simply surrogates for hidden, material forces: the dominant racial section does not dissolve into the bourgeoisie and the subordinate population into the proletariat; racial prejudice and group sentiment cannot be dismissed as superstructure or false consciousness."[1] Thus, contrary to Marxist theory, capital development in much of the modern world left race-connected practices largely intact.

Although race and ethnicity were often central to class struggles and Karl Marx recognized the importance of slavery in capitalist development, he and the neo-Marxists consistently marginalized or untheorized race. Manning Marable clearly documented that "capitalism underdeveloped black America."[2] But neither Marx nor Friedrich Engels ever theorized the underdevelopment of blacks in capitalist development. Racism negated any possibilities of English working-class consciousness in the eighteenth and nineteenth centuries, but, for racist or other reasons, Marx and Engel never questioned Anglo-Saxon supremacy—the historical right of one race to reduce another race to abject conditions of subjugation.

The critique of world capitalism often acquired force from racial and ethnic minorities, not just from movements of industrial workers in cities. Cedric Robinson noted, "The development, organization and expansion of capitalist society pursued essentially racial directions, so too social ideology." He also wrote,

> The English working class was never the singular social and historical entity suggested by the phrase [class]. . . . The negations resultant from capitalist modes of production, relations of production and ideology did not manifest themselves as an eradication of oppositions among the working classes.[3]

The racial stereotype of the Irish during Elizabethan England was often more derogatory than that applied to Africans, and traces of this stereotyping remained during the early phase of capitalist development in England, thereby negating working-class consciousness. Eventually the Irish assimilated with other Europeans as "whites" in the United States. The construction of whiteness for the Irish and other European immigrants provided the roots for conflict with black Americans that led to the underdevelopment of blacks.[4]

Yet, when conducting an analysis of the socioeconomic evolution of racism, Marx and Engels threw both materialism and dialectics to the winds.[5] Even the Frankfurt School, which influenced a generation of "new" leftists of various racial/ethnic groups—many of whom participated in or supported the struggle for racial equality—was not known initially for theorizing about "racial" problems.[6] Failure to apply Marxism and its critical analysis of capitalism to the black situation was, according to W. E. B. DuBois,

> a great loss to American Negroes. . . . Whatever he [Marx] said and did concerning the uplift of the working class must, therefore, be modified so far as Negroes are concerned by the fact that he had not studied at first hand their peculiar race problem in America.[7]

After the deaths of Marx and Engels, the official Marxian movement conceived of Marxism more as a theory of scientific socialism or as an instrument of political practice that provided for the ideology of left-wing political movements than as an instrument of critical social analysis.[8] Vladimir Lenin did raise the "Negro question" at the Second Congress of the Communist International in 1920 when he argued that the black proletariat in the United States was the most advanced sector of the black world. In 1928–1929, the Communist International Congress characterized the black belt of the southern United States an oppressed "nation." Yet, such presumptions were more a vulgarization of Marxism than a product of critical social analysis.[9]

A. Sivanandan wrote that capital "requires racism not for racism's sake but for the sake of capital."[10] Slavery as a mode of production provided the material base for racism. Race-connected practices are a function of processes and structures in social formations that relate to wider *intersocietal* dynamics of production and exchange.[11] Racism became so deeply implanted in social consciousness that it was easy to introduce racial divisions among workers even in large-scale industry. Birmingham capitalists made workers more aware of their race than their class condition to instigate competition between the races. The continuing use of race to force competition inhibited the solidarity necessary for effective strike power and ensured the segmentation of labor.

Capitalists will use any method to keep labor and other resources freely exploitable, even if doing so entails adapting to existing racial preferences.[12] In other words, racial subordination may be seen as instrumental to the pursuit of profit. Race-connected practices may vary from place to place and time to time.[13] Nevertheless, labor segmentation was one of the most common ways to fragment U.S. workers as a class. Daniel Fusfeld noted, "Much of the exclusion of Blacks and other minorities from higher-wage jobs, adequate education and training, and the mainstream society as a whole fits into a larger pattern of exploitation."[14] Furthermore, according to Raymond Franklin, "As this reality becomes experientially internalized on the part of blacks, a lack of motivation to fulfill more than minimal job requirements may begin to operate."[15] The hegemony of the dominant class was so complete that it was easier for blacks to follow the course of least resistance than to battle for what history had shown to be the right course. After all, as Paul Baran and Paul Sweezy noted, blacks who knew and kept their place were "tolerated and even liked by whites. What whites hated was the [black] who believed in and acted on the principle that all men are created equal."[16]

Marx's marginalization of race provided people of color with almost no understanding of how capitalism transformed their lives.[17] Marxian critical theory suffers from what Stanley Aronowitz calls a "will to uniformity."[18] According to Ernesto Laclau and Chantal Mouffe, it subsumed the question of race into the main, working-class cohesion debate and ignored it, linking the idea of the centrality of the working class in capitalism to

> (a) a vision of the collapse of capitalism as determined by the contradiction between forces and relations of production which would lead to increasing social misery—that is to say, to the contradiction between the capitalist system as a whole and the vast masses of the population; and (b) to the idea that capitalism would lead to proletarianization of the middle classes and the peasantry, as a result of which, when the crisis of the system came about, everything would be reduced to a simple showdown between capitalists and workers.[19]

In Birmingham the proletarianization did not take place, and there is no reason to assume that it will occur in the near future, especially in the postmodern world. The historical traditions of classical Marxism must not be permitted to overburden the analysis of race in U.S. capitalist development.

No matter how important racial categories are, they may not be so universal that class is obscured or takes on a profound racial dimension. As Jack Bloom noted, "The foundation for and dynamic of Southern racism as it was confronted by the civil rights movement rested upon the class system of the South."[20] Race-connected practices, wrote Greenberg, must contend with a powerful social schism: to one side, a dominant section with disproportionate control over economic resources, a presumptive privilege in social relations, and a virtual monopoly on access to the state; to the other side, a subordinate section with constrained economic resources and with little standing in social or political relations.[21]

Race-connected practices are understood best if they are viewed within the larger context of class struggle and capitalist development. However, Eugene Genovese writes, "To say that the race question has to be subsumed under the class question is not to make it a mere facade for class exploitation, nor to deny it a life of its own." Referring to the slave South, he continues,

Rather, it is a matter of arguing that racism restricted the options open to those charged with guarding class interests; that it forced the defense of class power into some channels rather than others; and that it helped form the ideology of the ruling class in such a way as to render it much more rigid than would have been the case without it. It is to argue that race gave shape to class hegemony, not vice versa.[22]

We must continue to embrace the importance of class in capitalist development, but we must not deny race its ontological status.[23] It affects all three levels of social formation: economic, political, and ideological.[24] In George Frederickson's comparative work on white supremacy in the United States and South Africa, he does not assign priority to either race or class. Rather he notes that any attempt to do so would prove vain; both are mutually reinforcing.[25] If we critically analyze race-connected practices within the context of capitalist development, we can avoid assigning a priority to race or class; they are relational. Racial relations must contend with class relations. Greenberg's work pays particular attention to the role of certain class actors in patterns of racial domination. Rather than transcending race, class formation breathed new life into racial categories. Greenberg wrote,

By understanding the developing class relations . . . we can understand much of the specificity and the dynamic in developing race relations. Racial domination is not an amorphous, all-encompassing relationship between groups distinguished by physical characteristics but, for the most part, *a series of specific class relations that vary by place and over time and that change as a consequence of changing material conditions.*[26]

In responding to these changing material conditions, capitalism transforms race-connected practices and place. It was the interactive effects of race and class that produced and transformed "America's Johannesburg."

NOTES

1. Stanley B. Greenberg, *Race and State in Capitalist Development: Comparative Perspectives* (New Haven, Conn.: Yale University Press, 1980), 406.

2. Manning Marable, *How Capitalism Underdeveloped Black America: Problems in Race, Political Economy and Society* (Boston: South End Press, 1983), 1–19.

3. Cedric J. Robinson, *Black Marxism: The Making of the Black Radical Tradition* (London: Zed Press, 1983), 2, 51.

4. Noel Ignatiev, *How the Irish Became White* (New York: Routledge, 1995), 111–12.

5. Carlos Moore, *Were Marx and Engels White Racists? The Prolet-Aryan Outlook of Marx and Engels* (Chicago: Institute of Positive Education, 1972), 35.

6. Lucius Outlaw, "Toward a Critical Theory of 'Race,'" in *Anatomy of Racism*, ed. Theo Goldberg (Minneapolis: University of Minnesota Press, 1990), 69.

7. W. E. B. DuBois, "Karl Marx and the Negro," in *W. E. B. DuBois: The Crisis Writings*, ed. Daniel Walden (Greenwich, Conn.: Fawcett, 1972), 399; see also W. E. B. Dubois, "Karl Marx and the Negro," in *Crisis* 40 (March 1933), 55–56.

8. Douglas Kellner, *Herbert Marcuse and the Crisis of Marxism* (Berkeley: University of California Press, 1984), 58–59.

9. Robinson, *Black Marxism*, 306.

10. A. Sivanandan, "Race, Class and the State: The Black Experience in Britain," *Race and Class* 17 (1976): 367.

11. Michael Peter Smith and Richard Tardanico, "Urban Theory Reconsidered: Production, Reproduction and Collective Action," in *The Capitalist City: Global Restructuring and Community Politics*, ed. Michael Peter Smith and Joe R. Feagin (Cambridge, U.K.: Basil Blackwell, 1989), 87.

12. Oliver C. Cox, *Caste, Class, and Race* (New York: Modern Reader Paperbacks, 1970), 333.

13. Raymond S. Franklin, *Shadows of Race and Class* (Minneapolis: University of Minnesota Press, 1991), 69–88.

14. Daniel R. Fusfeld, "Capitalist Exploitation and Black Labor: An Extended Conceptual Framework," *Review of Black Political Economy* 10, no. 3 (Spring 1980): 245.

15. Franklin, *Shadows*, 74.

16. Paul A. Baran and Paul M. Sweezy, *Monopoly Capital: An Essay on the American Economic and Social Order* (New York: Monthly Review Press, 1966), 253.

17. Robinson, *Black Marxism*.

18. Stanley Aronowitz, *The Crisis in Historical Materialism: Class, Politics and Culture in Marxist Theory* (Minneapolis: University of Minnesota Press, 1990), 90.

19. Ernesto Laclau and Chantal Mouffe, "Post-Marxism Without Apologies," *New Left Review* 166 (November/December 1987): 104; see also Ernesto Laclau and Chantal Mouffe, *Hegemony and Socialist Strategy: Toward a Radical Democratic Politics* (London: Verso, 1985), 159–75.

20. Jack M. Bloom, *Class, Race, and the Civil Rights Movement* (Bloomington: Indiana University Press, 1987), 58.

21. Greenberg, *Race and State*, 30.

22. Eugene D. Genovese, *The World the Slaveholders Made* (New York: Pantheon Books, 1969), 238.

23. Greenberg, *Race and State*, 406.

24. Robert Miles, *Racism and Migrant Labor* (London: Routledge and Kegan Paul, 1982), 99.

25. George M. Fredrickson, *White Supremacy: A Comparative Study in American and South African History* (New York: Oxford University Press, 1981), xx–xxi.

26. Greenberg, *Race and State*, 406. Emphasis added.

Bibliography

Abstract and Index of Ordinances of the City of Birmingham Passed Since the Adoption of the City Code of 1905. Compiled by J. P. Mudd, Assistant City Attorney, Birmingham, Ala. 9 August 1913.

Acts of Alabama, 1870–71. Montgomery, Ala.: W. W. Screws, State Printer, 1871.

Aglietta, M. *A Theory of Capitalist Regulation: The U.S. Experience.* Translated by D. Fernbach. London: NLB, 1979.

Agnew, John A. "Sameness and Difference: Hartshorne's *The Nature of Geography* and Geography as a Real Variation." In *Reflections on Richard Hartshorne's The Nature of Geography,* edited by J. Nicholas Entrikin and Stanley D. Brunn. Washington, D.C.: Association of American Geographers, 1989.

"The Alabama Decision." *Nation* 76, no. 1974 (30 April 1903): 346.

"Alabama: Its Iron Mountains and Coal Basin." *The Iron Age.* 15 July 1875.

Alabama Mine Inspector. *Coal Mine Statistics of State of Alabama for 1910.* Birmingham, Ala.: Grant and Pow, 1911.

"Alabama Miners: Many Delegates Present." *United Mine Workers Journal.* 25 June 1908.

Allen, James S. *Reconstruction: The Battle for Democracy (1865–1876).* New York: International Publishers, 1937.

———. *The Negro Question in the United States.* New York: International Publishers, 1936.

Allen, Theodore W. *The Invention of the White Race: Racial Oppression and Social Control.* Volume 1. London: Verso, 1994.

Alvarez, Eugene. *Travel on Southern Antebellum Railroads, 1828–1860.* Tuscaloosa: University of Alabama Press, 1974.

Andrews, George Reid. "Comparing the Comparers: White Supremacy in the United States and South Africa." *Journal of Social History* 20 (Spring 1987): 585–99.

Annual Report of the State Auditor, 1928.

Annual Report of the State Auditor, 1919.

Annual Report of the State Auditor, 1883, 1898.

Anti-Boycott Bill. No. 329, H. 518, 1903.

"Arbitration Commission Heard Much Testimony Yesterday." *Birmingham Age-Herald.* 16 August 1903.

Armes, Ethel. *The Story of Coal and Iron in Alabama.* Birmingham, Ala.: Chamber of Commerce, 1910.

Aronowitz, Stanley. *The Politics of Identity: Class, Culture, Social Movements.* New York: Routledge, 1992.

———. *The Crisis in Historical Materialism: Class, Politics and Culture in Marxist Theory.* Minneapolis: University of Minnesota Press, 1990.

"A Bright Future For Birmingham." *The Iron Age.* 12 April 1883.

Associated Press v. NLRB. 301 U.S. 103.

Bailey, Hugh C. *Liberalism in the New South: Southern Social Reformers and the Progressive Movement.* Coral Gables, Fla.: University of Miami Press, 1969.

Bailey, Richard. *Neither Carpetbaggers nor Scalawags: Black Officeholders During the Reconstruction of Ala., 1867–1878.* Montgomery, Ala.: Richard Bailey Publishers, 1991.

Baker v. Carr. 369 U.S. 186, 1962.

Baran, Paul A., and Paul M. Sweezy. *Monopoly Capital: An Essay on the American Economic and Social Order.* New York: Monthly Review Press, 1966.

Baruch, Basil. *The History of the New Deal 1933–1938.* New York: Capricorn, 1963.

Bates, Thomas. "Gramsci and the Theory of Hegemony." *Journal of the History of Ideas 36,* no. 2 (1975): 351–66.

Baughn, W. H. "Capital Formation and Entrepreneurship in the South." *Southern Economic Journal* 16, no. 2 (October 1949): 161–69.

Beiman, Irving. "Birmingham: Steel Giant with a Glass Jaw." In *Our Fair City,* edited by Robert S. Allen. New York: Vanguard Press, 1947.

Bendix, Reinhard. *Nation-Building and Citizenship: Studies of Our Changing Social Order.* Berkeley: University of California Press, 1977.

Benedict, Ruth. *Patterns of Culture.* Boston: Houghton Mifflin, 1934.

Bergstressor, Jack Roland, Sr. "Raw Material Constraints and Technological Options in the Mines and Furnaces of the Birmingham District, 1876–1930." Ph.D. diss., Auburn University, Auburn, Ala., 1993.

Berry, Brian J. L. *Long-Wave Rhythms in Economic Development and Political Behavior.* Baltimore: Johns Hopkins University Press, 1991.

Berry, Mary Frances. *Black Resistance, White Law: A History of Constitutional Racism in America.* New York: Meridith Corp., 1971.

Bhaduri, A. "A Study in Agricultural Backwardness Under Semi-Feudalism." *Economic Journal* 83, no. 329 (March 1973): 120–37.

Billings, Dwight B. *Planters and the Making of a "New South": Class, Politics, and Development in North Carolina, 1865–1900.* Chapel Hill: University of North Carolina Press, 1979.

Birmingham Racial Segregation Ordinances. Reprinted and Distributed by the Civil Rights Institute, Birmingham, Ala., 1992.

Blackburn, Robin. *The Making of New World Slavery: From Baroque to the Modern, 1492–1800.* London: Verso, 1997.

Blaut, James M. "Where Was Capitalism Born?" *Antipode: A Radical Journal of Geography* 8 (1976): 1–11.

———. "Imperialism: The Marxist Theory and Its Evolution." *Antipode: A Radical Journal of Geography* 7 (1975): 1–19.

Bloom, Jack M. *Class, Race, and the Civil Rights Movement.* Bloomington: Indiana University Press, 1987.

Bloom, Solomon F. *The World of Nations: A Study of the National Implications in the World of Karl Marx.* New York: Columbia University Press, 1941.

Blumer, Herbert. "Industrialisation and Race Relations." In *Industrialisation and Race Relations: A Symposium,* edited by Guy Hunter. London: Oxford University Press, 1965.

Bonacich, Edna. "Abolition, the Extension of Slavery, and the Position of Free Blacks: A Study of Split Labor Markets in the United States, 1830–1863." *American Journal of Sociology* 81 (November 1975): 617–28.

Bond, Horace Mann. *Negro Education in Alabama: A Study in Cotton and Steel.* New York: Octagon Books, 1969.

———. "Social and Economic Forces in Alabama Reconstruction." *Journal of Negro History* 23, no. 3 (July 1938): 290–348.

Bondi, Liz. "Feminism, Postmodernism, and Geography: Space for Women." *Antipode: A Radical Journal of Geography* 22, no. 2 (August 1990): 156–67.

"Boon to People." *Labor Advocate*. 26 April 1902.

Bowie v. B. R. And Electric Co. 125 Ala. 397.

Bowlby, Sophie, Jane Lewis, Linda McDowell, and Jo Foord. "The Geography of Gender." In *New Models in Geography: Political–Economy Perspectives*. Vol. 2, edited by Richard Peet and Nigel Thrift. London: Unwin Hyman, 1989.

Bowman, Shearer Davis. *Masters and Lords: Mid–19th-Century U.S. Planters and Prussian Junkers*. New York: Oxford University Press, 1993.

Brainerd, Alfred F. "Colored Mining Labor." *Transactions of the American Institute of Mining Engineers* 14 (1885–1886): 78–80.

Brandes, Stuart D. *American Welfare Capitalism, 1880–1940*. Chicago: University of Chicago Press, 1976.

Braverman, Harry. *Labor and Monopoly Capital: The Degradation of Work in the Twentieth Century*. New York: Monthly Review Press, 1974.

Brecher, Jeremy. *Strike*. San Francisco: Straight Arrow Books, 1972.

Brenner, Robert. "The Origins of Capitalism: A Critique of Neo-Smithian Marxism." *New Left Review* 104 (1977): 25–92.

Brenner, Robert, and M. Glick. "The Regulation Approach: Theory and History." *New Left Review* 186 (1991): 45–119.

Brinkley, Alan. "The New Deal and Southern Politics." In The *New Deal in the South*, edited by James C. Cobb and Michael V. Nomorato. Jackson: University Press of Mississippi, 1984.

Brody, David. *Steelworkers in America: The Nonunion Era*. Cambridge, Mass.: Harvard University Press, 1960.

Brownell, Blaine A. "Birmingham, Alabama: New South City in the 1920's." *Journal of Southern History* 38, no. 1 (February 1972): 21–48.

Bryan, Malcolm. "Address to the Rotary Club of Atlanta, 23 January 1961." In A. Meier and E. Rudwick, *Civil Rights During the Kennedy Administration, 1961–1963*. Part 1: *The White House Central Files and Staff Files and the President's Office Files*. Frederick, Md.: University Publications of America, 1986. Microfilm.

Caldwell, Earl. "Gaining Ground on Black Property," *Black Enterprise* (May 1978): 21–24, 48.

Caldwell, H. M. *History of the Elyton Land Company and Birmingham, Ala*. Birmingham, Ala.: Birmingham Publishing Co., 1892.

Calhoun, William P. *The Caucasian and the Negro in the United States*. Columbia, S.C.: R. L. Bryan Co., 1902.

Camejo, Peter. *Racism, Revolution, Reaction, 1861–1877: The Rise and Fall of Radical Reconstruction*. New York: Pathfinder, 1976.

Carroll, Charles. *The Negro a Beast: or, in the Image of God*. St. Louis: American Book and Bible House, 1900.

Cash, Wilbur J. *The Mind of the South*. New York: Alfred A. Knopf, 1941.

Cell, John W. *The Highest Stage of White Supremacy: The Origins of Segregation in South Africa and the American South*. Cambridge, U.K.: Cambridge University Press, 1982.

Chandler, Alfred D., Jr. *The Railroads: The Nation's First Big Business*. New York: Harcourt, Brace and World, 1965.

Cheung, N. S. *The Theory of Share Tenancy*. Chicago: University of Chicago Press, 1969.

Chicago Defender. 10 February 1917.

City Ordinance 709-F. 1949.

"City Zoning Law Declared Safe." *Birmingham Age-Herald*. 3 December 1926.

Clark, Thomas, and Albert Kirwan. *The South Since Appomattox*. New York: Oxford University Press, 1967.

Clark, Victor S. *The History of Manufactures in the United States*. New York: McGraw-Hill, 1929.

Cobb, James C. "Beyond Planters and Industrialists: A New Perspective on the New South." *Journal of Southern History* 54, no. 1 (February 1988): 45–68.

————. *Industrialization and Southern Society, 1877–1984*. Chicago: Dorsey Press, 1984.

————. *The Selling of the South: The Southern Crusade for Industrial Development, 1936–1980*. Baton Rouge: Louisiana State University Press, 1982.

The Code of Alabama, 1896. Vol. 2. Adopted February 16, 1897. Article 2, Sections 4476, 4477, and 4478. Atlanta, Ga.: Foote and Davies, 1897.

The Code of Alabama, 1907. Vol. 2. Adopted July 27, 1907. Article 2, Section 6528. Nashville, Tenn.: Marshall and Bruce Company, 1907.

The Code of the City of Birmingham. Birmingham, Ala.: City Commission. Enacted 18 September 1917.

The Code of Ordinances of the City of Birmingham. Birmingham Ala.: Mayor and Aldermen, 1905.

Cohen, William. *At Freedom's Edge: Black Mobility and the Southern White Quest for Racial Control, 1861–1915*. Baton Rouge: Louisiana State University Press, 1991.

Collins, Charles W. *The Fourteenth Amendment and the States*. Boston: Little, Brown, 1912.

Committee on Education and Labor. *Federal Employment Practices Act*. 81st Cong., 1st sess., 1949 H.R. Doc.

Commons, John R. "Horace Greeley and the Working Class Origins of the Republican Party." *Political Science Quarterly* 24, no. 3 (September 1909): 468–88.

Cone, James H. *For My People: Black Theology and the Black Church, Where Have We Been and Where Are We Going*. New York: Orbis, 1984.

Congressional Record. 3 April 1933.

Connerly, Charles E. "Urban Rivalry and the South: Atlanta and Birmingham." Paper presented at the Fifth National Conference on American Planning History, Chicago, Ill., 19 November 1993.

Connerly, Charles E., and Bobby M. Wilson. "Planning, Jim Crow, and the Civil Rights Movement: The Rebirth and Demise of Racial Zoning in Birmingham." Paper presented at the Association of Collegiate Schools of Planning Annual Conference, Columbus, Ohio, 31 October 1992.

Conrad, Alfred H., and John R. Meyer. *The Economics of Slavery and Other Econometric Studies*. Chicago: Aldine, 1964.

"Constitutionality of Segregation Ordinances." *Michigan Law Review* 16 (1917–18): 111.

"Convict Department, Its Management." Sworn Statement of Emmet O'Neal, Governor of Alabama. Investigating Committee. Montgomery, Ala.: Brown Printing Company, 1913.

Cooke, Philip. *Back to the Future*. London: Unwin Hyman, 1990.

Cooper, William J., Jr. *The South and the Politics of Slavery, 1828–1856*. Baton Rouge: Louisiana State University Press, 1978.

Copeland, Melvin T. *The Cotton Manufacturing Industry of the United States*. New York: A. M. Kelley, [1912] 1966.

Corbin, David A. "Class over Caste: Interracial Solidarity in the Company Town." In *Blacks in Appalachia*, edited by William H. Turner and Edward J. Cabbell. Lexington: University Press of Kentucky, 1985.

Corley, Robert Gaines. "The Quest for Racial Harmony: Race Relations in Birmingham, Alabama, 1947–1963." Ph.D. diss., University of Virginia, 1979.

County of Santa Clara v. Southern Pacific Railroad. 116 U.S. 138, 1132, 1886.

Cox, Kevin R., and Andrew Mair. "Locality and Community in the Politics of Local Economic Development." *Annals of the Association of American Geographers* 78, no. 2 (June 1988): 307–25.

Cox, Oliver C. *Caste, Class and Race: A Study in Social Dynamics*. New York: Modern Reader Paperbacks, 1970.

Cvornyek, Robert Louis. "Convict Labor in the Alabama Coal Mines, 1874–1928." Ph.D. diss., Columbia University, 1993.

Davis, George A., and O. Fred Donaldson. *Blacks in the United States: A Geographic Perspective.* Boston: Houghton Mifflin, 1975.

Davis, John P. "A Black Inventory of the New Deal." *Crisis* 42 (May 1935): 141.

DeCanio, Stephen J. *Agriculture in the Postbellum South: The Economics of Production and Supply.* Cambridge, Mass.: MIT Press, 1974.

Desimone, M. "Racial Discourse in a Community: Language and the Social Construction of Race." *Journal of Negro Education* 62, no. 4 (Fall 1993): 414–18.

de Souza, Anthony R. "To Have and to Have Not: Colonialism and Core-Periphery Relations." *American Geographical Society's Focus* (Fall 1986): 14–19.

Dix, Keith. "Work Relations in the Coal Industry: The Hand Loading Era, 1880–1930." *West Virginia University Bulletin* 78, no. 7-2 (January 1978).

Dobzhansky, Theodosius. *Mankind Evolving: The Evolution of the Human Species.* New Haven, Conn.: Yale University Press, 1962.

Dodd, Donald B., and Wynelle S. Dodd. *Historical Statistics of the South.* Tuscaloosa, Ala.: University of Alabama Press, 1973.

Dollard, John. *Caste and Class in a Southern Town.* Garden City, N.Y.: Doubleday, 1957.

Douglass, Frederick. *Narrative of the Life of Frederick Douglass.* Wortley, U.K.: J. Barker, 1846.

Dowd, Douglas F. "A Comparative Analysis of Economic Development in the American West and South." *Journal of Economic History* 16, no. 4 (December 1956): 558–74.

Dred Scott v. Sanford. 19 Howard 393. 1856.

D'Souza, Dinesh. *The End of Racism: Principles for a Multiracial Society.* New York: Free Press, 1995.

DuBois, W. E. B. "Karl Marx and the Negro." In *W. E. B. DuBois: The Crisis Writings*, edited by Daniel Walden. Greenwich, Conn.: Fawcett, 1972.

———. *The Autobiography of W. E. B. Dubois.* New York: International Publishers, 1968.

———. *The Negro Artisan.* New York: Octagon Books, 1968.

———. *Black Reconstruction in America.* Cleveland, Ohio: World Publishing Co., 1964.

———. "Federal Action Programs and Community Action in the South." *Social Forces* 19, no. 3 (March 1941): 375–80.

———. "Karl Marx and the Negro." *Crisis* 40 (March 1933): 55–56.

Duncan, Simon. "What Is Locality?" In *New Models in Geography: The Political-Economy Perspective.* Volume 2, edited by Richard Peet and Nigel Thrift. London: Unwin Hyman, 1989.

Eisner, Marc Allen. *Regulatory Politics in Transition.* Baltimore: Johns Hopkins University Press, 1993.

Elkin, S. L. *City and Regime in the American Republic.* Chicago: University of Chicago Press, 1987.

———. "Twentieth-Century Urban Regimes." *Journal of Urban Affairs* 7, no. 2 (1985): 11–28.

"Eloquent Speech of W. R. Fairley Explaining the Miner Side." *Labor Advocate.* 31 July 1908.

Engels, Friedrich. *The Condition of the Working Class in England.* 1844. Reprint, Moscow: Progress Publishers, 1977.

Erickson, Rodney A. "Corporations, Branch Plants, and Employment Stability in Nonmetropolitan Areas." In *Industrial Location and Regional Systems*, edited by John Rees, Geoffrey J. D. Hewings, and Howard A. Stafford. Brooklyn, N.Y.: J. F. Bergins Publishers, 1981.

———. "The Filtering-Down Process: Industrial Location in a Nonmetropolitan Area." *Professional Geographer* 28, no. 3 (August 1976): 254–60.

Evans, Chris. *The Histories of the United Mine Workers of America.* Vol. 2, *1890–1900.* Chicago: Library Resources, 1970. Microfiche.

Evans, Frank V. "The Social Equality Horror." *Birmingham Age-Herald*. 24 August 1908.

————. "Social Equality Talk Evil Feature of Strike." *Birmingham Age-Herald*. 22 August 1908.

————. "Striking Miners Rally Near Mines at Dora." *Birmingham Age-Herald*. 8 August 1908.

Ewen, Stuart. *All Consuming Images: The Politics of Style in Contemporary Culture*. New York: Basic Books, 1988.

Facts About Coalburg Prison: Doctor Parkes' Report Reviewed. Birmingham, Ala.: Archives, Birmingham Public Library, n.d.

Feldman, Marshall M. A. "Spatial Structures of Regulation and Urban Regimes." In *Reconstructing Urban Regime Theory: Regulating Urban Politics in a Global Economy*, edited by Mickey Lauria. Thousand Oaks, Calif.: Sage Publications, 1997.

Femia, Joseph. "Hegemony and Consciousness in the Thought of Antonio Gramsci," *Political Studies* 23, no. 1 (1975): 29–48.

Fields, Barbara J. "Ideology and Race in American History." In *Region, Race, and Reconstruction: Essays in Honor of C. Vann Woodward*, edited by J. Morgan Kousser and James M. McPherson. New York: Oxford University Press, 1982.

Fifth Biennial Report of the Inspectors of Convicts. September 1, 1902, to August 31, 1904. Montgomery, Ala.: State Printer.

Fine, Ben, and Ellen Leopold. *The World of Consumption*. London: Routledge, 1993.

First Biennial Report of the Board of Managers of Convicts. September 1, 1882, to August 31, 1894. Montgomery, Ala.: Brown Printing Co., 1894.

First Biennial Report of the Inspector of Convicts. October 1, 1884, to September 30, 1886. Montgomery, Ala.: Barrett and Company, State Printer and Binde, 1886.

First Biennial Report of the Inspector of Convicts. September 1, 1894, to August 31, 1896. Montgomery, Ala.: State Printer, 1896.

Fisher, James S. "Negro Farm Ownership in the South." *Annals of the Association of American Geographers* 63, no. 4 (December 1973): 478–89.

Fitch, John A. "Birmingham District: Labor Conservation." *Survey* 27, no. 14 (6 January 1912): 1527–40.

Fite, Gilbert C. *Cotton Fields No More: Southern Agriculture 1865–1980*. Lexington: University Press of Kentucky, 1984.

Fleisig, Heywood. "Mechanizing the Cotton Harvest in the Nineteenth-Century South." *Journal of Economic History* 25 (1977): 704–706.

Flynt, Wayne. *Poor But Proud: Alabama's Poor Whites*. Tuscaloosa: University of Alabama Press, 1989.

Flynt, J. Wayne. "The New Deal and Southern Labor." In *The New Deal and the South*, edited by James C. Cobb and Michael V. Namorato. Jackson: University Press of Mississippi, 1984.

Fogel, Robert William, and Stanley L. Engerman. *Time on the Cross: The Economics of American Negro Slavery*. 2 vols. Boston: Little, Brown, 1974.

Foner, Eric. *Free Soil, Free Labor, Free Men: The Ideology of the Republican Party Before the Civil War*. New York: Oxford University Press, 1970.

Fortune, T. Thomas. *Black and White: Land, Labor, and Politics in the South*. New York: Fords, Howard, & Hubert, 1884.

Fox, Ralph. *Marx, Engels and Lenin on Ireland*. New York: International Publishers, 1940.

Fox-Genovese, Elizabeth, and Eugene D. Genovese. *Fruits of Merchant Capital: Slavery and Bourgeois Property in the Rise and Expansion of Capitalism*. New York: Oxford University Press, 1983.

Franklin, Raymond S. *Shadows of Race and Class*. Minneapolis: University of Minnesota Press, 1991.

Fredrickson, George M. *Black Liberation: A Comparative History of Black Ideologies in the United States and South Africa*. New York: Oxford University Press, 1995.

———. *White Supremacy: A Comparative Study in American and South African History*. New York: Oxford University Press, 1981.

———. *The Black Image in the White Mind: The Debate of Afro-American Character and Destiny, 1817–1914*. New York: Harper and Row, 1972.

———. "Toward a Social Interpretation of the Development of American Racism." In *Key Issues in the Afro-American Experience*, edited by Nathan I. Huggins, Martin Kilson, and Daniel M. Fox. New York: Harcourt Brace Jovanovich, 1971.

Fry, H. *Financial Invasion of the U.S.A.: A Threat to American Society?* New York: McGraw-Hill, 1980.

Frye, Robert J. *Housing and Urban Renewal in Alabama*. Tuscaloosa: University of Alabama, Bureau of Public Administration, 1965.

Fuller, Justin. "History of the Tennessee Coal, Iron, and Railroad Company, 1852–1907." Ph.D. diss., University of North Carolina at Chapel Hill, 1966.

Fusfeld, Daniel R. "Capitalist Exploitation and Black Labor: An Extended Conceptual Framework." *Review of Black Political Economy* 10, no. 3 (Spring 1980): 244–46.

Garrow, David J. *Birmingham, Alabama, 1956–1963*. Brooklyn, N.Y.: Carlson Publishing, 1989.

———. *Bearing the Cross: Martin Luther King, Jr., and the Southern Christian Leadership Conference*. New York: William Morrow, 1986.

Gatewood, Lucien B. "The Black Artisan in the U.S., 1890–1930," *Review of Black Political Economy* 5 (Fall 1974): 19–33.

The General Code of the City of Birmingham. Enacted 21 October 1930. Birmingham, Ala.: City Commission.

Genovese, Eugene D. *Roll, Jordan, Roll: The World the Slaves Made*. New York: Pantheon Books, 1974.

———. *The World the Slaveholders Made*. New York: Pantheon Books, 1969.

———. *The Political Economy of Slavery: Studies in the Economy and Society of the Slave South*. New York: Vintage Books, 1967.

Gibson-Graham, J. K. *The End of Capitalism (as We Knew It): A Feminist Critique of Political Economy*. Cambridge, Mass.: Basil Blackwell, 1996.

Giedion, Siegfried. *Mechanization Takes Command*. New York: Norton, 1948.

Giles v. Harris. 189 U.S. 475, 1903.

Gilroy, Paul. "One Nation Under a Groove: The Culture Politics of 'Race' and Racism in Britain." In *Anatomy of Racism*, edited by David Theo Goldberg. Minneapolis: University of Minnesota Press, 1990.

Goldberg, David Theo. "'Polluting the Body Politic': Racist Discourse and Urban Location." In *Racism, the City and the State*, edited by Malcolm Cross and Michael Keith. London: Routledge, 1993.

Goldfield, David R. *Black, White, and Southern: Race Relations and Southern Culture, 1940 to the Present*. Baton Rouge: Louisiana State University Press, 1990.

Gordon, David. "Capitalist Development and the History of American Cities." In *Marxism and the Metropolis: New Perspectives in Urban Political Economy*, edited by W. K. Tabb and Larry Sawers. New York: Oxford University Press, 1978.

———. "Class Struggle and the Stages of American Urban Development." In *The Rise of the Sunbelt Cities*, edited by D. C. Perry and A. J. Watkins. Beverly Hills, Calif.: Sage Publications, 1977.

Gordon, David, Richard Edwards, and Michael Reich. *Segmented Work, Divided Workers: The Historical Transformation of Labor in the United States.* Cambridge, Mass.: Cambridge University Press, 1982.

Gonverneur, Jacques. *Contemporary Capitalism and Marxist Economics.* Totowa, N.J.: Barnes and Noble Books, 1983.

Gramsci, Antonio. *Prison Notebooks,* edited and translated by Quintin Hoare and Geoffrey Nowell Smith. New York: International Publishers, 1971.

Greenberg, Edward S. *Serving the Few: Corporate Capitalism and the Bias of Government Policy.* New York: Wiley, 1974.

Greenberg, Stanley B. *Race and State in Capitalist Development: Comparative Perspectives.* New Haven, Conn.: Yale University Press, 1980.

Griffith, David W. *The Birth of a Nation.* New York: The Epoch Producing Corporation, 1915.

Gross, Jimmie Frank. "Alabama Politics and the Negro, 1874–1901." Ph.D. diss., University of Georgia, 1969.

Gutman, Herbert G. *Work, Culture, and Society in Industrializing America: Essays in American Working-Class and Social History.* New York: Alfred A. Knopf, 1976.

———. "Black Coal Miners and the Greenback-Labor Party in Redeemer, Alabama: 1878–1879." *Labor History* 10, no. 3 (Summer 1969): 506–35.

———. "The Negro and the United Mine Workers of America: The Career and Letters of Richard L. Davis and Something of Their Meaning: 1890–1900." In *The Negro and the American Labor Movement,* edited by Julius Jacobson. Garden City, N.J.: Anchor Books, 1968.

Habermas, Jürgen. "What Does Socialism Mean Today? The Rectifying Revolution and the Need for New Thinking on the Left." *New Left Review* 183 (September–October 1990): 3–21.

Hacker, Andrew. *Two Nations.* New York: Charles Scribner's Sons, 1992.

———. "Do Corporations Have a Social Duty?" In *The Corporation in the American Economy,* edited by H. M. Trebing. Chicago: Quadrangle Books, 1970.

———. *The Corporate Takeover.* New York: Harper & Row, 1964.

Hall, P., ed. *von Thunen's Isolated State: An English Version of "Der Isolierte Staat."* Translated by C. M. Wartenberg. New York: Pergamon Press, 1966.

Hammond, J. L, and Barbara Hammond. *The Town Labourer, 1760–1832.* London: Longmans, Green & Company, 1917.

Handlin, Oscar, and Mary F. Handlin. "Origins of the Southern Labor System," *William and Mary Quarterly* 7, series 3 (1950): 199–222.

Harper, Ann. *The Location of the United States Steel Industry, 1879–1919.* New York: Arno Press, 1977.

Harris, Carl V. *Political Power in Birmingham, 1871–1921.* Knoxville: University of Tennessee Press, 1977.

———. "Reforms in Government Control of Negroes in Birmingham, Alabama, 1890–1920." *Journal of Southern History* 38, no. 4 (November 1972): 567–600.

Harris, Donald J. "Capitalist Exploitation and Black Labor: Some Conceptual Issues." *Review of Black Political Economy* 8, no. 2 (Winter 1978): 133–51.

Harris, Leonard. "Historical Subjects and Interests: Race, Class and Conflict." In *The Year Left 2: Toward a Rainbow Socialism, Essays on Race, Ethnicity, Class and Gender,* edited by Mike Davis, Manning Marable, Fred Pfeil, and Michael Sprinker. London: Verso, 1987.

Harrison, Shelby M. "A Cash-Nexus for Crime," *Survey* 27, no. 14 (6 January 1912): 1541–51.

Harvey, David. *The Condition of Postmodernity: An Enquiry into the Origins of Cultural Change.* Cambridge, Mass.: Basil Blackwell, 1989.

————. *The Urban Experience.* Baltimore: Johns Hopkins University Press, 1989.

————. *Consciousness and the Urban Experience: Studies in the History and Theory of Capitalist Urbanization.* Baltimore: Johns Hopkins University Press, 1985.

————. *The Urbanization of Capital.* Baltimore: Johns Hopkins University Press, 1985.

————. *The Limits to Capital.* Oxford, U.K.: Basil Blackwell, 1982.

Hawley, L. T. "Negro Employment in the Birmingham Metropolitan Area." In *Selected Studies of Negro Employment in the South.* Washington, D.C.: National Planning Association, Committee of the South Reports, 1955.

Haywood, Harry. *Negro Liberation.* New York: International Publishers, 1948.

Head, Holman. "The Development of the Labor Movement in Alabama Prior to 1900." Master's thesis, University of Alabama, 1955.

"Health as an Indication of Housing Needs in Birmingham, Alabama and Recommendations for Slum Clearance, Redevelopment and Public Housing." Jefferson County Board of Health, Geo. A. Denison, M.D., Health Officer. 12 April 1950.

Hearings Before the Committee on Investigation of United States Steel Corporation. House of Representatives, 62nd Congress, 2nd Session. House Report. 1127. Washington: Government Printing Office, 1911.

Hearings Before a Subcommittee of the Committee on the Judiciary Relating to the Absorption of the Tennessee Coal, Iron, and Railroad Company by the United States Steel Corporation. 60th Congress, 2nd Session. Senate Report. 1110. Washington, D.C.: Government Printing Office, 1909.

"Henry F. DeBardeleben." Birmingham Public Library, Archives, Hill Ferguson Historical Collection, File 3.36.

"Henry F. Debardeleben of the Tennessee Coal, Iron and Railway Company gives his views on the iron situation in the Birmingham District." *Birmingham Age-Herald.* 13 April 1894.

Higgs, Robert. *Competition and Coercion: Blacks in the American Economy, 1865–1914.* Cambridge, Mass.: Cambridge University Press, 1977.

Hilferding, R. *Finance Capital.* London: Routledge and Kegan Paul, 1980.

Hill, Herbert. "Myth-Making as Labor History: Herbert Gutman and the United Mine Workers of America." *Politics, Culture, and Society* 2, no. 2 (Winter 1988): 132–200.

"The History of the Tennessee Coal, Iron and Railroad Company, 1852–1932. Prepared by W. B. Allen. Archives, Birmingham Public Library, 1932.

Hoffsommer, Harold. *Landlord–Tenant Relations and Relief in Alabama.* Federal Emergency Relief Administration Research Bulletin, 2d ser., no. 9. Washington, 1935.

Holmes, John. "The Organization and Locational Structure of Production Subcontracting." In *Production, Work, Territory: The Geographical Anatomy of Industrial Capitalism,* edited by A. Scott and M. Storper. Boston: Allen & Unwin, 1986.

Honey, Michael. "Industrial Unionism and Racial Justice in Memphis." In *Organized Labor in the Twentieth-Century South,* edited by Robert H. Zieger. Knoxville: University of Tennessee Press, 1991.

Hornsby, Alton. "A City That Was Too Busy to Hate." In *Southern Businessmen and Desegregation,* edited by E. Jacoway and D. R. Colburn. Baton Rouge: Louisiana State University Press, 1982.

Horwitz, Morton. *The Transformation of American Law, 1870–1960.* New York: Oxford University Press, 1992.

"How Miners are Fleeced." *Labor Advocate.* 9 June 1894.

Hudson, Hosea. *Black Worker in the Deep South.* New York: International Publishers, 1972.

Hunt, Douglas L. "More Facts About Negro Housing." Parts 1 and 2, *Birmingham News.* 12, 14 November 1947.

Huntley, Horace. "Iron Ore Miners and Mine Mill in Alabama, 1933–1952." Ph.D. diss., University of Pittsburgh, 1976.

Ignatiev, Noel. *How the Irish Became White*. New York: Routledge, 1995.

"The Industrial South: Birmingham, Alabama." *Harpers' Weekly* 31 (26 March 1887): 213–15.

Ingalls, Robert. "Antiradical Violence in Birmingham During the 1930s." *Journal of Southern History* 47, no. 4 (November 1981): 521–44.

"Invites All North." *Chicago Defender*. 10 February 1917.

Jackson, Peter. "Geography, Race, and Racism." In *New Models in Geography: The Political-Economy Perspectives*. Vol. 2, edited by Richard Peet and Nigel Thrift. London: Unwin Hyman, 1989.

———. "The Idea of 'Race' and the Geography of Racism." In *Race and Racism: Essays in Social Geography*, edited by Peter Jackson. London: Allen and Unwin, 1987.

Jaynes, Gerald David. *Branches Without Roots: Genesis of the Black Working Class in the American South, 1862–1882*. New York: Oxford University Press, 1989.

Jessop, Bob. "Post-Fordism and the State." In *Post-Fordism: A Reader*, edited by Ash Amin. Oxford, U.K.: Basil Blackwell, 1994.

Joll, James. *Antonio Gramsci*. New York: Penguin Books, 1978.

Jones, Lewis W. "Fred L. Shuttlesworth: Indigenous Leader." In *Birmingham, Alabama, 1956–1963*, edited by David J. Garrow. Brooklyn: Carlson Publishing, 1989.

Jordan, Winthrop D. *White over Black: American Attitudes Toward the Negro, 1550–1812*. New York: W. W. Norton, 1977.

Katznelson, Ira. *Black Men, White Cities: Race Politics and Migration in the United States, 1900–30, and Britain, 1948–68*. London: Oxford University Press, 1973.

Kayatekin, Serap Ayse. "Sharecropping and Class: A Preliminary Analysis." *Rethinking Marxism* 9, no. 1 (Spring 1996/97): 28–57.

Kelley, Robin D. G. *Race Rebels: Culture, Politics, and the Black Working Class*. New York: Free Press, 1994.

———. *Hammer and Hoe: Alabama Communists During the Great Depression*. Chapel Hill: University of North Carolina Press, 1990.

Kellner, Douglas. *Herbert Marcuse and the Crisis of Marxism*. Berkeley: University of California Press, 1984.

Kemmis, Daniel. *Community and the Politics of Place*. Norman: University of Oklahoma Press, 1990.

Kent, Russel. "Senate Hears of Distress in City." *Birmingham Age-Herald*. 6 January 1932.

Kiessling, O. E. "Coal Mining in the South." *Annals of the American Academy of Political and Social Science* 153 (January 1931): 84–93.

Kilson, Martin. "Black Politicians: A New Power." *Dissent* (August 1971): 333–45.

King, R. J. "Capital Switching and the Role of Ground Rent 1, Theoretical Problems." *Environment and Planning A* 21 (1989): 445–62.

Kleniewski, Nancy. "From Industrial to Corporate City: The Role of Urban Renewal." In *Marxism and the Metropolis: New Perspectives in Urban Political Economy*. Edited by William K. Tabb and Larry Sawers. New York: Oxford University Press, 1984.

Kolchin, Peter. *First Freedom: The Responses of Alabama's Blacks to Emancipation and Reconstruction*. Westport, Conn.: Greenwood Press, 1972.

Kondratieff, N. D. "The Long Waves in Economic Life." *Review of Economic Statistics* 17, no. 6 (November 1935): 105–14.

Krebs, Sylvia H. "Will the Freedmen Work? White Alabamians Adjust to Free Black Labor." *Alabama Historical Quarterly* 36, no. 2 (Summer 1974): 151–63.

Kulik, Gary. "Black Workers and Technological Change in the Birmingham Iron Industry, 1881–1931." In *Southern Workers and Their Unions, 1880–1975*, edited by Merl E. Reed, Leslie S. Hough, and Gary M. Fink. Westport, Conn.: Greenwood Press, 1981.

Kutler, Stanley I. *The Dred Scott Decision: Law or Politics.* Boston: Houghton Mifflin, 1967.

Kuznets, Simon. "Innovations and Adjustments in Economic Growth." *Swedish Journal of Economics* 74 (1972): 431–51.

———. *Capital in the American Economy: Its Formation and Financing.* Washington, D. C.: National Bureau of Economic Research, 1961.

"The Laborers War." *Labor Advocate.* 2 April 1898.

Laclau, Ernesto, and Chantal Mouffe. "Post-Marxism Without Apologies." *New Left Review* 166 (November/December 1987): 79–106.

———. *Hegemony and Socialist Strategy: Toward a Radical Democratic Politics.* London: Verso, 1985.

LaFever, Mortier W. "Workers, Machinery, and Production in the Automobile Industry." *Monthly Labor Review* 19, no. 4 (October 1924): 735-60.

Lamonte, Edward S. "Politics and Welfare in Birmingham, Alabama: 1900–1975." Ph.D. diss., University of Chicago, 1976.

Larson, M. S. "Proletarianisation and Educated Labor." *Theory and Society* 9 (1980): 131–75.

Lash, Scott. *Sociology of Postmodernism.* London: Routledge, 1990.

Lauria, Mickey. "Introduction: Reconstructing Urban Regime Theory." In *Reconstructing Urban Regime Theory: Regulating Urban Politics in a Global Economy*, edited by Mickey Lauria. Thousand Oaks, Calif.: Sage Publications, 1997.

Laws Governing State and County Convicts. Article 2. Alabama code of 1896.

Lefebvre, Henri. *The Production of Space.* Translated by Donald Nicholson-Smith. Oxford, U.K.: Basil Blackwell, 1991.

———. *The Survival of Capitalism.* London: Allison and Busby, 1976.

Leighton, George R. "Birmingham, Alabama: The City of Perceptual Praise." *Harper's* 175 (1937): 225–42.

Lembeck, Jerry. "Class Analysis and Studies of the U.S. Working Class: Theoretical, Conceptual, and Methodological Issues." In *Bringing Class Back In: Comparative and Historical Perspectives*, edited by Scott G. McNall, Rhonda F. Levine, and Rick Fantasia. Boulder, Colo.: Westview Press, 1991.

Lerner, Jack Leonard. "A Moment of Shame: The Convict Lease System in Alabama." Master's thesis, Samford University, 1969).

"Let Us Have Peace." *Labor Advocate.* 19 July 1890.

Lewis, W. David. *Sloss Furnaces and the Rise of the Birmingham District: An Industrial Epic.* Tuscaloosa: University of Alabama Press, 1994.

———. "Joseph Bryan and the Virginia Connection in the Industrial Development of Northern Alabama." *Virginia Magazine of History and Biography* 98, no. 4 (October 1990): 613–40.

Liberson, Stanley, and Arnold R. Silverman. "The Precipitants and Underlying Conditions of Race Riots." *American Sociological Review* 30, no. 6 (December 1965): 887–98.

Lichtenstein, Alex. *Twice the Work of Free Labor: The Political Economy of Convict Labor in the New South.* London: Verso, 1996.

———. "Racial Conflict and Racial Solidarity in the Alabama Coal Strike of 1894: New Evidence for the Gutman-Hill Debate." *Labor History* 36, no. 1 (Winter 1995): 63–76.

———. "Twice the Work of Free Labor: Labor, Punishment, and the Task System in Georgia's Convict Mines." In *Race, Class, and Community in Southern Labor History*, edited by Gary M. Fink and Merl E. Reed. Tuscaloosa: University of Alabama Press, 1994.

Lincoln, Abraham. *Collected Works*. Vol. 5, edited by Roy P. Basler. New Brunswick, N.J.: Rutgers University Press, 1955.

Lindgren, James M. "'First and Foremost a Virginian,' Joseph Bryan and the New South Economy." *Virginia Magazine of History and Biography* 96, no. 2 (April 1988): 157–80.

Lipietz, A. "New Tendencies in the International Division of Labour: Regimes of Accumulation and Modes of Regulation." In *Production, Work, Territory: The Geographical Anatomy of Industrial Capitalism*, edited by A. Scott and M. Storper. Boston: Allen & Unwin, 1986.

Litwack, Leon F. *North of Slavery: The Negro in the Free States, 1790–1860*. Chicago: University of Chicago Press, 1961.

Loeb, Harold. *The Chart of Plenty: A Study of America's Product Capacity Based on the Findings of the National Survey of Potential Product Capacity*. New York: Viking Press, 1935.

Logan, John R., and Harvey L. Molotch. *Urban Fortunes: The Political Economy of Place*. Berkeley: University of California, 1987.

Logan, Rayford W. *The Negro in American Life and Thought: The Nadir, 1877–1901*. New York: Dial Press, 1954.

Lopez, Ian F. Haney. *White by Law: The Legal Construction of Race*. New York: New York University Press, 1996.

Luke, Timothy W. *Social Theory and Modernity: Critique, Dissent, and Revolution*. Newbury Park, Calif.: Sage Publications, 1990.

Lumpkin, Katharine DuPre. *The South in Progress*. New York: International Publishers, 1940.

Luraghi, Raimondo. *The Rise and Fall of the Plantation South*. New York: New Viewpoints, 1978.

———. "The Civil War and the Modernization of American Society: Social Structure and Industrial Revolution in the Old South Before and During the War." *Civil War History* 18, no. 3 (September 1972): 230–50.

Mancini, Matthew J. *One Dies, Get Another: Convict Leasing in the American South, 1866–1928*. Columbia: University of South Carolina Press, 1966.

Mandel, Ernest. "Explaining Long Waves of Capitalist Development." In *Long Waves in the World Economy*, edited by Christopher Freeman. London: Butterworths, 1983.

Mandle, Jay R. *The Roots of Poverty: The Southern Plantation Economy After the Civil War*. Durham, N.C.: Duke University Press, 1978.

Mann, Susan A. "Sharecropping in the Cotton South: A Case of Uneven Development in Agriculture." *Rural Sociology* 49, no. 3 (Fall 1984): 412–29.

Mann, Susan A., and James M. Dickinson. "Obstacles to the Development of a Capitalist Agriculture." *Journal of Peasant Studies* 5, no. 4 (1978): 466–81.

Manufacturers' Record 27. 7 June 1895.

Manufacturers' Record 15. 6 April 1889.

Manufacturers' Record 14. 3 November 1888.

Marx, Karl. "Wage Labour and Capital." *New Rhenish Gazette*, No. 266. 7 April 1849.

Marable, Manning. *Race, Reform, and Rebellion: The Second Reconstruction in Black America, 1945–1990*. 2d ed. Jackson: University Press of Mississippi, 1991.

———. *How Capitalism Underdeveloped Black America: Problems in Race, Political Economy and Society*. Boston: South End Press, 1983.

Marks, Carole. *Farewell—We're Good and Gone: The Great Black Migration*. Bloomington: Indiana University Press, 1991.

Markusen, Ann. *Regions: The Economics and Politics of Territory.* Totowa, N.J.: Rowman & Littlefield, 1987.

Marshall, F. Ray. *Labor in the South.* Cambridge, Mass.: Harvard University Press, 1967.

———. *The Negro and Organized Labor.* New York: Wiley, 1965.

Marshall, Michael. *Long Waves of Regional Development.* New York: St. Martin's Press, 1987.

Marshall, T. H. *Class, Citizenship and Social Development.* Chicago: University of Chicago Press, 1964.

Marx and Engels on the United States. Compiled by Nelly Rumyantseva. Moscow: Progress Publishers, 1979.

Marx, Karl. *Capital: A Critique of Political Economy.* Vol. 1. Translated by Ben Fowkes. New York: Vintage Books, 1977.

———. *Political Writings.* Vol. 2, *Surveys from Exile.* Baltimore: Penguin, 1974.

———. *Grundrisse: Foundations of the Critique of Political Economy.* Translated by Martin Nicolaus. New York: Vintage Books, 1973.

———. *Karl Marx to P. V. Annenkov, Brussels, 28 December 1846.* Reprinted in Karl Marx, *The Poverty of Philosophy.* New York: International Publishers, 1971.

———. *Capital.* Vol. 1. New York: International Publishers, 1967.

———. *Capital.* Vol. 2. Moscow: Progress Publishers, 1967.

———. *Capital.* Volume 1. Translated by Eden and Cedar Paul. New York: E. P. Dutton and Co., 1930.

Marx, Karl, and Friedrich Engels. *The Communist Manifesto.* New York: Penguin Books, 1967.

———. *The Communist Manifesto,* edited by Samuel H. Beer. New York: Appleton-Century-Crofts, 1955.

Massey, Douglas S., and Nancy A. Denton. *American Apartheid: Segregation and the Making of the Underclass.* Cambridge, Mass.: Harvard University Press, 1993.

Matthews v. City of Birmingham. No. 286046, N. D. Ala., 1947.

McAdam, Doug. *Political Process and the Development of Black Insurgency, 1930–1970.* Chicago: University of Chicago Press, 1982.

McFeely, William. *Yankee Stepfather: General O. O. Howard and the Freedmen.* New Haven, Conn.: Yale University Press, 1968.

McKelway, A. J. "Conservation of Childhood." *Survey* 28 (6 July 1912): 1530.

McKiven, Henry M., Jr. *Iron and Steel: Class, Race, and Community in Birmingham, Alabama, 1875–1920.* Chapel Hill: University of North Carolina Press, 1995.

McLaughlin, G., and S. Robock. *Why Industry Moves South.* Washington, D.C.: National Planning Association, Committee of the South, 1949.

McLaurin, Melton Alonza. *The Knights of Labor in the South.* Westport, Conn.: Greenwood Press, 1978.

Mensch, Gerhard, Charles Coutinho, and Klaus Kaasch. "Changing Capital Values and the Propensity to Innovate." In *Long Waves in the World Economy,* edited by Christopher Freeman. London: Butterworths, 1983.

Meyer, David R. "The Industrial Retardation of Southern Cities, 1860–1880." *Explorations in Economic History* 25, no. 4 (October 1988): 366–86.

Miles, Robert. *Racism and Migrant Labor.* London: Routledge and Kegan Paul, 1982.

Mill, John Stuart. *Principles of Political Economy.* Vol. 2. Boston: Charles C. Little and James Brown, 1848.

Miller, Randall M. "Daniel Pratt's Industrial Urbanism: The Cotton Mill Town in Antebellum Alabama." *Alabama Historical Quarterly* 34, no. 1 (Spring 1972): 5–35.

Mills, Frederick C. *Employment Opportunities in Manufacturing Industries in the United States*. National Bureau of Economic Research Bulletin no. 70. New York, 1938.

Milner, John T. *Alabama: As It Was, as It Is, and as It Will Be*. Montgomery, Ala.: Barrett and Brown, 1876.

———. *Report to the Governor of Alabama on the Alabama Central Railroad*. Montgomery, Ala.: Advertiser Book and Job Steam Press Print, 1859.

Miner, Claudia. "The 1886 Convention of the Knights of Labor." *Phylon* 44, no. 2 (June 1983): 147–59.

"Miners Convention." *Labor Advocate*. 18 June 1904.

"Miners, Pratt City in the Tells." *Labor Advocate*. 30 March 1894.

Mitchell, Martha. "Birmingham: A Biography of a City of the New South." Ph.D. diss., University of Chicago, 1946.

Mitchell, Wesley C. "A Review." In *Recent Economic Changes in the United States*. Report of the Committee on Recent Economic Changes, President's Conference on Unemployment. Vol. 2. New York: McGraw-Hill, 1929.

Mollenkopf, John H. *The Contested City*. Princeton, N.J.: Princeton University Press, 1983.

Monk v. City of Birmingham. 87 F. Supp. 538, N. D. Ala., 1949.

Montagu, Ashley. *Man's Most Dangerous Myth: The Fallacy of Race*. New York: Oxford University Press, 1974.

Moore, Barrington, Jr. *Social Origins of Dictatorship and Democracy: Lord and Peasant in the Making of the Modern World*. Boston: Beacon Press, 1966.

Moore, Carlos. *Were Marx and Engels White Racists? The Prolet-Aryan Outlook of Marx and Engels*. Chicago: Institute of Positive Education, 1972.

Mullins, Betty Hamaker. "The Steel Corporation's Purchase of the Tennessee Coal, Iron & Railroad Company in 1907." Master's thesis, Samford University, 1970.

Myers, J. "Black Human Capital: The Freedmen and the Reconstruction, 1860–1880." Ph.D. diss., Florida State University, 1974.

Myrdal, Gunnar. *An American Dilemma: The Negro Problem and Modern Democracy*. New York: Harper & Brother, 1944.

Nelson, Daniel. *Managers and Workers: Origins of the New Factory System in the United States, 1880–1920*. Madison: University of Wisconsin Press, 1975.

Nelson, R. *The Merger Movement in American Industry, 1895–1956*. Princeton, N.J.: Princeton University Press, 1959.

Nguyen, Dan Thu. "The Spatialization of Metric Time: The Conquest of Land and Labour in Europe and the United States." *Time and Society* 1 (1992): 29–50.

Nikolinakos, M. "Notes on an Economic Theory of Racism." *Race* 14 (1973): 365–81.

NLRB v. Jones & Laughlin Steel Corp. 301 U.S. 1.

NLRB v. Freuhauf Trailer Co. 301 U.S. 49.

NLRB v. Friedman-Harry Marks Clothing Co. 301 U.S. 58.

Noble, David. *America by Design: Science, Technology and the Rise of Corporate Capitalism*. New York: Alfred A. Knopf, 1977.

Norrell, Robert J. "Caste in Steel: Jim Crow Careers in Birmingham, Alabama." *Journal of American History* 73, no. 3 (December 1986): 669–94.

Northrup, Herbert R. *Organized Labor and the Negro*. New York: Harper & Brother, 1944.

———. "The Negro and Unionism in the Birmingham, Ala., Iron and Steel Industry." *Southern Economic Journal* 10, no. 1 (July 1943): 27–40.

Northrup, Herbert R., and Richard L. Rowan. *Negro Employment in Southern Industry: A Study of Racial Policies in Five Industries*. Philadelphia: University of Pennsylvania Press, 1970.

O'Brien, Michael. "The Nineteenth-Century American South." *Historical Journal* 24, no. 3 (September 1981): 751–63.

O'Connor, James. *Accumulation Crisis.* Oxford, U.K.: Basil Blackwell, 1984.

Ofari, Earl. *The Myth of Black Capitalism.* New York: Monthly Review Press, 1970.

Olmsted, Frederick Law. *A Journey in the Back Country.* New York: Schocken Books, 1970.

———. *The Cotton Kingdom.* New York: Modern Library, 1969.

———. *A Journey in the Seaboard Slave States, with Remarks on Their Economy.* New York: Dix & Edward, 1856.

Omi, Michael, and Howard Winant. *Racial Formation in the United States: From the 1960s to the 1980s.* New York: Routledge and Kegan Paul, 1986.

Only Six Million Acres: The Decline of Black Owned Land in the Rural South. Sponsored by Clark College of Atlanta and the Rockefeller Brothers Funds. New York: Black Economic Research Center, 1975.

"Only Way to Remedy." *Labor Advocate.* 23 March 1901.

Outlaw, Lucius. "Toward a Critical Theory of 'Race.' " In *Anatomy of Racism,* edited by David Theo Goldberg. Minneapolis: University of Minnesota Press, 1990.

Page, Brian, and Richard Walker. "From Settlement to Fordism: The Agro-Industrial Revolution in the American Midwest." *Economic Geography* 67, no. 4 (October 1991): 281–315.

Painter, Nell I. *The Narratives of Hosea Hudson: His Life as a Negro Communist in the South.* Cambridge, Mass.: Harvard University Press, 1979.

Park, Sam O., and James O. Wheeler. "The Filtering-Down Process in Georgia: The Third Stage in the Product Life Cycle." *Professional Geographer* 35, no. 1 (February 1983): 18–31.

Parker, Edward W. "Coal." Department of Interior, U.S. Geological Survey. Mineral Resources of the U.S. Washington, D.C.: Government Printing Office, 1904.

Parkes, Thomas D. *Report on Coalburg Prison.* Birmingham, Ala.: Committee on Health of Jefferson County Medical Society, 1895.

Pearce, R. "Sharecropping: Towards a Marxist View." *Journal of Peasant Studies* 10, no. 213 (1983): 42–70.

Peet, Richard. "Inequality and Poverty: A Marxist-Geographic Theory," *Annals of the Association of American Geographers* 65, no. 4 (Dec. 1975): 564–71.

The Penal Code of Alabama. Adopted by the General Assembly at Session, 1865–1866. Montgomery, Ala.: Reid and Screw, 1866.

Perlo, Victor. *The Negro in Southern Agriculture.* New York: International Publishers, 1953.

Persky, J. J., and J. J. Kain. "Migration, Employment and Race in the Deep South." *Southern Economic Journal* 36, no. 1 (July 1970): 268–76.

Phillips, Ulrich Bonnell. *American Negro Slavery: A Survey of the Supply, Employment and Control of Negro Labor as Determined by the Plantation Regime.* New York: Appleton & Company, 1918.

Phillips, William B. *Iron Making in Alabama.* Tuscaloosa: Geological Survey of Alabama, 1912.

Philo, Chris, and Gerry Kearns. "Culture, History, Capital: A Critical Introduction to the Selling of Places." In *Selling Places: The City as Cultural Capital, Past and Present,* edited by Gerry Kearns and Chris Philo. Oxford: Pergamon Press, 1993.

Piven, Frances Fox, and Richard A. Cloward. *Poor People's Movements: Why They Succeed, How They Fail.* New York: Vintage Books, 1979.

———. *Regulating the Poor: The Function of Public Welfare.* New York: Pantheon Books, 1971.

Plessy v. Ferguson. 163 U.S. 537, 1896.

Post, C. "The American Road to Capitalism." *New Left Review* 133 (1982): 30–51.

Powell, Lawrence N. "The Prussians Are Coming." *Georgia Historical Quarterly* 71, no. 4 (Winter 1987): 639–67.

Prentice, George. "Neighboring Counties Favor Boundary Change." *Montgomery Advertiser.* 18 December 1957.

"President Mitchell in District No. 20: His Utterance Display Wisdom, Moderation and Firmness." *Labor Advocate.* 11 February 1905.

Proceedings of the Constitutional Convention of Alabama, III, IV, 1901.

Proceedings of the Joint Convention of Alabama Coal Operators Association and United Mine Workers of America. Birmingham, Ala., 22 June 1903.

"Proceeding of the Labor Convention: Wednesday, January 4, 1871." *Weekly State Journal.* 6 January 1871.

Prunty, Merle C. "Two American Souths: The Past and the Future." *Southeastern Geographer* 17, no. 1 (May 1977): 1–24.

———. "The Renaissance of the Southern Plantation." *Geographical Review* 45, no. 4 (October 1955): 459–91.

Quadagno, Jill. *The Color of Welfare: How Racism Undermined the War on Poverty.* New York: Oxford University Press, 1994.

Quadrennial Report of the Inspectors of Convicts, September 1, 1910 to August 31, 1914. Montgomery: Brown, 1910–14.

Quarles, Benjamin. *The Negro American.* Glenview, Ill.: Scott, Foresman and Co., 1967.

Rakove, Milton. *Don't Make No Waves . . . Don't Back No Losers.* Bloomington: Indiana University Press, 1975.

Ransom, Roger L. *Conflict and Compromise: The Political Economy of Slavery, Emancipation, and the American Civil War.* New York: Cambridge University Press, 1989.

Ransom, Roger L., and Richard Sutch. *One Kind of Freedom: The Economic Consequences of Emancipation.* Cambridge, U.K.: Cambridge University Press, 1977.

Raper, Arthur F. *Preface to Peasantry.* Chapel Hill: University of North Carolina Press, 1936.

"Registration of Negro Voters in Alabama in 1954." G. E. Pierce, Research Secretary, Alabama State Coordinating Association for Registration and Voting, Birmingham, Ala. Unpublished paper, n.d. In Southern Research Council File 41.2.16.3.3. Archives, Birmingham Public Library.

Reich, Michael. *Racial Inequality: A Political-Economic Analysis.* Princeton, N.J.: Princeton University Press, 1981.

Report of the Special Committee of the Alabama General Assembly to Investigate the Convict Lease System. Unpublished. Montgomery, Ala., 1889.

Rex, John. *Race Relations in Sociological Theory.* 2d ed. London: Routledge and Kegan Paul, 1983.

Rifkin, Jeremy. *The End of Work: The Decline of the Global Labor Force and the Dawn of the Post-Market Era.* New York: G. P. Putnam's Sons, 1995.

Rikard, Marlene Hunt. "An Experiment in Welfare Capitalism: The Health Care Services of the Tennessee Coal, Iron, and Railroad Company." Ph.D. diss., University of Alabama, 1983.

———. *The Black Industrial Experience in Early Twentieth Century Birmingham.* Birmingham: Alabama Center for Higher Education, 1979.

———. "George Gordon Crawford: Man of the New South." Master's thesis, Samford University, 1971.

Roback, Jennifer. "The Political Economy of Segregation: The Case of Segregated Streetcars." *Journal of Economic History* 46, no. 4 (December 1986): 893–917.

Robinson, Cedric J. "Race, Capitalism, and the Antidemocracy." In *Reading Rodney King/Reading Urban Uprising,* edited by Robert Gooding-Williams. New York: Routledge, 1993.

——. *Black Marxism: The Making of the Black Radical Tradition.* London: Zed Press, 1983.

Roediger, David. *Towards the Abolition of Whiteness: Essays on Race, Politics, and Working Class History.* London: Verso, 1994.

——. "Precapitalism in One Confederacy: A Note on Genovese, Politics and the Slave South." *New Politics* 9, no. 11 (Summer 1991): 90–95.

——. *The Wages of Whiteness: Race and the Making of the American Working Class.* London: Verso, 1991.

Rogers, William Warren. *The One-Gallused Rebellion: Agrarianism in Alabama, 1865–1896.* Baton Rouge: Louisiana State University Press, 1970.

Rogers, William Warren, Robert David Ward, Leah Rawls Atkins, and Wayne Flynt. *Alabama: The History of a Deep South State.* Tuscaloosa: University of Alabama Press, 1994.

Roy, William G. "The Organization of the Corporate Class Segment of the U.S. Capitalist Class at the Turn of This Century." In *Bringing Class Back In: Contemporary and Historical Perspectives,* edited by Scott G. McNall, Rhonda F. Levine, and Rick Fantasia. Boulder, Colo.: Westview Press, 1991.

Sawers, Larry. "New Perspectives on the Urban Political Economy." In *Marxism and the Metropolis: New Perspectives in Urban Political Economy,* edited by William K. Tabb and Larry Sawers. New York: Oxford University Press, 1984.

Saxton, Alexander. *The Rise and Fall of the White Republic: Class Politics and Mass Culture in Nineteenth-Century America.* London: Verso, 1991.

Schechter Poultry Corp. et al. v. United States. 295 U.S. 490, 1935.

Schumpeter, Joseph A. *Business Cycles: A Theoretical, Historical, and Statistical Analysis of the Capitalist Process.* 2 vols. New York: McGraw-Hill, 1939.

Schwartz, Michael. *Radical Protest and Social Structure.* New York: Academic Press, 1976.

Scott, Emmett J. *Negro Migration During the War.* New York: Arno Press and *The New York Times,* 1969.

Scott, Emmett J., and Lyman Beecher Stowe. *Booker T. Washington: Builder of a Civilization.* New York: Doubleday, Page and Company, 1916.

Sennett, Richard. *Flesh and Stone: The Body and the City in Western Civilization.* New York: W. W. Norton, 1994.

Sharpe, Elizabeth Ann. "Was There a Dictatorship of the Proletariat in New Orleans During Reconstruction?" Paper presented at Southern Labor Studies Conference, Birmingham, Ala., 21–24 October 1993.

Shufeldt, Robert W. *The Negro: A Menace to American Civilization.* Boston: R. G. Badger, 1907.

Silver, Christopher. "The Racial Origins of Zoning: Southern Cities from 1910–40." *Planning Perspectives* 6 (1991): 189–205.

Sitkoff, Harvard. *A New Deal for Blacks, The Emergence of Civil Rights as a National Issue.* Vol. 1, *The Depression Decade.* New York: Oxford University Press, 1978.

Sivanandan, A. "Challenging Racism: Strategies for the '80s." *Race and Class* 25 (1983): 1–11.

——. "Race, Class and the State: The Black Experience in Britain." *Race and Class* 17 (1976): 347–68.

Sixth Biennial Report of the Inspection of Convicts, September 1, 1904 to August 31, 1910. Montgomery, Ala.: Roemer Printing, 1904–6.

Smith, Douglas L. *The New Deal in the Urban South.* Baton Rouge: Louisiana State University Press, 1988.

Smith, Mark M. *Mastered by the Clock: Time, Slavery and Freedom in the American South.* Chapel Hill: University of North Carolina Press, 1997.

Smith, Michael Peter, and Richard Tardanico. "Urban Theory Reconsidered: Production, Reproduction and Collective Action." In *The Capitalist City: Global Restructuring and Community Politics*, edited by Michael Peter Smith and Joe R. Feagin. Oxford, U.K.: Basil Blackwell, 1987.

Smith, William B. *The Color Line: A Brief in Behalf of the Unborn*. New York: McClure, Phillips & Co., 1907.

Snowden, Frank. *Blacks in Antiquity*. Cambridge, Mass.: Harvard University Press, 1970.

Soja, Edward W. *Postmodern Geographies: The Reassertion of Space in Critical Social Theory*. London: Verso, 1989.

Sowell, Thomas. *The Economics and Politics of Race*. New York: William Morrow & Company, 1983.

———. *Ethnic America: A History*. New York: Basic Books, 1981.

———. *Race and Economics*. New York: David McKay Co., 1975.

Sparrow, Hugh W. "Area with 30 Percent of State's People has Over Half of Voters." *Birmingham News*. 20 May 1956.

Spencer, Samuel R., Jr. *Booker T. Washington and the Negro's Place in America*. Boston: Little, Brown, 1955.

Spero, Sterling D., and A. L. Harris. *The Black Worker: The Negro and the Labor Movement*. New York: Athenaeum, 1968.

Stark, David. "Class Struggle and the Transformation of the Labor Process: A Relational Approach." *Theory and Society* 9, no. 1 (January 1980): 89–130.

Starobin, Robert S. *Industrial Slavery in the Old South*. New York: Oxford University Press, 1970.

Statistical Abstract of the United States: 1940. Washington, D.C.: U.S. Government Printing Office, 1941.

"Steel Corporation Acquires Tennessee Coal & Iron Co.," *The Wall Street Journal*, 7 November 1907.

Stein, Judith. "Southern Workers in National Unions: Birmingham Steelworkers, 1936–1951." In *Organized Labor in the Twentieth Century South*, edited by Robert H. Zieger. Knoxville: University of Tennessee Press, 1991.

Stiglitz, J. E. "Incentive and Risk Sharing in Sharecropping." *Review of Economic Studies* 41, no. 126 (April 1974): 219–55.

Stocking, George W. *Basing Point Pricing and Regional Development: A Case Study of the Iron and Steel Industry*. Chapel Hill: University of North Carolina Press, 1952.

Stone, Katherine. "The Origins of Job Structures in the Steel Industry." In *Labor Market Segmentation*, edited by Richard C. Edward, Michael Reich, and David M. Gordon. Lexington, Mass.: D. C. Heath and Company, 1975.

Storper, Michael, and Richard Walker. *The Capitalist Imperative: Territory, Technology, and Industrial Growth*. New York: Basil Blackwell, 1989.

Straw, Richard A. "The Collapse of Biracial Unionism: The Alabama Coal Strike of 1908." *Alabama Historical Quarterly* 37, no. 2 (Summer 1975): 92–114.

Taeuber, K., and A. F. Taeuber. *Negroes in Cities: Residential Segregation and Neighborhood Change*. Chicago: Aldine, 1965.

Taft Research Notes on Alabama Labor History. "Black Workers." Birmingham, Ala.: Archives, Birmingham Public Library, n.d.

Taylor, Frederick W. *Principles of Scientific Management* (New York: Harper & Brother, 1911.

Taylor, Joseph H. "Populism and Disfranchisement in Alabama." *Journal of Negro History* 34, no. 1 (January 1949): 410–27.

Testimony of John Rutledge Before the U.S. Senate Committee on Education and Labor. *Report of the Senate Upon the Relations Between Labor and Capital and Testimony.* IV. 48th Congress, 2nd Session, 1885.

Tharin, Robert S. *Arbitrary Arrests in the South.* New York: John Bradburn, 1863.

Thompson, E. P. "Time, Work-Discipline, and Industrial Capitalism." *Past and Present* 38 (December 1967): 56–97.

Thompson, Edgar. *Plantation Societies, Race Relations and the South: The Regimentation of Populations.* Durham, N.C.: Duke University Press, 1975.

Thompson, Robert A., Hylan Lewis, and Davis McEntire. "Atlanta and Birmingham: A Comparative Study in Negro Housing." In *Studies in Housing and Minority Groups*, edited by Nathan Glazer and Davis McEntire. Berkeley: University of California Press, 1960.

Thornton, J. Mills, III. *Politics and Power in a Slave Society: Alabama, 1800–1860.* Baton Rouge: Louisiana State University Press, 1978.

Tindall, George Brown. *The Disruption of the Solid South.* Athens: University of Georgia Press, 1972.

———. *The Emergence of the New South: 1913–1945.* Baton Rouge: Louisiana State University Press, 1967.

Todorov, Tzvetan. "'Race,' Writing, and Culture." In *"Race," Writing, and Difference*, edited by Henry Louis Gates, Jr. Chicago: University of Chicago Press, 1986.

Trattner, Walter I. *Crusade for the Children: A History of the National Child Labor Reform in America.* Chicago: Quadrangle Books, 1970.

Turner, Frederick Jackson. *The Frontier in American History.* Washington, D.C.: Government Printing Office, 1894.

U.S. Bureau of the Census. *Abstract of the Twelfth Census of the United States, 1900.* Washington, D.C.: Government Printing Office, 1904.

U.S. Bureau of the Census. *1978 Census of Agriculture.* Vol. 1, *State and County Data.* Part 1, *Alabama.* Washington, D.C.: Government Printing Office, 1981.

———. *1978 Census of Agriculture.* Vol. 1, *Summary and State Data,* Part 51. Washington, D.C.: Government Printing Office, 1981.

———. *Compendum of Ninth Census, 1870.* New York: Arno Press, 1976.

———. *1959 Census of Agriculture.* Vol. 2, *General Report.* Washington, D.C.: Government Printing Office, 1962.

———. *Census of Agriculture, 1940.* Vol. 3. Washington, D.C.: Government Printing Office, 1946.

———. *The Social and Economic Status of the Black Population in the United States: An Historical View, 1790–1978.* Current Population Reports, Special Studies Series P-23, no. 80. Washington, D.C.: Government Printing Office, 1979.

———. *Census of Population, Characteristics of the Population,* Alabama, 1940. Washington, D.C.: Government Printing Office, 1942.

———. *Sixteenth Census of the United States: 1940 Population.* Washington, D.C.: Government Printing Office, 1942.

———. *Census of Agriculture, Part @, The Southern States.* Washington, D.C.: Government Printing Office, 1927.

———. *Census of Manufactures,* 1900. Washington, D.C.: Government Printing Office, 1902.

———. *Census of Manufactures,* 1890. Washington, D.C.: Government Printing Office, 1895.

———. *Census of Manufactures,* 1880. Washington, D.C.: Government Printing Office, 1883.

―――. *Population of the U.S. in 1860, Eight Census.* Washington, D.C.: Government Printing Office, 1864.

―――. *Seventh Census of the United States, Manufactures.* Washington, D.C.: Government Printing Office, 1859.

―――. *Eighth Census of the United States, Manufactures.* Washington, D.C.: Government Printing Office, 1865.

―――. *1870 Census of Population, Ninth Census.* Washington, D.C.: Government Printing Office, 1872.

―――. *Population of the U.S. at the Tenth Census,* 1880. Washington, D.C.: Government Printing Office, 1883.

―――. *U.S. Census of Population.* 1890, Vol. 1. Washington, D.C.: Government Printing Office, 1895-97.

―――. *U.S. Census of Population.* 1900, Vols. 1 and 2. Washington, D.C.: Government Printing Office, 1901-1902.

―――. *U.S. Census of Population.* 1910, Vol. 2. Washington, D.C.: Government Printing Office, 1913.

―――. *U.S. Census of Population.* 1920, Vol. 1. Washington, D.C.: Government Printing Office, 1921.

―――. *U.S. Census of Population.* 1930, Vol. 4. Washington, D.C.: Government Printing Office, 1933.

―――. *U.S. Census of Population.* 1940, Vol. 3. Washington, D.C.: Government Printing Office, 1943.

―――. *U.S. Census of Population.* 1950, Vol. 2. Washington, D.C.: Government Printing Office, 1953-54.

―――. *U.S. Census of Population.* 1960, Vol. 1, Characteristics of the Population. Washington, D.C.: Government Printing Office, 1961.

―――. *U.S. Census of Population.* 1970, Vol. 1, Characteristics of the Population. Washington, D.C.: Government Printing Office, 1972.

―――. *U.S. Census of Population.* 1980, Vol. 1, Characteristics of the Population. Washington, D.C.: Government Printing Office, 1983.

―――. *U.S. Census of Population.* 1990, Vol. 1, General Population Characteristics. Washington, D.C.: Government Printing Office, 1992.

U.S. Bureau of Labor. *Annual Report of the Commissioner of Labor, Convict Labor.* Washington, D.C.: Government Printing Office, 1905.

U. S. Circuit Court of Appeals, Fifth Circuit. *City of Birmingham et al. Appellants v. Mary Means Monk et al. Appellees.* 185 F.2d 859. Brief and Argument of Horace C. Wilkinson, Attorney for Appellants, 1949.

U.S. Congress. *Absorption of the Tennessee Coal and Iron Co.* 62d Cong., 1st sess. S. Doc. 44, Serial 6101. Washington, D.C.: Government Printing Office, 1911.

―――. Committe on Education and Labor. *Federal Employment Practices Act.* 81st Cong., 1st sess. 1949 H.R. Doc.

―――. Report of the Joint Committee on Housing. *Slum Clearance.* 80th Cong., 2nd sess. Washington, D.C.: Government Printing Office, 1948.

U.S. Department of the Interior, U.S. Geological Survey. *Mineral Resources of the U.S.,* 1902. Washington, D.C.: Government Printing Office, 1904.

U.S. Industrial Commission. *Report of the Industrial Commission on Prison Labor.* Washington, D.C.: Government Printing Office, 1900.

U.S. Senate Committee on Education and Labor. *Report of the Senate upon the Relations Between Labor and Capital and Testimony,* IV. 48th Congress, 2nd Session, 1885.

U.S. Senate. *Reports of the Immigration Commission, Immigrants in Industries.* Part 1, Bituminous Coal Mining, 2 Vols. 61st Congress, 2d sess., Senate Doc. 633, VII. 1910.

U.S.A., The Permanent Revolution. New York: Prentice-Hall, 1951.

United Mine Workers Journal. 25 June 1908.

United States v. United States Steel Corporation. 251 U.S. 417, 1920.

Urry, John. "The Growth of Scientific Management: Transformations in Class Structure and Class Struggle." In *Class and Space: The Making of Urban Society,* edited by Nigel Thrift and Peter Williams. London: Routledge and Kegan Paul, 1987.

———. "Capitalist Production, Scientific Management and the Service Class." In *Production, Work, Territory: The Geographical Anatomy of Industrial Capitalism,* edited by Allen J. Scott and Michael Storper. Boston: Allen & Unwin, 1986.

Valocchi, Steve. "The Racial Basis of Capitalism and the State, and the Impact of the New Deal on African Americans." *Social Problems* 41, no. 3 (August 1994): 347–62.

van Alstyne, William. "Rites of Passage: Race, the Supreme Court, and the Constitution." In *Race Relations and the Law in American History,* ed. Kermit L. Hall. New York: Garland Publishing, 1987.

van der Berghe, Pierre L. *Race and Racism.* New York: Wiley, 1967.

van Evrie, John H. *White Supremacy and Negro Subordination: or, Negroes a Subordinate Race.* New York: van Evrie, Horton and Company, 1868.

"Vice-President White Tells Why Strike Was Called Off." *Labor Advocate.* 25 September 1908.

Vittoz, Stanley. *New Deal Labor Policy and the American Industrial Economy.* Chapel Hill: University of North Carolina Press, 1987.

Voegeli, V. Jacques. *Free but Not Equal: The Midwest and the Negro During the Civil War.* Chicago: University of Chicago Press, 1967.

von Thunen, J. H. *Der Isolierte Staat in Beziehung auf Landwirtschaft und Nationalokonomie.* Berlin: Weegandt, 1875.

Wagstaff, Thomas. "Call Your Old Master—'Master': Southern Political Leaders and Negro Labor During Presidential Reconstruction." *Labor History* 10, no. 3 (Summer 1969): 323–45.

Walker, Richard A. "A Theory of Suburbanization: Capitalism and the Construction of Urban Space in the United States." In *Urbanization and Urban Planning in Capitalist Society,* edited by Michael Dear and Allen J. Scott. New York: Methuen, 1981.

———. "Two Sources of Uneven Development Under Advanced Capitalism: Spatial Differentiation and Capital Mobility." *Review of Radical Political Economics* 10, no. 3 (1978): 28–37.

Ward, Robert David, and William Warren Rogers. *Convicts, Coal, and the Banner Mine Tragedy.* Tuscaloosa: University of Alabama Press, 1987.

Warner, William L. "Introduction." In *Deep South,* edited by Allison Davis, Burleigh Gardner, and Mary Gardner. Chicago: University of Chicago Press, 1941.

Washington, Virginia & Maryland Coach Co. v. NLRB. 301 U.S. 142, 1937.

Watts v. Housing Authority of the Birmingham District. 150 F. Supp. 552, 1956.

West, Cornel. "Race and Social Theory: Toward a Genealogical Materialist Analysis." In *The Year Left 2: Toward a Rainbow Socialism, Essays on Race, Ethnicity, Class, and Gender,* edited by Mike Davis, Manning Marable, Fred Pfeil, and Michael Sprinker. London: Verso, 1987.

"What U.S. Steel Has Acquired In the Purchase of T.C. 1I.," *The Wall Street Journal,* 8 November 1907.

Whatley, Warren C. "Labor for the Picking: The New Deal in the South." *Journal of Economic History* 43, no. 4 (December 1983): 905–29.

White, Joseph L. *The Psychology of Blacks: An Afro-American Perspective.* Englewood Cliffs, N.J.: Prentice-Hall, 1984.

White, Marjorie L. *The Birmingham District: An Industrial History and Guide.* Birmingham, Ala.: Birmingham Historical Society, 1981.

Wiener, Jonathan. "Class Structure and Economic Development in the American South, 1865–1955." *American Historical Review* 84, no. 4 (October 1979): 970–92.

———. *Social Origins of the New South: Alabama, 1860–1885.* Baton Rouge: Louisiana State University Press, 1978.

———. "Planter Persistence and Social Change: Alabama, 1850–1870." *Journal of Interdisciplinary History* 7, no. 2 (Autumn 1976): 235–60.

———. "Planter–Merchant Conflict in Reconstruction Alabama." *Past and Present*, no. 68 (August 1975): 73–94.

Wiley, B. I. "Salient Changes in Southern Agriculture Since the Civil War." *Agricultural History* 13, no. 2 (1939): 65–76.

William, Eric. *Capitalism and Slavery.* New York: Russell & Russell, 1961.

William v. Mississippi. 170 U.S. 213, 1898.

Williams, Gwyn A. "The Concept of 'Egemonia' in the Thought of Antonio Gramsci: Some Notes on Interpretation." *Journal of the History of Ideas* 21, no. 4 (1960): 587–99.

Williamson, Joel. *The Crucible of Race: Black–White Relations in the American South Since Emancipation.* New York: Oxford University Press, 1984.

Wilson, Bobby M. "Black Housing Opportunities in Birmingham, Alabama." *Southeastern Geographer* 17, no. 1 (May 1977): 49–57.

Wilson, Carter A. *Racism: From Slavery to Advanced Capitalism.* Thousand Oaks, Calif.: Sage Publications, 1996.

Wilson, William Julius. *The Declining Significance of Race: Blacks and Changing American Institutions.* Chicago: University of Chicago Press, 1978.

Wolters, Raymond. "Section 7a and the Black Worker." *Labor History* 10, no. 3 (Summer 1969): 459–74.

Wood, Ellen Meiksins. *Democracy Against Capitalism: Renewing Historical Materialism.* Cambridge, Mass.: Cambridge University Press, 1995.

Wood, Phillips J. *Southern Capitalism: The Political Economy of North Carolina, 1880–1990.* Durham, N.C.: Duke University Press.

Woodburn, James A. *The Life of Thaddeus Stevens.* Indianapolis: Bobbs-Merrill Co., 1913.

Woodman, Harold D. *King Cotton and His Retainers: Financing and Marketing the Cotton Crop of the South, 1800–1925.* Columbia: University of South Carolina Press, 1990.

———. "Post–Civil War Southern Agriculture and the Law." *Agricultural History* 53, no. 1 (1979): 319–37.

Woodson, Carter G. *The Mis-Education of the Negro.* Trenton, N.J.: Africa World Press, 1990.

Woodward, C. Vann. *The Strange Career of Jim Crow.* 3d ed. London: Oxford University Press, 1974.

———. "Yes, There Was a Compromise of 1877." *Journal of American History* 60, no. 1 (June 1973): 215–23.

———. *Origins of the New South, 1877–1913.* Baton Rouge: Louisiana State University Press, 1951.

———. "Tom Watson and the Negro in Agrarian Politics." *Journal of Southern History* 4, no. 1 (February 1938): 14–33.

Woofter, T. J., Jr. *Landlord and Tenant on the Cotton Plantation.* Research Monograph 5, Works Progress Administration Division of Social Research. Washington, D.C.: Government Printing Office, 1936.

Worthman, Paul B. "Black Workers and Labor Unions in Birmingham, Alabama, 1897–1904." *Labor History* 10, no. 3 (Summer, 1969): 375–407.

Worthman, Paul B., and James Green. "Black Workers in the New South, 1865–1915." In *Key Issues in the Afro-American Experience*, edited by Nathan Huggins, Martin Kilson, and Daniel Fox. New York: Harcourt Brace Jovanovich, 1971.

Wright, Angie, and Duna Norton. "Land Ownership and Property Taxation in Alabama." Appalachian Land Ownership Task Force, Program for Rural Services and Research. Tuscaloosa: University of Alabama, 1980.

Wright, Gavin. *Old South, New South: Revolutions in the Southern Economy Since the Civil War*. New York: Basic Books, 1986.

———. *The Political Economy of the Cotton South: Households, Markets, and Wealth in the Nineteenth Century*. New York: W. W. Norton, 1978.

Yarrow, Michael. "The Gender-Specific Class Consciousness of Appalachian Coal Miners: Structure and Change." In *Bringing Class Back In: Contemporary and Historical Perspectives*, edited by Scott G. McNall, Rhonda F. Levine, and Rich Fantasia. Boulder: Westview Press, 1991.

Zeichner, Oscar. "The Legal Status of the Agricultural Laborer in the South." *Political Science Quarterly* 55, no. 3 (September 1940): 412–28.

Zinn, Howard. *A People's History of the United States*. New York: Harper & Row, 1980.

Index

Note: **Boldface** numbers indicate illustrations.

GEOGRAPHIES OF JUSTICE AND SOCIAL TRANSFORMATION